THE ROMANCE OF MOUNTAINEERING

I. 'CLEAR OF THE BROODING CLOUD'

R. L. G. IRVING

(Member of the Alpine Club, French and Italian Alpine Clubs)

THE ROMANCE OF MOUNTAINEERING

WITH 41 COLLOTYPE
REPRODUCTIONS, AND
MAPS AND DIAGRAMS

NEW YORK

E. P. DUTTON AND CO. INC.

TO MY WIFE

TO MARY AND VINCENT

AND

TO ALL WHO HAVE SPENT THEMSELVES

AND FOUND CONTENT UPON HIGH MOUNTAINS

PREFACE

THIS book is an attempt to tell the story of the great heritage of
adventure and enjoyment in which every climber of the present
generation may have a share.

The early chapters will show how men came to discover potent
charms in rocks and snow that had long repelled or terrified them,
and how in the pursuit of those charms they found a treasure that
enriched the whole manner of their life. The second and longest
portion of the book describes the pleasures and dangers attendant on
the possession and use of so much wealth. In the concluding
chapters I have tried to collect some of the teachings of experience on
the surest methods of securing our heritage against deterioration from
age or misuse; to find some assurance that mountaineering may be to
this and to succeeding generations as full of adventure as it has been
to our predecessors, and that mountains may remain to each one of
us as we grow old as full of promise as the mountains of youth,
though they carry all the memories, the friendships, and the visions
with which they have blessed the intervening years.

Footnotes, references, and statistics have been deliberately omitted;
my excuse is in the title of the book, however far its contents fail to
justify the word 'romance.' That word is used in the double sense
of the story of mountaineering adventure and of the relationship of
mountain to man.

Nearly everything that has been written about mountaineering has
some bearing on my subject. The difficulty has been to make a
selection from this embarrassing wealth of material. In my choice
of climbs to illustrate my story I have given some preference to what
is likely to be less familiar to the average reader, if it seemed to serve
my purpose as well as what must be already known to all.

When an incident has been a famous subject of controversy in
Alpine history, such as the first ascents of Mont Blanc or of the
Jungfrau, I have given the version which I believe to be the truest,
after checking the evidence by such knowledge and experience as
I possess.

Where alternative spelling is defensible, I have preferred the form that is familiar from past use to that which is the latest fashion: Kanchenjunga to Kangchenjunga, Vélan to Velan, cornice to corniche, etc. I apologize to any readers whom the practice may offend.

My grateful acknowledgments are due to a very large number of authors for the help they have given me in my task, and in several cases for actual passages which I have quoted. If the list that follows is incomplete, I hereby tender my sincere apology for any omissions that may occur.

First and most important in the collection of material, the *Alpine Journal* and its editor, Col. E. L. Strutt, then the following:

The publications of other Alpine clubs, especially the French and Italian, of which I have been a member more than twenty years.

The books written for the Mount Everest Committee.

Josias Simler et les Origines de l'Alpinisme, by Coolidge.

Voyages dans les Alpes, by Saussure.

Voyages en Zigzag, by Töppfer.

Travels Through the Alps, by Forbes.

Scrambles Amongst the Alps, by Whymper.

The Playground of Europe, by Leslie Stephen.

Climbing in the Sierra Nevada, by Clarence King.

The Mountains of California, by John Muir.

Life of De Saussure ; The Exploration of the Caucasus ; Below the Snow Line, by Freshfield.

Climbing in the Himalaya and other Mountain Ranges, by Norman Collie.

Mountain Memories, by Conway.

Monte Cervino ; Alpinismo Acrobatico, by Guido Rey.

On High Hills, by Geoffrey Young.

Les Crêtes du Mont Blanc, by Jacques and Tom de Lépiney.

Alpine Pilgrimage, by Kugy (Mr. Tyndale's translation).

Climbs and Ski Runs, by Smythe.

Fontaine de Jouvence, by Lammer (French translation by Ch. Sénéchal and E. Gaillard.

I also acknowledge my debt, and I think you will agree it is not small, to the artists in photography and black-and-white for the illustrations that bear their name.

There are two more debts even greater than any I have mentioned.

One is to Mr. H. E. G. Tyndale for all the help and encouragement he has given me, both in the criticism of the manuscript and in the reading of the proofs. The other is to him again, and to other young climbers, who have loved what I have loved and so made all things new for me. They are my sureties, who have enabled me to go on increasing the immense debt I owe to mountains. I hope that my fellow-climbers, whatever be their age or skill, may find in what I have written some small acknowledgment of their own debt as well as of mine.

R. L. G. I.

1935.

PREFACE TO THE SECOND EDITION

In the first chapter I expressed a hope that those whose treasure was already in the hills would find it suffer no depreciation in my book. And therefore I have altered one or two of the titles to the illustrations in which I am accused of undue levity. A few mistakes have been noted and corrected. An Index has been asked for and supplied.

It has given me particular satisfaction to find with what generous appreciation the book has been read by some who would make no claim whatever to be considered climbers.

R. L. G. I.

May 1935.

CONTENTS

PART I.—BIRTH AND EARLY YEARS

PART II.—SIGNS OF MATURITY

PART III.—PERPETUAL YOUTH

LIST OF ILLUSTRATIONS AND MAPS

xiii

DIAGRAMS

PART I

BIRTH AND EARLY YEARS

They waited, watching through the centuries,
To drop their magic in unheeding eyes,
    And make the love-light play
In features held accursèd, unendowed;
And now, with torch upheld, they point the way
    Clear of the brooding cloud.

CHAPTER I

IT is a good and pleasant thing to be thankful, and to say so; that is why it has been a labour of love to write the story of mountaineering from its beginnings to the present day, praising therein famous men and the climbing fathers that begat us. The courage to undertake the task comes from the possession of this one qualification : that I have studied the subject all my life.

My very earliest recollections of a summer holiday centre round the ascent of a Welsh hill. It was a domesticated hill that rose a paltry six hundred feet above the shore, but it was enough; something that would always remain had appeared upon the background of my life. Above and behind this hill a heathery slope rose to a higher point; I was told I was too small and young for this greater ascent; it was said to be over a thousand feet above the sea, and I cried nearly all the way home at the thought of what I had lost. From that day there was only one thing that really mattered in the choice of places for the August holiday: the height of the hills within reach. The best weeks in every year were those in which mountains were trying to teach me what men can learn by climbing them.

One early lesson in the Lake District, when I was about fifteen, impressed itself vividly on my memory. The mist was thick and night was closing in as I came cautiously and wonderingly down the steep southern face of Great Gable, while my parents away in the vale of Newlands were sending out a man to blow a horn upon the hills, in the hope that the missing son was near enough to hear. It was my first taste of the awful thrill which the close presence of steep mountains can inspire.

Another peculiarly vivid memory some ten years later is of Mont Blanc. The Bosses ridge was dazzlingly bright under new snow; the blue sky had the unfathomable depth of night with all the radiant energy of day. The lesson of that day was unforgettable; absolutely alone with Mont Blanc, without a trace of any other soul upon it after three days and nights of bad weather which I had spent at the Tête Rousse. With that ascent the promise made to the very small boy in Wales, that happiness for him would be found in climbing mountains, seemed to find complete fulfilment. Since that day gratitude and praise have been more necessary accompaniments of all the best hours of life.

By that time the Alps themselves had taught me nearly all I knew of how and why men ought to climb them, before I had come to any knowledge of Alpine literature or guide-books. It may be that this primitive and direct method of approaching mountains has helped me to enter into the spirit of the pioneering days; and I am sure that I owe to it, at any rate in part, that the years have brought no disillusionment. Difficult routes have not dulled the taste for easy ones, and familiarity has never bred contempt. To climb a peak has not been to conquer it, but to be admitted to intimacy. That is one reason why a second, a third, or an ascent of which I have lost count has given as great pleasure as the first. And the other reason has been the presence of a younger generation whose appreciation has given new value to what was there before.

By far the greater part of my climbing career has been spent in taking the young into the mountains, to see if they will drink the draught that may prove to be for them also an elixir of life. For many it is not that, refreshing as it always is. Whenever it has proved so to be, that wonderful source of health, of happiness, and of knowledge, which knows no limitations of quantity, has filled my own big cup a little fuller.

And now I find myself about to write the romance, and, thank God, the unfinished romance of mountaineering. It is not a book of reference. The man who buys it as such is hereby warned that he will have poor value for his money.

The place of mountains in history, their geographical arrangement, the application of iron and concrete to the development of the steeple-jack side of mountaineering—these are details of the story which demand a special knowledge and a special interest which I shall never have. On the mountains I have always felt as a child, and it is as a child that I have accepted what they had to give, the zest of life that grows in the hard playing of a strenuous game, a game where effort never fails to bring some measure of success; and with it the invitation to read eternal truths, written in characters larger, clearer, and more exquisitely illuminated than any in the world. How men came to find these, how they are finding them in ever

increasing numbers, and how they may contrive to find them is what
I am going to try to tell.

My own share in that achievement is negligible, but one hope
I have.   It is that those whose treasure is already in the hills
will find it suffers no depreciation in these pages.   Experience will
not allow me to hope for more.   Words will never give the fingers
to feel or the eyes to see what is offered by the rocks and the snow.

Why, then, write at all?   My best excuse is that it is impossible
to receive so much and to say nothing.

The story of mountaineering was already old before I was born;
and therefore I owe much to the circumstances that enabled me to
approach mountains with the simplicity and enthusiasm of the early
pioneers.   Almost every great peak I have climbed has given me the
pleasure, without the fame, of an explorer's ascent.   A bad memory
and an entire absence of notes have enabled me to enjoy similar and
even greater pleasures on a later visit.

I have climbed with a companion elected to the Alpine Club in
1872, which gives me a link with, shall we say, the middle ages of
mountaineering; and I have climbed for several years with one who
only this year attains the age that makes him eligible for election.
So that, although my own mountaineering life will add nothing to
the succession of great adventures which will form the main part of
this history, it may help to bind the tale of those achievements into
a single whole.

Where shall we begin the tale?

The origins of any great human activity are almost as elusive as
the origins of life itself.   The great commercialized streams of mountaineering activity, that now flow through Zermatt, Grindelwald, or
Chamonix, are as different from the early advance of exploration above
the snowline as are the lower reaches of the Rhine from its beginnings.
And as we might trace that river back to the trickles on the glacier,
to the snow, and so back into the sky itself, so it is with mountaineering.
That takes us back to a contemplative side of mountaineering where
the appearance of a sport is lost; it is too far for us.

The birthplace of the Rhine may fairly be said to be the spot
where it emerges as a definite stream from the dark cave that
opens at the glacier's end.   And we shall begin the story of
mountaineering where it first emerges from the darkness of the
Middle Ages as a sport, that is to say, a pastime, in which the
overcoming of physical obstacles by conscious muscular effort is an
essential element of enjoyment.

CHAPTER II

1492 is a great date in the world's history. In that year Columbus made his famous voyage which led to the settlement of America and the enormous development of the material resources of the world which resulted from it.

The dangers of this sudden growth of riches, which has outstripped the capacity to make intelligent use of them, have become more and more evident in the last few years. To most things that, taken in excess, may poison us, there is an antidote. And a kind Providence ordained that in this very year 1492 we may place the authentic beginning of a pursuit that has been, and will continue to be, a particularly efficacious remedy for the physical and spiritual deterioration threatened by a period of mass production, in which a man's life is assumed to consist 'in the abundance of the things which he possesseth.'

There are records of mountain ascents before 1492: I know the Emperor Hadrian went up Etna to see the sun rise; that is an imperial whim rather than a mountaineer's ascent. There is an ascent of the Canigou at the west end of the Pyrenees by King Peter III of Aragon about the year 1280, but there is an imaginative flavour about the story that compels me to place it in the Tartarinesque annals of mountaineering. He began the ascent accompanied by two knights 'honoured by his affection,' who swore never to leave him. A thunderstorm comes on and the knights fall wellnigh senseless on the ground. A little higher their exhaustion and terror are such that the king has pity on them and tells them to wait while he goes on, which they gladly do. Ancestors these two knights might be of Tartarin and Bompard, who swear at the Grands Mulets to perish rather than cut the rope, the same rope that is found later across the snow ridge with both ends cut.

Peter finishes the climb alone and on the summit finds a lake. Like many a later climber, he cannot resist throwing a stone into it, and 'there arose out of it a horrible dragon of enormous size which

7

began to fly hither and thither, darkening the air with its breath.' After which Peter climbed down to his companions, and all that he had seen and accomplished he related to them, describing it 'without reserve.' Yes, Peter, without reserve. Even allowing you the dragon, the nearest lake is a long way from the summit. No *Alpine Club Journal* would accept this ascent.

There is no doubt whatever as to the authenticity of the ascent of 1492, that of the Mont Aiguille in Dauphiné. It is a remarkable mountain nearly seven thousand feet in height, whose large, flat summit is cut off from access on all sides by cliffs hundreds of feet high. It is a challenge to any man with the instincts of a climber urgent within him. Antoine de Ville, Lord of Domp Julien, was such a man, and was ordered by King Charles VIII to go and climb it. His account shows clearly that the order was carried out completely and willingly, and he himself is a true prototype of the modern mountaineer. It was written on the summit to the president of the Dauphiné Parliament.

When I left the king he charged me to try and climb the mountain known as the Inaccessible, and with the use of mechanical devices (*subtilz engins*) I have by the grace of God found means to reach the top. For three days I have been there with more than ten others, both clergy and gentry, with a king's ladder- man (*eschelleur*) and I will not come down till I have a reply from you, in order that, if you should wish to send men to see us on the top, you may be able to do so. I warn you that you will find few men who, when they see where we are and the way we have contrived thither, will dare to follow us, for it is the most horrible and awful way I ever saw or any man of our company.

I write this on the 28th June on Agulle fort [spelled also, Equille; the word had probably never been written], called the Inaccessible, for the people call it the Agulle, and that it may not be forgotten I have had it named in the name of Father, Son, and Holy Ghost, and of Saint Charlemagne for love of the king's name. I have also had mass said upon it and have set up three high crosses in the corners.

To give you an idea of the mountain, the summit has a circumference of nearly a league, it is a quarter of a league in length and a cross-bow shot in breadth and it is covered with beautiful pasture. We found a fine preserve of chamois which can never get away, with young ones born this year, one of which we killed on arrival, inadvertently killed, for I would not have any taken till the king's will is known.

There is a half-league of ladders to climb up and a league beside, and the summit is the most glorious place you ever saw.

On receipt of this important letter, the president convokes the Parliament of Dauphiné, and it is resolved to send the usher to see if the account is true.   The usher comes back on 5th July and makes his report.   He finds that ladders have been placed in the rocks at the beginning of the climb, and although he saw Domp Julien and many others on the top 'he had no wish to venture up.   In the face of such obvious danger of death and the impossibility of getting up he feared he would be tempting the Providence of God if he risked it, for at the mere sight of the mountain all were terrified.'

Various other witnesses testify to seeing Domp Julien on the top; indeed, no other ascent has ever been so fully certified!   The official report by François de Bosco, Domp Julien's almoner, gives the names of the climbing-party.   Among them, besides the ladder-man, we find a professor of theology, two lawyers, a carpenter, etc.   It is good to hear that they ate, drank, and rested (he does not say slept) upon the mountain.   He gives the size of the meadow on the top as rather more than forty men could mow (in a day).   He also notices birds, including our friends the red-legged choughs.   The way he describes is even more fearful to descend than to ascend, and he mentions that Domp Julien had a house put up in a couple of days and that a clerical friend brought up some tame rabbits to establish on the summit pasture.

How clearly, in this wonderful tale, do we see foreshadowed the latest developments of mountaineering!   'By order of the king' so easily passes into: 'By invitation of the Everest Committee'; the 'subtilz engins' of Domp Julien into the rings and pitons of *Die Technik schwerster Eisfahrten* of L. Maduschka.

There is a familiar ring, too, in the jolly swagger, the French *panache* of the victor, warning other men not to attempt what he has done.   'The hazard of the ascent of the slabs above the two-hundred-foot chimney—unless a rope were fixed above—removes the climb outside the class of those that can be justifiably or even sanely led by more than two or three men now living.'   These are the words of an English Domp Julien of the twentieth century, whose only 'subtilz engins' were the skilful management of a guide's exceptional powers.

Quite recently a Slovene Domp Julien, who appears to combine in his own person the offices of carpenter, ladder-man, and guide, follows with a companion a route made by an adventurous pair, male and female, and shows a pride and chivalry not unworthy of our fifteenth-century hero.   'They agree in declaring that this route and their own "Black Gully" are the most difficult ascents by far as yet achieved in the Julian Alps.'   And just to show that the

Gallic cock still crows in the country that speaks the language of Domp Julien, let us notice in *La Montagne* in 1920: 'That day we had little doubt we had attained the extreme limit of what is possible on an ice-slope.' Never were there so many gallant cocks crying victory from eminences difficult of attainment as at the present day.

Further, this fellow Domp Julien might be credited with second sight, seeing the precaution he takes to have the authenticity of his ascent established beyond all doubt. It makes us grieve for the simplicity of later pioneers.

Think what a vast output of literary skill and effort might have been directed to other uses if J. R. Meyer had taken proper steps to have the ascent of the Finsteraarhorn properly certified in 1812. True, there were obvious difficulties in one or two remaining on that sharp, high summit while a messenger descended to fetch a com-missioner of oaths from Brigue or Berne. The lush grass, the tasty chamois, and the materials and emplacement for a shelter are all lacking. These difficulties would have been foreseen by the great Domp Julien.

For many years travellers who reached the summit of Mont Blanc obtained certificates signed by a Chamonix peasant that they were not like unto those who go 'not quite to the top, as far as Pierre Pointue.' I will give one more instance to show how careful pioneers must be. In an *Alpine Journal* of 1932 you will find a certificate duly signed and witnessed, not to prove but to disprove the claim to a first ascent. In 1893 an Italian gentleman, Count Lurani, much respected and beloved in his generation, climbed a rocky point, the Cima Sant' Anna or Badilet. The top consists of two blocks of rock. There was a thick mist, and Count Lurani inadvertently sat down on the wrong one. Some years later a Major Tanner ascended the peak and sat down on the right one, which was higher. For some reason mountaineering circles continued to credit Count Lurani with the first ascent and to slight the achievement of Major Tanner. Therefore, in 1932, Major Tanner, to establish the truth, made another ascent. He found his block of rock to be several centimetres higher than Lurani's, and separated from it by a practically unjump-able gap of nearly seven feet. Moreover, there was no evidence of Lurani's (or of his own) ascent beyond a record several yards away from the true summit. The logic of Major Tanner's guides shows how well he had chosen his men. Their first premise, 'the top of a mountain is not reached till the actual summit has been attained,'

(a) THE CHALLENGE

(b) THE FACE CLIMBED

2. MONT AIGUILLE

will hardly be disputed.   Their second, 'that Count Lurani had not sat on the highest rock,' was admitted by the count himself.   *Ergo,* Lurani's claim to the first ascent is not worth—a tanner.

Have you quite an easy conscience in this matter, reader? If you have ever climbed in North Wales, you must have been up Tryfaen. You know the two great blocks on the top that look like two men from the road below.   Have you never described yourself as having been up Tryfaen, when you have not only omitted to take a micrometer to make sure which *is* the highest, but have not attempted to ascend either?   It is true the gap is jumpable, so that I have at least one ascent to my credit out of some fifty or sixty spurious ones.

What might be described as the levelling spirit that appears in later Alpine literature, and cannot bear to see a peak unconquered, is entirely absent in Domp Julien.   It belongs to the age of democracy, an envious age.   This is how a citizen of Philadelphia records the triumph of a first ascent: 'Thus fell the haughty monarch of the Selkirks . . . and ruddy, throbbing countenances were the only evidence that the peerless primate of the range had at last submitted to the yoke of iron-shod boot.'   If only he had read of Domp Julien's example, he might have christened the peak Melchizedek, in the name of the United States of America.   But perhaps he thought the name, Sir Sandford, was already punishment enough.

The baptismal ceremony, instituted by Domp Julien, has lost something in beauty and romance.   The local name is often set aside or rejected when discovered.   Chomolungma, the 'goddess mother of the country,' a name peculiarly suited to the highest summit in the world, remains Mount Everest.   Successful ascents are no longer attributed to the grace of God.   There is certainly a cross on the top of the Viso and a statue of the Virgin on the Aiguille du Géant.   Such cases are rare enough to be remarkable.   No British climber, save one who knew his solitude was unobserved, would dare to do anything suggesting a profession of faith upon a mountain, and it would be a violation of good taste to mention it.

There is no other ancient record of an ascent which conveys to us the atmosphere of modern mountaineering, with its pride and its delight in the difficulties overcome.   Leonardo da Vinci, whom we welcome to the rank of mountaineers, reached the fringe of perpetual snow on one of the ridges falling south from Monte Rosa, probably Monte Bò, about eight thousand five hundred feet.   His notes of the ascent are mainly scientific and have stood the test of time less well than his artistic work. This modest peak, according to Leonardo, 'is so high that it rises above almost all the clouds, and snow rarely falls there; sleet falls there only in summer when the clouds are floating at their greatest height, and the sleet remains as sleet so long there, that if the rising and falling of the clouds were not so rare—such a thing does not happen twice in a summer—the accumulated sleet would form a very great mass of ice.' Fortunately for the prospects of winter sports in the district these observations on the snowfall are based on insufficient data!

A long account in Latin verse of an ascent of the Stockhorn, by a large, cheerful party, in 1536, might be taken as a forerunner of an off-day for a modern climbing-party that does not take its pleasure too seriously, or of a club-meet. The importance of meals is given full recognition; a quarter of chamois and well-matured cheese are added to what Ceres and Bacchus can provide; a good standard to set in this department of mountaineering. Dean Inge would be right in doubting whether progress is the word to apply to the long succession of meals described in Alpine literature of the last seventy years.

Various ascents of the peaks of Pilatus are recorded. Special permission from the authorities in Lucerne was required owing to the danger of disturbing Pontius Pilate and his wife, who repose in a couple of small lakes, or rather marshes, on the upper slopes of the mountain. The danger of careless stone-throwing into such places has been already indicated in the account of Peter of Aragon's ascent of the Canigou; and Pontius Pilate and his wife would be expected to take the very worst vengeance that a guilty conscience could suggest. Conrad Gesner, a most enlightened man, was brave enough to suggest that the Roman governor had never been near the place, and that if he had been he would have received no power to benefit or hurt the living. The worst he could do would be to impose on the superstitious the penalties of their superstition. Let us hope that Gesner did not suffer for this open scepticism learned upon his beloved mountains.

More than a passing word is due to Gesner. The peaks he climbed offer little scope for the display of technical skill; they were enough to bring out a singularly complete appreciation of the other sides of mountaineering. Never have the praises of water-drinking been sung so entrancingly. Like Epicurus, he loves it, 'not only for the simple, natural pleasure that it gives, but for the sensation of mental sanity and freedom that it induces on the morrow.'

Intensity of bodily pleasure [he says] depends on the increase or decrease of the contrary sensation. . . . Is it not then evident that the drinking of clean, cool water can never be so pleasant as when we are overcome by heat and thirst and weariness? . . . How can a man fail to feel the extreme of pleasure in that moment when he relaxes weary limbs, when cool airs succeed to extreme heat, when burning thirst is quenched, when food is there to satisfy an appetite that has a sharpened edge—above all, when the mind is particularly serene and sure?

One almost suspects Ruskin of plagiarism in the fourth volume of *Modern Painters* as one reads: 'Nowhere else as much as among mountains is such variety found in so small a space; seeing that in a single day, to give but one example, one may both see and feel all the seasonal changes of the year.'

Gesner bids us conclude—and we are only too ready to do so—that 'every day spent with friends upon the mountains will be a source of supreme pleasure, a day of keen enjoyment to every sense we have, provided nothing in the shape of the weather or in that of mind or body comes to thwart us. . . . If the mind is suffering, if it has not banished care and passion, these pleasures of body and of sense are sought in vain.' Oh, Gesner, how true that is! And how true it is also, that the higher we rise, the more easily do cares and passions sink back into the plains!

And Gesner sees the great merit in mountaineering, that its highest pleasures are within the reach of all.

Give me a man endowed in fair measure with physical and moral qualities, who has had a liberal education and is not the slave of idleness or sensuality; I would have him also an observer and admirer of nature, so that in the very contemplation and admiration of these mighty works of the Supreme Architect, and of the infinite variety of nature revealed in mountains as parts of one great whole, a joy of soul may increase the joy of harmony of all our senses. Is there (for such a man) in all nature's realm, a recreation more worthy of honour, more complete within itself in all respect?

No, Gesner, none, if I may answer for the average man you mention! Nor can we better your approach to the aesthetic side of mountaineering. Your climbing methods are more open to criticism. 'We mount a long slope that is pathless and so steep that in places we get up by grasping clods of earth, and over roots and stones with great labour we at last attain the summit.'

Could anything be worse to the twentieth-century climber, missing the path on the ground up to the climb, clutching sods, and finally going up scree? And yet even in the twentieth century we sometimes read of short cuts that prove long, and scree slopes are still with us, while as for the sods, even the English cragsmen who have Abraham to their father are not guiltless. We may read in *Rock Climbing in North Wales* how, on the eastern buttress of Lliwedd, Abraham himself confesses: 'I remembered the words of the poet: He that stands upon a slippery place makes nice of no vile hold to stay him up, and *hung on to my sod.*' (The italics are mine.)

Mountaineering has taken a remarkable hold of members of the learned professions; they need more than others the antidotes it provides! And our last name among the great pioneers of the sixteenth century must be Benoît Marti, a distinguished professor of Greek and Hebrew in the Academy of Berne. The Niesen and the Stockhorn are again the chosen peaks.

'Who would not admire, who would not regard with delight and affection, who would not come to climb places of this sort? Assuredly, men who are not moved by beauty such as this deserve, in my opinion, to be called idiots, fools, simpletons, fishes, slow tortoises!'

That seems to be going a little too far, especially in regard to flying men and road-hogs, if there be any among them—and it is to be feared there are—who are insensible to the attractions of mountains! But it is the language of an enthusiast. On the Niesen he found a stone on which was scratched in Greek: ὁ τῶν ὀρῶν ἔρως ἄριστος (The love of mountains is best).

Where is that stone now? Cannot you imagine the Alpine clubs of the world bidding against each other for its possession if it were ever auctioned at Lucerne? And would you not love to meet the ghost of the man who engraved it wandering in the high places? For my part, I feel I know him better than some of the people I meet constantly; and I would rather meet him on a visit to the land of shades than Napoleon or Alexander, whose talents must have lost much of their value when they passed into the realm of spiritual things.

Towards the end of the sixteenth century a dark cloud seems to have descended on men's minds. Topographical knowledge grows, but the true light of mountaineering is dimmed for nearly two hundred years. The energies of Europe are devoted to fighting or persecution. High mountains are left to the dragons and evil spirits from which Gesner and his like had begun to free them. Even Scheuchzer includes in his voluminous treatise on mountain phenomena, pub-lished in 1723, a *classified list* of dragons that inhabit the highest regions of the Alps. We have to wait nearly three hundred years before the unsuspected wealth of the heritage is revealed in the epic of Mont Blanc. And it is long after that that the true heir of Domp Julien and Gesner appears, the climber who combines sheer joy in pitting skill and strength against the challenging tilt of a colossal nose or brow, with an appreciation of the beauty and spiritual significance of mountain forms.

CHAPTER III

THE WINNING OF MONT BLANC

'DES personnes sont visibles au Mont Blanc.' Almost any fine morning in August this notice may be seen hung upon telescopes of varying size at favourable street corners in Chamonix, or outside the restaurants on the slopes above that command views of the great mountain opposite. The apathy of the crowds that pass by unheeding is a wonderful testimony to the growth of mountaineering. What a mere tourist may do any fine day is clearly not worth looking at!

It is a remarkable change from 1850, when crowds went up to the Flégère to watch an ascent and waited to give the successful climbers a great reception at Chamonix in the evening. And yet 1850 is a very long time after 1787, the great year of Saussure's ascent.

That ascent is far the most important in the annals of mountaineering. In all ages, including the present, the impression made upon the world by the accomplishment of a feat depends on the person who performs it as well as on the feat itself. Indeed, a thing which would not be remarkable at all if you or I performed it, such as a round of golf, a ride on a push-bike, or a modest climb, may become a thing worthy of head-lines if a person sufficiently famous or sufficiently rich elects to do it. And Saussure was a very eminent man through his position, his wealth, and his scientific learning. That such a man should actually choose to employ his wealth and his time in climbing a mountain, that is to say, in pursuing a form of activity which the world then regarded as one of the disagreeable additions to the struggle for existence suffered by peasants who were unfortunate enough to live among the Alps, was something like the starting of a revolution in social life.

The outstanding nature of the peak and its central position in Europe gave to the feat a special character. For the pre-eminence of Mont Blanc is not, like that of Everest, a matter that all but a few of mankind must accept on the word of a surveyor. Whether we are looking from the famous viewpoints round Chamonix and Cour-mayeur, which show its features in detail and make us bend our necks to measure its immense height; or whether we see its faintly golden snows from the distant summits of the Maritime Alps or of eastern Switzerland, there is no rival to the majesty of Mont Blanc.

Many years before any attempt to climb it had been made, travellers had come to wonder at the great cataracts of ice, the glaciers that flowed down from its sides into the valley of Chamonix. The visit of Windham and Pococke, in 1741, is evidence of the growing fame of the district and also of the entire absence of any desire to climb the higher peaks. The men of Chamonix considered it extraordinary that any one but a crystal seeker or a chamois hunter should wish to ascend as high as the Montenvers, and great precautions were taken before the Englishmen and their guides ventured so far. The names of these two brave adventurers were carved on a huge stone near the Montenvers.

The eighteenth century saw a vast demolition of artificialities and venerable conventions and prejudices in men's attitude to nature as well as in their relations to one another and to established order. Rousseau is the greatest among many writers who express the change of mind that helped to bring about the new order. He cannot justly be called a prophet of mountaineering, for he made no attempt to penetrate or to describe the higher zones of the Alps, the region that was regarded as fearful and desolate, a place accursed, to be shunned by man. He hardly touches even the zone of high valleys and villages near the upper tree limit. 'Jean-Jacques,' says Sainte-Beuve, the great French critic, 'had acquaintance only with the lowlands, the lakes, the cottages, and orchards. . . . He never explored, or described in detail, even the middle zone. . . . The highest regions may be said to be the discovery and the conquest of the famous scientist, Saussure.' Rousseau, nevertheless, by his passionate advocacy of a return to nature and his invitation to men to follow him into the pleasant places that lie among the foothills of the Alps, must have the credit for inducing succeeding generations to come and look upon the peaks with eyes that were prepared to find in them a potential source of beauty and delight.

Saussure was born in 1740, just a year before the visit of Windham and Pococke to Chamonix. However strongly he himself urges scientific research as the motive of his climbing adventures, it is not hard to find in his pleading an excuse for a love of mountaineering that was far in advance of the age in which he lived. Quite early in his life, when he was still a boy scrambling among the hills round Geneva to find botanical specimens for his mother and himself, he was at heart a mountaineer. 'I have had from childhood the most positive passion for the pleasures of the mountains. I still remember the sensation I felt when, for the first time, my hands touched the rocks of the Salève, and my eyes enjoyed its points of view.' We need no excuse of the botanist or the geologist after that confession of true mountaineering faith!

In 1760 he paid his first visit to Chamonix, and before he left he had posted in all the parishes of the district offers of a handsome reward for the man who should first ascend Mont Blanc, and a compensation for time spent in looking for the way. No serious attempt to win that reward was made for another fifteen years.

After this visit Saussure's passion for Mont Blanc grows steadily greater, for he writes: 'It became for me a kind of illness. I could not even look upon the mountain, which is visible from so many points round about, without being seized with an aching of desire.'

He made several long expeditions to various parts of the Alps, climbing nothing that can be described as difficult or high, but exceedingly adventurous for the time, and therefore a source of anxiety to his wife and family. He was a model for husbands who climb, taking every measure to alleviate their fears. Despite all such measures it must have been trying waiting for him during his dis-appearances into the recesses of the Montagnes Maudites, full of dangers real and imagined, and but lately rid of the dreadful dragons seen by Alpine peasants in their cups and so carefully classified by Scheuchzer only a generation before.

Saussure, then, is the great figure in the epic of Mont Blanc, and a most attractive personality as well as great. An aristocrat with all the advantages of birth and wealth, he never domineers but uses all his resources in furtherance of aims that may fairly be called idealistic. An ardent scientist, he is prepared to go through hardships of any kind to get nearer to the knowledge of the truth. His ascents are all made in pursuit of knowledge, and scientific instruments are carried up that leave no doubt of the serious character of his researches; but— and this is where he is of special interest to us mountaineers—in an age when climbing for its own sake was still unheard-of folly, we see the true climber's nature coming through this clothing of scientific culture. 'I simply live for a nearer view of the High Alps, which look so majestic from our Geneva hills.' That shows a desire that goes beyond scientific research.

Chamonix grew rapidly in favour as a resort for sightseers in the middle of the eighteenth century. After the adventurous trip of

Windham and Pococke, visits to the lower portion of glaciers developed the profession of guide, and increased the knowledge and experience of walking on ice. Mont Blanc still appeared immeasur-ably higher than any point reached in these modest excursions, and so completely inaccessible that it was not till 1775 that an attempt was made to earn the reward offered by Saussure.

Any one looking at Mont Blanc from the Brévent, or even from Chamonix, sees that the first point to aim for is the Grand Plateau, the great snowy basin below the steep snows and ice of the summit, and that the Montagne de la Côte offers a convenient tongue of solid ground running far up into the glacier. This was the route chosen, and the first party of four guides did well to get as high as the Grands Mulets rocks. Fatigue, indisposition, and fear, rather than any climbing obstacles, prevented further advance. We must remember that they started from low down, that they had never been high enough before to get acclimatized to a height of ten thousand feet, that they probably ate, and almost certainly drank, what would upset most of us on our first day in the Alps; and, above all, they were entering deeper with every step into a region which their imagination filled with all sorts of perils. Such difficulties as the ascent of Mont Blanc from Chamonix offers occur below the Grands Mulets. Remove all traces of the way taken by porters and climbing-parties on their way through the ice-fall, and there will be a problem in route-finding which I believe would not be solved without some delay by many modern parties.

It was not till eight years later that another attempt was made, and this time the party reached the Petit Plateau, where one of them felt ill and all hurried back. Lack of appetite and a general feeling of exhaustion were again a serious trouble. Men are as frightened now, as then, of illness whose origin is quite mysterious, and normally strong, healthy men are often the most frightened by a *malaise* that may be trifling. One great hefty fellow in the party, nicknamed 'Le Grand Jorasse,' declared it was useless to carry provisions, and that next time he should take nothing but a parasol and smelling-salts! This pronouncement by a robust guide, so evidently stronger and more experienced than himself, made a great impression on Saussure, and he began to look upon success as absolutely impossible. His opinion was shared by most of the wise men of Chamonix.

Now is the chance for a keen rival; and one existed in the person of Bourrit. Bourrit is the journalist explorer, writing bombastic descriptions, jealous of the exploits of others. He was a man of

c

humble birth, whose good voice and considerable artistic talent
had got him the post of precentor in the cathedral of Geneva. He
was a genuine lover of the Alps; he painted them, he occasionally
took visitors, if sufficiently distinguished, among them, and he loved
above all things to talk and write about them. He was vain. His
longing to be able to boast of having climbed Mont Blanc burned
with a fiercer flame than Saussure's hopes of scientific discovery from
the ascent. Poor Bourrit! It is a tragedy that he never reached the
top. He was a most indifferent climber—in that respect a marked
contrast to the expert journalist climber of the present day. He
was jealous too, though he owed too much to Saussure's generosity
to show it spitefully towards him, as he did towards humbler men.
When Saussure wrote him a very friendly letter, warning him against
an attempt on the mountain, suggesting that his health and strength
were not equal to such an effort, he was not likely to regard it as a
deterrent. He made his attempt.

Bad weather compelled a return after a bivouac on the Montagne
de la Côte. The chief interest the attempt has for us is that Dr. M. G.
Paccard was one of the party.

Paccard is the second great figure after Saussure in our epic. He
had had a good education and practised as a doctor in Chamonix.
Saussure, after his first meeting, describes him as a fine-looking,
intelligent fellow, with a taste for botany and a desire to climb Mont
Blanc. He was a vigorous, athletic man, with plenty of character,
and he was a far better climber than Saussure or Bourrit; but he
occupied the sort of ambiguous position, between a peasant like the
local guide and a gentleman like Saussure, that was a serious hindrance
to simple and cordial relations with either class. He soon showed
he meant business despite his slender resources and limited time.
In 1784, the year following Bourrit's fruitless attempt, we hear of
him reconnoitring Mont Blanc from new directions. With a single
companion he slept on rocks at the edge of the Glacier du Tacul,
and tried to get through the great Géant ice-fall. They failed, as
might be expected, and they saw nothing to encourage the idea that
the great mountain was more accessible from this other side than
from Chamonix. Later in the same year Paccard had a look at the
rocks of the Aiguille du Goûter, though there is no evidence of his
having made a serious attempt to climb it.

Paccard is the type of young, athletic man whose success after a
very short apprenticeship is rather galling to older men who have
found greater difficulties, and have taken far longer to reach or have

failed to reach the same proficiency. It was not till more than a hundred years later that Paccard's true part in the story of Mont Blanc was rescued by diligent seekers after truth from the mass of misrepresentation under which the jealousy of Bourrit and the ambition of Jacques Balmat had concealed it.

In September of the same year two chamois-hunters were reported to have reached the top of the Aiguille du Goûter, and Bourrit comes up from Geneva to have another try with six guides. His persistence in spite of the general discouragement is the best feature of his mountaineering. Alas! he himself fails almost at once on the lower rocks of the Aiguille. Two of his guides go on to the top and push on as far as the Dôme du Goûter, and apparently reach the rocks where the Vallot hut now stands. Saussure's hopes revive after this partial success, and next year, 1785, a very wet year, the weather at last gives him a chance in September to make an attempt by this route. No one but his guides generally accompanied Saussure; it was a special concession to Bourrit, as in some ways the pioneer of the route, that he was allowed to join the party, with his son. Saussure had had a tent put up on a small plateau below the steep rocks of the west face of the Aiguille, and here they passed the night. The physical experiments were rather a failure. There were compensations, and those who have watched the change from day to night from the Tête Rousse will know the depth and the sincerity of Saussure's feelings when he writes:

The beauty of the evening and the splendour of the sunset as I watched it from my vantage-point, brought consolation for the disappointment. . . . I went back there when night had closed in upon us; the heavens were clear without a trace of cloud; only deep in the valleys the light mist still floated; the brilliance of the stars, which at this height had ceased to twinkle, cast over the mountain-tops a pale glow, extremely faint, but enough to show their power and distance. The restfulness and the utter silence reigning in the vast spaces spread out before my eyes, which imagination pictured vaster still, inspired in me a feeling akin to terror; I seemed to be the sole survivor of the universe, and that it was its corpse I saw stretched beneath my feet. Sad as such ideas may be, they possess an attraction which the mind resists with difficulty. My eyes kept turning to those dark solitudes more often than towards Mont Blanc, where snows gleaming with a sort of phosphorescent light suggested thoughts of movement and life. But the cold, keen air on this isolated point soon drove me back into the hut.

Honest as well as human to add that last acknowledgment! There we see a simple, strong nature in contemplation of the new world into which countless mountaineers have entered since his day. And there we have also the greatest discovery of all that Saussure made, that in the highest, loneliest snows of all, farthest from the bustle of the plains, suggestions of movement and of life remain when everything below seems wrapped in the sleep of death.

Next morning the climbing did not go well. Bourrit was so afraid of the cold that he delayed the start till 6.15, and wore on his feet things more like fur slippers than boots, the heels of which came off. After five hours they were still many hundred feet below the top of the Aiguille. Fresh snow lay on the rocks. The leading guide went on and reported much more snow above, and the attempt was given up. It was not at all a competent party for climbing steep, broken rocks. It numbered twelve persons. Saussure was roped to three guides, one above and two below, in descending. The elder Bourrit had a hand on the shoulder of a guide, while another held him up by the coat-collar. The son clung on to the coat-tails of another guide. No wonder they did not get up. It is just the sort of place where the reasonably athletic will move faster than the unathletic with more experience. If the same rib is followed from the base, the last few hundred feet are decidedly steep; generally parties cross a couloir, where stones fall frequently, to a more southerly rib, which offers no difficulties if the easiest route is taken. The rock is loose, and where it is steep I have been glad to be alone on most of the nine occasions I have been up or down.

Saussure halted on the rocks to make observations, and found the Bourrits starting for the valley. He spent a quiet night at the hut and must have been glad to be rid of them. They had the impudence to ascribe the failure to Saussure's deficiencies as a climber! In an attempt afterwards to excuse himself for this perversion of truth, Bourrit could only object to Saussure's practice of making the guides go behind him in descending, where they might have sent stones on to him, and to his adoption of a facing-outwards position from which he might have fallen backwards. The reader can get an idea of Bourrit's technique from these criticisms.

It is sad to have to note a serious blot in Saussure's mountaineering record. In a letter to his friend the Prince de Ligne describing this ascent he says: 'As I toiled with such effort up these steep rocks I envied the lot of aeronauts, who rise to those great heights sitting at ease in their gondolas. I even wondered if it would be possible to use these air-carriages to reach inaccessible peaks such as Mont Blanc.'

In the very next year Saussure's reward was won. Early in June two parties set off from the Dôme du Goûter, one ascending by the

Aiguille du Goûter, the other direct from Chamonix by the Montagne de la Côte and the snow slopes above it. The latter party, consisting of Paccard and two guides, won the race easily, and, after being joined by the others, all pushed on to the ridge of the Bosses du Dromadaire. It is not surprising that it stopped them. The first *bosse* is steep and its side may be nearly pure ice. With an alpenstock and a meat-chopper I should not like leading up it at the end of a long climb, and I have had to check the slip of a competent young climber with an ice-axe in descending it. On a fine, calm day, when dozens of guides and amateurs have hewn and tramped a great track over it, it is tame enough.

They turned back, but not all of them. A young crystal-seeker, Jacques Balmat, had attached himself as a by no means welcome addition to the winning party. He is the third great figure in the epic of Mont Blanc, not so outstandingly great as his own vanity, the jealousy of Bourrit, and the imagination of the great Alexandre Dumas have portrayed him, but still a great figure. A wonderfully tough, strong fellow, this Balmat, rather a boaster, bold, and ready for anything that offered a good reward. He parted from the others, or they left him behind, to look for crystals among the rocks, very likely those on which the Vallot hut is built. His subsequent movements have been variously related, for at this point of the story we enter upon the famous controversy of Balmat versus Paccard which has caused rivers of ink to flow in Alpine literature. After Balmat has had all the credit from three or four generations, the champions of Paccard have arisen and destroyed the image of Balmat that was set up, though they have not quite put Paccard in his place.

In this work of demolition they have had a very much better case than that of the iconoclasts who have tried to prove Shakespeare did not write Shakespeare, or that England and France were as much to blame for the war as any one else. They have on their side the more trustworthy documentary evidence, and also the whole weight of common mountaineering sense. The story I shall give you is based entirely on these last two sources. Monsieur H. F. Montagnier and Mr. E. H. Stevens have been indefatigable workers in the cause of truth, and but for their researches the work of constructing what I believe to be as true a version as can be given would have been most difficult.

Balmat followed his companions' track till darkness, cloud, and hail came on and made it too dangerous to venture farther. He spent the night on the snow, probably close to a crevasse near the edge of the Grand Plateau; and in the morning returned to Chamonix, reaching it as early as eight o'clock, little the worse for his night out. The tale told by Balmat to the great novelist Dumas, when Dr. Paccard was dead, and commonly believed for long afterwards, is impossible to accept. It is worth giving, and it need not make us too hard on Balmat. Climbers, fishermen, and sportsmen of all sorts have been guilty of drawing the long bow, and Balmat's is such a beautiful great bow that we can easily forgive him. In these less imaginative days of climbing, few indeed among genuine mountaineers would dare to try to draw it.

This is Balmat's version. He had come back from two nights and a long day on the upper snows, crystal-hunting or looking for a way up the mountain; and as he enters Chamonix he meets Paccard and the two guides preparing to start. He hastens home, eats, dries his clothes, fills his gourd with wine and his knapsack with barley-cake fried in linseed oil, and sets off again to catch up his rivals. Left alone to brave the perils of the first *bosse*, he climbs it till it becomes so steep that he can only go up astride, pressing with his knees, and finally the angle stops him dead. It is four o'clock when he is back near the rocks below the *bosse*. He descends to the Grand Plateau, crosses it, and after one failure passes a big crevasse and gets on to steep snow above; he climbs this, making holes with his alpenstock right up to the ridge from which he sees the Italian face. Clouds are down on Mont Blanc, and after an hour's halt he comes down, night falling when he reaches the foot of the steep slope (the *ancien passage*). He passes the night, his fourth night out, just above the great crevasse. He is all but frozen, maintaining circulation by violent gymnastics, and in the morning he feels compelled to descend to his home, where he sleeps for twenty-four hours!

Now let us return to the more realistic version of the tale. Paccard had already been studying the mountain from the Brévent. The Bosses ridge having been proved too difficult for men furnished with very rudimentary instruments for dealing with steep slopes of hard snow or ice, some way had to be found of reaching the broader ridge that runs north-by-east from the summit. Marie-Couttet, one of the best of the Chamonix guides, whose name figures in all the early ascents of the mountain, had considered that it was not possible to reach this ridge. Paccard was not content to take that view, and determined to make an effort to prove it could be done. The one really useful bit of knowledge that Jacques Balmat's recent experience had gained was that a night could be spent high up the mountain without fatal results, thus disposing of one of the greatest of the fears that had haunted the minds of all the local men.

Two men were now filled with an ardent desire to reach the summit, and even in Balmat's case we need not regard the hope of the reward in cash as the only source of that desire. He must have known of Paccard's projected attempt, and offered himself and was accepted as an *ouvrier,* that is to say, as a porter. We need not bother over Balmat's status. It is refreshing to be able to put away all the vanity and jealousy and controversy that came after and have obscured the story of this first ascent, and think of the two men setting out, thrilled with hope and imbued only with the sort of spirit that fills two young, strong, adventurous men, who are ready, each of them, to do their utmost for the attainment of a common aim. A friend of one of them, a *marchande de sirop,* was told to look out for them next morning near the Dôme du Goûter. She was almost certainly Balmat's friend and not, as stated in some later accounts, a *bonne amie* of the doctor; for Balmat indiscreetly admits in his own story that at the rocks of the Petits Mulets he was thinking of her looking out for them near the Dôme du Goûter. Balmat was under the impression they were to have another try at the Bosses ridge, while Paccard had in mind the way actually followed up to the northerly ridge from the Grand Plateau.

They left Chamonix early in the afternoon of 7th August, after three weeks of unsettled weather. They were heavily laden, for they had to pass a first night out on the Montagne de la Côte, with a probability of a second night out somewhere high up on the snow. Accordingly they carried a blanket as well as sufficient provisions. No rope was taken, nor the short-handled axe that was used for chopping steps in hard snow, only alpenstocks shod with heavy iron points. Paccard had a compass, and, as a gentleman with scientific aims as well as a mountaineer, he had also a thermometer and a barometer with a tripod stand. The latter must have been a most tiresome extra burden for Balmat.

They left the shelter at the top of the Montagne de la Côte at four o'clock on the morning of the 8th; it would be then just light enough to see their way. They made their way across the very broken glacier towards the chain of rocks on which the Grands Mulets hut now stands. The difficulties were great. Balmat had been on this part of the glacier two months earlier, and no doubt he led over it. It was now much later in the season, and the crevasses had opened. Four times they broke through snow bridges and had to cross by laying their two poles side by side and sliding across on them. They had to make many detours, and it was midday when they passed the last of the chain of rocks and bore away to the right under the Dôme du Goûter (the Gros Mont, as Paccard calls it). Here they left the route followed in June by Paccard and the two guides across the slopes of the Dôme, and went over the Petit Plateau, where they met with deep snow accumulated by the previous week of bad weather, and they had no glasses to protect their eyes from the intense glare. Balmat was inclined to turn back here, especially as an infant child was very ill at home, but Paccard encouraged him to keep on, relieving him of some of the heavy load he was carrying.

At three o'clock they reached the Grand Plateau. Immense resolution must have been needed to go on, great as was their longing to succeed. The summit is still nearly three thousand feet above, and they had no experience to tell them that on the highest slopes the wind would have swept away most of the snow that was causing them such labour. On the Grand Plateau the snow was still lightly crusted. Balmat found the exertion of making the track so great that he refused to go on unless Paccard could do his share of leading. This Paccard did, and they led in turns from here to the summit.

Paccard led the way up from the plateau by the route he had had in mind at starting. In the illustration of Mont Blanc you see two snowy ledges sloping up, the one above the upper band of rocks (the Rochers Rouges), which is the *ancien passage* used in all subsequent ascents till 1827, the other between these two bands of rock. It was this last that Paccard chose.

These slopes must now be more broken and difficult than they then were; the shrinkage of the ice would account for it. Bold and adventurous as these two men were, it was hardly possible to believe, when I looked at the route from the Bosses ridge in 1933, that the lower portions, either of the ledge they followed or of the *ancien passage,* could have been passed by men unroped and without axes. Fortunately the snow was in good condition, hard, and therefore in no danger of avalanching under their weight, and providing fairly good foothold in the holes scooped out with the heavy iron point of the pole.

At five o'clock they were up the steepest part, and as they pushed on to the ridge and up it to the right, a cold wind met them. Breathing was becoming difficult, and they must have been very weary. At the Petits Rochers Rouges Balmat looked for a place to bivouac, while Paccard did his duty as a scientist and looked for geological specimens. There was nothing that offered any shelter, and they gallantly decided to make a last effort to reach the summit before turning back. It was then 5.45.

The snow was very good; nevertheless they had to stop, at first every hundred steps, then at increasingly frequent intervals, till it came down to every fourteen steps! They led in turn. It was bitterly cold, and Balmat lent the doctor one of his fur gloves in exchange for one of the doctor's leather ones.

The last rocks of all, the Petits Mulets, provided an excuse for a short halt to collect specimens and observe the vertical stratification. It sounds better than the fastening of a bootlace or the admiring of the view. From here Paccard took the last slope straight up; Balmat, more heavily laden, took it in zigzags, and had to run the last few yards to reach the top at the same moment as the doctor. It was 6.23 by the watch of Baron von Gersdorf, whose eye was glued to the telescope down below.

They planted the barometer-stand in the deep powdery snow and took an observation. Either the instrument was a bad one, or it had been damaged on the way. It read much too low, both on the summit and on the Montagne de la Côte, suggesting that air had got into the tube. The result gave over seventeen thousand feet to Mont Blanc. Paccard had been intelligent enough to note the difference of height at the two levels pretty accurately, and a subsequent observation with a new 'English' barometer, on the Montagne de la Côte, enabled him to calculate the error and bring out a result of 15,545 feet, only a little more than two hundred feet lower than the present accepted height. In a short stay of thirty-five minutes on the top Paccard made many other observations. The temperature was nearly 14° F. below the freezing-point, which means very severe cold, with a strong wind. He took compass readings to check the magnetic variation, and he had a strip of blue paper in twenty different shades to help him estimate the depth of blue of the sky. All this besides taking in the general topographical features of a view unparalleled for extent in the Alps.

It is remarkable that any man at such an hour could devote the precious minutes to scientific observations of such little value. To be on the summit of Mont Blanc, when the sun is sinking and throwing lights and shadows of bewildering beauty over the surrounding sea of mountains, is a sufficiently impressive experience in itself. To be the first man ever to stand there, as well as to stand there at that time, is a thing we can only hope for in our dreams.

Since five o'clock the two men had been in full view of the telescopes at Chamonix, at Bourrit's house, and at other points on the north slopes of the valley, and their movements on the last part of the ascent were faithfully recorded in minutest detail by an important observer, the Baron von Gersdorf. It was close on seven o'clock, a few minutes before sunset, when they left the summit. The rocks of Mont Blanc de Courmayeur, a few hundred yards away to the south, seemed to offer no prospect of a shelter from the icy wind, and they hurried, in fact ran, down to the Rochers Rouges in six minutes. Taking it in turn to pick up their tracks they made good progress down the steep slope, and reached the Grand Plateau just before dark. Bright moonlight helped them to follow their tracks, and the snow bridges were frozen firm, so that they got off the ice where the Montagne de la Côte runs into the glacier just before midnight. There they could rest at ease and count the comparatively trifling cost.

Both had mild frostbite in the hand that had worn a leather glove, first wet and then frozen, on the windswept ridge and summit. Paccard's hand was black, Balmat's white. Paccard being a doctor, Balmat a peasant who grubbed among the rocks, one would have expected it the other way round. Circulation was restored to both by rubbing, though Paccard's finger-tips remained without sensation for several weeks. Then they wrapped themselves in the one blanket and went to sleep.

Next morning both woke to the knowledge that they were severely burnt by the sun on the fresh snow, and Paccard was so nearly blind that Balmat had to lead him by the hand down to the priory. I think this sight may have helped to win acceptance for the version of the story that took shape in Balmat's mind on his return.

It is regrettable that the selfish side of human nature should have cast its ugly shadow over this splendid adventure. The truth has come to light at last, but it is at the expense of Balmat, and it shows how easily a man's head is turned and his generosity destroyed by the pride of achievement. Bourrit is greatly to blame, for he was a recognized authority on Alpine exploration. The disappointment of seeing the glory of the first ascent taken from him by Paccard the amateur, the young man without influence or long experience, was too much for him, and it is at the expense of Paccard that he finds an outlet for his spite. There was no doubt of the ascent itself; scores of people had witnessed it. The whole credit of the achievement is transferred to Balmat, and we have to admit that Balmat was only too ready to receive it.

So the false tale was started and given wide circulation in a published account by Bourrit, in which Balmat figures as the discoverer and sole hero of the ascent, Paccard playing as secondary a part as it is possible for a climbing companion to play. A very few sentences from a translation of Bourrit's account in the *Scots Magazine* for November 1786 will show its nature. I choose the passage which describes the first stage; it shows Bourrit at his most Bourrit-like.

The heaven, which appeared in volumes above them, was more and more so as they advanced. . . . They seemed as if they were wafted on beautiful clouds. . . . They imagined that they belonged to a species of beings superior to human nature; and the more they ascended, the more the illusion approached to probability. . . . The doctor began to be out of health, his knees stiffened, and the cold prevented him from advancing; his companion, more active and hardy, encouraged him . . . a summit appears before them, they are in doubt if it is the last. Balmat resolved to be convinced, moves alone . . . the snow is firm, and he sees that but a few paces remain to come at the top of the mountain: he gains it. What joy! the whole earth is beneath his feet! He announces his success to his companion with his shouts; he goes down to meet him, animates and assists him. . . . They are beheld from Chamonix; strangers saw them through their glasses.

They did indeed, and it is doubtful if justice could have been done to Paccard if they had not! Balmat received plenty of encouragement from Bourrit in magnifying the part he had played, and in belittling Paccard. The distortion of facts became so bad that Paccard had to make Balmat sign a certificate, witnessed by two other Chamoniards, contradicting the libels on his conduct.

It is a very great pity that we can never see Paccard's own account of the ascent, and we must conclude it was never published; all efforts to trace it have failed; only his prospectus inviting subscriptions to defray the cost has survived. The discovery of the doctor's diary, though it only gives a few lines about the actual ascent, was one of the most valuable finds made by those who have searched diligently for evidence.

The story spread by Balmat and Bourrit had a start which caused it to be believed till long after the three great figures in the story, Paccard, Balmat, and Saussure, were dead. So that almost simultaneously with this great first ascent, in which mountaineering was born as a splendid, healthy infant, appears a bad fairy godmother of selfish rivalry and competition, with ugly features of jealousy and suspicion, who can still exercise a baneful influence upon it.

It is a rare thing, it may be unique, that the first ascent of a famous peak should not be the most famous in its history. With Mont

Blanc this is so. The ascent by Paccard and Balmat could not have done for mountaineering what was done by Saussure's ascent.

Saussure lost no time in preparing to profit by the opening of the route. Before Paccard and Balmat were back from the summit, Tairraz the innkeeper had sent off an express messenger to Geneva with news of the success that had been witnessed by the watchers at the telescopes. Saussure's reply to Tairraz shows well his ardour, his generosity, and his modesty.

I was delighted to be the first to hear the news. . . . And now I am going to tell you something you must keep quite secret; I am hoping to make the ascent myself by their route. Not that I flatter myself I can get right to the top; I have neither the youth nor the agility of the doctor—but I hope at any rate to be able to reach a great height and carry out observations which for me would have importance.

He goes on to ask Tairraz to send up at least half a dozen men to do what they can to make easier the earlier part of the route through the ice-fall between the Montagne de la Côte and the Grands Mulets rocks. He tells him to put Jacques Balmat in charge and to pay him extra, and he suggests the building of a hut at the top of the Montagne de la Côte, to serve as a shelter for the men as well as sleeping quarters for himself the night he comes up. He also gives orders for the construction of another hut much higher up, on some rocks at two-thirds or three-quarters of the distance from the Montagne de la Côte to the summit. This he did, knowing he could not possibly climb this whole stage without a night out. Unfortunately there are no rocks so situated on the early route.

He went up on 20th August. Very bad weather came on and he came down disconsolate to Chamonix, where he remained hoping vainly for settled conditions for several days, till all hope of an ascent that year had to be abandoned. Next year, 1787, preparations were pushed forward in June and July, and Jacques Balmat, with two other guides, Cachat le Géant and Alexis Tournier, made the second ascent of the mountain. They left the sleeping-place on the Montagne de la Côte at 2.20 a.m., and reached the top at 3 p.m. This ascent is hardly noticed in Alpine literature, a typical instance of the way that fame overlooks what is not done with pomp and circumstance.

The main interest of this second ascent from a historical point of view is that the party almost certainly reached the northerly ridge of Mont Blanc from the Grand Plateau by the snow terrace above the higher Rochers Rouges, not that between the two bands of rock which Paccard chose the year before.

At last, on 1st August, Saussure set off in fine weather with every prospect of success. The story of his climb is so familiar that only a brief reference need be given here. It was a huge caravan of twenty persons: Saussure and his valet, with eighteen guides led by Jacques Balmat. In addition to great provision of food and drink they carried many scientific instruments, some of them heavy instruments capable of giving very accurate readings. They had black crape masks to keep off the glare, the usual iron-shod alpenstocks, some short-handled axes, crampons, ropes, and a ladder, and there was a tent which must have been of considerable size, for the whole party squeezed into it on the Grand Plateau.

The night on the Montagne de la Côte was not too cold or comfort-less, several of the guides sleeping in convenient niches in the rocks or in Saussure's old shelter, while he himself shared the tent with his valet and two or three of his regular guides. Next morning squabbles over the loads delayed the start till half-past six. It was not the labour of carrying the weight, but the fear that it would break the snow bridges, that made them reluctant to carry a pound more than was their share.

The Grands Mulets rocks were reached soon after nine o'clock. Marie-Couttet had all but fallen through a snow bridge, and the sight of the chasm disclosed by the hole he made so unnerved the guides that they were afraid of anything but rock or bare ice. The time taken is far shorter than that taken by Paccard and Balmat, showing that a good deal of route-finding and of step-cutting had been done beforehand. Saussure had difficulty in persuading the guides to go higher than the rock to sleep. Jacques Balmat's account of his experiences of a night out the year before would, we may be sure, lose nothing in the telling. And greater even than the fear of unendurable cold was the fear that the warmth and weight of twenty bodies would cause the snow to give way and precipitate the party into one of the horrible chasms with which they believed the whole glacier to be undermined. Saussure had to threaten to go on himself with any men that were ready to accompany him before they would leave the solid rocks. On the Petit Plateau they walked over the débris of two huge avalanches that had fallen from the Dôme du Goûter since the ascent of the three guides less than a month before.

The night in the tent on the Grand Plateau, with twenty tired, unwashed men in it, must have been horrible. Saussure came out

3. SAUSSURE'S PARTY ON THE 'ANCIEN PASSAGE'

to get a breath of cool, pure air, and he tells us what he saw. 'The moon shone with dazzling splendour in a sky black as ebony. Jupiter was just coming out, flashing a brilliant ray from behind the highest point east of Mont Blanc, and the light reflected upon the vast basin of snow was so dazzling that no stars could be distinguished but those of the first and second magnitude.' The dreamer and the scientist find happy union in Saussure.

In the night the rumble of a great avalanche close at hand woke them with a start. They actually had to walk over it in ascending the *ancien passage* in the morning. This is where the critical part of the ascent begins. The dangers of the glacier, magnified by ignorance and imagination, now lie behind them, the real dangers only partially appreciated are beginning. With our better knowledge of snow conditions we can see how fortunate they were to escape disaster.

Saussure's account enables us to reconstruct the conditions with great exactness. The day was perfectly clear and fine, the sky being, as he tells us, of the darkest possible blue, whose intensity is dimmed by no suspicion of cloud; possibly the third day after a bad period, when the wind has died down so as to be unnoticed below the highest ridges of the higher peaks. The long, snowy ledge ran up steeply in front of them for at least a thousand feet to the broad skyline ridge. Its angle is about forty degrees, that is to say, considerably above the angle at which loosely lying snow may avalanche on open slopes. On the right, above them, was the steep face broken by ice-cliffs, threatening the lower part of the way they must take and from which the avalanche had passed down in the night. The whole way up on the left the ledge ended suddenly in a great ice-cliff, set on the top of a high belt of vertical rocks, a constant reminder of the fate of any one who slipped over the edge.

On the lower part, where the recently fallen snow had been exposed to the sun and out of the wind, it had melted sufficiently for the cold of the night to freeze the surface hard. Higher up, on the colder, more exposed position, the crust was too thin to bear a man's weight, and they broke through into several inches of loose powdery snow lying on a lower hard surface of ice or hard snow.

What a hopelessly incompetent party they would seem to us now if we saw them strung out at irregular intervals along this famous *ancien passage*. Let us hope that in the size of the party, which to us is an added source of danger, they all found mutual assurance! First there is Balmat, and one or two other guides, breaking the track, slipping a few inches now and then on the slippery surface beneath,

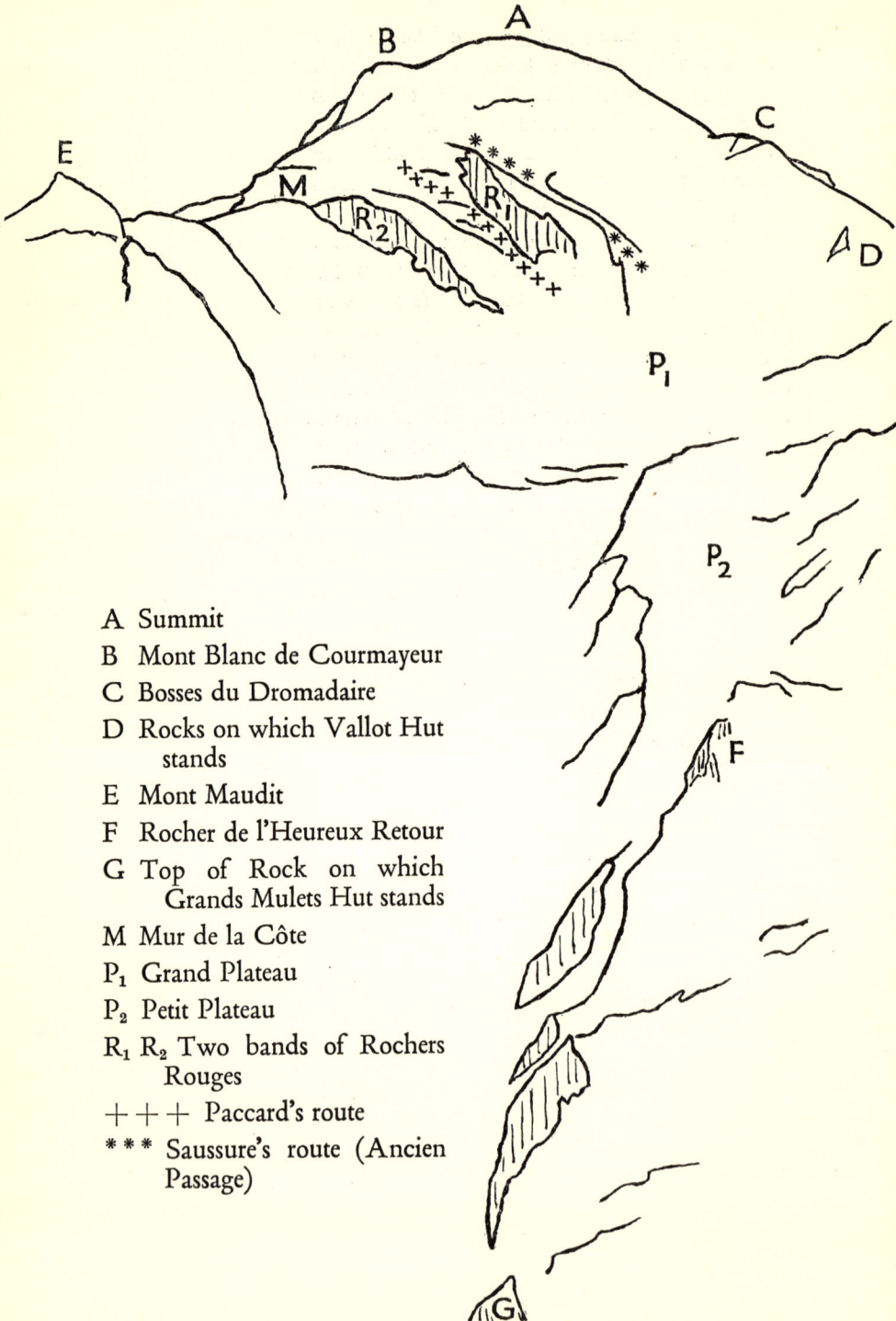

A Summit

B Mont Blanc de Courmayeur

C Bosses du Dromadaire

D Rocks on which Vallot Hut
stands

E Mont Maudit

F Rocher de l'Heureux Retour

G Top of Rock on which
Grands Mulets Hut stands

M Mur de la Côte

P_1 Grand Plateau

P_2 Petit Plateau

R_1 R_2 Two bands of Rochers
Rouges

+ + + Paccard's route

* * * Saussure's route (Ancien
Passage)

4. MONT BLANC FROM THE AIR

and held up only by the pressure of the thin crust against the calves of their legs. Then Saussure himself, intent now only on success and putting all thought of danger from his mind. He plods up gallantly, getting very breathless and exhausted now, one hand leaning on a rail consisting of an alpenstock held between him and the precipice by his guides, the other hand trying to get purchase on his own alpenstock to check the slipping of his feet.

Where the crust was harder the guides chopped steps with the stout axes some of them carried, and, as has happened to many a party, rather too far apart for the comfort of those following, whose balance is less secure. A great *sérac* at one point compelled them to go quite near the edge. Behind Saussure would come his faithful, suffering valet, drawing a false assurance of safety, like his master, from the extemporized handrail. Finally the rest of the guides in irregular order, the laggards still stumbling over the blocks of ice and balls of avalanche snow that had fallen a few hours before.

Fortune smiled on this courageous company, under this early and greatest discoverer of the snowy Alps, and not a single one of the twenty was lost on the expedition. The last nine hundred feet up the north ridge, entirely free from danger but capable of filling the legs of the most expert mountaineer with lead, was a long, breathless fight to keep the body moving up.

The time taken from the last Rochers Rouges to the summit, nearly two hours, from a little after nine o'clock till eleven o'clock, is long compared with two and a half hours for the previous stage up from the Grand Plateau. Paccard and Balmat took only thirty-eight minutes, and they had climbed three times the height from their sleeping quarters. Saussure trampled the last few feet of snow with a feeling of anger at the time and effort exacted by the last resistance of Mont Blanc, which it makes by simply holding us high enough in the air to paralyse our powers. He stayed for four and a half hours on the summit, working hard at his experiments and bewailing his inability to work at normal speed. For us the ascent of Mont Blanc is made for the pleasurable emotions it can give; for Saussure it was a unique opportunity to penetrate farther into the undiscovered realm of physical research that was beginning to draw men into it. The scientist in him would not spare a single one of those precious hours for the indulgence of the dreamer at the great moment of his life. Fortunately the most lasting impressions of such Alpine pilgrimages are the work of moments. We need not doubt that Saussure had a satisfaction that finds no expression in the record of his observations

D

of temperature, of barometric pressures, of topographical discoveries, and of the effect of height on the sound of pistol-shots. The nature of the impression made by the reaching of the goal, like a great joy or a great sorrow, is often not realized till later. He lets us know something of his feelings as a climber and not as a scientist, when he rushes into the arms of an old Swiss friend whom he meets on the way back to Geneva, exclaiming: 'Congratulate me; I come from the conquest of Mont Blanc,' and later also, after he has returned safely home, when he says: 'I can now look upon Mont Blanc with real pleasure, and without the painful disturbance of the emotions which the sight of it aroused in me before.'

The descent was safely carried through. Some of the guides were sufficiently alive to the dangers of the *ancien passage* to look for a better way down while the lengthy experiments were being carried out on the summit. We are not told where they looked, but we may surmise that one short glance at the Brenva slopes would rule them out as an alternative, and even the Mur de la Côte, which in 1827 became the regular route, would appear to them, especially if it was icy, more difficult than anything they had ascended. They descended in their tracks. The trampling of the fresh snow by many feet must have caused some adherence to the underlying surface which would compensate for the melting by many hours of sunshine of the supporting crust. Where the far-spaced steps had been chopped in the harder snow, which would have been very awkward to descend, they could now plunge down on their heels with comparative ease and safety.

At sunset they reached and proceeded to baptize the Rocher de l'Heureux Retour, almost the highest of the chain of rocks that begins a little below the present Grands Mulets hut. There they set up the tent for the night, and Saussure began to taste the joys of retrospect which are to mountaineers such a generous and unfailing return for the wise outlay of energy they have made.

In the morning they found that some of the snow bridges had collapsed; a guide occasionally put a leg through or slipped on a steep slope in avoiding a crevasse, and the ladder was of great service. They were all thankful to reach terra firma at the top of the Montagne de la Côte. There they met Bourrit, who tried to persuade some of the guides to stay with him that night and climb Mont Blanc again. They were weary and anxious to attend mass at Chamonix, and they refused. So Bourrit had to come down to Chamonix with Saussure and see him receive the congratulations of his family and friends.

And they owed a good deal to fortune. The fact that such a

party achieved the ascent without any sensational accident, and the ease with which Mont Blanc may be climbed from Chamonix at the present time, are apt to make us forget the very real dangers of the expedition, not so much the obvious dangers to individuals of crossing the lower crevassed portions of the glacier unroped, as the risk of disaster from a slip or from avalanche on the *ancien passage*.

Saussure was too keen to discover what the Alps had to tell him to remain content with his great feat. One other expedition that he made deserves a mention in any history of mountaineering: his passage of the col, known vaguely as the Tacul, and named by him the Col du Géant, after the famous rocky peak that was only conquered by the use of pitons in 1882. This expedition, made in the following year, with a stay in camp of sixteen nights on the col itself, is, by modern standards, a bigger mountaineering undertaking than the ordinary ascent of Mont Blanc. As in the case of Mont Blanc, Saussure was not the first to make the climb successfully, and yet his is again the most famous of all passages of the col. He is so far from having the later climbers' attitude that, instead of being fiercely jealous of those who anticipate him in achievement, he seems absolutely content, indeed pleased, to have had the possibility of the route demonstrated by another!

Bourrit must certainly have derived immense satisfaction from anticipating his famous rival in crossing what was spoken of in Chamonix as the Grand Col. The credit we wish to give Bourrit for this fine expedition is sadly diminished by the exhibition of jealousy and exaggeration which characterizes his account of it. Bourrit's was the third authentic crossing. In 1786 M. Exchaquet, a manager of mines at Servoz, made an attempt, and it is humiliating to find that he failed through the incompetence of an English companion. Early the next summer he engaged a couple of guides to come with him, but one of these slipped off the day before with a friend and robbed him of the honour of the first authentic traverse of the col. Exchaquet was an enterprising amateur and capable mountaineer, like Paccard, just the type of whom Bourrit was particularly jealous, and we find that Bourrit makes no mention of his success, though he mentions that of the two guides who had got across the day before.

Bourrit's passage of the col was made in the late August of 1787. Being much later in the season than that of Exchaquet, the *séracs* of the Géant ice-fall would be more difficult, and their terrors lose

nothing in his description. 'The guides, all four of whom had been
with Saussure on Mont Blanc, admit that the difficulties of that
mountain do not approach those of this expedition. . . . These
towers and shattered walls often rose three or four hundred feet above
us.' The easy descent on the Italian side is compared to the rocks
of the Aiguille du Goûter, on which Bourrit and his son gave, as
we have seen, a poor exhibition of climbing. Had it really been as
steep, Bourrit and his son would certainly not have reached Courmayeur that night. Writing in the third person, Bourrit tells us
that 'he returned to Geneva from this memorable expedition with
the most extraordinary pictures and the honour of having passed in
one day into Piedmont, through countless perils, perils which gave
him an added satisfaction by showing what man can do when
spurred on by the desire of fame.'

Saussure's account of his expedition in 1788 is strikingly different
in its simple sincerity. Though it was early in July, his guides
thought it best to turn the Géant ice-fall by the rocks of La Noire
on the right bank of the glacier. 'Our guides warned us that this
route is much more dangerous than the one taken the previous year,
but I do not lay much stress on their statements, partly because the
dangers of the moment always appear greater than those that are
past; partly because they think their employers will be flattered by
being told that they have come through very great peril.' Saussure
mentions steep slopes of snow in which the guides had trodden
steps the previous afternoon, and which would otherwise have presented difficulty to a party without axes when the surface was hard.
He makes no mention of the only real danger, that of falling stones.
One of the guides had a nasty fall into a crevasse, but the obvious
course of roping does not seem to have been adopted on the long,
snow-covered Géant Glacier, any more than on Mont Blanc.

Saussure stayed sixteen days on the col. The scientific observations he made have no place here, though the making of them at all
times of the day, and on different days, was the object of his long
visit. More interesting to us is that in the course of his prolonged
study of scientific phenomena he found that mountains show themselves in new and unexpected lights to those who spend long periods
in the high places which they keep secluded from the world of men.
He became intimate with them as never before. To his imaginative
mind propinquity with these great peaks gave a new understanding
of the significance they might hold in life. They ceased to be wild,
unapproachable things of which men must be afraid. Saussure

could look from close at hand with wonder and admiration at these immense features of rock and ice in which men had hitherto found only a cold, relentless hostility.

His last evening, when the observations were ended and the records made, brought him a splendid reward for his long labours.

That sixteenth evening, the last we spent upon the Col du Géant, was supremely beautiful. All the high peaks seemed to have conspired to make us regret our parting from them. The cold wind that had made most of our evenings here so comfortless, refrained from blowing. The crests that towered above us, and the intervening snows, put on the loveliest shades of rose and carmine. Over Italy a broad band of purple extended along the whole horizon, and above the band the full moon rose in queenly majesty, vermilion-tinted. The air around us was as pure and perfectly limpid as Homer imagines that of Olympus to have been, while the valleys, filled with the vapours that had formed there, looked like abodes of thickest darkness.

But how shall I find words to describe the night that followed on this lovely evening, when the twilight ended and the moon shone in solitary glory, pouring floods of silvery light upon the immense amphitheatre of snow and rock that encircled our humble shelter. These fields of snow and cliffs of ice, too dazzling to be looked at in the day, what a wondrous and enchanting spectacle they present under the soft beams of the torch of night! What a magnificent contrast the dark granite rocks afford, standing out in sharp, bold outlines against the gleaming snow! Was ever such a moment given for meditation? What pains and hardships are not paid in full by moments such as these! The soul of man is lifted up, a wider, nobler horizon is offered to his view; surrounded by such silent majesty he seems to hear the very voice of Nature, and to become her confidant, to whom she tells the most secret of her operations.

Remember it is Saussure, the pattern of sincerity, who writes, and judge how he was moved; and remember also that these words were written several years before Ruskin was born.

Saussure is a true father of mountaineering, however much the value of the part he played in its history may fluctuate as one generation succeeds another. The twentieth century has opened as one of material achievement, diminishing the interest and the belief in spiritual matters. Men do not want in Alpine literature attempts to convey the contemplative pleasures it affords; the barest and most business-like record of achievement is what they demand. Progress in mountaineering is measured and conceived in terms of metres and angles and time. And so Saussure is, for the time, not quite so great a figure as he was. Both Paccard and Placidus a Spescha were far better climbers, and their individual enterprise and achievements much greater from the technical point of view. The present generation has rehabilitated these two, who were not honoured in their time as they deserved.

Why do neither of them occupy as great a place as Saussure held, and will always hold, in the history of mountaineering? Paccard, the village doctor in Chamonix, Placidus, the monk in Disentis, lived in the midst of the high mountains, the Mont Blanc and the Tödi group, in which their climbs were made. They were comparatively poor men to whom worldly pleasures were strictly limited by circumstances. Both were men of considerable education, to whom the Alps offered an excellent way of developing their interests in topography, or in physics or botany. The cynic of these days could say of both: 'They climb mountains because they have nothing better to do.' The most ill-natured cynic would not have thought of saying that of Saussure. Here was a man with every advantage of wealth and position, cultured, married to a young wife to whom he was devoted; every pleasure that a great city could offer was his for the asking. And he chose to climb the Accursed Mountain! He was too big a man, too intelligent, too generous and broad-minded, to be dismissed as a crank. And this strange choice of his was no mere whim of a man who had temporarily tired of other diversions, for he went on making mountain expeditions after his greatest and most famous climb.

Just as the support of a financial magnate may cause some undertaking that has been unconsidered or despised before to be quoted on the list of shares for which men anxious to get rich will bid, so did Saussure cause mountaineering to appear among the occupations on which men deliberately choose to spend their time.

Climbers may say that his aims were merely scientific; so might we say that the aim of Elizabethan explorers was the search for gold. There was a divine curiosity that underlay those aims. There were many scientists in Saussure's day, and none of them but he had a longing to climb Mont Blanc or cross the Col du Géant.

The greatest service that man can render to any human activity is to give it a new value that was unrecognized before. We pay our debt of adulation readily to a personal achievement that is attainable only by exceptional capacity, such as a very difficult climb, or the breaking of a record. Those who give new value to what is attainable by nearly all, place us under an obligation so immense that it is beyond our power to pay. Saussure had the opportunity to give a new value to mountaineering, and he took it, using it with a generous enthusiasm which makes his name beloved as well as honoured by all who know the part he played in the winning of Mont Blanc. Through his ascent the belief came to mankind that the Alps might be what they have now become for us, the most gloriously profitable portion of all the world in which to pass those hours of leisure when wise men seek and find the adventure that is life.

CHAPTER IV

THE GROWTH OF UNDERSTANDING

SAUSSURE was a great man. He held up a light, not that it migh shed lustre on himself, but that men might follow in the path that leads to knowledge of the truth. And they followed almost too faith-fully, too literally, being for many years content to tread exactly in the track which he had opened up into the new world above the snow line.

For two or three generations after Saussure, Chamonix is the only place where regular mountaineering occurs, and the records of ascents made there read like faint echoes of his great adventure. An attempt to climb Mont Blanc remains in the eyes of the world an act of folly, a sin against the usages of society which must be charitably covered by the excuse of scientific research.

An Englishman, Colonel Mark Beaufoy, is the first man to reach the summit after the local heroes whose exploits were recorded in the preceding chapter. His ascent was made with his servant and ten guides only six days after that of Saussure. We know that 'he suffered much, thought he had gone blind, got a swelled face, and regretted he had undertaken such a thing.'

However, from the manuscript of our old friend the village doctor, Paccard, we learn that 'he walked up like a guide,' and that he observed the latitude (45° 50′ 11″) and the altitude of the sun (59° 42′ 26″). The fact that these observations were taken to a second of angle shows what a seriously substantial instrument he must have had carried up to save his reputation for sanity!

Bourrit consoled himself on this occasion with the society of the colonel's attractive young wife, aged nineteen, whom he describes as imaginative and very well educated. In fact it was she 'who worked out with ease the results of the readings taken on the summit, which proves what great attention is paid to women's education in England.' One can almost forgive Bourrit his jealousy and his bombastic exaggeration for that!

Poor Bourrit all but achieved his ambition the next year, when he accompanied Mr. Woodley as far as the rocks called the Petits Mulets, only a few hundred yards from the top, but he could not quite do it, and had to see the others finish the climb without him.

No other ascent occurs till that of Baron Dorthesen and M. Forneret in 1802. The former 'walked on the snow like a Russian.' Whether this implies a better or worse technique than Colonel Beaufoy's must be left to the reader's judgment. They built a hut on the Grands Mulets on arriving there, the old one evidently having disappeared in the storms of several winters. They observed an electrometer and took various temperatures. Their progress was retarded by 'une chaleur intérieure' which afflicted M. Forneret, and which would presumably be translated 'a chill' by the doctor in the drawing-room. Their faces were protected with tallow, whose smell must have intensified the usual distaste for food above the Grand Plateau.

The first American ascent, by Dr. Jeremiah Van Rensselaer and Dr. William Howard, was made in 1819. Both wrote accounts of their climb, and that of Dr. Jeremiah almost makes one suspect a relationship to the author of Lamentations. On the Grands Mulets 'night soon closed upon us and rendered our situation still more appalling; the dead silence of darkness was broken only by the groans of the weary, or by the loud thunder of a fallen avalanche that roused us from an imperfect sleep.' Descending the *ancien passage,* 'part of one of the avalanches that threatened us in our ascent had already fallen and lay scattered over our path, and the part that yet hung suspended above us seemed ready to follow its fallen half. Dreadful indeed was the silence in which, with hurried step, we hastened down the sidehill. Fearing to raise a look from the pathway, and scarcely daring to breathe, we arrived at the bottom.' On the return to Chamonix 'we went immediately into a darkened room, and, after washing in cream, went to bed, but not to rest. Our eyelids were glued together and our faces entirely blistered.' Even the retrospect is not too rosy. 'Thus our journey has been of no avail in adding to our knowledge of the rarefaction of the air at the top, yet we are satisfied with having made the attempt.' The practice of roping the party had certainly been introduced before this ascent.

The manuscript of Dr. Paccard already alluded to has many interesting notes on these early ascents. The doctor is often mentioned as lending instruments or ministering to sufferers. Repeated references to Paccard himself as the discoverer of the *ancien passage* suggest that the doctor's part in the first ascent had been unfairly judged and that someone was trying to steal the credit that was his due.

In 1819 we find him lending Captain J. Undrell a thermometer, a compass, a prism, and a sextant. In 1823 one of the guides of Mr. H. H. Jackson had his face red and puffed and his eyes were painful and inflamed, an affliction which Dr. Paccard relieved 'by rubbing it with beer-foam,' the liquid below the foam being no doubt reserved for the internal use of the patient to give him confidence in the cure.

The number of guides continues to be absurdly large, five being the minimum. Jacques Balmat seems to have led every one of the first six ascents, but after 1802 his name disappears from the lists recorded.

In 1820 the accident which was bound to happen sooner or later on the *ancien passage* occurred, several guides of Dr. Hamel's party being swept by an avalanche into the crevasse at the foot and three buried so deeply that they were never seen again. Relics of the accident appeared at the foot of the Bossons Glacier about forty years later. This was the first genuine mountaineering accident, and it made a deep impression in Chamonix.

Mr. Jackson's was the first ascent after the accident. In the account of it in the *Journal de Savoie* of Chambéry it is interesting to note this reference to the *ancien passage*: 'This way which M. Paccard had discovered before his ascent in 1786 was then less dangerous because the snows were low, which is not the case during a period of increase of the glaciers. M. Paccard considers that in such a period another route might be made above the Grand Plateau "sur le piédestal de rocher tronqué, qui embrasserait celui-ci et le rocher rouge."' The reader can decide for himself whether this refers to the way by the corridor and Mur de la Côte or a way nearer the *ancien passage*. Paccard's own ascent was almost certainly made by the ledge below the *ancien passage*; no doubt there were reasons at the time for preferring it to the *ancien passage,* which he says he had previously discovered and which runs above the higher band of the Rochers Rouges.

In a letter to the same paper in 1825 describing the next ascent, that of Captain Sherwill and Dr. Clark, Paccard himself writes: 'The steep slope above the Grand Plateau (the possibility of which, as a way up, I was the first to ascertain from the Brévent before my ascent) was clear of snow, owing to an avalanche similar to that which swallowed up the guides in August 1820; it had left the ice bare, and a staircase had to be cut in it with the axe.' He also tells us the height of the barometer (15 inches 9·6 lines), which shows that the scientific side of the adventure was still taken seriously.

Weather was some excuse for the neglect of science by MM. Chenal and Viallet in 1834. They had hardly time to consult the themometer, which marked 12° (C.) below zero. An unfortunate pigeon, almost blind after two days' captivity in a basket, and ex-hausted by constant shaking, refused to make for Chamonix, where its young awaited it. 'We had to give up the other experiments we had meant to carry out.' No wonder! There was a violent wind and thirty-four inches of snow. In fact there was some doubt expressed as to whether they ever reached the top, the doubt being increased by their having taken two young porters at a lower tariff than usual.

Count Henri de Tilly is the first Frenchman to climb Mont Blanc, later in 1834. The number of guides is still large, six on this occasion, and apparently excessive, for only two reached the top with the count, two of them a quarter of an hour after, and two gave up altogether! The ascent was still regarded as a severe ordeal in which something more than mere discomfort might be expected. Tilly himself was frostbitten badly enough to make the doctors consider the amputation of the limb. Mr. Waddington's ascent in 1836 is described as 'one of the most fortunate that have ever taken place. It was accomplished in two days without serious accident; one guide had a foot frostbitten, two others the nose: every one suffered severely in the eyes, but no one's health suffered seriously.' And the account continues: 'It is to be hoped that Mr. Waddington, who did not make the expedition merely to go up the mountain, will publish an account of his ascent and the scientific observations he was able to make.' On this occasion we read of five guides, three 'volunteers,' and five assistants. The latter did not get farther than the Glacier des Bossons. The *malaises* described by the few persons who have reached the summit of Mont Blanc, the results of which undermined the health of the celebrated Saussure, began immediately above the Grand Plateau and after a breakfast of 'volaille gelée et du vin en sorbet.' Some of the guides descended from the summit at once, leaving Mr. Waddington and 'two other persons' to make the necessary sacrifices to science and presumably also to find their way safely down the Mur de la Côte, which had become the recognized route after its discovery in 1827.

The first Italian ascent, by the Marchese Imperiale di Sant' Angelo, took place in 1840. Only one guide out of the whole party had his feet frostbitten. And we are told, as something surprising, that 'the marquis is now in Geneva in excellent health.'

Even as late as 1850 a man could not make this ascent, so soon to be degraded to a 'mere snow-grind,' without causing grave anxiety to his nearest and dearest. *The Times* of 9th September 1850 contains an account of an ascent made by Mr. S. A. Richards and Mr. W. K. Gretton. 'Crowds assembled to witness the start; as the arduous nature of the adventure was well known, the guides left their watches and little valuables behind, and the two gentlemen made their wills and prepared for the worst. Great anxiety was expressed on many a face as the little band, headed by our two countrymen, disappeared in the forest at the foot of the mountain.' Cannons were fired to celebrate the arrival, not only at the summit but at the Grands Mulets on the afternoon of the first day. 'The Flégère and the Brévent were crowded with anxious observers.' And the return was a veritable triumph. They reached Chamonix once more at half-past seven, when, 'preceded by the best music Chamonix afforded, and carried on the backs of some enthusiastic Frenchmen, they were received at the Hôtel de Londres with loud cheers, firing of cannons, and expressions of delight at their safe return.'

And that is written sixty-three years after Saussure's ascent. In another thirty years we find Mummery expressing quite other views, when his friends have taken him up to the Grands Mulets owing to the weather having put rock-climbing out of the question. He was almost tricked into the drudgery of an ascent. 'When we awoke the next morning, we found ourselves half-way up to the Grand Plateau, Burgener and Venetz being evidently under the impression that we intended to spend the rest of the day in the treadmill-like occupation of ascending Mont Blanc.'

It would be a diverting spectacle to see the present members of the Groupe de Haute Montagne offering their backs as saddles for the triumphant return of those who ascend Mont Blanc by the ordinary route from Chamonix!

One of the most romantic episodes in the history of mountaineering is the discovery of the route now generally followed from Chamonix, the route by the Bosses du Dromadaire. Its discoverer was one of the many Couttets, and of the only slightly less common Marie-Couttets; not the Joseph Marie-Couttet whose name occurs in almost all the early ascents of Mont Blanc at the beginning of the nineteenth century, but a strange creature who prowled about the hills and glaciers alone, 'thin, with piercing eyes and pointed nose, wearing a red coat, worn at the shoulders and scanty, faded to a tawny brown by the sun'; whence his nickname, 'Moutelet,' a patois word for weasel. A pioneer of 'l'alpinisme acrobatique' apparently.

One day he was guiding an Englishman who bore himself with more than the usual amount of British phlegm. All sorts of climbing difficulties elicited no sign of emotion from his employer, and at last in exasperation Moutelet makes for a half-uprooted pine hanging over a thousand-foot precipice. 'He walks boldly along the trunk; having reached the end he lies down, hangs by his feet, and sways to and fro above the drop. The Englishman watched him, still unmoved; but when Moutelet rejoined him, he put a piece of gold into his hand, saying: "Take this! But don't do it again!"'

On another occasion he fell 150 feet down a steep face consisting of a long series of rocky steps, and he bumped grievously on every one. It was thought he was dead; however, after a time he opened his eyes, and the priest who had come to give extreme unction told him to thank God for not having been killed on the spot. 'I thank God!' he cried. 'He didn't let me off a single step!'

He was considered rather a loony, and this, coupled with his decrepit appearance, prevented the acceptance of his frequent offers to take climbers over the Bosses ridge. One day, after dismissal by a party which he had attempted to join at the Grands Mulets, he went off by himself. On the Grand Plateau they found him sitting on the snow and passed on to the corridor. A few jokes at his expense may have acted as a goad to the poor old weasel. As the party reached the top of the Mur de la Côte, they saw a man descending from the summit. As he came near he stopped and bowed gravely, hat in hand, like a householder welcoming his guests. He was then eighty-four, a fine age to make the first crossing of a ridge whose appearance had turned back every guide and amateur who had approached it.

There is no reason to doubt the validity of this first ascent. The route was definitely opened by Charles Hudson's party, with Melchior Anderegg and other guides, in 1859. It was not descended till 1869. Charles Hudson, coming over the Aiguille du Goûter and Dôme du Goûter in 1855, actually descended to the Grand Plateau and reascended to Mont Blanc rather than risk the Bosses ridge. But the age of mountaineering as a pastime had then begun. The subsequent history of Mont Blanc is beyond the limits of this chapter.

Let us see what has been happening in the Oberland. In the few glimpses it is possible to give in a single chapter of the growth of mountaineering in the early nineteenth century, my aim has been to concentrate attention on those early mountaineers in whom some innate longing to climb great peaks for the sake of pure adventure transcends the aim of the scientist or the explorer. And by his own confession Johann Rudolf Meyer II was such a one. His father, J. R. Meyer I, was an explorer and topographer, but his younger brother and his son, Johann Rudolf Meyer III, were climbers like himself, and both were famous athletes.

On 29th July 1811 J. R. Meyer II, with his younger brother and with three servants, set off from Aarau on an expedition which is famous in Alpine history, not only because it resulted in the first ascent of a great peak, the Jungfrau, but because it caused a flood of controversy from the pens of jealous contemporaries and from those of great Alpine historians, notably Dr. Dübi and Mr. Coolidge.

The party reached the Grimsel and crossed it on 30th July, picking up a porter on the way. The way to Concordia over the Oberaarjoch and the Grünhornlücke was considered too long and hazardous, so they descended into the Rhône valley, left it somewhere between Fiesch and Naters, and made their way in a single day by the Riederalp, the Riederfurke, across the lower Aletsch Glacier and up the Ober Aletsch Glacier to the Beich Pass and down to Gletscherstafel. Most of us would think such a walk entitled us to take it easy next day. Not so the Meyers!

At Gletscherstafel they persuaded a couple of chamois-hunters to accompany them for 25 batzen (about 3½ Swiss francs) a day, and started at 5 a.m. for the Lötschenlücke. From there the three servants were sent back, the crevasses and the appearance of the surrounding peaks being too much for their nerves. We can believe they turned back gladly, and they might well have been at the end of their tether.

The remaining five bivouacked somewhere on the north side of the Grosser Aletschfirn. The Meyers had brought a good equipment, 'warm clothing, ropes, a ladder, alpenstocks, dark veils, and a big black linen sheet to act as a tent, and also as a flag to be set up on the summit'; but they were without scientific instruments, *esteeming such things a hindrance for adventurous climbers.*

The afternoon had been spent in reconnoitring: one of the Meyers thought he had identified the Jungfrau from the lower slopes of the Aletschhorn. From such a position it is extremely difficult to realize all that lies between the Gletscherhorn and the final peak of the Jungfrau.

It happens that in 1907, being then ignorant of Alpine history, I approached the Jungfrau from the Lötschental and covered much of the ground over which the Meyers must have gone. After reading and re-reading the different views of the pundits on the wanderings

of the pioneers on 2nd and 3rd August, with which I will not confuse the reader, I will give him what emerges for me as the most likely story.

Let us put ourselves in the position of the Meyers, and try to realize how difficult identification of peaks must have been for them and how obscure the relative position and origin of glaciers. The failure of Bullock and Mallory, both experienced men, on the first Everest expedition in 1921, to identify the easy approach by the East Rongbuk Glacier is an instance of the puzzling nature of glacier topography.

A comparison of the two maps, the accurate modern map and the Meyers' map, made in 1813, is essential to an understanding of the route followed. What do we notice that can help us to trustworthy conclusions?

1. The orientation of the map suggests that magnetic north was taken for true north. This would have the effect of making a point which lay considerably north of east appear east. South-south-east becomes almost due south. For it is a curious coincidence that the deviation of the compass needle to the west of north attained a maximum in 1818 and must have exceeded 20° in the Oberland in 1812.

2. The portion of the map which concerns us, that south of the Jungfrau, is much more sketchy and inaccurate to the west of the ridge called Kranzberg in the modern map than it is to the east of it. The reason is that the tracks of 1811 are to the west, and those of 1812, as to which there is no possibility of doubt and which would be fresh in Meyer's memory, lie up the Jungfraufirn on the east. The position of the Lötschenlücke, where the Anengrat joins it from the north, is clearly indicated close to where the track of 1811 begins to be marked. But the positions of the Grosshorn and Mittaghorn are badly misplaced. This portion of the map bears evidence of reconstruction from memories already hazy.

3. The Gletscherhorn is not indicated at all. This is important, for it is almost certain that the Meyers, on 2nd August, mistook the Gletscherhorn for the Jungfrau and the highest point of the Kranzberg east of it for the Mönch.

4. There is no route whatever marked across the Concordiaplatz from the Vorjähriges Nachtlager (1811 bivouac) to the Zweites Nachtlager (1812 bivouac). If the latter represented the second night's bivouac it is inconceivable that the route would not be marked joining one to the other.

Other points that occur will be noticed as we follow the party up. The bivouac on 2nd August was on some rocks where the Lötschen

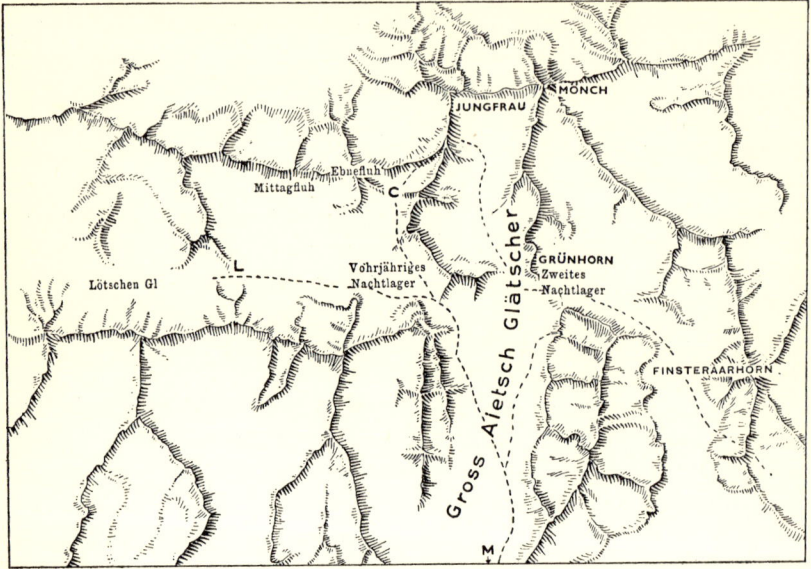

(a) After Meyer

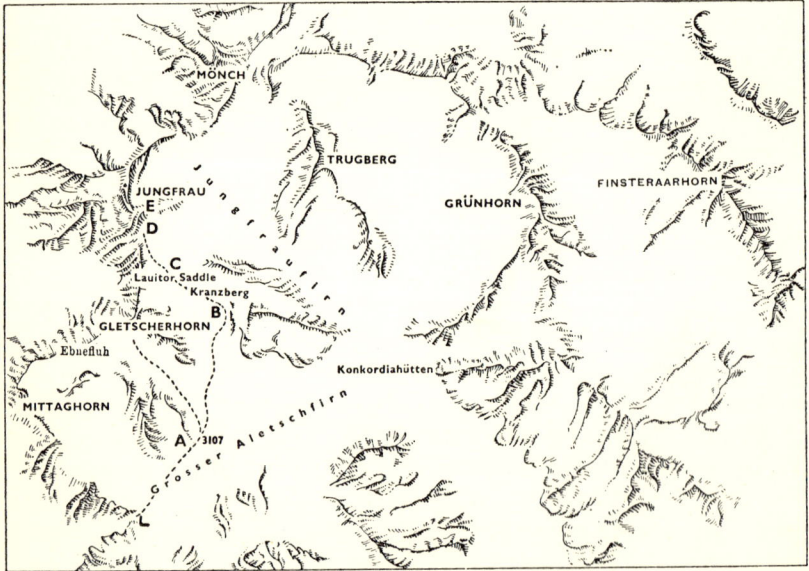

(b) After Siegfried

6. MAPS OF J. R. MEYER'S EXPLORATIONS. *See Notes on page 317*

Glacier joins the Aletsch Glacier. Meyer's map marks the Lötschen Glacier as west of the Lötschenlücke: there is no name for any of the glaciers falling south from the Ebnefluh and the Gletscherhorn into the Grosser Aletschfirn, or for this last. The position of the bivouac is almost certainly wrongly marked on their map. There is nothing in the nomenclature to prevent our placing it where other considerations suggest we must put it, at the foot of the spur descending from the Ebnefluh, where the Ebnefluhfirn joins the Grosser Aletschfirn, near the point 3,107 m. Nothing on the map contradicts the description of this point in Meyer's text, 'where the Lötschen Glacier unites with the Aletsch Glacier.'

Next morning they started up the crevassed glacier between the Ebnefluh and Gletscherhorn, which latter they took for the Jungfrau. This glacier, remembering the orientation of the Meyers' map, would be correctly described as falling south from the Jungfrau. The ladder was requisitioned more than once to cross awkward crevasses, so progress would be slow. By ten o'clock they estimated the summit of the Jungfrau to be only six hundred feet above them. This would fit in very reasonably with the assumption that to them the Gletscherhorn was the Jungfrau. The weather deteriorated and a *Föhn* wind drove them back. We may presume there was cloud on the highest points and that the going was heavy. They were back at the bivouac at two o'clock, and then these tireless fellows set out to reconnoitre afresh.

They ascended 'another glacier more to the east, likewise descending from the Jungfrau,' and they now learned the connection between the Aletsch and Fiescher Glaciers, as well as the continuous connection between these and the Lauteraar, Finsteraar, and Oberaar Glaciers.

Now no one can discover all that without going up high, and they must have got a good view enabling them to make the discovery from high up on the Kranzberg, a very easy mountain to climb and the obvious one to climb for a view in the few remaining hours of daylight.

They returned to the previous night's bivouac and moved their camp and equipment to 'a point of considerable height, farther east and half an hour south of the Mönch' (i.e. the Kranzberg). This camp was probably not far below the figure 3,622 on the Swiss map. It is possible that the marking of the route across the lower part of a ridge of the Kranzberg suggests where it was, but the problem of placing on their map the exact position of the first and second bivouacs would be an enigma to them as well as to the historians. The map

E

shows that their memories, unchecked by any previous map, are quite uncertain as to the two 1811 bivouacs, and they have vaguely suggested a position with no indication as to whether it was that of 1st August or 2nd August.

Now for the great day of 3rd August. The porter was sent over the Lötschenlücke for provisions, so only the two Meyers and the two chamois-hunters remained. What impression did the events of this day leave on the Meyers from which to construct their map?

They started 'as the first rays of the sun reddened the rocks of the Jungfrau *close before us,*' and they then proceeded up the slopes of snow and ice descending from that peak, hoping, as the mountain was now close, to reach the top by ascending these slopes. A vain hope; what they took for a continuous snow-field was an optical delusion, for suddenly in front appeared a descent of forty or fifty feet; on both sides the slopes fell steeply and *'the way down to the final peak of the Jungfrau '* lay along a sharp snow ridge.

Now this is just what would happen to a party that had imagined the Gletscherhorn to be the Jungfrau or part of the Jungfrau, and arrived on the small snow plateau near the Lauithor. From here the Rottalhorn and Jungfrau appear practically one peak.

The descent was difficult. An alpenstock was driven deep into the snow, and the party slid down one by one with a leg each side of the narrow ridge. Then they came 'to the foot of the final peak, to which they got very close, going in and out between some points of rock projecting from the ice.' The saddle was reached at eight o'clock, about three and a half hours going from the bivouac. Almost certainly this saddle was not the Rottalsattel. The following year the Meyers took about two hours from the Rottalsattel to the top and said that progress was slow owing to step-cutting. From the saddle reached in 1811 at 8 a.m. it took them *six hours.* The historians have forgotten this enormous difference. Moreover, there is no descent such as that described in reaching the Rottalsattel, either over the ridge or across the flank of the Rottalhorn. The impression of the 1811 climb clearly left on the mind of the Meyers is of an ascent of a glacier followed by a descent and then a long ridge.

They have endeavoured to show this in marking their track, which crosses a lightly but definitely marked ridge joining the Ebnefluh to a point east-south-east of it, and then follows the ridge up to the Jungfrau. What has not been understood is that this ridge begins at the foot of the *Rottalhorn,* and they followed *close under the rock of this peak* and up a steep slope, where rocks came through the ice, on to the top of the snowy spur descending east from the Rottalhorn, and so without difficulty in normal conditions to the Rottalsattel, where the 1812 route is joined. The only really misleading error in the Meyers' map is the short piece of ridge forming the east side of the small enclosed triangle east of the word 'Ebnefluh.' Such an enclosed triangle is, of course, an impossibility; the ridge of the Kranzberg actually starts in the nearly level small plateau east of the Lauithor.

In 1907, after my party had made the first ascent of the Rottalhorn by the south ridge, Mr. Coolidge suggested to me that the Meyers might have ascended by this ridge. My note in the *Alpine Journal* tells me that we took three and a half hours to climb the six or seven hundred feet of ridge, and that the rocks were uniformly difficult. Three of our party of four had the week before traversed the Bietschhorn from the hut to Ried in under nine hours, so that we were not a slow party, and it is impossible that the Meyers should have not mentioned a long stretch of rocks as difficult as these; besides, their account corresponds well with an ascent close under the rock face. What they did was to follow a long south ridge of the Jungfrau, turning the great gendarme called the Rottalhorn by steep snow on its east side. The comparatively modern practice of subdividing mountains into separate peaks was unknown to the pioneers.

The leader—we are not told which of them it was—secured the others by fixing a rope, presumably to an alpenstock driven into the snow, if no rock was available and they had no ice-axes or crampons to help them. A crevasse near the top, possibly near the Rottalsattel, gave some trouble, but they reached the top at last at two o'clock. The flag was set up and half an hour was spent in 'enjoying the view and the topographical instruction it afforded.' No one felt any ill effects from fatigue or altitude. What grand men these Meyers were, and what a contrast their great adventure offers to Chamonix mountaineering of the period, with its organized bureau forcing an absurd number of guides of very varying capacity on untrained tourists desirous of gaining glory on Mont Blanc!

On the way down, somewhere by the Rottalhorn, one of the chamois-hunters collapsed from strain, and being also almost blind from the glare he had to be led on the rope with his eyes covered.

The porter, evidently no ancestor of the being so often reviled in later Alpine literature, had returned safely alone over the long glacier pass from Gletscherstafel with fuel and firewood, and they must have spent a glorious hour on getting back to camp just before dark.

Early next morning they were off again to the Lötschental, where the two hunters left them with assurances of their readiness to go with them 'wherever they chose to go.' *The same day* these wonderful Meyers, with the porter, must have gone over the Beich Pass and across the mountain-sides to Fiesch, and on 5th August they crossed the Grimsel and made the first record of their amazing expedition in the visitors' book at the Hospice.

As far as was possible in the case of such honest men as the Meyers, doubts were expressed as to the genuineness of the ascent. A storm must have quickly flung down the big black flag, set up though it was on a side of the ladder deeply buried in the snow, for jealous eyes at the ends of telescopes could see no trace of it on the summit later in August.

In 1812 younger members of the family, Johann Rudolf III and Gottlieb, sons of Johann Rudolf II, added fresh glory to the family.

These two, with their father and uncle Hieronymus, the heroes of 1811, and a Dr. Thilo, a teacher at Aarau—an early instance of the hold mountaineering has on pedagogues—crossed the Oberaarjoch with guides and built a hut on the Gemslücke, a pass about eleven thousand feet in the ridge running south-east from the Finsteraar-horn. Bad weather drove them back to the Grimsel, but on 15th August Johann Rudolf III started with the guides to attempt the Finsteraarhorn.

From a bivouac on the Oberaarjoch the party attacked the steep east face of the ridge between the Gemslücke and the top of the Finsteraarhorn. Here, again, the historians have found great matter for controversy, but I have no hesitation in giving, as most correct, the version of the story arrived at by Captain Farrar, who is, on every sort of ground, a first-rate judge of this case.

The party was well equipped and wore 'foot-irons.' The wall that rose in front of them was extremely steep, and there must have been much fresh snow, for 'they buried the arm deep in the cold snow to support the insecure foothold.' In places steps were hewn in bare ice for hand and foot. Progress was more secure on the rocks.

They crept under a great boss of ice 'which swung out far over the gorge, full of cracks filled with lovely glacier green. Icicles hung from its overhanging pinnacles like stalactites in a rock grotto, and from time to time fell past us, awakened by our steps, and rattled down to the depths of the Finsteraar Glacier below.'

Johann Rudolf III had the proper eye for beauty. But in this case it was a treacherous beauty. The huge *sérac* had crashed on to the

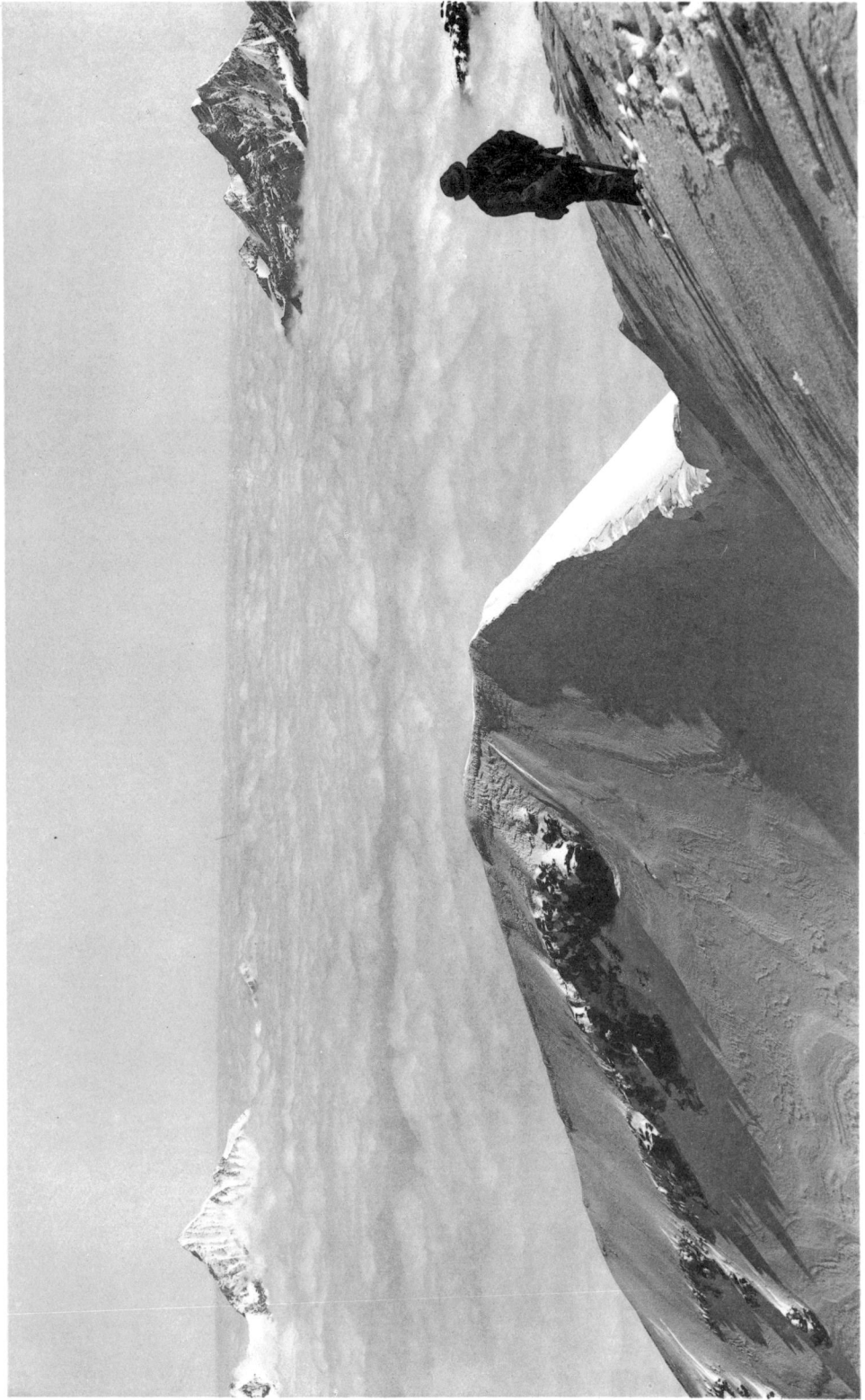

7. WEISSHORN AND MISCHABELHÖRNER

glacier next time the chamois-hunters passed.   Later, in 1907, it had
a shot at Captain Farrar and H. V. Reade, who fled for cover into the
bergschrund.   For six hours they toiled up the wall, and when they
reached the *arête* at the point of the ridge marked 3,902 m. Johann
Rudolf could go no farther, or at any rate felt his going on would
prevent the possibility of the guides' reaching the top.   This point
is generally known now as Meyer's Peak.   From here the point
4,165 m., known as the Vorgipfel, would look like the highest
point to any one who did not look carefully for a farther, higher
point, which is just visible, but with difficulty distinguishable, beyond
it.   Three of the guides climbed the ridge to this lower summit.   It
is not an easy ridge, and the time they took to ascend and return,
four and a half hours, is a fair time for experienced climbers.   It
would be exceptionally fast time for a visit to the true summit by
a party of present-day experts.

Meyer's own words, 'three hours had been needed to cover this
way, which was expected to take a quarter of an hour,' are almost
conclusive in proving that the ridge climbed by the guides was in
full view from Meyer's Peak.   The considerable stretch of jagged
ridge that connects the Vorgipfel with the summit is quite out of sight.

Their claim that they reached the actual summit, as they told
Meyer on their return, cannot be allowed.   The descent was made
by the much easier slopes below Meyer's Peak on the west side of the
ridge.   But if Johann Rudolf's gallant attempt on the Finsteraarhorn
failed to achieve complete success, doubt has never been cast on the
authenticity of Gottlieb Meyer's ascent of the Jungfrau in September
of 1812.

With a couple of guides, Volker and Bortes, he left the Märjelenalp
on 2nd September, and reached the hut built by the family at the
foot of the 'Grünen Horn' late that evening.   The site of the hut
is called Zweites Nachtlager on Meyer's map.   Their route up the
Jungfrau, from the Jungfraufirn, is that followed by almost all parties
from Concordia or the Jungfraujoch.   One of the guides was ill
and they went slowly, not reaching the great *bergschrund* below the
Rottalsattel till 11 a.m.   Two poles destined for flagstaffs were laid
across the *schrund.*   Up these the leading guide swarmed and cut
steps in the steep slope above.   Gottlieb and the other guide followed
on the rope and the poles were dragged up.   Steps were needed in
the final *arête,* and one of the guides was left behind, the other two
men reaching the top at two o'clock.   The other guide managed to
join them later, but both guides were very exhausted.   The flag was

stuck up and was actually seen in process of erection by Johann Rudolph III from the Strahlegg.

The steep wall below the Sattel was descended face inward, and they jumped the *bergschrund*. The 'Grünen Horn' hut was reached at seven o'clock. Next day a projected attack on the Mönch was defeated by bad weather and they returned to the Märjelenalp. This time storms failed to dislodge the flag on the summit, for it was reported as visible by a 'trustworthy man' in 1842!

There is no space to tell of the many glacier passes crossed for the first time by various members of the family in this year 1812; and with 1812 this brilliant outburst of mountain adventure ended. For many years the big peaks are left alone.

In 1828 a daring attempt was made by two Englishmen, Brown and Slade, to scale the Jungfrau from the Rottal side with four guides, two of whom bore the name of Lauener, which became famous in the next generation.

In 1829 the highest point of the Finsteraarhorn was reached by Hugi's guides, though not by Hugi himself, by the *arête* leading from the saddle in the north ridge that bears Hugi's name.

Towards the middle of the century the exploration and mapping of the High Alps was progressing rapidly and preparing the ground for the great era of climbing that was to follow. No account, however summary, of the development of mountaineering, can pass by without mention of two of the most attractive personalities that have ever found the great treasure of their life in the Alps, and have invited others to share that treasure with them.

One is a Scot, J. D. Forbes. His aim was the study of glaciers, but round that central aim he gathered so many of the things that belong to mountaineering that he must be regarded as the father of the English climbers who made the Alps their playground.

Those who have neither the leisure nor the means to visit the great distant ranges of the world may find in Forbes's writing a wisdom which does not lose its value with age.

The Alps rise to all the elevation which is necessary in order to convey to the imagination the fullest sense of the sublime in such objects, whilst their dimensions—gigantic, no doubt, compared to the mountains of the British islands—do not present the unwieldy extent of the Andes or Himalaya. There is no transverse valley in the Alps—that is, one leading directly from the plains to the highest ridge—up which an active man cannot walk in two days, and the actual passage of the chain may usually be effected in one.

Now, any great increase upon such a scale necessarily wearies the traveller with monotony, even though it be the monotony of grandeur, while it tasks his physical powers by keeping them too long upon the stretch. The circuit of Mont Blanc or Monte Rosa is quite as long as most people will consider necessary to give them a vivid conception of an immense hill; and if we accurately examine the slow progress which the uneducated eye makes to a correct estimate of magnitudes and distances in the Alps, we find that, practically, their scale is sufficiently great to afford, to at least nine-tenths of travellers, the most majestic conception with which such objects can at all inspire them.

All I have read of climbing in distant ranges, all I have heard from the lips of men who have taken part in Himalayan expeditions, confirms the view the Scottish philosopher expresses in these words.

Forbes had found out the secret that unlocks the treasure-chest of all great mountains. In later life he writes: 'My heart remains where my body can never be. . . . My yearnings towards the Colinton banks [his Scottish home as a boy] and towards the Swiss mountains are much on a par—*both home-sickness.*'

And again:

Happy the traveller who, content to leave to others the glory of counting the thousands of leagues of earth and ocean they have left behind them, and established in some mountain shelter with his book, starts on his first day's walk amongst the Alps in the tranquil morning of a long July day, brushing the early dew before him, and, armed with his staff, makes for the hill-top, begirt with ice or rock, as the case may be, whence he sees the field of his summer's campaign spread out before him, its wonders, its beauties, and its difficulties, to be explained, to be admired, and to be overcome.

> 'Ignotis errare locis, ignota videre
> Flumina gaudebat; studio minuente laborem.'

The second name is that of Töpffer. No mountain-lover was ever more modest about his climbing powers, and it must be admitted he had reason to be. But he is a father of all the lighter side of mountaineering—the special jokes and names that are shared by a party that know each other well, the small mishaps, the good deeds and the misdeeds of guides, of porters and innkeepers; and with it all a full appreciation of the freedom of life, the variety of beauty, and the width of view offered by an Alpine tour. It is this perpetual contrast of deep spiritual impressions with all sorts of incidents and obstacles of the way that call for muscular effort, good temper, and good-humoured chaff that makes mountaineering, whether it results in the accomplishment of climbing feats or not, such an admirable refreshment for soul and body.

M. Töpffer as a climber hardly ranks at all, but we shall not love him less. In the following passage from his *Nouveaux Voyages en Zig-zag* we shall see him scared by an ordinary steep hill-side, while encouraging the younger generation to do better, and have a glimpse of an unknown English hill-wanderer whose son, if heredity counts for anything, must have had some share in the conquest of the Alps by Englishmen in the succeeding generation.

Töpffer with his usual large party of young people is at the Great St. Bernard.

Jean Payod [the guide] mentioned the Chenalette, a peak almost opposite the door of the monastery, whence one has a view over the main chain, similar to the one we had admired in the morning, but far more extensive. Directly after dinner we set off on this expedition. A pretty tough job it looks! Instead of a path a series of small couloirs as steep as walls, by which we climb from one small platform to the next. Beware of straying from the right way here!

At last a level place with some boulders to sit on, and some red snow to make snow ices with! From here the top is in sight, and the monks have set up a cairn on it. But in full view also is the precipitous slope by which it must be reached, and its aspect is enough to make M. Töpffer give up all idea of any Chenalette for himself and all his charges. Finally, however, under the persuasion of Payod and the entreaties of five of his nimblest and most experienced young friends, he gives permission for the climb, but only for these five and under the stipulation that he is to be with them.

The start is made. First débris slopes of big laminated rocks that wobble as you tread upon them or rapidly slip down when your weight is on them. Then bare walls dipping straight into the red snow, and then a first great couloir of horrible aspect. . . . At this point M. Töpffer's knee-tremble begins. Enough of the Chenalette for him! No more stipulation that he is to accompany the party! But seeing the five others in excellent form and Jean Payod quite free from anxiety, he lets them go on and makes for the level place they started from, with all speed, and yet with every precaution to avoid reaching it too quickly by way of the laminated rocks. On the level all is well. The telescope is set up, and while every one in turn is engaged in following the party's progress, an Englishman, alone and limping, turns up. Scarcely has he had time to take in what is going on when he is off, alone and limping, for the Chenalette. M. Töpffer, having been on it, can't get over it!

After being out of sight for half an hour, the party reappears, six small nine-pins threading their way along the edge of a precipice. While they are carefully helping each other down what they have struggled up, the Englishman, alone and limping, appears too. Quite calmly he zigzags, lets himself slide, leaps, and crawls to such good purpose that he gets to the bottom without the slightest harm by his own special route and at the same moment as the others, who are astounded to see him again alive. In fact, on the top of the Chenalette this strange man indulged in pranks that terrified even Jean Payod. From that narrow crest poised above a fearful precipice, he ventured to stride across to a rather lower ridge close by; from there, planting a foot on a projecting rock and finding within reach some cracks to cling to with his hands, he leant with apparent pleasure over the abyss.

Surely no modern climber will refuse to see a pioneer in this nameless Englishman of 1843.

The philosophical reflections of Töpffer, engendered by the atmosphere of the Alps, are hardly matter for this chapter, but a stirring appeal in a number of the *Rivista Mensile* for 1933 to Italian youth, to seek out the most arduous and dangerous climbs and to find in mountains both an altar and a home, wings for the soul and food for the mind, and in so doing to obey the commands of the Duce, makes me think the latter has been reading passages of *Nouveaux Voyages en Zigzag,* especially this one, that follows almost immediately after a description of arrival on the Stelvio, then on the Tyrolese frontier.

Politics (at such a time and place) may easily seem to be a sorry collection of doubtful principles which rival parties have substituted for the wholesome rules of common sense, a dangerous arsenal of weapons in the hands of wounded selfesteem, of unfair privilege, of restless ambition, of every fierce and jealous passion. It makes one think that the fewer men there are who hold a key to this arsenal, the less chance there is of the mass of peaceful, hardworking citizens being ceaselessly worried and tormented and hampered in the pursuit of profitable and lawful enterprise, by the activities that enrich a host of officials and inspectors who constitute themselves socalled protectors of the public. . . . It is not so much governments as parties, that delay the coming of peace, order and stability, not so much laws and regulations as the disorder of opinions and principles we call politics.

Certainly enthusiasm for climbing was never greater than it is at present in Italy and Germany. Töpffer is right enough when he claims that mountains make the dividing ridges of party strife seem ludicrously small.

Before the middle of the century John Ball had amassed much of the extraordinary knowledge of the whole Alpine chain that marked him out as the first president of the Alpine Club, and fitted him to be the father of guidebooks on the Alps for real mountaineers. He was so eminent as a botanist, a scientist, and an explorer that his claims as a climber are often forgotten. Already in 1845 he was leading through the steep and intricate Schwärze Glacier to the Schwarztor a local chamoishunter whose heavy countenance, 'denoting neither energy nor enterprise,' proved too true an indication of his character. And a single passage from his description of the descent of the Italian side of the pass shows him to have been one of those convinced optimists on whom Fortune smiles.

My next thought was to attempt the descent by the middle of the glacier; three times I went forward, and each time was obliged to return, by the breaking of the snow bridges over which I attempted to pass. The last of these presented the most striking scene I have ever witnessed. I was over a great *bergschrund* completely roofed in with a thick coating of snow; towards the crown of the arch the roof gave way with me, and though the position is not a comfortable one, I had become so far used to it in the course of that day, that I paused for a second to glance down into the vault over which I hung suspended. The chasm appeared to be about thirty feet wide and went down to a depth that was veiled in blue darkness. . . . The glance was but a momentary one, for there was no time to be lost in withdrawing from so unusual a position; my arms remained above the snow, and with a little help from the rope, I had no difficulty in regaining the solid bank. I may say, once for all, that where two men are united by a strong rope, there is no danger from the falling in of snow bridges, provided the man who remains behind keeps the rope stretched, and is attentive to give a moderate degree of assistance at the moment when it is wanted.

In 1857 he had to leave his so-called guide behind and complete the ascent of the Pelmo alone.

If we accept the ascent of the Wetterhorn by Alfred Wills in 1854 as the beginning of modern mountaineering, we may regard John Ball as one of the last and most beneficent of those who prepared the ground for the great game. In the next chapter the players will take possession.

CHAPTER V

THE GREAT PEAKS ARE WON

ENGLISHMEN—using the word to include all Scotsmen, Irishmen, citizens of the British Empire, and Americans who speak English— have always loved any form of activity that combines sport and adventure. The part they played in the years when the Alps were suddenly changed from an unknown wilderness into a vast playground is a thing of which we may well be proud, but it is so astonishing that we must look for other causes than mere racial character.

Forget all the later development of mountaineering, whereby the climber has come to rank a peak according to the opportunities it offers for daring, technical skill, and thrilling situations, and consider which were, at the beginning of the second half of last century, and still are, the great mountains whose names are familiar to the crowds that wonder at them, and which stand out as the giants of their company in any distant view.

In the Mont Blanc range, Mont Blanc itself, then the Grandes Jorasses and the Aiguille Verte.

East of Mont Blanc in the Pennine Alps, the Grand Combin and the great Zermatt peaks, the Weisshorn, the Dent Blanche, the Matterhorn, the Lyskamm, Monte Rosa, and the Mischabelhörner, culminating in the Dom.

In the Oberland, the Finsteraarhorn, the Aletschhorn, the great trio of Eiger, Mönch, and Jungfrau, and the most distinguished, the Bietschhorn. Farther east the Bernina and the Disgrazia, and beyond these the Ortler and Königsspitze, and south of Mont Blanc the Gran Paradiso and the Grivola in the Graians; in Dauphiné, the Ecrins, Mont Pelvoux, and the Meije, and farther south Monte Viso.

Previous to 1855 Mont Blanc, Monte Rosa (for it would be pure pedantry to refuse to accept ascents of the Grenzgipfel and Ostspitze as ascents of Monte Rosa), the Finsteraarhorn, the Jungfrau, the Ortler, and Mont Pelvoux had been ascended. These ascents were excep^ tional expeditions made many years before the age of mountaineering as a sport began.

61

The other great peaks were awaiting the invaders. The Mönch fell to an Austrian, the Grand Combin to a trio of local chamois-hunters, the Meije, long after the others, to a Frenchman, and all the rest were won by English enterprise.

Sport is a comparatively recent growth outside Britain. The word 'sport,' in the same spelling but in varying pronunciations, becomes French, German, or Italian, according to the nationality of the user. The idea the word conveys to English minds is too elastic, too elusive, and too permeated with the English view of life to be understood and accepted by other nations. Attempts in recent publications of other European Alpine clubs to give a clear logical definition of the word show it is a growth grafted on the life of a people, and not a natural growth. The fact is that comparative peace gave Englishmen the opportunity to turn their combative instincts to sport, while the peoples of Europe were struggling with each other to alter political boundaries or political régimes.

Another cause was that England had produced a great mountain prophet in Ruskin. A succeeding generation may feel a sense of superiority in decrying his greatness, for they take off from the higher levels which he had won against the Philistines. History will have to acknowledge the immense power he exerted over the minds of his generation, not only in England, but in Europe. And Ruskin had shown to men ready to lift their eyes that mountains may be supremely beautiful. The immense masses that before had had something evil in them acquired a quality of moral grandeur. Induce men to go and see what is at once beautiful and truly great, and you cannot fail to inspire in some of them the longing for closer knowledge, for an intimacy that will infuse something of that beauty and that greatness into their own personality.

And it was natural that the peaks which stood out from the others should be the first approached. Out of a dozen persons chosen at random, would you expect to find a single one who would not wish to be introduced, and if possible to have a few moments of intimacy, with a personage of acknowledged greatness and attraction? The conversation you have may be commonplace, or it may be one you will never forget; the occasion is memorable.

And so it is with the highest peaks. The actual way may be easy, little more than a walk, or it may call for the exercise of all the faculties; in any case a climber who is a sound judge of mountain values will realize he is in contact with that which has the essential quality of greatness. Javelle had climbed many more difficult peaks, including

8. THE ITALIAN SIDE OF THE MATTERHORN

the unroped Matterhorn, before he climbed Mont Blanc by the ordinary route from Chamonix; yet he was moved to tears by the greatness of the occasion in his life.

The highest peaks, the monarchs of the different Alpine groups, were climbed first; the satellites, often more brilliant and attractive, were approached later.   From the vast number of early first ascents it is difficult to select some for special mention, and the publication of a popular edition of *Peaks, Passes, and Glaciers* has placed most of the accounts within reach of all who wish to read them.   As far as possible I have avoided quoting from what is easily accessible to all.

Among the eager band that poured across the Channel to take possession of the Alps professors and clergymen figure prominently. Let us pick out a few representative figures.

Take Professor John Tyndall, a scientist and a very fine mountaineer too.   If you will try to follow him up the Weisshorn with his famous guide Bennen, you will probably admit his claim.

He and Bennen and a second guide, Wenger, arrive at Randa. The great white pyramid of the Weisshorn is hidden behind the *séracs* of the Bies Glacier and the steep cliffs that hold it up high above the valley.   From the Oberland, and especially from the slope above Belalp, where Tyndall afterwards built his Alpine home, the Weisshorn is the grandest object in the great chain of the Pennines.

Tyndall was unwell, exciting the pity of the waitress Philomène as he refused the food she offered.   In the hot afternoon they climbed the steep pine-clad slopes to a bivouac not far from the Schallenberg Glacier.   Tyndall was racked with thirst.   They reached a chalet; milk was poured into a small tub.

With my two hands I seized the two ends of a diameter of this vessel, gave it the necessary inclination and stooping down, with a concentration of purpose which I had rarely before exerted, I drew the milk into me.   Thrice I returned to the attack before that insatiate thirst gave way.   The effect was astonishing. The liquid appeared to lubricate every atom of my body, and its fragrance to permeate my brain.   I felt a growth of strength at once commence within me; all anxiety as to physical power with reference to the work in hand soon vanished, and before retiring to rest I was able to say to Bennen: 'Go where thou wilt to-morrow, and I will follow thee.'

Only a science professor could have described a long drink in such language, and only a very stout-stomached mountaineer could have cured an internal upset in such a way!   What is one man's meat . . .! Compare Conway on his return from the Pelvo d'Elva: 'With utter

lack of foresight I drank a litre of cold milk at once; before long I
was in a fever and it was late the following day before I could quit
my bed.' Still, that was at Casteldelfino before Mussolini's régime.
You may stop a bullet climbing near Monte Viso now, but you are
less likely to be killed by a germ.

The effect of milk on guides or porters might be interesting, but I
can recall no instance in Alpine literature of a mention of its being
taken; they seem to have preferred fermented liquors; perhaps excess
of milk diet in childhood is the reason.

An eave of overhanging rock was the roof of the bivouac; the
removal of the stones laid bare some dry clay, and an ice-axe stirred
this into sufficient softness. Tyndall lay and watched the sunset
fires die out along the great range from the Mischabel to the Breithorn,
and the moon sail up like 'a vast balloon' from behind the
Rimpfischhorn.

A short reconnaissance before turning in for the night had shown
a couloir, 'fearfully steep,' that offered access to the east arête. Beyond
that they hoped for the best, but where Leslie Stephen had failed two
years before, in 1859, and Charles Mathews, with the redoubtable
Melchior Anderegg, had again failed the following year, there must
be formidable obstacles.

Restless, as most of us are before a big climb, they got up too early,
drank their coffee, and had to wait for dawn. It was absolutely
cloudless, removing all threats from the weather. Unroped on the
hard-frozen snow, they crossed an intricate bit of glacier and the
bergschrund and cut up the couloir to the arête.

A long climb over its débris-covered towers followed. Attempts
to save time by crossing the innumerable icy couloirs by which the
south face of the ridge is furrowed only proved that the ridge itself
was best. A curious stretch of the ridge, topped by an uncorniced
edge of pure white snow, was crossed by Bennen, and Tyndall
followed 'as a boy walking along a horizontal pole, with toes turned
outwards.' The professor, in his account, cannot resist a full description of such a perfect example of Faraday's principle of regelation,
but he gallantly admits:

My guide, unaided by any theory, did a thing from which I, though backed
by all the theories in the world, should have shrunk in dismay.

The day is hot, the work hard, and our bodies are drained of their liquids as
by a Turkish bath. . . . A bottle of champagne . . . furnished Wenger and
myself with many a refreshing draught. Bennen fears his eyes, and will not
touch champagne.

The ridge provided good sport. 'There is scarcely a position possible to a human being which, at one time or another during the day, I was not forced to assume. But there was overmuch of it.' After three hours on the ridge Bennen says (as translated by Tyndall): 'I have not only good hopes, but I do not allow myself to entertain the idea of failure.'

After six hours of the ridge he laid his face on his axe for a moment; a kind of sickly despair was in his eyes as he turned to me remarking: 'Lieber Herr, die Spitze ist noch sehr weit oben.'

However, a sip of champagne changed this into 'Herr! wir müssen ihn haben.' The last granite rock is passed and a knife-edge of pure white snow is followed to the sharp point where three great ridges meet in the summit.

Two men from Randa had been descried on the glacier following their tracks on to the ridge, evidently rivals anxious to share the prize. Now they are seen far below on one of its many towers. 'Again and again the roar of triumph was sent down to them.' The roars reached them, for they turned back and endeavoured to make the people of Randa believe that the great Weisshorn had been scaled, but it took a long time, especially as one of the alleged conquerors was a man with such a poor stomach for food as Tyndall had shown himself to be.

Bennen's ice-axe was sacrificed as proof of the victory; its head was knocked off, and the handle, with a red handkerchief floating from it, was stuck up and later shown to Bennen himself from the Riffel Hotel.

The wonder of Alpine views and of Alpine sunrises and sunsets was new, and the accounts of the early climbers are full of them; only the very brave or the very foolish attempt to describe them now. They are still part of the bread of life to many climbers, but there are obvious limitations to the use of bread as literary material, however fresh may be the appetite with which we return to it in the morning or the evening. From the concluding words of Tyndall's description, these few will show how deep he could drink of the cup of enjoyment.

I had never witnessed a scene which affected me like this. Bennen once volunteered some information regarding its details, but I was unable to hear him. An influence seemed to proceed from it direct to the soul; the delight and exultation experienced were not those of Reason or of Knowledge, but of Being. I was part of it and it of me. . . . I opened my notebook to make a few observations, but I soon relinquished the attempt. There was something incongruous, if not profane, in allowing the scientific faculty to interfere where silent worship was the reasonable service.

Our next representative shall be E. S. Kennedy, second president of the Alpine Club.

In Val Masino two carriages were toiling up to the 'Grand Ancient Italian Bathing Establishment.' In the first are Kennedy and Leslie Stephen, driven by the head-waiter, in the second Melchior Anderegg and Thomas Cox, Kennedy's valet, driven by a boy in blue. Their goal is Monte Disgrazia. Invalids were welcomed at the baths, but no such horribly robust men as these, who wish to be called at an unearthly hour in the morning.

They collected some food, managed to wake themselves, and under escort of a lantern-bearer, who knew a man who knew the path up the valley leading towards the peak, they sallied forth at 1 a.m. At the village of San Martino the lantern-bearer woke an old man and disappeared. Meanwhile the sky darkens and the rain descends. They return to the establishment to find their rooms occupied by a burial party and a corpse.

At last, after having got up, dressed, and entered upon the day's work three times in less than twenty-four hours, they make the final start, along a track which Melchior and Cox had explored on what was thought of as the previous day, but was actually still the same day. The track was lost; that miserable experience, so often repeated and to be repeated as long as we continue to climb, of stumbling in the dark along a pathless ravine, was endured, and a high alp reached at dawn. Is there any climber of experience who can boast that in his case this history has never repeated itself?

The band of desolation that separates the pastures from the snows was crossed, and a rampart of rocks ascended till an amazing view of the Bregaglia Alps burst upon them, a quite unexplored region 'of jagged peaks interspersed with craggy precipices, with hanging glaciers and with towering pinnacles,' that will always be associated for later generations with the name of Christian Klucker. In ten minutes there appeared above this wild confusion of sharply outlined and deeply shadowed peaks the Monte Rosa range, the Weisshorn, and the Mischabel, in softest possible tones of light and shade.

They appeared like some creatures of the sky that had no connection with things of earth; below them, below us, and now apparently at our feet, while the great space between the near and distant ranges was wholly lost, were the rugged and contorted masses that might well constitute the remnants of a battle-field whereat had striven, with monstrous implements of war, the gigantic children of the Titan race.

A difficult passage occurred where the ridge dividing the Predarossa Glacier merges in its upper slopes; Kennedy suggested that Stephen and Melchior should complete the ascent alone, but they refused to accept such an offer. The ledge they are crossing on a steep face above the glacier is interrupted by 'an insurmountable buttress.' Melchior, fastened to both ends of the rope, held by the other three, is let down the side and makes his way round the buttress till he can fix the rope to a rock where the ledge is continued. The rope is drawn tight round the buttress and fixed on their side. Melchior crosses back, and the traverse is effected with the fixed rope as an effective support.

From the farther ledge the glacier is soon gained, and at the top of its steep slopes a notch (the Sella di Pioda) in the west arête. It is only 1862, and yet Kennedy speaks of the ridge-climb in tones of almost contemptuous familiarity.

This embraced the usual characteristics of a mountain ridge, a snow cornice on our left, steep contours of ice varied with ribs of rock on our right; our actual line of advance over some rocky tooth, up a steep slope of snow, an occasional descent, and finally, a general scramble that placed us at half-past eleven on the final peak.

What are Kennedy's reflections?   He himself asks and answers the question.

What was our first thought? Was it 'How shall we get down again?' or 'How magnificent is the panorama!' or 'Where is the top that I may pocket it?' or 'Can we find any stones wherewithal we may build up a memorial?' or 'What have we got to eat and drink?' or 'Who has the tobacco-pouch?' or 'Where is the barometer and boiling-water apparatus?' or was it—if it may be called a thought—the simple passive consciousness of success? The descent is trying, and gladly would I avoid it. The view is sublime and I enjoy it. The top is an object in every way worthy of attainment, and as an heirloom to posterity would I transmit it. The memorial to succeeding generations raises a feeling gratifying to the pride of a man, and I am a partaker in it. The crust of bread recreates exhausted strength and I devour it; the wine is nectar itself, and I relish it, the pipe is universal, but I nauseate it. The scientific observation is of the utmost importance, and with most unfeigned satisfaction do I behold others trying to keep their hands warm while they are conducting it. But, to my mind, each and every one of these sources of gratification sink into insignificance when compared with the exhilarating consciousness of difficulty overcome, and of success attained by perseverance.

F

A long vista of moments spent upon Alpine summits is evoked by these words, and even now we shall not greatly quarrel with the conclusion.

Kennedy on the Disgrazia, even more than Tyndall on the Weiss-horn, reveals the great change that has suddenly come over men's way of regarding the Alps. There is a sense of confidence, of mastery, and there is genuine enjoyment. There is humour. Humour that serves the Englishman not only to extract a smile from the crossest moods of Fortune, but as a defence against the strong emotions which might push him off the path of dignified restraint.

Peaks that had been shorn of imaginary terrors and on which no real difficulties occur, such as Monte Viso, the Grivola, the Gran Paradiso, fell at the first contact, like ripe plums, into the hands of those who came to gather them. In one or two cases the dangers are hardly realized. The first ascent of the Lyskamm was something like an extempore picnic. The Rev. J. F. Hardy, in later years a genial autocrat of the Riffel table d'hôte, has described the attack on this great mountain, which was to earn the sinister name of 'the Man-eater.' Coming out of Seiler's hotel at Zermatt one fine morning of August 1861 he was greeted by invitations from his friends.

'I say, old fellow, we're all going up Monte Rosa to-morrow, won't you join us? We shall have capital fun.'

'What, is that Hardy? Oh yes, do come, there's a good fellow.'

Before I had time to answer, a voice, afterwards discovered to be J. A. Hudson's, was heard to mention the Lyskamm, upon which hint I spake.

'Ah, the Lyskamm! that's the thing. Leave Monte Rosa and go in for the Lyskamm; anybody can do Monte Rosa, now the route's so well known; but the Lyskamm's quite another affair.'

'Yes, indeed, I expect it is. Why, Stephen couldn't do it.'

'He was only stopped by the bad state of the snow.'

'Well, Tuckett failed too.'

'He was turned back by a fog.'

'So may we be.'

'Certainly we may, also we mayn't, and in the present state of the weather the latter's the more likely of the two.'

Eventually no less than fourteen persons set off, six of them guides. No, it was fifteen, for when they came to rope up in two parties of seven, 'a supernumerary porter, name and ability unknown,' was discovered and attached, after dispute as to which seven should sacrifice themselves, to the first rope. He was left on the col at the foot of the east ridge to enjoy, let us hope, the remains of a huge breakfast, while

Perren began to tread steps in the powdery snow that lay upon the narrow edge that leads to the summit. All went well, and the steps were well consolidated by many pairs of feet.

On the summit Perren shows an exuberant satisfaction, especially with his employer, such as only very genial clergymen excite. After making way for Hardy to set foot first upon the highest point, 'he shrieks and chuckles, and seizing both my hands dances round me; then he puts his arm round my shoulder, and pats and fondles me, as though he were caressing a young horse that he had tried and not found wanting.' One of the other guides strikes up a German hymn, but, 'at a hint from Perren, he changes it into *God Save the Queen,* and out burst fourteen voices.'

If any ghost or dragon still lingered round about, that must have finished it! 'Sibson's mixture,' consisting of equal parts of red wine and champagne, invented for the occasion by Dr. Sibson, who was on Perren's rope, counts for something in this sudden access of the club-meet spirit in an English party.

The number of new peaks and passes collected by individuals in these wonderful years was a sore grievance to a later generation that had no chance of coming in on the ground floor when the shares in Alpine fame were offered so cheap. Mr. F. F. Tuckett was one of the most notorious cases. Appearing in every part of the Alps, this wonderful man, who remained for long a legend in comparatively unknown districts, gathered in upwards of forty new peaks and passes between 1856 and 1865. And his bag included such big prizes as the Aletschhorn in 1859, Monte Cristallo and the Königsspitze in 1864.

Bear with me, reader, in the hopeless task of compressing a great decade of Alpine history into this chapter. Fancy dismissing the ascents of the Bietschhorn and Rothorn and the crossing of the Eiger-joch in a single line. It must be done. It would be a crime to compress or divide any of the gems of Alpine literature that Leslie Stephen collected and gave to the public when he christened the Alps *The Playground of Europe.* That book is the classic of the period, and it is readily accessible to readers.

Let us turn now to the best-known climber of the period, to Edward Whymper. It is true that Whymper made his living largely as an illustrator and popularizer of the Alps and that in his expedition to the Canadian Rockies many years later he was acting as an advertising agent for the Canadian Pacific Railway. The suggestion of an invasion of the noblest of sports by commercialism was resented by many of Whymper's contemporaries. The resentment is under-standable. The idea that a climbing expedition could be undertaken with any consideration of its marketable value as a story in the daily press or in a book was abhorrent to the men who founded the Alpine Club, and it is still in the nature of a profanation to some. We are more tolerant or less squeamish about profanation now.

There is nothing in all Whymper's early campaigns in the Alps to indicate that he was urged on by anything but a young and burning enthusiasm for climbing. He is an outstanding figure. His first great book, *Scrambles Amongst the Alps,* is a boy's book as well as a man's book. It stands easily first in the number of converts to mountaineering it has made.

In 1861 he had his first scramble on the Matterhorn; in 1863 he made his sixth attempt. And here are his *first ascents* in 1864 and 1865: Brèche de la Meije, Pointe des Ecrins, Col de la Pilatte, Mont Dolent, Aiguille de Trélatête, Aiguille d'Argentière, Moming Pass, Grand Cornier, Grandes Jorasses (west peak), Col du Mont Dolent, Aiguille Verte, Col de Talèfre, Ruinette, and the Matterhorn.

In the history of mountaineering the first ascent of the Matterhorn is not comparable in importance to Saussure's ascent of Mont Blanc; the element of discovery is lacking. It was an inevitable incident in the advance along a path that had been found by others. Never-theless, there are features of that ascent which have made it for ever remarkable. There is no other great mountain in the Alps to com-pare with the Matterhorn in dramatic isolation from its neighbours; its grim precipices bluffed the men of Zermatt and many famous guides into a belief in its inaccessibility.

Up to 1857 not a man in Valtournanche had dreamed of climbing 'La Becca.' That was the local name for the famous peak that takes entire possession of a young climber's heart when it reveals itself at last to his impatient eyes as he is driven up the valley from Châtillon. Then English visitors began to appear, inquiring if the ascent had ever been attempted, and the idea of such a possibility is born in the minds of the natives, and with one of them it becomes an obsession. He was Jean Antoine Carrel, a born leader, a splendid cragsman, but intolerant of service under others and jealous of his native rights upon the peak.

He was the only guide who persistently refused to regard the mountain as inaccessible, and all his energies were directed to conquering it from the Italian side. For long Whymper's efforts also were made from this side, sometimes with the co-operation of Carrel, sometimes without.

When he came to examine the east face he discovered that its angle was far less steep than had been supposed and that the rocks were favourable for climbing. With this discovery victory was assured to the first resolute and capable party that made their attempt under good conditions.

In July 1865 Whymper believed he had secured the services of the two brothers Carrel for an attempt from the Zermatt side before they renewed their efforts along the old line of attack from Breuil. Actually the Italians were already preparing for a serious reconnaissance on behalf of Signor Giordano and the Italian minister Sella. Whymper regarded himself as having been completely duped with the connivance of Favre, the innkeeper at Valtournanche, for whom a victory from the Zermatt side would be most unprofitable. At Breuil, while he was vainly trying to find a man to help him transport his baggage over the Théodule, appeared a young Englishman fresh from a first ascent of the Gabelhorn, Lord Francis Douglas, with a young Taugwalder. Whymper's suggestion for an attack on the Matterhorn was accepted, and old Peter Taugwalder, who had been far enough up the Hörnli ridge to dissipate some of its terrors, was engaged.

At Zermatt they found Charles Hudson with the famous Michel Croz, Whymper's guide on many of his greatest first ascents; they too had planned an ascent of the Matterhorn for the same day. Unfortunately Hudson insisted that if they joined the parties his young friend Hadow, a fine walker but an inexperienced climber, should accompany them.

Whymper proved right. Only the final rocks above the shoulder were difficult, and very early in the afternoon they looked down from the summit on their Italian rivals, still several hundred feet below. Hadow slipped while Croz, immediately in front of him, was descending the steep rocks above the shoulder, where the chains are now fixed. He knocked Croz over, Hudson and Lord Francis were dragged off, and the two Taugwalders, with Whymper between, were almost certainly saved by the breaking of the rope that attached them to the men in front. If only such a great struggle could have been free from disaster and from ugly rivalry!

Among all the characters in the battle to penetrate the many defences of the great mountain, two attractive figures stand out, free from the slightest trace of jealousy or cupidity, eager, enduring, and generous, and filled with supreme happiness upon its highest rocks.   One is the hunchback porter, Luc Meynet, always obliging, always content with the remnants of food and the worst seat at a resting-place, who kneels in adoration and bursts into tears of joy at his first sight of the vast panorama revealed on the Col du Lion, and who, when at last after many years he was privileged to reach the summit, declared he heard the angels singing and exclaimed: 'Now I can die content.'   The other is a young Italian, the Abbé Gorret, and it is the latter's story of the first ascent of the Italian side that I shall give.

Gorret was a godson of the hunter J. J. Carrel.   He was studying to be a priest, but he returned to a peasant's life in the holidays. In the summer of 1857, when twenty years of age, he sets out with his godfather and Jean Antoine Carrel to try to climb the Becca.   They spend some of the morning idly flinging stones into a lake and only reach the Tête du Lion.   Below them they see the Col du Lion, not at all, as was believed in the valley, a way over to the Val d'Hérens!

The attack so lightly begun was to last eight years.   In 1858 Kennedy comes to reconnoitre, and writes his conclusion that 'from Breuil all access to the summit appears to me out of the question.'   Vaughan Hawkins, Tyndall and Bennen, foolishly underestimating Carrel's ability, try and fail.   Slowly the farthest point is pushed higher and higher.   Two men only, all through the series of defeats, never lose their belief in a final victory, Carrel and Whymper.   But for their jealous rivalry these two might have shared a victory that would have enriched the rest of their lives.   In the event, the Matterhorn became for Whymper a fearful tragedy, for Carrel a crushing disappointment.

The Abbé Gorret had been away at a theological college.   He came back on holiday to Valtournanche in July 1865.   On the 15th July an exploring party of guides under J. A. Carrel, sent out by the Italian engineer Signor Giordano, returned in profound discouragement.   Their rivals had carried off the victory that very day by climbing the peak from Zermatt by the Hörnli ridge.   The Italian party had been descried on the shoulder near the Pic Tyndall by Whymper on the summit and greeted with cries of exultation: '"Croz, Croz, don't you see them down there? Ah, the *coquins*! They are low down. . . . Croz, we *must* make them hear us, they *shall* hear us!"   I seized a block of rock and hurled it down.'

The Abbé Gorret was not a whit less keen to go up.   Only Carrel was ready to go with him.   Later in the evening they persuaded two others to join them, J. B. Bich and J. A. Meynod, servants of the hotel at Le Giomein. Carrel refused to take Giordano. Gorret and and the other two, he knew, were as good as guides, but he would not be responsible for a tourist. Gorret made it a condition that, as Giordano was providing everything necessary for the expedition, not one of them should receive any pay. 'We were going as volunteers to avenge our country's honour.'

At 4 a.m. next day they started from Valtournanche, and after a halt at the chapel of Breuil they made the final arrangements. Gorret put on his hunting clothes, tucked his trousers into his socks, took his alpenstock, and set off, carrying the ropes as his share. Two porters were to accompany them up to the bivouac. Carrel had his soldier's haversack; the other four put the provisions and equipment in sacks 'so arranged as to be carried on the back, leaving the move ments unimpeded and the hands free for climbing rocks, a way of carrying sacks that greatly tickled us owing to the picturesque appear ance it gave our caravan.' We have ceased to connect our rucksacks with ornament or amusement!

It was a dry season and there was exceptionally little snow under the Tête du Lion; the Col du Lion is passed and the huge final pyramid confronts them. 'I could not analyse my feelings,' says Gorret. 'I felt my heart beating; I would have liked to hug to it this wonderful Mont Cervin.'

The chimney is climbed 'sweep fashion, using elbows, knees, feet, and hands.' Early though it is, the tent is set up, on Carrel's advice, in the old place below the Grande Tour, and not carried higher.

Next morning the difficult climb to pass the Tour has to be tackled at once. They move one at a time, belaying the rope. One by one the now famous stages of the climb are passed; the dangerous couloir on the south face; 'a small plateau of extremely hard snow' (the Linceul); the slabby rocks where the ridge is regained. Only a string was left here where Tyndall had fixed a rope a few years before, and they replaced it with another rope before crossing.

At ten o'clock they passed the flag pole on the Pic Tyndall and took it with them to serve for their flag on the summit. They halted for food and rest at the foot of the final crags, which a sensational gap (the Enjambée) cut off from the ridge they had been following. Across the gap they faced the last, unknown defences.

Gorret was for continuing up the ridge, the best route, but Carrel led off along a ledge of reddish rock across the face that rises sheer above the glacier four thousand feet below.

We were crawling, stretched full length on the solid rock, half-way across the face above the Zmutt valley when icicles and rocks loosened from the top gave us a great fright as they fell past. We could see no way on. We started, there-fore, to climb up an almost perpendicular rock; this was the part that cost us most time and effort. At last we reached the foot of the final crags which slightly overhung and where we could watch the icicles pass over our heads without any possibility of hitting us, and crash on the rocks we had just been climbing.

Although the place is not more than a couple of yards broad and is inclined at an angle of nearly 40°, we gave it all sorts of nice names: the gallery, the railway, etc. With hands clinging to the rock above, we glided along this gallery. . . . 'No sen fer!' (We're stuck!) cries Carrel, who is leading. 'A good job too!' answers Meynod from the rear; he thought Carrel had said *fouer* (We're through!). A couloir a few yards wide, which had been out of sight before, cut us off from the ridge in front, on which we could see a safe and easy way.

Carefully examining the position, we saw that about twenty-five feet below us it was possible to cross on to the ridge and gain the summit.

We must let ourselves down! Yes, but what from? We simply have not the time to fix an iron ring in the rock; we shall never get away in daylight, and just a few steps more will do it! Once past this difficulty there is nothing more!

Well, we discussed it; I was the heaviest and strongest; not for all the gold I could carry would I have agreed to be the one left. But someone had to make the sacrifice, and I did it. Planting my heels on the edge of the cliff, my back against the rock, my arms pressed to my chest, I let two of my comrades down, one by one; the third chose to stay behind with me; I was happy.

A few minutes later, the two were out of danger on easy ground, galloping up. I felt then what I had given up; I sat astride of the ridge and watched them, shouting words of encouragement, and with my heels I spurred the Mont Cervin, as though I would make him move, and make him feel he had found his master: 'You're for it, you brute.'

I was trying to find some way of letting myself down into the couloir and of making it practicable for tourists, when the others rejoined me. I pulled them up with the rope; they clasped my hand; I congratulated them; then I took my place on the rope again and we started back again.

There is no more attractive figure in all the annals of climbing than this young priest, with all the difficulties of a great climb conquered, with his back to the rock, paying out the rope to the men that are to gather all the glory; and yet happy in the doing of it.

Is it not he who has really carried off the prize?

PART II
SIGNS OF MATURITY

CHAPTER VI

THE EXTENSION OF THE PLAYGROUND

WITH the ascent of the Matterhorn almost simultaneously by two entirely different routes, the work of the early climbers may be regarded as finished. No peak will henceforth be allowed to be inaccessible, however forbidding the appearance of its walls of rock and ice. The very scaling of these walls has ceased to be a price to pay for the contemplative pleasures of the summit; it is an end in itself. The spirits of Domp Julien the cragsman and of Gesner the dreamer on the height have stood together as godfathers to modern mountaineering and loaded the lusty babe with gifts.

The terrible drama in which Whymper's victory had ended drew the attention of the world to a new craze, to which it had not yet accorded the name or privilege of sport. What was this folly that had cost the lives of four men, including a young lord? Walking up a mountain to see the view or to make scientific observations was a recognized incident of travel or exploration; deliberately going on to parts of the mountain that were dangerous was a thing that called for a protest of the strongest nature. Englishmen did not yet recognize mountaineering as a sport.

In sport the element of danger was admitted. Cricket would not be cricket if played with a soft ball; soccer and rugger without charging and vigorous tackling would be a poorer kind of football; in boxing and hunting the risks were still more obvious; a man might be seriously injured or even killed at these great games without incurring any charge of folly.

Indeed, the absence of risk for long excluded lawn-tennis—so long called pat-ball—from the aristocracy of sport. By all means let those to whom nature had denied the special gifts that bring success in popular games console themselves by walks upon the hills, but they must not claim the privileges accorded to real sportsmen.

This attitude to mountaineering, regarding it as a refuge for the unathletic, died hard. It must have been a surprise to the county committee when a keen cricketer like myself refused the chance of making a first appearance in first-class cricket because it would mean missing the early days of August in the Alps.

It is true that a large proportion of the early climbers, strong and tough as they were in body, were intellectuals rather than athletes and sportsmen. A kind Providence saw to that. They understood the value of the heritage which they were passing on to the generation that followed. The great Austrian climber, Dr. Kugy, has called them 'the bearers of an incomparable tradition,' and it is in this tradition that the stewards of the heritage were trained.

We may regard the formation of Alpine clubs as an important step in its preservation and development, and the English Alpine Club was the first of all Alpine clubs. It was born at a small dinner-party in 1857; a dinner remains the great annual celebration of its life. Fifty years later over 120 clubs or associations were in existence in all parts of the world to encourage mountaineering.

The authority that a club can exercise is more limited in mountaineering than in any other sport. The game is played by individuals on grounds of their own choosing far from any possibility of control. The Alpine Club is no M.C.C. whose decisions are accepted with a submissiveness that is almost beyond the dreams of a Fascist autocrat. No punishment is attempted beyond a censure that only flatters the folly that deserves it. No climber can be suspended—except by his immediate companions and at his own request! None but Scottish landlords and suspicious governments have attempted to close the climbers' playgrounds. And, as a result, the stewards of our mountaineering heritage have had no unpleasant enforcement of discipline to spoil the pleasure of their task, which is the keeping of the annals and the development and extension of the great estate.

Good maps cost time and money, and in consequence good maps existed only for those regions where the serious business of fighting could be carried on, just the regions devoid of interest to climbers. Map-making in a new Alpine district may have all the romance of exploring the future domain in the company of the best-beloved. It is always exhilarating to climb a wall and see what is on the other side. And when the wall is thousands of feet high, the other side may contain surprises of all sorts—a pleasant or unpleasant descent for the climber, a topographical surprise for the geographer or cartographer, and perhaps the surprise of finding a previous map or record wrong. The number of professional men among the early climbers was large, and in these the habit of putting others right has developed into an instinct, which, when duty does not compel, it is a pleasure to indulge.

Alpine publications are sometimes mere inventories of peaks and passes acquired, with the date and manner of acquisition and title-deeds of the men who claimed them first; sometimes they attempt to record the emotions as well as the incidents of a day. Nothing can be less suggestive of romance than the bald summaries contained in a Climbers' Guide; the thrilling hours that may have won the right to that brief entry are hidden from all but a few individuals. An announcement in the press that a marriage has been arranged and will shortly take place between A. B. son of —— and C. D. daughter of —— is bald enough, yet a good many of us can imagine from our own experience a romantic prelude. A poster in the street says: 'Test Match, Bradman not out 334.' That means nothing to a Frenchman, a great feat to a cricketer; it recalls the most faultless batting they ever saw to several thousands of spectators, and a great deal more to Bradman. But the countless hours of adventure that go to the making of a Climbers' Guide are so varied in the scene and in the efforts and emotions that fill them that none but the men who have lived those hours, even if they are climbers, can picture what they mean.

Here are a couple of comparatively expansive passages from Climbers' Guides. In the first, picture yourself on a part of the huge wall of ice and rock that closes the valley of Lauterbrunnen:

The rocks begin at a height of about 10,000 feet and are good till a vertical rock wall blocks the way. This is turned by a succession of short but difficult traverses to the left or north, and a direct climb up very steep rock, three hours being spent on this bad bit of less than 300 feet.

That is a clear statement, as useful as such an indication can be. This is how the turning of the rock wall appears in the journal of the party written a day or two after.

But when, at about 12.15, we stood directly beneath it [the vertical wall] there appeared no way except one leading round to the left. Accordingly we took this way to the left, and I think I am voicing the general opinion of the party in saying that we are all thankful at the prospect of never repeating this traverse. It was necessary to edge along beneath a bulging rock wall, moving ever to the left until snow could be reached. First, we crept along a thin ledge, and surmounting a small platform of rock, somewhat glazed, wormed our precarious way round a bulging rock to a small recess beneath an overhanging chimney. Finding this impossible to ascend, Graham kept well round to the left on a level, being well belayed by the second man, and passing over a vertical face of rock, with good holds in places, reached a platform of rock some forty feet to our left. The second man then unroped, and passed round the traverse, the rope between the other two being stretched tight and belayed behind two splinters of rock; the last man in traversing loosed the rope, and the party tied on once more at the rock platform. Our position was a sensational one, and we could now choose one of two routes; either we could cut down and along an excessively steep slope of hard snow, which gave place now and then to ice, thus rounding the left end of the overhanging rock wall; or we could keep almost at a level, and traverse over snow, not quite so steep at first, close beneath the wall of rock. The leader chose the latter, and cutting admirable steps in very steep snow—the angle I should estimate at 65°—reached a small ridge in this large patch of snow. The traverse needed the utmost care, especially in one place where the snow lay thin upon ice, and the steep wall above prevented the cutting of a proper step. At this corner in the snow-patch the other two waited, while the leader kicked his way round a considerably steeper slope of snow, which appeared to have an inclination of some 80°, and with difficulty effected a lodg-ment upon a small patch of rocks. This traverse called forth a piece of leadership, of which the other two, anxiously engaged in passing the rope round a doubtful belaying-pin, were unwilling witnesses.

And now it appeared that the crux of the climb was to come. From my position at the corner, I could see a vertical rock wall, which seemed to promise little hold; I could also see the leader attempting it, and it was with great relief that we saw him at the third attempt surmount it in safety. He then passed from our sight, and we shouted to him to get as much above us as possible. Our only answer was a call for more rope, in response to which Guy unroped and we fastened the spare rope to the sixty-foot one with which we had been climbing. For some time further we heard the sound of the leader's axe grating upon the rocks, before he pronounced himself firm and called to the second man to come. The rope unfortunately hung a little too much to the left, as a result of which the second man was forced to attack an entirely hopeless face of rock; however, after being helped up this he mounted rapidly, and having reached the leader's position, waited there while the latter cut up another seventy feet of very steep snow.

Meanwhile, I had time to look around me. Below, the snow-slopes ran down for five hundred feet with appalling steepness, and the next thing visible was the sloping snow-covered Schmadrirück, two thousand feet below. A few sparkles in the far distance indicated the lake of Thun, and on the opposite hillside I could see the hotel, and even thought to distinguish figures watching our move-ments. To the right was the wall beneath which we had crept, and above to the left the sun was playing on a patch of rocks which for the last three hours had seemed to come no nearer to us.

Soon it was time to ascend, and with vigorous aid from the rope, I scrambled somehow up the short rock wall, and saw above Guy seated comfortably on a huge stone, looking perfectly happy, and Graham higher up, outlined against the dark sky.

That is word for word as it was recorded a few days after in the minutes of a private record. It tells a good deal more to any climber than the lines of the Climbers' Guide, and it brings back to the men who were there as much as memory can recall of such a day.

Here is another example from a foreign Climbers' Guide; this time the scene is the Mischabel.

At about 600 feet below the summit, this couloir ends in a sort of chimney whose walls form a very obtuse angle, about 100 feet high, very steep and in part overhanging. This difficult place was brilliantly climbed by Franz Loch matter; the other members of the party were hauled up by the rope. . . .

Read Mr. Geoffrey Young's ten pages of description of that piece of climbing in his book *On High Hills*. If you are not a climber, it will impress you as something desperately dangerous and thrilling; if you are, your fingers and toes will feel themselves clawing at the wrinkles of an imaginary and pitiless slab against that terrible pull back into the abyss. And still we shall be far away from what the five men hanging on that grim precipice saw and felt.

The two passages quoted are typical of hundreds of pages of others like them. These Climbers' Guides are sufficient proof of the persistence with which the Alps have been and are being forced to yield what is steadily set before the climber as his ideal, the making of a new route. As with an oil-well that is beginning to run dry, the cost of maintaining the yield grows more and more difficult. The effect of this will be noticed elsewhere.

The decade which ended with the conquest of the Matterhorn has been called the golden age of mountaineering. The ideal expedition was the first ascent of a great peak. This was the pure gold of mountaineering, and upon it was based a gold standard for succeeding generations. Departures from the gold standard must be considered later. Such a thing was not dreamed of by the well-known climbers born in the golden age, whom one may regard, and who certainly regarded themselves, as stewards of the mountaineering inheritance. For them, therefore, the Alps after 1865 could no longer offer the prizes of the last few years. Men with sufficient means and leisure to try to win these prizes in other great ranges of the world were soon engaged in the attempt.

The first well-equipped party of climbers reached the Caucasus in 1868; an ideal party to explore, to appreciate, and to describe a new playground: D. W. Freshfield, A. W. Moore, C. C. Tucker, with François Dévouassoud, the Chamonix guide. Elbruz and Kasbek, the two best-known peaks, fell easily before them. The wonderful wall formed by Shkara and Janga, Dych Tau, and the two-headed Ushba, the Caucasian rival of the Matterhorn, were left for succeeding parties.

Comparing the Caucasus with the Alps, Mr. Freshfield writes:

The supremacy of Caucasian scenery lies in the heart of the chain: it consists in the form of the peaks, their lavish glaciation, and the richness of the flowers and forestry that clothe many of the upper valleys. Its inferiority, compared to Alpine scenery, will be found in the outskirts of the mountains. The strength has to be sought; the weaknesses, on the countrary, are obvious at first sight.

And like all who have found a new thing, he looks upon it as a parent on his child. Speaking of the Alps in 1902 he says:

They can hardly be to another generation what they have been to their discoverers, to the men who forty years ago joined to fill up a gap in the maps of Central Europe, to survey the chain of Mont Blanc and the Graian Alps, the then untrodden snows of the Ortler, the Adamello, and the Grand Paradis.

And Clinton Dent, who went out in 1886, gives the Caucasus one of the best advertisements a range has ever had:

We have found at the other end of Europe a strange country, where giant peaks wait for you—remote, sublime, inaccessible to all but their most patient lovers. If you worship the mountains for their own sake; if you like to stand face to face with Nature where she mingles the fantastic and the sublime with the sylvan and the idyllic—snows, crags, and mists, flowers and forests—in perfect harmony; where she enhances the effect of her pictures by the most startling contrasts, and enlivens their foregrounds with some of the most varied and picturesque specimens of the human race—go to the Caucasus.

The last word of that fine appeal might be changed to that of any great range, even to the Alps, without becoming untrue, but it breathes an enthusiasm that was infectious. Even Mummery tore himself away from the 'bulging ice of the gullies, and the brown slabs bending over into immeasurable space,' so generously provided by the Chamonix Aiguilles, to climb Dych Tau in 1888.

The subjugation of the chain was complete when the twin peaks of Ushba were traversed by H. Pfann and two friends in a great expedition which necessitated four successive nights without shelter of any kind.

One of the most memorable episodes in the story of the Caucasus is the search for traces of Donkin and Fox, who with their two guides disappeared in 1888 and were never seen again. Donkin was one of the first to bring back photographs of the High Alps that gave an

9. USHBA, THE MATTERHORN OF THE CAUCASUS

idea of their beauty. It meant adding to the load carried a $7\frac{1}{2}''$ by $5''$ plate camera with changing box, the whole weighing eighteen pounds without the tripod. Now excellent pictures can be taken with apparatus whose total weight is about a pound.

Dych Tau, a splendid peak of over seventeen thousand feet, and then still unclimbed, was their goal. The last message that reached another English party out in the same year said that they were going to approach it from the south by crossing the Ullu-auz Pass. An attempt the previous day on the north ridge had failed.

Four Englishmen — Freshfield, Dent, Woolley, Powell — and a brother of one of the lost guides, Fischer, with three Swiss guides, set out in 1889 to look for traces of their friends. Rumours of foul play by the natives had spread, and it was important to obtain, as far as possible, conclusive evidence of an accident. The party reached the foot of the Ullu-auz Pass and looked up a broad, steep gully that led up to it. Anywhere on the rocks beside the gully seemed a possible place for a bivouac; a search with the telescope revealed no place as specially likely. The night might even have been passed on the other side of the ridge. They started up towards the pass.

Two long ribs of rock lying on the right of the ice gully offered the best means of access. Both looked feasible, but it was only after a moment's hesitation that the left-hand one was selected, as it seemed more broken, was broader and ran up higher. If the right-hand rib had been chosen, we might conceivably have missed the object of our search altogether. We made our way up the rocks without any great difficulty. Half-melted masses of snow constantly hissed down the ice gully as we ascended, and the great chasm that extends along the base of the cliff was choked for the most part with avalanche snow. The rocks were steep, but so broken as to afford good hand- and foot-hold. Still, the mind was sufficiently occupied in attending to the details of climbing to prevent the thoughts from wandering. Insensibly we began to think of little save of the view that would be revealed from the top of the pass. From time to time an opportunity would be found of gazing to right or left, but progress was tolerably continuous. Maurer, who was leading, looked upwards now and again as he worked out the best line of ascent, but the rocks were so steep that he could only see a very few feet.

Just about midday, as he stopped for a moment to look upwards, I saw his expression suddenly change. 'Herr Gott!' he gasped out, 'der Schlafplatz!' I think I shall never forget the thrill the words sent through me. We sprang up, scrambling over the few feet that still intervened, and in a moment were grouped on a little ledge just outside the bivouac.

There was little enough to be seen at the first glance save a low horseshoe-shaped wall of stones, measuring some six feet by eight, and carefully built against

G

an overhanging rock. The enclosure was full of drifted snow, raised up into a hump at the back, where it covered a large rucksack. On a ledge, formed by one of the stones, a little snow spectacle-box caught the eye as it reflected the rays of the sun. For a few moments all was excitement as the presence of one object after another was revealed. 'See here,' cried Maurer, as he scooped away the snow with his hands, 'the sleeping-bags!' 'And here a rucksack,' said another. 'Look, they made a fire there,' called a third, 'and here is the cooking-kettle and the revolver.' Then came somewhat of a reaction, and for a few minutes we could but gaze silently at the place that told so clear a tale, and endeavour to realize to the full the evidence that had come upon us with such overwhelming suddenness.

Later on, before the native audiences that crowded into the visitors' room in every village, Powell, who spoke Russian, would tell the story to some native in authority, who would interpret it to the rest, pointing out that the district was exonerated from all suspicion. Then various articles would be brought and shown, particularly the rusty revolver. And the chief would speak to this effect: 'We are indeed rejoiced that you have found these traces. It relieves our people from an irksome and unjust suspicion. It is well that English-men came to our country for this search, for we believe that no others would have accomplished what you have done. We are all very grateful to you.' And in many villages simple words of genuine sorrow were spoken: 'We remember well Donkin and Fox; they were brave and good men, and we loved them. It is very sad to us us to think that they are lost.'

This long, difficult journey, undertaken to try to clear up the mystery of the death of friends when the fact of their death was certain, is a fine page in the history of mountaineering. The twentieth century has produced more and better climbers than the Victorian age; it has not yet produced finer men.

The Himalayas could not be left long uncoveted. Up to 1860 there had been no mountaineering beyond such as was necessary to satisfy the men whose ambition is to slay the animals that share our liking for the snows. In 1864 and 1865 an exceptionally enterprising member of the Indian Survey, Mr. Johnson, ascended several peaks over twenty-one thousand feet. He slept at nearly twenty-two thousand feet, and it remains a mystery whether he actually climbed a peak of nearly twenty-four thousand feet. The Indian Survey did not encourage climbing that offered no great benefit to the mapping of a district; moreover it invented names for these splendid snow-peaks of the Himalayas that would discourage any romantic adventure with them.   The peak Mr. Johnson may or may not have ascended is E 61!

The first notable achievement in Himalayan climbing is Mr. Graham's ascent of Kabru, a snow mountain of approximately twenty-four thousand feet close to the mighty Kanchenjunga.   There is no reason to doubt the genuineness of Graham's ascent.   The fact that he and his guides in good training suffered no special inconvenience from the height is not at all remarkable if we remember that two Norwegians in 1907 spent over a week within 1,500 feet of its summit, and that greater heights still have been reached by members of the later Everest expeditions without discomfort.

Well-equipped expeditions followed, but so far the tide of invasion has beaten in vain against the real defences of the Himalayas.   In 1892 Sir Martin Conway made a great voyage of mountain exploration in the Karakorams, far the greatest if we reckon greatness by the magnificence of the peaks that flung their challenge down from precipices greater than any on which man had looked before.   The great Hispar Glacier, forty miles long, was ascended, to the Hispar Pass.   On the far side a great snow lake, with no apparent exit and covered with slush under the fierce sun, was crossed, and at the far side the outlet was disclosed.

The wide, level snowfield of the Biafo at the outlet of the snow-lake is floor to a glorious avenue of peaks.   They rise on both sides of the glacier for some fifteen miles, one way and another, a series of spires, needle sharp, walled about with precipices on which no snow can rest, and separated from one another by broken couloirs, wherein tottering masses of snow are for a while arrested till each in turn is dislodged and falls with an overwhelming crash on the slopes far below.   The aiguilles of Chamonix possess an impetuosity of outline that impresses every spectator, but these Braldu pikes outjut them in steepness, outnumber them a hundred, perhaps a thousandfold in multitude, and outreach them in size.

Here is work to keep our modern experts busy for several years more: a thousand super-Charmoz, a thousand super-Grépons, a thousand super-Requins, a thousand super-Fous . . . It will be long before the natives have learned to distinguish the last from the climbers themselves.

The Baltoro Glacier, when the party had advanced two days' march up its narrow beginning, widened to disclose an array of still greater giants.   The highest of these splendid peaks, only surpassed in height by Everest and gloriously inaccessible, is K 2 to the official world.   Masherbrum, Gusherbrum, the Hidden Peak, the Broad

Peak, the Mustagh Tower, are all over twenty-four thousand feet, and if difficulty is the measure of value, climbers have here a potential source of incalculable wealth. If enjoyment or romance is our measure of value, the experience of Conway and of the later Himalayan expeditions forbids us to esteem the Himalayan peaks as highly as the Alps. To be surrounded by them, to look up at their unapproach-able crests, is an unforgettable experience. To climb them is to lose capacity for any feeling beyond a weariness that gradually overcomes the power, if not the will, to push on.

On Pioneer Peak, on which Conway reached a height of 22,600 feet, he tells us:

> The views in these upper regions, except in so far as they commanded very distant prospects, did not differ in character from those beheld about the high *névés* of any mountain-range. . . . We merely saw larger extensions of snow-field and bigger mounds, ridges and pyramids of snow rising out of them. There was little that was unusual in the glacial features which, high aloft, are the same all the world over. Romance, I suppose, was vanishing. Exaltation of heart was wearing out.

The next generation confirms in more definite terms this suggestion that the exaltation of heart, the expansion and gladness of the mind which we associate with Alpine heights, fades out in apathy when a height is reached at which man can with difficulty breathe and live. In a later chapter you will hear something of what men feel as they approach a height of twenty-seven thousand feet on Everest.

In 1909 the Duke of the Abruzzi took out another well-equipped expedition to the Karakorams. The main purpose was to climb K 2. They never got through the first defences and they had little hope of ever doing so, for the results of reconnoitring were not en-couraging. 'On every side the walls and ridges offer impossible angles. Precipitous *arêtes* are flanked by couloirs glittering with pure ice, above which at from six to ten thousand feet hang glaciers broken into tottering *séracs*.'

A height of over 24,500 feet was reached on the Bride Peak, under conditions much resembling those found by Conway on the adjoining Golden Throne. This remained the greatest height reached by climbers till the second Everest expedition of 1922.

Less elaborately organized expeditions carried out exploration and ascents more after the fashion of ordinary Alpine parties, the ascent of Trisul, well over twenty-three thousand feet, being accomplished by Dr. Longstaff with a couple of Italian guides. Something like

10. A HIMALAYAN SPIRE

six thousand feet were climbed on the last stage above the final camp, the height and pace achieved being very similar to that of Graham's party on Kabru. The cost of this expedition was trifling compared with that of the recent Everest expeditions.

These great extensions of mountaineering activity in the region above the snowline are in no way different in nature from moun-taineering in the Alps. The implements used are the same, the obstacles larger and more fatiguing, the pleasures rarer, the trials more severe; the emotions stirred are similar. Below the snowline the country and the inhabitants are entirely different, and it is the latter that give to books of Himalayan mountaineering their distinctive atmosphere.

The same is true of other ranges. It is the forests and lakes of the Canadian Rockies and the primitive conditions still existing there that give them their special character. Above the snowline, except in the Selkirks, the rocks are worse, the forms of the peaks less varied and less beautiful, the glacier work less attractive than in the Alps. Most of the peaks can only be reached by a long trek through forest, and the climber rarely sleeps under a roof more solid than canvas. The joys of camp life are forced upon him, and he learns what they can be.

Man is made like that; he goes to the ends of the earth to find the pleasures that lie almost at his door. On the pastures that give the Alps their name, and make them the one perfect range in the world, there are ideal camping-grounds. A forest is beautiful, but it is not better than a pasture, and it harbours all sorts of creatures that can easily penetrate a skin softened by hot baths, and make serious inroads on the hours of peaceful contemplation. The freedom of camp life, the isolation from the world below, the rushing stream, the starlight nights, the stories by the camp-fire, whose praises are sung by men returning from the Rockies, can be enjoyed in the Alps; and not one climber in a hundred will forsake the hut or the hotel in order to enjoy them!

In the Rockies the rosy light of novelty is over all. The mere presence of a hotel within ten miles will make this rosy glow fade into the light of common day. The same man who complains of an extra thousand feet to be climbed from his hotel before he reaches snow, who makes every effort not to lose the path among the trees and undergrowth, will find attraction in forcing his way for hours, even days, through pathless forest to reach the base of his peak if only it is in a range five thousand miles away. Perhaps it is the fault of city life. So keen are we to refresh ourselves with a glimpse of nature completely untainted by our fellow-men that the more Nature tries to hide some portion of herself from us, the more curious we are to see it. Logic is no part of the climber's make-up. He loves Nature to have secrets from him, and yet he does his utmost to reveal those secrets and publish them to other climbers in the pages of a journal. All he asks is that he shall be first to reveal them!

This pride of priority looms terribly large in the annals of moun-taineering. The jealousy over first ascents, the desire to belittle the achievement of earlier climbers, betrays itself over and over again, and especially in the case of the most famous peaks. It is remarkable how often, in this connection, history repeats itself. Mont Blanc is climbed by Dr. Paccard; doubts are cast on his ascent, and his fair share in the honour is denied for generations. The first ascent of Elbruz is claimed by Freshfield's party: a claim of priority is put in by a Russian party, who, with the possible exception of one native, did not get within many hundred feet of the summit. Chimborazo is climbed by Whymper: the first ascent is claimed by a Frenchman, M. Jules Resny, on the ground that a thermometer, admittedly out of order, dipped into boiling water, gave a reading that showed (on incorrect calculations) a height within three feet of the height attributed to the summit by surveyors.

Kabru, the first famous peak of the Himalayas to be ascended, is climbed by Graham and Boss with a Swiss guide; the ascent is disputed. The Grand Teton in the United States provides us, as we might expect, with a regrettably perfect example. When America takes up an activity previously established in Europe, she is apt to seize on the external features.

In 1898 Mr. Owen, of Wyoming, U.S.A., claimed the first ascent. After enumerating the many unsuccessful efforts previously made since 1843 to climb this famous peak south of the Yellowstone National Park, Mr. Owen describes his successful climb. Let us join him six hundred feet below the top, on a shelf above which

the wall rises with a slope of only 20° from the vertical in one sweep of glassy granite. . . . It is as neat a piece of rock-work as one would wish to see, and is certainly not surpassed by anything in North America. Having reached the head of the first crevice, we stood face to face with another, fully 160 feet long and nearly vertical. Thanks to the ragged nature of this niche, we were able to pass it in safety, and soon had an opportunity of standing upright once more with a level granite slab under our feet. Three hundred feet higher we left the west face and passed round to the east side, halting at the upper margin of the immense snowfield on the south face of the peak. The sight was most impressive. A single step southward and we should be hurled into eternity—an unbroken leap of 3,000 feet! The slope of the snowfield is steep almost beyond belief, and it is a mystery to me still how it retains its position, seemingly in opposition to the law of gravitation. We were now but 100 feet below the summit, and could see that victory was to be our portion. Passing squarely round to the east side, we scaled the last fifty feet without difficulty, and at 4 p.m. stood upon the topmost rock of the Grand Teton, where never before rested man's foot.

Now read these words from a letter published after the appearance of Mr. Owen's account:

The pride of Mr. Owen in his recent achievement has, it is to be regretted, led him into the folly of attempting to magnify it by the claim that his is the first ascent, which pretension he attempts to maintain by attacking the veracity of Captain Stevenson, who has been dead many years, and of Mr. Langford, an honoured resident of St. Paul, Minn. It is an act of simple justice to the memory of Captain Stevenson, a man of the highest and most unquestionable veracity, and only fair to Mr. Langford, who is an author of distinction, one of the founders of Yellowstone National Park, and a citizen of the highest reputation, to state the fact of their first ascent of the peak [in 1872].

And here is the modern generation on Mr. Owen's route. The party had made the first ascent of the east ridge, which they report as likely 'to initiate a new cycle in the mountaineering importance of the Teton.'

'At 4.30 we started down. Knowing the simplicity of the ordinary route, we had already taken off the rope and stowed it in a rucksack, and we now literally ran down the mountain, reaching camp again, with the toilsome climb up out of Bradley Canyon included, in exactly three hours.'

Literally ran down! How small Mr. Owen must have felt if he read that, and how climbers will insist on forcing the least attractive features of mountaineering into notice!

Novelty draws climbers to all parts of the great backbone of the Americas. Climbing gets less and less attractive as we follow it south. Aconcagua offers one wonderful effect, the great shadow of its summit projected by the rising sun to the horizon of the Pacific two hundred miles away, and travelling over the water and the plain till it reaches the climbers' very feet. But it exacts a heavy price. One who has climbed in more ranges of the world than any other admits it. 'For its vast scale there is nothing meaner in mountain architecture than this north-west slope of Aconcagua . . . a slope of débris from bottom to top.' And such débris! . . . 'It was now and again relieved by short rock scrambles, but otherwise it was one heart-breaking pound, three steps lost by sliding back for every four taken.' And the dry, cold wind adds much to the trials of the climber. 'The stuff under foot became looser the higher we climbed. If we yielded to the desire to halt, the cold drove us to move on. Clothes, though of thickest fur, and wolf-skin gloves, seemed no better protection than so much muslin. Above twenty-one thousand feet, with a temperature probably below zero Fahrenheit, we felt colder than I ever remember.'

Farther south still, the peaks of Tierra del Fuego attract by their mystery and repel any advance for closer acquaintance with awful storms and livid snows. Conway is, as far as I know, the only man who has made a serious attempt on Mount Sarmiento. It is a shy peak, but it can blush in a manner that invites to closer acquaintance.

Suddenly—so suddenly that all who saw it cried out—far away above this cloud, surprisingly, incredibly high, appeared a point of light like a glowing coal drawn from a furnace. The fiery glow crept down and down as though driving the mist away, till there stood before us as it were a mighty pillar of fire with a wreath of mist round its base, and downward a wonderful pink wall and cataract of ice to the black forest and reflecting water. We had seen the first peak now—a tower of ice-encrusted rock, utterly inaccessible from the western side.

And this is how the invitation is followed up:

The darkness in the north, before it descended upon us, was truly appalling. It seemed not merely to cover, but to devour the wintry world. The heavens appeared to be falling in solid masses, so dense were the skirts of snow and hail that the advancing cloud-phalanx trailed beneath it. Black islands, leaden waters, pallid snows, and splintered peaks disappeared in a night of tempest, which enveloped us almost before we had realized that it was at hand. A sudden wind shrieked and whirled around us; hail was flung into our faces, and all the elements raged together. The ice-plastered rocks were accounted for; we came to resemble them ourselves in a few moments. All landmarks vanished; the snow beneath was no longer distinguishable from the snow-filled air. To advance was impossible.

No repulse could have been colder or more conclusive.

The men who will enjoy climbing Sarmiento will have to follow a régime that brings them nearer in bodily habit to the natives. Conway saw, in an open canoe of bark and skins, 'as ill-looking and unclean specimens of humanity as can be imagined. They wore loose pieces

11. NATURE'S LAST STRONGHOLD

of fur hitched on to them in casual fashion, but most of their bodies were naked, and the falling snow melted upon them. They were fat—greasy of aspect, resembling seals or other blubber-covered animals.'

The other extremity of the continent, where the great mountains of Alaska rise fifteen thousand feet above the snowline in the middle of summer, has played its part in the romance of mountaineering in America. The conditions in those high latitudes belong rather to polar exploration than to what we mean by climbing, and it is the approach to the peaks that presents the greatest obstacle to their ascent.

The Duke of the Abruzzi was the first to conquer one of the giants, Mount St. Elias. The story is a record of efficient organization and of perseverance under monotonous and trying conditions. Many days are occupied in dragging sledges over the lower slopes. 'The scenery is grand but monotonous; all element of contrast is lacking, while the abundant snow destroys any boldness of outline in the peaks and ridges.' A camp is set up on a col at over twelve thousand feet, and the start is made up the north ridge at midnight.

The ascent is monotonous, without the smallest difficulty, now on the wide crest of the *arête*, now on one or other of the slopes. . . . We were forced to halt for five or six minutes every quarter of an hour. At last we sighted above us a sharp pinnacle of ice, and a little beyond it to the right the great snowy dome of the summit. We climbed this slope in zigzags, pausing for breath every ten minutes. Suddenly Petigax and Maquignaz stop and stand aside, and the prince is the first to set foot on the summit of St. Elias. We hasten up panting and exhausted to join in the hurrah. I will not attempt to describe our sensations. Difficulty of breathing, throbbing at the temples, exhaustion, all disappeared instantaneously in the excitement of that moment. . . . The Italian flag fluttered on an ice-axe, and we crowded round our chief to join with all our might in his cheer for Italy and the king.

Happy those breathless climbers who under such circumstances need only one word for their country and one syllable for its ruler! Fancy with your last gasp having to cheer for the Union of Socialist Soviet Republics! But such fanatical levellers as Communists might prefer removing a peak to climbing it.

Other ascents more difficult, and involving some of the special difficulties both of Arctic and of Himalayan explorations, were successfully accomplished. Allen Carpe's name will always be associated with this district. Only here could he find mountain country that completely satisfied him.

This country has lost none of its fascination for me in the last four years, which
have changed so much else in my life. . . . It is wild and sombre, very different
from those Canadian mountains you visited. It is more like Alberta than Jasper
or Robson, but is probably more like Norway or some parts of Scotland. Those
places we visited in Canada one can readily think of as casual vacation resorts,
but this country stays with me. It has haunted me for years, as you know, and
I doubt if I will ever be really satisfied until I have tried to live in it.

He took part in the first ascent of Mount Logan in 1929, an undertaking that involved weeks of alternating sunshine and awful cold,
of disappointment, retreat, and ultimate success. The base of the
peak has a circumference of a hundred miles, and at ten thousand
feet it measures sixteen miles from east to west and eight from north
to south.

Later, in 1931, he pushed on with a single companion in the face
of real mountaineering difficulties to the summit of Mount Fairweather.
Its godfather was evidently an optimist, by Allen Carpe's account:

We were alone on the mountain. . . . At night the wind came up strong.
We had to take the tent-pole down and gather the straining canvas in our hands
lest it be torn to shreds or carried over the precipice. The wet snow melted
through and converted the interior into a lake which we bailed out with an
empty tin. Small avalanches passed with a swish close to the tent. Waterfalls
of drier snow poured over the cliffs high above. Once, while we looked, the
whole surface sheet of powder snow coasted silently off the hidden reaches of the
shoulder, took the air in great rolling waves, and quickly filled the glacial chute
at our feet. There was no sound whatever.

They started off when the weather improved, taking with them

a sleeping robe, a tarp, shovel, and food enough for several days, ready to dig in
and bide our chance if the storm should resume . . . the going was pretty deep.
We crawled, Indian fashion, on all fours, distributing our weight on knees and
forearms. It was very cold, certainly well below zero. As we approached
the *arête* we measured the grade with a clinometer: 55° was maintained
over a long slope, and the steepest place touched 60°. The surface was not
what one would choose for walking at this angle but it held up surprisingly
well. High up everything was changed. Fantastic and unstable cornices
draped the ridge, and twice broke under our feet. In the west the shadow of
the mountain lay clear and immense upon a carpet of low sea-clouds; and around
a point on the silhouette, corresponding to our own station on the mountain,
was an iridescent halo. By it we observed our slow progress toward the shoulder.
Here at perhaps 6 a.m. the welcome sun met us. Without a halt we went on
to the ice steps of the preceding climb [when they had been driven down by the
blizzard]. Above them, we followed the crest of the ridge straight to the top;

this seemed the easiest way. It was clear, windy, and bitterly cold. . . . We tied the *parka* to our tent-pole and set it up on the summit facing the sea.

The sun, even in this high latitude, 'became roasting hot,' and the condition of the snow was dangerous on the descent. 'With some care and more luck' they reached the tent again in the afternoon. Next day was no day of rest.

The descent of the remaining four thousand feet [to the glacier] was a night-mare. Sun and rain had got in their work, the season of night frosts was passing, the snow was wet and treacherous. Wide bands of hard, old ice had opened in the steepest places, requiring slow cutting. We were directly in the path of falling rocks. Despite an early start, it was afternoon when we reached the site of the glacier camp.

Next year, in 1932, a party returning from an ascent of Mount McKinley brought the news of Allen Carpe's death. Ski-tracks on the snow-covered glacier led to a broken bridge over a big crevasse, and told the tale. Either Carpe or his one companion had fallen through; the other had stood on the lip of the crevasse to look down and had also fallen in. Carpe's companion had struggled out despite severe injuries, and perished in the snow. A member of the rescue party all but met a similar death while the body was being dragged down with the only rope. Carpe's companion on Mount Fairweather says of him: 'I have known no other mountaineer more careful than he, nor have I ever seen or known of his making a false step.' Compare that statement with the manner of his death and meditate on the conclusion you should draw.

The brief glimpses it has been possible to give in this chapter have shown the spread of mountaineering from the Alps to all the great ranges of the world. In almost every case the aims and methods of the climbers who have brought these new ranges within the conquered fields of man's activities have been those of the early climbers in the Alps. Exploration and mountaineering have gone hand in hand.

There are many mountain regions that have not received a men-tion. There are mountains in Japan, and there is an admirable saying of the Japanese as they set out upon their climb: 'May our five senses be pure and may the weather on the honourable mountain be fine.' There are high mountains in Africa; and of them I must confess that if the tales of their explorers are true and the results of their photography are genuine, there is not one that would compensate me for the loss of a single expedition in the Alps.

Weather is the one great drawback to climbing in the splendid range of the New Zealand Alps. The latitude corresponds to that of Switzerland and the snowline is about three thousand feet lower; that tells a tale! Mr. Harold Porter, who has climbed and photo-graphed almost every route there that can tempt a mountaineer, told me that one and a quarter days per week was the average number he expected to be good. Four fine days in succession is a blessing rarely vouchsafed. It was thoughtful of Nature to provide this fine playground at the Antipodes for those who would otherwise have found it impossible, even in the twentieth century, to enjoy the world above the snowline in a holiday of three or four weeks.

For the remaining ranges, forgotten or ignored, perhaps one that is specially beloved of you, the reader, I can only say: 'Forgive me for what I have left undone.'

It is time to consider developments in the nature and ideals of mountaineering, to see whether, with the opening up of all but a few peculiarly inaccessible and less attractive mountain systems, there has been left only a second best for the generation that is 'born out of due time.'

12. IN THE CANADIAN ROCKIES

CHAPTER VII

THE OLD LEADING-STRINGS ARE DROPPED

WHAT was the position of the ardent climber when tradition and standardization had begun to enfold the sport of mountaineering within their meshes?

The great men, Leslie Stephen, Freshfield, Whymper, and Moore, had made his mouth water, as I hope they still make mouths water, with their descriptions of great new ascents in the early numbers of the *Alpine Journal* and in the books that have become classics. And at the same time they provokingly denied to him the choicest fruits of all. The position, as they saw it for him, was something like this: 'Here in the Alps is laid out a feast of good things, and the feast is offered now to you, but we regret'—and few regrets have been expressed with such shameless exultation!—'that the only perfect vintage at moderate price, the Grand Cru des Premières, is exhausted, for we have drunk it all! There is a Caucasian bin ready for drinking and a large Himalayan bin maturing, and a few others of this exceptional vintage, but it has become a rich man's wine. However, we have left a lot of sound second-quality stuff, and there are excellent servants whom we can strongly recommend and who will show you where to get and how to enjoy what you want.'

Young appetites proved too strong to be content with this. Almost simultaneously two methods of satisfying them appeared, both of which have drawn the censure of the established great. The first was the production of a new sort of Cru des Premières, fortified with a spirit of danger that had been absent from the original Grand Cru. The second was to dispense with the servants and enjoy the feast without them.

Both developments were inevitable. If you persuade a man that a first ascent is the one thing that opens the door to supreme enjoyment and to fame, he is likely to push through somehow without bothering his head about approval of his methods. The only answer the old men could expect was: 'If risks beyond any you accepted are the price for this wine of life, we are ready to pay that price.'

The second alternative, the enjoying of the good things without the guides, arose from a trait in human nature that has nothing to do with danger. Much guideless climbing nowadays is done because the expense of guides is quite beyond the purses of thousands who refuse to be denied participation in a great sport, but the early guideless climbers were seldom men who could not have spared the wages of the best professionals. They were the men who discovered that the whole pleasure, if not the fame, of a new ascent is open to those who have to find their own way upon a mountain. And more than that; there is in many men a special satisfaction in reliance on their own resources. It dates from schooldays. Did not the very same quality of sausages, of bacon, or of herring that were just the 'same old stuff' when cooked in the house kitchen and served in the house hall become ambrosial when prepared over a primus stove, eaten in a room that had no sort of claim but privacy to be a dining-room? A peak climbed guideless may have all the pleasures of a first ascent.

Only one great Alpine peak, the Meije, lived on unconquered into the last quarter of the nineteenth century. And a grand antagonist it was, disdaining any armour of ice and artillery of stones, simply offering its great, bare, rugged breast to the wrestler's hold. It fell after a great struggle to Père Gaspard, who lived at its foot and who led a French soldier up its southern precipices to the Glacier Carré and the final defences above it. Gaspard and several sons of his enormous family came to know every rocky wrinkle that marked its few weak spots. Familiarity bred something like contempt. Père Gaspard, by example and precept, approved the making of a will as the prelude to the first ascents. Later he is reported to have approached a tourist with the words: 'Come up the Meije; an umbrella is all you need.'

The last great peak had fallen; how could the Alps be made to yield something that might fairly be called a first ascent? The answer was soon given, and the double solution of the problem has the merit of giving an inexhaustible supply. Either find a new route up a peak already climbed, or confer the dignity of peaks on unclimbed spurs of larger peaks. All that succeeding generations have to do, when the supply of new material fails, is to subdivide mountain faces into smaller facets and to lower the standard of isolation required by individual peaks. The process has already been carried far. On British rocks there are routes claiming a separate existence within a few feet of one another; in the Alps they are rarely at present within a stone's throw of each other, though in some cases the showers of stones or ice which the mountain is liable to discharge might possibly kill two parties in adjacent modern routes at one discharge.

The search for new routes began while many important peaks were still unclimbed.   At first these routes were made in the genuine desire to find the most practicable route up a mountain by a totally different side from that of the first ascent.   The Matterhorn is an exceptional case of two entirely different routes up a famous peak being opened almost simultaneously.

Mont Blanc, by its unique prestige and the immense extent of its base, had its obvious possibilities as a gold mine for the prospectors of new routes.   The present generation will hardly believe that the famous Brenva route was first climbed in a genuine attempt to discover a good route up Mont Blanc from the Italian side—and in those days a good route meant a route free from objective dangers and excessive difficulty.   The ascent by the Rocher du Mont Blanc was not made until 1872, the easiest Italian route by the Dôme Glacier not until 1890 by a party which included Achille Ratti, now Pope Pius XI.

A. W. Moore, one of the party led by Melchior and Jakob Anderegg, who opened the Brenva route in 1865, writes: 'The summit of Mont Blanc is three hours distant from the Dôme.   No one has yet reached it starting from the Col du Miage or *is ever likely to do so* . . . from the level of the southern glacier'!   And the concluding words of his account seem almost as strange in these days: 'As regards practical utility I fear that the Brenva route up Mont Blanc possesses few advantages over that by the Mont Blanc du Tacul.   But it has one merit which the latter lacks, that of direct-ness.   It is also incomparably more interesting and exciting.   I trust therefore that someone will be found sufficiently enterprising to give it another trial.'   His trustfulness has been amply justified.

The story of this Brenva ascent is one of the best-known in Alpine history.   The famous sharp *arête* half-way up the face has been chosen by a popular novelist to serve a murderer's aims.   Melchior Anderegg's splendid icemanship prevented Moore from recognizing that the gravest difficulty of the climb will generally be found on the ice-slopes below the wall of *séracs* that threatens to refuse, but can generally be made to concede, a way up to the broad easy ridge that leads to the summit of Mont Blanc.   Melchior's caution in insisting on the crossing of the *arête* astride and his alarming words on reaching its farther end: 'We must get up, for we cannot go back,' exaggerated for Moore the difficulty of this sensational portion of the climb.   But

Moore's own words indicate how serious may be the position of a party below the final difficulty: 'Our position was, in fact, rather critical. Immediately over our heads the slopes on which we were terminated in a great mass of broken *séracs,* which might come down with a run at any moment. It seemed improbable that any way out of our difficulty would be found in that quarter. But where else to look? There was no use in going to the left—to the right we *could* not go—and back we *would* not go.' A weak spot in the icy wall was found and climbed by Melchior.

It was here also that Güssfeldt, led by Emile Rey, in 1892, began to feel those awful icy 'shades of the prison-house,' one might say of the condemned cell, closing in. It is one of those places where the climber is most likely to be threatened with an irrevocable shutting of the door of escape, when the grey wings of death cast their shadow on the glittering grey slopes. Up to the present courage and resource have always found a successful issue. Güssfeldt writes in his notes:

> We begin to fear there is no possible way out. We know not which way to turn. Everywhere, steep slopes, where every step demands sixty strokes of the axe, and costs sixty seconds of our time. An hour later I write: 'Situation desperate.' The ice is white like snow and yet hard as clear ice. To right and left bluish layers of sparkling *névé*! Nowhere a way out! We advance with deadly slowness. Suddenly the way out appears. The moment may be compared to that in which the shipwrecked man has his first glimpse of the lifeboat approaching through the waves.

A famous guideless party, Mummery, Hastings, and Collie, spent the hours of an afternoon trying to cut a way out of these pitiless slopes of sticky ice, that got ever steeper and steeper. They were forced to descend to spend the night on a tiny islet of rock not far above the narrow *arête* below, and only got through the wall of *séracs* by thrusting their axes to form hand- and foot-hold for the leader. Another famous guideless party, Wilson, Wicks, and Bradby, found the ice-wall without a breach of any sort, and were faced with the necessity of cutting their way to the Col de la Brenva across a truly appalling ice-slope. It was already 5 p.m., and the shadowed face was intensely cold.

> Steep, slippery ice, of a hardness unknown to us before, with a curious quality, unique in our experience, born probably of great cold and enormous pressure— a quality of viscosity, which gave the impression of cutting into something which would not chip, but whose particles clung together like stiff tar. And every step had to be a fairly ample one—some to take both feet—and everywhere a rail of

hand-holds undercut to get a grip. Our gloves froze to these holds and to the slippery coat of ice which covered completely the stocks of the axes; and if by any chance a bare hand touched the metal, it stuck to it as if adhering to thick glue.

At 7 p.m. they reached the *séracs* on the far side of the slope. There the leader could embrace a stalactite of ice and swing up into a cave; this was quitted by a jump into a choked crevasse, and beyond the farther wall of the crevasse—at last the longed-for slope of snow, 'where even a roll would not be attended by serious consequences.'

In the official records the first party alone has the credit of a first ascent. The other three parties had everything else a climb can give, uncertainty till the very end, the need for judgment, skill, and boundless courage. Can we deny to any one of these three later ascents the perfection of quality in mountaineering? When we weigh our joys in scales that register true values the additional worth of this label of first ascent is no more than that of the scrap of paper that is covered by its mention in the Climbers' Guide.

The Brenva route is one that has suffered less degradation of prestige than others during the development of climbing technique and the decrease in the margin of safety that has taken place since the first ascent. The two last ascents referred to show the immense advance made by guideless climbing, for it is a severe test of a party's strength. In many years there is certainly a danger of falling ice, and accidents have occurred on this route from this cause despite the comparative infrequency with which it has been taken.

In 1865 the crowning wall of ice must have appeared solid from below, for it is as certain as anything can be that neither Melchior Anderegg nor Moore nor the Walkers would have deliberately exposed themselves to a known danger of this kind while cutting laboriously up the last steep slopes.

A far more dangerous climb, the ascent of Monte Rosa from Macugnaga, was made on the word of a great guide, Ferdinand Imseng, that it was 'reasonably safe.' The crossing of the great couloir named after the Italian Marinelli, who was killed there with Imseng in 1881, is always a gamble. Avalanches, sometimes of huge size, *may* fall down it at any time. It is fair to the party of 1872 to say that the danger was not appreciated when the expedition was undertaken.

The making of new routes in the face of recognized and unavoidable danger from falling stones or ice was the work of the naughty boys of the various Alpine clubs. Two of the naughtiest in the late seventies

H

were Thomas Middlemore and Oakley Maund. An expedition of Middlemore's with the guide Jaun, which produced a great commotion in the Alpine Club, was the traverse of the Col des Grandes Jorasses. It was not by any means the most dangerous of the climbs with which he shocked the greybeards, but it indicates a change of attitude to the deliberate taking of risks. The Col des Grandes Jorasses is the square, well-marked notch to the right of the terrific wall of the peak that fronts the gazers at the Montenvers. It had been reached from the north after a difficult ice-climb by an English party in 1864; the descent on the Italian side they considered 'hopelessly impossible, a sheer drop of many hundreds of feet.'

This was just the sort of thing to tempt Middlemore. He failed to persuade a companion, a very fine climber, T. S. Kennedy, to come with him, but his guide Jaun was of like mind with him. Let us join them on the last bit of the ascent on the Italian side, a very steep couloir.

Before we reached the foot of the rocks we saw that the scaling them would be a tougher job than Jaun had foretold. . . . The only feasible side of attack was on the eastern flanking wall. The rocks here were very rotten, as bad indeed as any you could find on the Italian slopes of the great chain, baked into rottenness by the glare of the southern sun. The foot-hold was bad, the hand-hold was worse, and both feet and hands had to be used. I find it far easier to graduate the pressure of the feet than of the hands in climbing loose rocks. Our course lay along a line which followed the bottom of the couloir, and was raised a little above it. Sometimes we were nearly forced into the gully, and with our axes could have almost touched the ice, stones, and such small debris as from time to time whistled down it. Of course, so long as we kept quite clear of the couloir, which we managed to do the whole time, so long this cannonade gave us amusement without a particle of risk.

Mr. Middlemore is a convinced optimist about the behaviour of mountain missiles. The marks on the rocks at the sides of couloirs indicate that the deviations of missiles from the grooves assigned to them by hopeful climbers are often large. The path, especially, of a 'whistling' missile after it strikes is as uncertain as that of a ball from a spin bowler on an extremely bad wicket. However, let us note that the party avoided the main danger of stones from this source.

There was another source of falling stones, which, if not risky, was anyhow not pleasant. This source was ourselves. The rocks were so steep and broken that, with the best care, we each of us kept disengaging stones. This inconvenience Jaun, who led us, treated with marvellous good temper. I, who came next, was not so serene. Two of the axes, which from time to time had to be perched,

14. DEFENCES OF THE AIGUILLE VERTE

had been already carried away by falling stones. My hand had been cut by another stone, which was immediately followed by a third, bruising my shoulder, and so paining me as to make me feel quite sick. My language, I fear, became expressive.

No reference is made to the third man on the rope, Joseph Rey; but he was only engaged as porter, and the tradition of early Alpine climbers in regard to porters seems to be *nil nisi malum*. The ascent of the rocks of the couloir took over five hours. They emerged on to the steep snow at its head, where they 'saw that the gully was the natural drainpipe, down which the débris of the whole col was sent.'

It was now four o'clock, so we pushed our way up the wall of snow that stood between us and the top of the pass. This, a work of five minutes with three axes, took us half an hour with only one. Indeed, as it was, there seemed some likelihood of our manning a raft of snow down the couloir, but with the help of our hands and legs sunk well in the snow, we reached the top of the pass at half-past four.

Rey had been offered twenty to forty francs according to the difficulty of the climb. Mr. Middlemore decided 'to comfort him with a hundred francs.' Rey thanked him for a sum greatly exceeding any expectations, and said he would not repeat the climb for a thousand francs: 'and he evidently meant it.' Middlemore adds: 'I told Jaun, and we both laughed heartily.' Their adventures were not quite over,

for, hurrying close together, with only a few feet of rope between each man, down the end of the stream where the Mont Mallet Glacier debouches into the Echaud [now generally written Leschaux], on a surface which seemed scarcely streaked by a ripple, where one would be inclined to scoff at the idea of a crevasse, Jaun, who was first, suddenly disappeared, descending by a clean drop of some twenty or thirty feet to the end of his rope. I straightway grounded myself in the soft snow. Rey was equal to the occasion: he jerked the rope under my armpits, and then with great presence of mind proceeded to strangle me. At first he treated with indifference my prayers for life. He was evidently acting under a stern sense of duty, and would not be influenced by a mere appeal to his feelings. But at last, as he saw that tugging at me did not affect Jaun's case, he gave me rope, and joining our strength we pulled Jaun to the surface. We landed him *sans* hat, *sans* axe (so we had not the wherewithal to gaff him), a bit cut about the face, very purple there, and almost breathless. On the whole, however, not much the worse. Slightly scared, perhaps, but no doubt pleased to find that his *facilis descensus* was not such warm work as he had feared.

All in the day's work, as you might say, if it is a day with Middlemore! It is surprising to read of such utterly careless mountaineering by a capable guide, but in this matter of crevasses my own experience inclines me to think that *very few men indeed,* if any at all, fully realize the danger of a deep fall into a crevasse, by any member, but especially the leader of a roped party descending, until such a thing has happened. When they have hung on the rope or helped to pull up a man who has been hanging, several feet down, between the horrible walls of a crevasse lit only by light through the hole he has made in the rotten ceiling above—then, but not till then, will they cease to regard the danger as negligible. The ambition of every young climber in this matter should be to equal the record of Christian Klucker, who at the end of a long, distinguished career as a guide could boast of 'never having both feet in the same crevasse at the same time.'

Middlemore's account of this climb makes one think highly of Kennedy's judgment in refusing to accompany him. A stone that can hit the second on the rope hard enough to 'make him feel quite sick' is likely to do something much worse to a fourth on that rope. Subsequent ascents of the col on the Italian side have been made with less risk, and it is obvious that every ascent of such rotten rock clears away a great amount of the loose stuff.

We must take one more look at Middlemore, this time with the other naughty boy of the Alpine Club, Oakley Maund, and a Frenchman of the same type, M. Cordier. And their guides were a fine, bold trio: Jaun, Jakob Anderegg, and Maurer. The north-east face of the Aiguille Verte, on which we find them, is as fine a place as one could wish for an exhibition of naughtiness. No other peak combines so grandly as does the Verte the characters of an aiguille and of a great peak. Its easiest ridge, the Moine ridge, is a difficult climb; its only face which offers a comparatively easy route by a broad couloir, mainly hard, steep snow in favourable years, is swept by stones after the upper rocks are loosed from frost.

A glance at the illustration of the north-east face will show that it offers an alternative of a terribly long and difficult rock ridge falling from left of the summit to an island of rock in the glacier, or of a face or couloir of very steep ice grooved by missiles from above. The couloir that starts from the ridge to the right of the summit and is menaced by a great mass of *séracs* from above it on the left is the one chosen by the naughty boys for their new route.

Hardly were Anderegg and Cordier established on the hard ice of the upper lip of the *bergschrund* than a stone whizzed past Maurer, who had begun to follow; another just missed Middlemore; Maund describes how they remained for twenty minutes crouched in the shelter of the *bergschrund*, himself in the least secure portion of the soft snowbridge, with icy drips trickling down his neck, while Jaun cut across the couloir to get out of the line of fire. Higher up an impracticable slab compelled them to recross the couloir. On the far side

the climbing was most exciting, and but for the fact that the rocks were hard frozen would have been quite impossible. Every foot we gained, however, the difficulties increased, and we were again forced to cross the couloir. It was here no more than forty or fifty feet wide, but it was terrifically steep, the ice was black and hard, and its width necessitated our all being in it together. While crossing I was struck by a small stone on the knee, which, though cutting it and producing great pain for a few minutes, did not even oblige us to halt.

Yet once more the couloir was crossed near the top before they reached the last patch of rock and the last steep slope that gave access to the ridge. This proved unexpectedly narrow, and an hour's cutting in hard ice was required before it ran into the steep snow of the white crown that marks this splendid summit. A storm caught them late in the afternoon descending the great couloir in the south-west face. Hail poured over the rocks and made them slippery. Luckily they picked up tracks after crossing the couloir. Torrents of rain soaked them, lightning lit up the gathering gloom; the stones must have all missed them or waited till, just before complete darkness fell, they had crossed the *bergschrund*. It was a day after their own heart. 'If we imagine three Momings, interspersed with rockwork on a par with the best bits of the Gabelhorn, we get a fair notion of the treat that kind Heaven vouchsafed us.'

To make a new route up a famous peak was becoming a difficult task. The elevation to the Alpine peerage of attendant aiguilles, some of them mere spikes on ridges, provided a new supply of first ascents, but in few cases were they such as could be lightly undertaken. In saying that the Meije was the last great peak to be climbed, I am aware that I am excluding from that select category some of the best beloved of peaks. The two to which it was hardest to deny the distinction are the Géant and the Dru; they pose so magnificently before the crowds that flock to Courmayeur and Chamonix, and the challenge they fling down to the rock-climber is so unmistakably clear and defiant.

The Géant was the first peak on which a modern climbing-party drove pitons into the rocks to obtain a victory. It is obvious that any peak, even Everest, can be made accessible by a sufficient expenditure of time, hard work, and money. The amount of preparation varies with the skill of the climber. A few pitons will enable an expert party to cross a rock-face that could only be made accessible to the ordinary tourist by expensive blasting operations; the principle is the same in both cases. If there were not abundance of other peaks able to confer favours as great as those of the Géant, by all means make it accessible to as many as possible who wish to enjoy those favours. As it is, it seems a pity it was not left free from perpetual bondage in fixed ropes, even if it was not accessible by the eclectic route nature has provided on the north face. There are men who cannot see a wild bird or animal of any size without wanting to slay it, or to keep it in captivity, but many positively prefer to leave it untouched. Why not have left just one or two of nature's citadels in the Alps unclimbed? It is too late now for such a wish!

The Dru was coveted by all who saw it, and it fell at last to the men who deserved it before all others, Clinton Dent and Alexander Burgener. Time after time Dent had assaulted its defences, and every time bad weather, or ice upon the rocks, or the sheer steepness of its walls beat off his attack. He used a ladder; but if it be a sin to use a ladder, then Saussure must fall into the same condemnation, for the sinfulness is the same whether the wall against which the ladder be leaned is of granite or of ice. It was used to save time rather than to get over an otherwise impossible obstacle.

Dent, who had returned from the Alps to England, 'utterly dispirited' by the vile treatment of the weather, was summoned by telegram to Chamonix, and a few days later the party of four, encouraged by a final reconnaissance of the route, were grouped round the camp-fire beside the Charpoua Glacier: Dent and Burgener, J. W. Hartley and Kaspar Maurer.

The ladder was used to cross the couloir that ran up from the head of the glacier. From this point nothing but Dent's own account can begin to do justice to this grand climb.

Next we fastened a double rope, about twenty feet in length, and swung ourselves down a rough cleft as if we were barrels of split peas going into a ship's hold. Up again, and the excitement waxed stronger as we neared the doubtful part. Then Alexander lay flat on his stomach, and wriggled round a projecting rock, disappearing suddenly from view. We followed, progressing like the skates down the panes of glass in an aquarium tank, and found ourselves huddled together on a little ledge. An overhanging rock above compelled us to assume the anomalous attitudes enforced on the occupant of a little-ease dungeon. What next? An eager look up, and part of the doubt was solved. There was a way —but such a way. A narrow, flat couloir, its angle plastered with ice from top to bottom, invited, or forbade, further progress. Above, a pendulous mass of great icicles, black and long like a bunch of elephants' trunks, crowned the gully. We tucked ourselves away on one side, and the guides performed the best feat of rock climbing I can imagine possible. Unroped they worked up, hacking out the ice, their backs and elbows against one sloping wall and their feet against the other. The masses of ice dashing down, harder and harder as they ascended, showed how they were working. Suddenly a slip above—a shout—a crash of falling ice. Then a brief pause, broken after a few minutes by a triumphant yell from above, and the end of a rope dangled down close to us. Using this latter aid considerably, we mounted, and found the top of the couloir blocked up by a great overhanging boulder, dripping still where the icicles had just been broken off. 'Come on,' said voices from above. 'Up you go,' said a voice from below. I leaned as far back as I could, and felt for a hand-hold. There was none. Then right, then left—still none. So I smiled feebly, and said: 'Wait a minute.' Thereupon, of course, they pulled with a will, and, struggling and kicking like a spider irritated with tobacco-smoke, I topped the rock gracefully. How the first man did it is, and always will be, a mystery to me. Then we learned that a great mass of ice had broken away under Maurer's feet while in the couloir, and that he must have fallen had not Alexander pinned him to the rock with one hand. From the number of times that this escape was described to me during the next day or two I am inclined to think it was a near thing. 'The worst is over,' said Alexander. I was glad to hear it, but, looking upwards, had my doubts. The higher we went the bigger the rocks seemed to be. Still, there was a way, and it was not so unlike what I had often pictured.

Another tough scramble, and we stood on a comparatively extensive ledge. Already we had climbed more than half of the only part of the mountain as to the nature of which we were uncertain. A few steps on, and Burgener grasped me suddenly by the arm. 'Do you see the great red rock up yonder?' he whispered, hoarse with excitement; 'in ten minutes we shall be there, and on the arête—and then——' I felt that nothing could stop us now; but a feverish anxiety to see what was beyond, to look on to the last slope, which we knew must be easy, impelled us on, and we worked harder than ever to overcome the last few obstacles. The ten minutes expanded into something like thirty before we really reached the rock. Of a sudden the mountain seemed to change its form. For hours we had been climbing the hard, dry rocks. Now these appeared to vanish, and—blessed sight—snow lay thick, half-hiding, half-revealing the last slope of the arête. A glance showed that we had not misjudged. Even the cautious Maurer admitted that as far as we could see all was well; but he added: 'Up above there, possibly——' And now, with the prize almost within our grasp, a strange desire to halt and hang back came on. Alexander tapped the rock with his axe, and let out his pent-up excitement in a comprehensive anathema of Chamonix guides. Already we could anticipate the half-sad feeling with which we should touch the top itself. The feeling soon gave way. 'Forwards!' we cried, and the axe crashed through the layers of snow into hard blue ice beneath. A dozen steps, and then a bit of rock-scrambling; then more steps along the south side of the ridge—some more rock, and we topped the first eminence. Better and better it looked as we went on. 'See there!' cried Alexander suddenly; 'the actual top.' There was no mistaking the two huge stones we had so often looked at from below. A few feet below them, and on our left, was one of those strange arches formed by a great transverse boulder, and through the hole we saw blue sky. Nothing could lie beyond, and, still better, nothing could be above. On again, while I could hardly stand still in the great steps the leader hacked out. A short, troublesome bit of snow-work followed, where the heaped-up cornice had fallen back from the final rock. Then Hartley courteously allowed me to unrope and pass him, and in a second I clutched at the last broken rocks, and hauled myself up on to the flat, sloping summit. There for a moment I stood alone, gazing down on Chamonix. The dream of five years was accomplished. The Dru was climbed.

And was the pleasure over? Far from it. Dent himself tells us how it recurs:

Would you recall these mountain pictures? Draw close the curtains, stir the coals into an indignant, crackling blaze, and fashion in the rising smoke the mountain vista. How these scenes crowd back into the mind, with a revivability proportionate to the impression originally made! What keener charm than to pass in review the memories of these simple, wholesome pleasures; to see again, as clear as in the reality, every ledge, every hand- and foot-hold; to feel the fingers tingle and the muscles instinctively contract at the recollection of some tough scramble on rock or glacier?

The Dru is still a climb the modern expert considers worth the doing. It demands some judgment as well as ability to climb its steep rocks when there is no party in front to show the way. We may regard its ascent as the beginning of an epoch in which the element of exploration is insignificant compared with the joy of battle with obstacles that tax courage, endurance, and skill to the uttermost. And the figure that stands out in the history of moun- taineering as typical of this lust of battle is Alexander Burgener.

There have been better rock-climbers; there have been none so undismayed by difficulties, none that have uttered more exultant yells when the adversary is beneath him. The sort of place where he was at his very best was where a wicked bulge of green ice has changed what might have been an exhilarating passage on steep rock into a prolonged trial of nerve and endurance; a place where strength of arm and wrist must be applied with a nicety of touch that can carve out a path without breaking the glassy crust, and can fashion the holds in which the numbed fingers of one hand can hold the body steady, while the other plies the axe, or while the feet are moved into the narrow steps.

15. HUMAN GRANITE

Without Burgener's support, Venetz would never have tackled the bulge of ice that tried to bar him and Mummery from the summit of the Charmoz. Nothing shows the character of the man better than the early history of the Col du Lion. He might have been aptly nicknamed the Cœur de Lion among guides. It is all that a pass should not be as a way of getting from one place to another. Whymper's description of the Swiss side is famous. 'Throw a bottle down to the Tiefenmatten; no sound returns for more than a dozen seconds.' Allowing, as we safely may, that it is the remark of a man who has transferred the contents of the bottle to himself, it is hardly an exaggeration if the bottle is well thrown. And the bottles thrown on Whymper's recommendation are very far from being the only missiles to be feared.

The difficulties of the first ascent made by Burgener and Mummery were very formidable. Long, steep ice-slopes above the *bergschrund* lured the climbers up on a thin crust of frostbound snow that would be useless for a descent later in the day, and then led up to an almost perpendicular wall heavily glazed with ice. Even Burgener would have retreated here, had not return been almost certain death, when the sun had loosed the snow and the missiles waiting up above. The only way of passing was to cut a continuous ledge along which the feet could shuffle; the work, with only one hand for the axe, being terribly severe. On the ice-slopes higher up were ribbons of snow, 'of the worst and most powdery description,' only trusted because the hundreds of feet of steep ice on which they lay made the labour of an alternative unthinkable.

The final cliff, 'of loose, disintegrated rock' held together by a plaster of snow and ice, is climbed, the cornice broken through, and Burgener's hand grasps the ridge of the col. It is easy to understand his yell of triumph as he does so, and it is hard to believe that any man would be ready to repeat the experiences of the previous hours. The very next year Burgener leads Dr. Güssfeldt down these fearful slopes. Showers of stones from the cliffs of the Matterhorn and Tête du Lion sweep the couloir below the upper ice-slopes, bare that year, on which long hours have been spent. The night is spent in great peril and discomfort in the middle of the couloir; in the morning frost holds back the stones, and they escape alive.

Yet a third time Burgener crosses the col with Herr von Kuffner and Alois Kalbermatten. Conditions on later ascents have been rather less severe. There have been few of these, but, as far as I know, Burgener is the only man who has ever returned to storm those icy battlements.

No son of the Alps was ever better endowed with their rude strength and their unshakeable heart. He loved the triumphs snatched out of the hands of Chamonix rivals, but he was generous in acknow' ledgment of real skill. Dr. Julius Kugy was descending with him from the Théodule when they met an Englishman riding up the path on a donkey, his long legs almost trailing on the ground. 'Who's that poor fellow?' asked Kugy. 'That's Mummery,' answered Burgener. 'He climbs better than I do.'

I met him once in 1902 in the Dom hut above Randa. There was no veneer of politeness in Alexander, and his contempt for his *Herr*, a rather clumsily built Teuton, was undisguised. But even then, many years after Mummery's death in the Himalayas, his voice broke as he spoke of this beloved comrade of his greatest years.

A great avalanche overwhelmed him, with other guides, as they were crossing the rocks below the Bergli hut, coming from the Eismeer station of the Jungfrau railway, a strange place to prove fatal to the man who had three times faced and conquered the precipices of the Col du Lion.

He did as much as any single man to push up the standard of climbing towards the limits of the possible. Franz Lochmatter, Joseph Knubel, Armand Charlet, and others may have pushed it higher still, but in a way they may be said to have stood on Burgener's shoulders.

Outside the professional ranks, the standard of performance shows a marked advance in the eighties. Partly this is due to increased knowledge of what is possible and a greater assurance in attacking what had passed for inaccessible, partly to the greater physical advan' tage of the generation that followed that of the sixties. It has been my privilege to introduce many young people of varying aptitude to the pleasures of mountaineering. Only experience can prove, as only experience can make, a first-rate mountaineer, but it is certain that a young, loosely built, athletic man will learn to climb far more quickly than one who is of stiffer build and who has little aptitude for other sports. The man who can kick a football accurately with either foot in any position is able, almost at once, to move well on rocks and to judge distance accurately, so that he can place his foot quickly and securely upon small holds. Gymnasts are generally good at difficult obstacles requiring strength of arm and finger, where slow, deliberate movement is required. A supple wrist and a good forearm readily acquire the flick of the axe that brings out a nice big piece of ice, and a good eye helps to hit the slope in just the right spot. Knowledge of snow and ice, and of the trustworthiness of rocks, judgment of conditions, of route, and of weather can only come through experience, and even then the longest experience without mountaineering instinct may fail to equip a man to be a leader on a big mountain. The early climbers were of the imaginative, contemplative type, rather than the athletic, though in those days the two were more often found in combination than they are now. They did not realize that a man whose hands and feet have been trained by other sports to carry out the wishes of his eye exactly and in the minimum of time, may develop very quickly indeed into a good climber. The ascent of the Meije by three Englishmen, who climbed the south wall to the Glacier Carré by a route more difficult than that discovered by Gaspard, opened their eyes to the possibility of guideless expeditions.

The opening of our home playgrounds in Lakeland, in North Wales, and northern Scotland played a great part in the rapid development of English climbing. In 1873 a February ascent of Glydr Fawr was considered a feat worthy of a page and a half of the *Alpine Journal*. Twenty-five years later Owen Glynne Jones's book on Lakeland appeared, and the faces of Scafell, of Lliwedd, and of the Coolins were scored all over by the nails of climbing-boots, the rocks surmounted being as difficult as any to be found on the well-known Alpine routes.

The Swiss and Austrians had their playgrounds too, and, the conditions being those of the Alps themselves, a generation of fine guideless climbers grew up, and all the more quickly where cricket and football were unknown; there was no rival to absorb the attention and energies of the best athletes. The Zsigmondys and Purtscheller were the Austrian counterpart of the Mummery generation of famous British climbers.

The complete absence of glacier-work tended to concentrate the attention of young British climbers on rock-climbing. And I must let that statement stand, even after remembering that one of the severest bits of ice-work I have ever done was on the face of Ben Nevis one April day. Good cragsmen and indifferent mountaineers, with a somewhat limited and unimaginative way of regarding mountains, is a not unfair description of a very numerous type that was produced. At the same time British climbing must not be held altogether responsible for a lack of imagination in some British climbers; it is noticeable in any country. Rock-climbing attracted a large number of men who found in the struggle with walls and chimneys the satisfaction that had been given or denied them in the games they played at school. How can we ever thank nature enough for the physical thrills that reward a sharp muscular effort when that effort achieves any immediate and palpable result, whether it be the dispatch of a ball to the exact place where we would have it go, or the raising of the body against the grim push of the unrelenting rock and the pull of our earthly chain? If climbing meant nothing more than this it would still remain a grand sport.

A striking feature in the record of British climbing is the compara-tive immunity from accidents it has enjoyed. Our home playgrounds are almost entirely free from the objective dangers. How often does a climber hear the ping or crash of a falling stone on British hills, except such as may be dislodged by a careless or tidy-minded climber? Another reason is that, despite the incitement produced by the grading of routes and the publication of sensational feats, the essentially sound attitude to sport inherited from the past enables the majority of British climbers to climb for enjoyment. The Swiss, more than any other continental nation, climb for the same reason; rivalry in the accomp-lishment of dangerous feats occurs, but it is a feature rare in them as in ourselves, and the result is that they share with us a happy immunity from accidents.

It is well to recognize the savage character of the fetish that may be worshipped under the name of first ascent. The strain of explora-tion in the excellent cross, produced in the sixties, between that strain and the climbing strain was becoming almost unrecognizable in the Alps at the beginning of the century. The production of virgin peaks by subdivision has not really succeeded in maintaining it. A ridge that is sufficiently like a comb may satisfy the longing to become godfather to a tooth in quite a number of expert climbers. If it has been gazed at by thousands, and been almost within a stone's throw of men on neighbouring peaks, the only reason for its neglect being the difficulty of traversing a comparatively short stretch of difficult slabs, the element of exploration has gone.

There is something rather pathetic in this belief of the climber that he makes peculiarly his own the route or summit which his boots have been the first to tread. The rocks of a peak I have been the first to climb are no whit dearer to me than those on which others have preceded me. Most of us have often been on ground where nobody has been before, and our sensations have not been those of pride of possession, but of annoyance, and very bluntly expressed annoyance, at getting off the correct mountaineering route.

The attraction of a first ascent is in the element of uncertainty.

Even when the details are visible the element remains. That steep pitch of rock near the top, will it go? What happens round that corner? And that element of uncertainty would remain for climbers on countless Alpine peaks, but for that pestilent habit of publishing achievements! Accord this book at least this merit, that it will not remove that glorious uncertainty from a single fresh route!

Every district in the Alps is being forced to produce peaklets that aspire to maintain themselves in independence. The Chamonix Aiguilles are admirably adapted for the purpose, and the development of the process there is typical of what has been happening in every range where the supply of virgin peaks is getting low.

Can you believe that the Charmoz and the Grépon were referred to by the *Alpine Journal* as parts of the same peak? Yet this crime of *lèse-majesté* was actually committed. 'The lower peak of the Charmoz' was climbed by Mummery, Burgener, and Venetz in July 1881; the two highest points on the ridge of the highest peak of the Charmoz [*sic*] by the same party on 3rd August 1881. The crime is repeated in the *Guide de la Chaîne du Mont Blanc,* compiled by Louis Kurz and published in 1892; the name Grépon is attached to the small peak of about nine thousand feet now known as the Aiguille de l'M. The matter has been hushed up in later publications of Mummery's books, but you see what a childlike view of mountains the earlier climbers took. And a habit, dating from childhood, of judging the attraction of mountains by their form and height, led me to make the same mistake. To me these two popular rock peaks, at the foot of whose pitches queues of climbing-parties stand waiting on a fine summer morning, appeared to be two points of a summit inferior in form and general attraction to the Blaitière. Let me finish the confession, now I have begun. It was the Blaitière I chose to climb; we lost our way in the dark early hours among the nut-trees between Chamonix and the upper slopes; we judged the *séracs* of the Nantillons Glacier to be an objective danger which it was bad mountaineering to incur, and in ignorance of the usual route below them, spent precious time in cutting up the steep, bare glacier under the Blaitière, reaching the Col des Nantillons after midday. We did not return to it till six o'clock in the evening after climbing the two highest peaks of the Blaitière; there were no tracks or climbers on the peak. In the fear of being benighted on the glacier we followed the tracks down below the threatening *séracs* and groped our way down to Chamonix before midnight. It was a good day, and, having looked down upon the Charmoz and the Grépon from so near, I have never burned with desire to climb them. I realize that this puts me beyond the pale for the modern climber. It is, however, one of my few special qualifications as a historian of mountaineering that I can so easily put myself in the position of the early mountaineers. The point of view makes all the difference. I agree that you cannot look into any shop in Chamonix where photographs are displayed without feeling that, viewed from a certain angle, the Grépon is a wonderful bit of creation and has a striking independence. And you must agree with me that from the summit of Mont Blanc, if not from the Blaitière, it is permissible to have doubts as to 'that being greatest which did nothing seem.' Looking up at the red walls of slabs that rise to the summit of the Grépon from the Mer de Glace you will have a very different impression. For the ordinary man that is the side from which to view it, and the side from which he will not seek to climb it unless he is led by a cragsman whose powers, even among the experts, are exceptional.

The Blaitière and the Plan have provided in their connecting ridge a family of virgin peaks whose wild charms have been successfully wooed by those irresistible love-makers the French. And they have such endearing names! The tallest, next the Plan, is the Crocodile, then the Caïman, then two small, pert things, virgin till 1910, then a great tall one, the Aiguille du Fou, a small, sharp double tooth called Les Ciseaux, and then the Blaitière.

In 1920, Monsieur J. de Lépiney, after two refusals, overcame the resistance of both the still virgin peaklets, and the higher now bears his name. Thanks to M. de Lépiney himself, we can obtain a fleeting glimpse of the methods of courtship of the Groupe de Haute Montagne, a typically French society, selected from the more adventurous spirits of the French Alpine Club, which M. de Lépiney and his brother Tom helped to found. Only by first bestowing his attentions on the taller sisters is M. de Lépiney able to approach the object of his affections. The rocks above the glacier under its east face are unclimb- able. A point nearly as high as the objective is reached almost under the Plan; the couloir between the Plan and Crocodile, and that between the latter and the Caïman, are crossed in a descending traverse; and the bivouac is made where the party had been benighted on a previous attempt, on the *arête* descending from the Caïman. On that occasion the lower of the two virgin peaklets had been reached and received the name of the Chevalier, the godfather being M. de Lépiney's companion. This time Tom de Lépiney, his brother, is with him. The descending traverse of the precipice is continued

16. AIGUILLE DU PLAN

G   F   E   D   C   B A

G_2

G_1

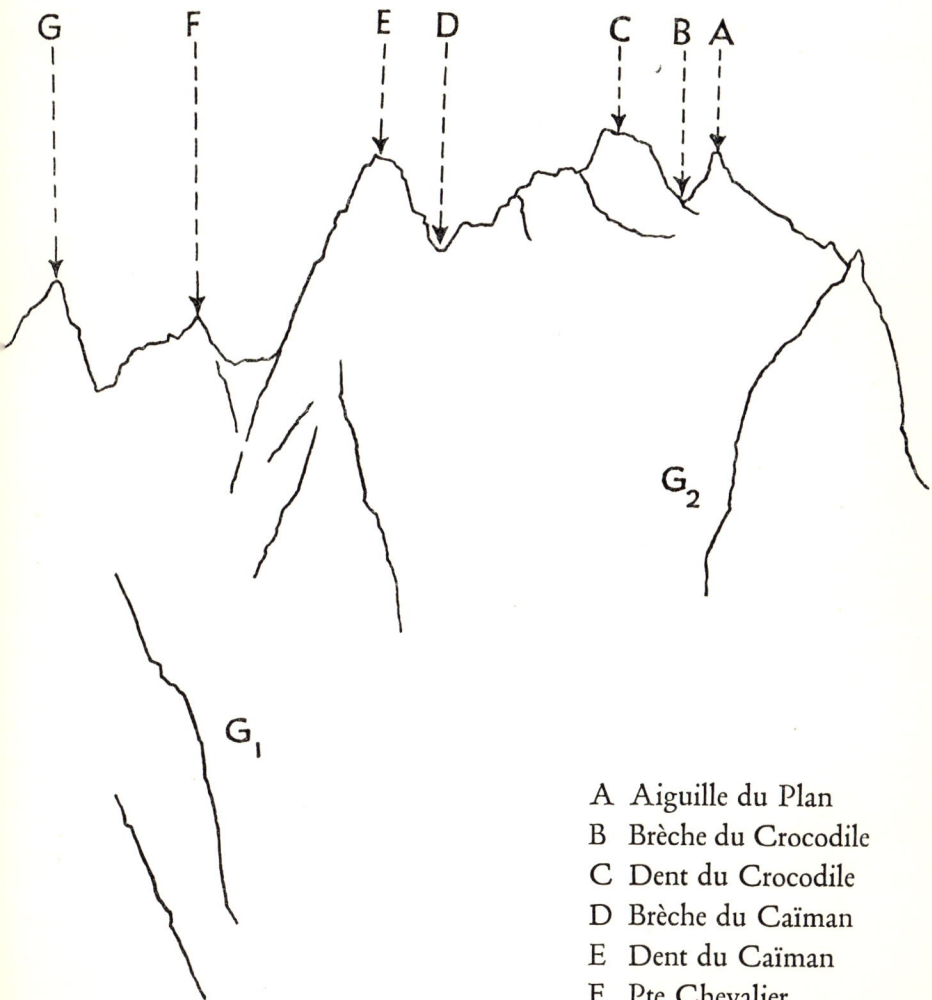

A Aiguille du Plan
B Brèche du Crocodile
C Dent du Crocodile
D Brèche du Caïman
E Dent du Caïman
F Pte Chevalier
G Pte de Lépiney
     (*not shown on
     photograph*)
G_1 Glacier de Blaitière
G_2 Glacier du Plan

See also Notes on page 319

and the couloir descending from the small col to the right of the Caïman is reached.

A short descent on the rope, a bridged position in the narrow couloir, and then a take-off from a friendly shoulder, enables them to reach the rounded slabby ridge descending from the Point Chevalier. From there they gradually mount over splendid slabs into the couloir descending from the Col de Blaitière. The weight of the rope, seventy metres in length, is felt in the ascent to this col. The peak now rises straight above them. A first shoulder is reached, and a traverse on the Chamonix face enables them to reach the *arête* descending to the Col du Fou on the far side. Horizontal ledges help them to attain what seems the only possible route, a chimney leading to the south-east *arête*. They have already all but circled the small peak.

The overhang at the start is too much for our first attempts; but determined to win a way we make another assault after a brief truce. Thanks to a shoulder to the left of the chimney, the leader reaches a good hold, makes a small swing like a pendulum which allows him to get into the chimney, and gets a few metres up it. Then a fresh check and a hard struggle to emerge on to the *arête*.

There is still a final block to climb; it is like a blunt knife, about ten feet high, and six or seven feet wide at the base. A pull-up is sufficient to land them on it. 'A more delicate and sensational operation is to stand up, straight and steady, on the topmost point.'

At seven o'clock they are back on the *arête* of the Caïman, where another night out is inevitable. And at eleven o'clock it begins to snow! At four o'clock big flakes are coming down and they crouch over the rope to protect it. The descent when daylight comes has become intensely perilous, for the slabs of the Plan – Crocodile couloir are swept by torrents of snow, except when a lull in the storm temporarily curtails the supply. Tom de Lépiney runs out fifty metres of rope in crossing, held by the rope from as high as possible. His brother looks in vain for a belay for doubling the rope which, as it is held by Tom de Lépiney 120 feet below and 150 feet away, offers no real security of any kind. Luckily there is a temporary cessation of the snow flood, which allows him to descend close to the avalanche groove in snow resting on ice, not quite so dangerous as the slabs. Montenvers is gained after a day of twenty-seven hours. The expedition is an extraordinary testimony to the attraction of a few metres of virgin rock. And it is sound mountaineering too. Any party may be trapped by bad weather or by force of circumstances into a

17. FURGGEN RIDGE

dangerous situation; that is a very different thing from the deliberate acceptance of certain danger in order to accomplish a feat which experienced men will only attempt if they are as reckless as they are brave. This gradual toleration of danger which no skill can avoid, and the actual cult of danger to which it leads, is a development which is too recent and too important to introduce into this chapter. An earlier chapter and an earlier epoch in mountaineering was closed by the first ascent of the Matterhorn. This one shall also close upon the Matterhorn.

If an observing angel were to offer me a choice of half a dozen scenes depicting crises on great climbs, I should certainly choose for one of them the small shoulder of the Furggen ridge, just below the last great corner of partly overhanging cliff that towers up and hides the Swiss summit of the Matterhorn.

First I see Mummery, Burgener, and Venetz halted there. A furious gale was tearing icicles and stones from the summit rocks, and forbade any attempt upon the terrible cliff. A traverse to the shoulder on the north-east ridge was to them the only possibility. Dodging the missiles in the early part of the traverse, Burgener, 'at racing speed, led us to a secure ledge' below a crag. 'Immediately in front, the long, pitiless slabs, ceaselessly swept by whizzing, shrieking fragments of all sorts and sizes, suggested to Burgener . . . that it would be well to drink our Bouvier, and consume our other provisions, before any less fitting fate should overtake them.' The stones missed them as they hurried across, and the final traverse, bare and holdless, pronounced by some guides watching from the shoulder to be 'quite impossible,' was safely passed by Burgener.

Then I see a famous five crouching on the same small shoulder. There is Geoffrey Young, with his back to the final tower and a leg over each of the precipices that fall to Switzerland and Italy, Knubel next him, astride of the narrow edge of snow, Ryan with two of the Lochmatters perched on some stones under the overhanging rocks. On one side lay the traverse followed by Burgener; on the other, what Young describes as a 'peeling shaly shelflet' ran under the cliff across the Italian face. Not only did it offer small security of hold; it was under perpetual bombardment from above. Straight up the corner was the way that Guido Rey tried to follow *on a rope let down from above,* and had failed. And stones were coming down the only possible line of approach to this precipitous edge.

Ryan, regardless of risk, is for an attempt upon the corner. All the guides are painfully alive to the fearful risk, and it is not mainly

I

of themselves that they are thinking.   Young inclines to the traverse
taken by Burgener, and it is this traverse that is chosen.   It was a
choice that is a credit to British mountaineering, for it is the route on
which the climbers are under fire from the mountain's missiles for
the shortest time.

It is interesting to note that this party, one of the strongest ever
strung out upon a critical traverse, found the difficulties worthy of
their utmost skill.   Burgener and Mummery, who preceded them by
more than twenty years, had already reached very near the limits
of the possible.

Guido Rey has described in thrilling pages his passion to make
this great ridge his own.   Perhaps no other climber could have
made us view through his eyes the extraordinary sequel to his failure
to get up that long, hanging three-hundred-foot rope, when he was
let down by a rope ladder till his feet and hands had made contact
with all the details of the last pitch that had beaten back all efforts
from below.   We do not expect or want normal behaviour from
lovers as passionate as he!

Dr. Piacenza, with his two brave guides, one of them appropriately
named Carrel, the other Gaspard, appears now upon the famous
shoulder, burning to succeed where other great climbers had, in their
view, failed.   Previous reconnaissances from the Col Félicité, on the
ordinary Italian route, had been sufficiently thrilling.   Ropes and
pitons were left upon the Italian face to hasten the return when
stones began to fall.

In turn held by the others, we scrambled across vertical bits.   As soon as
we heard from the depths the cry of: 'That will do, pull the rope!' the work
of hauling up our invisible companion began.   The silence was dramatic
at such a moment, nothing could be heard but the gaspings and oaths of our
friend attempting to climb up and being continually crushed by the rope against
the sides of the gullies.

And then, when the sun rose, 'rock-slides wrecked the faces and
couloirs, leaping, whistling, and thundering down towards the
glaciers which fringe the peak.'   This is on a mere reconnaissance
made to achieve by a particular portion of its final cliff the ascent of a
peak that had been climbed scores of times before!

And at last the reconnaissances are over and the party assembles
on the Furggen shoulder, in the fixed determination to start off along
that 'shelflet' described by Mr. Young, that ran across the precipice
on the Italian side, and of which he says, in reference to Dr. Piacenza's

ascent: 'That a later party should have actually started upon this route after seeing what we saw is even more surprising than their luck in escaping from it alive to the summit.' Gaspard had already been severely hit by a stone, but did not think of turning back. Beyond a twenty-yard traverse a holdless block or rock was climbed by the entire party, standing on each other's shoulders, like a storming-ladder set up under fire from the wall above. More slabs and crevices led to the snow ribbon below the final crag. 'The snow was speckled with stones, a sure proof of constant rock-falls.' Under a great boss on the crest that still soared up, dividing Italy from Switzerland, they sheltered from the stones dislodged by other parties. Seeing Swiss parties on the Hörnli ridge they feel that 'the glory which will accrue to the men of Valtournanche is lost for ever to those of Zermatt.' We are getting near to the delirium of climbing. An attempt to climb a slab some distance from the crest failed, but another slab was found which could be surmounted by setting up another three-piece ladder. Another half-hour's wait and Piacenza joins the two guides upon a tiny platform.

At that moment 'an enormous mass fell from the mountain, and raising a cloud of smoke, plunged down the couloir with a hideous crash. The guides no longer see how to advance; everywhere impossibilities confront us. Nothing else is left but the avalanche-swept couloir, feasible only at night when frost has bound the debris.' They almost decided to wait there through the long afternoon and evening, but instead they made up their minds to risk a most dangerous traverse back to the ridge. 'We securely belayed a rope, and then with infinite care Carrel crawled up towards a great boulder, a few stones breaking away beneath his feet with a dreadful clamour; he kept his balance, however, and at length we saw him safe and sound by the boulder.' Another bare slab is traversed on a fastened rope, and then once more the ridge is gained with a view over the Swiss side. 'We are certain of victory! . . . Proudly and full of confidence we advance. . . . Twenty minutes more, and at 1.30 p.m. we attain the top. . . . We are mad with joy. . . . We embrace and wave a red flag as a token of victory to our friends at Le Giomein.'

All of these three climbs by Mummery, by Young and Ryan, and by Piacenza were ascents of the Matterhorn by the south-east ridge. It would be absurd to refuse that name to the route taken by the first two parties merely because they turned an obstacle on the ridge which it would have been bad mountaineering to attempt to climb direct.

The difference in the technical skill of these famous amateurs, as well as in that of their guides, must have been extremely small. All of them were capable of climbing rocks that were near the limit of what is possible for men without artificial aids. For Mummery the route was entirely new, the element of exploration so constantly present, that there can have been no sense of failure in traversing below the final cliff across to the neighbouring ridge. For him there was no other possible finish to the climb. Young and Ryan must have set out with designs on the direct route. In their case there was a decision to be made. Was the desire for the personal satisfaction of a new victory, of doing what Mummery had failed to do, to overrule all considerations of safety for themselves and for the men in their employ?

The whole energies of Piacenza's party are concentrated on that final terrific step. To do what others have failed to do is the motive that drives them to the desperate venture. Man is no longer contend-ing with nature alone; he is using nature as a means of contention between himself and other men.

Which of these parties made the best ascent of the peak by the Furggen ridge, the ascent which you would most have liked to share? This book leaves no doubt of the answer its author would have you make; but what is your answer? That is what concerns him.

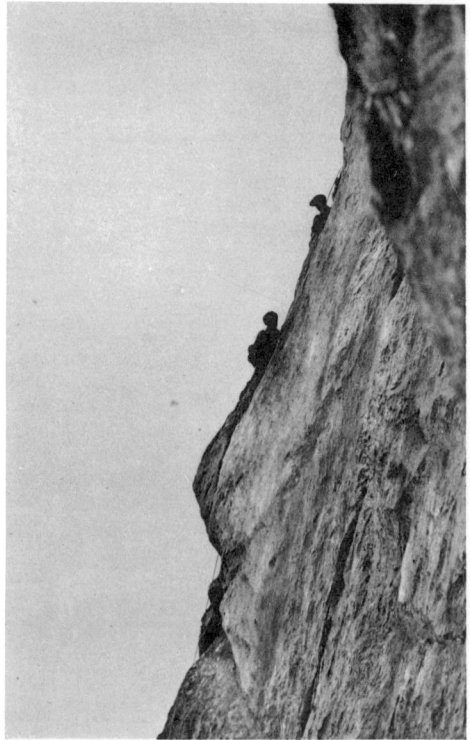

18. STEEPLEJACK CLIMBERS AT WORK BELOW AN OVERHANG

CHAPTER VIII

MECHANIZATION AND THE CULT OF DANGER

WHEN a new generation reaches the stage of life at which it emerges from the restraints of tutelage it is faced with a number of choices which may greatly affect its future. The very purpose of its activities may present itself as a problem that has not hitherto been put before it. There is generally a reluctance to accept the limitation of sensations and of pleasures which reality has imposed on older beings, and there is a refusal to believe that it needs experience to distinguish permanent values from values that fluctuate with fashion. It is these last that affect judgment powerfully in every rising generation. Every new generation is almost bound to believe that the ideas of those who are still young enough to be thought of as contemporaries are better than those of the preceding generation—till it has put them to the test itself; that is to say, till a still younger generation takes its place.

Mountaineering, as it approaches its full development, is exceedingly vigorous and exceedingly alive, and it has not escaped the problem of choosing the path along which it shall travel and the purpose it shall have in view. It has been strongly affected by the ideas and tendencies of the age, and this must be borne in mind in any attempt to appreciate the developments shown in modern climbing.

This is an age of mechanization. Our view of the universe and everything in it is more mechanical, more material, than in the early days of mountaineering. The actual instruments used in climbing have recently acquired a peculiar importance which may affect our whole view of the sport. It is curious that until quite lately no implements were used which were not in use in similar but more rudimentary form hundreds of years ago, before mountains were thought of as anything but obstacles to be passed with the least possible risk.

The rope as a security against danger on a glacier was in use in the sixteenth century. It is mentioned in Simler's book on the Alps, published in 1574. 'The guides tie a rope round them, to which the travellers who follow are attached; the leader sounds, as he goes along, with a pole, and carefully looks for crevasses in the snow, and if he happen by mischance to fall in, his companions on the rope hold him up and pull him out.'

Snow-shoes for deep snow were known even to the Greeks, in the form of small sacks for horses' feet, and in the Alps in Simler's time we are told of a form almost identical with the raquettes sold now by sports outfitters, consisting of 'hoops of wood like those used to bind casks, laced across with cords.'

The use of paper as a protection against cold was also known over three hundred years ago; 'paper or parchment is a perfect guarantee for the chest against cold.' The paper used by the modern bivouacker is that used for modern journalism and can hardly claim any advance, either in the matter written upon it or in protective quality.

Crampons are mentioned by Strabo as being used in the Caucasus in the wars of Pompey against Mithridates. They were made of hide, shaped like cymbals, and carried sharp points. In the Middle Ages in the Alps the type is a stout sole with three spikes. Saussure mentions crampons made of leather with heel-spikes and attached by straps.

Glissading was well known, and the fashionable winter sports are, like jazz music, an instance of a return to primitive delights practised by savages. Plutarch describes how the Cimbri paraded in front of the enemy by sitting on their shields and tobogganing down steep slopes. The pleasures of both roller-skating and ski-ing were to some extent enjoyed together by the future Emperor Leo the Isaurian when he crossed the snows of the Caucasus on 'cyclopodes,' a species of large skates provided with wheels.

The ice-axe is the most original and successful improvement on the old implements, combining, as it does, in handy form the old alpenstock and the peasants' chopping-axe. The discovery that hard ice is easily split by a thin-pointed tool, and is almost unaffected by a cutting edge, made the ascent of ice-slopes possible. Some of the big expeditions of the early sixties, such as the passage of the Eigerjoch and Moming, would have been impossible without something like a modern ice-axe. The glacier has now become an unimportant item of the modern climbing day, which is spent on precipices where the axe, where it is not simply a nuisance, is used as a piton or for cutting steps close to the stomach or the nose. Consequently the handle of the axe has shrunk till its length approximates once more to that of the old chopper and can be stuck in a rucksack with the pointed end protruding. The climber who returns carrying his axe otherwise than in this latest way is liable to be placed among the old fogies.

The great invention with which this mechanical age has endowed the climber is the piton, which varies from a rough, stout peg of iron to an elegant, fragile leaf of steel. It can be adorned with a ring, so that the proudest rock-faces and the most domineering of profiles suffer the degradation foretold by the prophet: 'Behold I will put a ring in thy nose.' This ring opens like the clip at the end of a watch-chain, hence the name *mousqueton* in French, *moschettone* in Italian; in German it is a *Karabiner*. There is no English word for it. It is, in fact, decidedly un-English in name and in nature.

All implements used in mountaineering are essentially utilitarian. In common with all mechanical devices their object is simply to reduce labour and facilitate the achievement of results. Every increase in their use increases the proportion of the purely utilitarian in mountaineering. In the Jungfrau railway we have a proportion which is a hundred per cent; it is the increase of mechanical aids carried to its furthest limit. Any mountain, even in the Himalayas, can be ascended by a sufficient expenditure on mechanical means; but every increase in mechanical equipment affects the ethical value of our contest with the mountain, which has no capacity for increasing its powers of resistance.

Our use of mechanical devices will therefore depend greatly on our aim. If our aim is at all costs to reach the summit, and we measure the value of our success by the speed and ease with which the result is achieved, the ideal climber being like the ideal machine, then the more perfect and complete our mechanical equipment the better. In so far as an aesthetic or moral value is attached to the ascent, the use of mechanical devices cannot help us, and it may hinder us. The windows through which the artists and writers of the present day invite us to view these latter values are so distorting that the modern generation may well be excused for doubting the real existence of any stable abstract values, and for concentrating its attention on what can be measured in mathematical units, speed records, scoring records, height records. Times are given for ascents, not so much for affording any indication of the normal time required as for demonstrating the superior speed with which the party moved. An American tourist gets a guide to take him up and down the Matterhorn from the Hörnli hut in little more than three hours, and perhaps he even finds added glory in the fact that his guide is ill in bed for several days as a result. Some climbers, fascinated by the magic of numbers, and accustomed to measure heights in metres, form an ambition to climb every peak in the Alps that exceeds four thousand metres. These unfortunate men live under the perpetual menace of having to go, like Karl Blodig in 1932 at the age of seventy-three, and climb some new point of a ridge which the process of subdivision had brought into the category of four-thousand-metre peaks. The enormous heights above the earth's surface lately attained by aeroplanes and balloons have diminished the thrill of pushing up the height record in the Himalayas, but it remains the natural ambition of climbers. The use of gas in this, as in other contests, has been adopted as a means of establishing ascendancy over the adversary. It may be necessary to have tow-ropes from machines in the air to help or even to lift the climber bodily over portions of the way before the least accessible of the Himalayas are trodden under foot, but if we have to assert the supremacy of men over mountains in this way, it will be done. The achievement of standard climbs of high-grade difficulty is clearly of a different and more easily measurable nature than that which may be experienced on climbs in which mountaineering sense is required, and in which the element of mystery and exploration is still present.

The introduction of the piton and the detachable ring has not improved man's natural capacities, but it has allowed places to be climbed which Nature intended should remain untouched by human feet, and it has enabled young men to combine with rock-climbing the love of playing with machinery. To the Teuton it has given to rock-climbing the essential character of a 'sport.' This word 'sport' had been known and understood in Britain for many generations; even the modern passion for records and results induced by the dominance in our life of the machine has not succeeded in obscuring the basic idea in regard to sport, that it must be carried out under fair and loyal conditions. Any deviation from this fairness is not sporting.

The superficial attributes of 'sport,' its rivalries, its standardization, and the glorification of results have been adopted with the word itself by other nations of Europe at a time when a mechanized view of life was already established, and it is these superficial attributes that have been accepted as the essential character of sport rather than the idea of it which still remains part of the Englishman's upbringing. To many of the early mountaineers the use of the piton and the fixed rope was anathema. Every aid of this kind upon the Matterhorn was regarded with positive loathing by my old friend Frederick Morshead, one of the fastest and best of the Victorian climbers. We can take no personal credit for this 'sportsmanlike attitude'; it is bred in us, just as a love of animals is bred in us, or the quality we call reserve at home and which easily takes on the appearance of quiet arrogance when we go abroad. An Englishman never thinks of trying to define sport; abroad definitions are constantly appearing and changing. Here is an expert Teutonic climber's attempt: 'Sport is any activity which manifests itself by measuring force against resistance, and the motives of which are the attainment of personal distinction.' This is how an Italian climber regards it: 'The essential object of sport is the development and direct recognition of force and quality under clearly defined conditions.'

Munich, being near the Bavarian Alps, has given its name to the most famous of the new schools of climbing, which have been described as the 'sporting-heroic-arithmetic' type. It is a necessity of this school that climbing prowess should be capable of accurate measurement. For this purpose it has established six grades of difficulty ranging from 'easy' to 'quite exceptionally difficult.' This grading is becoming common in the Dolomites and in the Julian Alps, and is beginning to spread towards the west in the Italian Alps.

The proximity of one or two fine rock-faces, easily reached in these days of rapid transport by students on a week-end holiday, has suggested the organization and standardization of climbing on the lines of other games. And in Britain we have been familiar with 'grading' for nearly forty years. Before many of the present generation had begun to climb, we had been given our lists of graded climbs for the Lake District, for Wales, and for the Coolins; less methodical than our Teuton friends, we had only four unnumbered categories, Easy, Moderate, Difficult, Exceptionally Severe. How many hundreds upon hundreds of young Britons have felt their self-respect growing as they passed from easy 'moderates' to the harder 'moderates' and then to 'difficults,' and then in diminishing numbers to 'exceptionally severes,' and some few farther still to the highest and proudest region of exaltation, where they might be privileged to describe a new climb up rocks considered impossible by the inventor of an exceptionally severe!

And if this most coveted thing, the making of a new climb almost worthy of a grade to itself, which to-day must generally be 'beyond the limits of what is humanly possible' (in the current year), is unprocurable, the next best thing is to accomplish with comparative ease and in a fraction of the time a climb that has cost its inventor hours of terrible effort and the constant fear of immediate dissolution. About the time when the professors of the Munich school were beginning to test their hand-holds on their mother's finger, the Guglia de Amicis was, 'humanly speaking, impossible.' When Tita Piaz, the famous Dolomite guide, reached the top by lassoing the point with a rope flung from an adjacent point and executing a fearsome traverse through the air, the climbing world saw the beginning of a new invasion of points inaccessible by the old methods. Piaz was a modern, greedy for novelty, speed, and sensation, a new type of guide, with his elegant little house, his motor-bike, his love of dangling on ropes over appalling precipices, and his self-assurance, that would keep a famous climber who employed him waiting outside the inn a whole hour before starting, while he took a leisurely meal at his ease in the hotel. Try to imagine Melchior Anderegg or François Dévouassoud behaving like that, and you will see what a gulf separates modern climbing in the eastern Alps from the mountain-eering of the sixties. A few years later the Guglia de Amicis was climbed direct by three men and a woman! In 1931 it was the object of a sort of club meet of twenty-one persons, five of whom were women.

Still, the Guglia is admitted to the fifth grade of Munich, that is to say, the highest but one, and will only fall into a lower place when a seventh grade, reserved for entirely superhuman achievements, is created.

But while we may feel sorry for the feeling of inferiority suffered by those whose inferior technique or greater modesty confines them to the lower grades, there is consolation for them in the opportunity that publicity gives them for worship of the great sixth-graders. It may be the only form of worship that a material view of life has left them! As to the sixth-grade men themselves, the satisfaction they must find in surmounting the sheer, stark walls and overhangs, against which they match their strength and their machines, is the modern compensation for a complete absence of anything that demands mountaineering sense. And this satisfaction of personal achievement is supplied in glorious abundance. Even the hammering of pitons, which absorbs a large part of the leader's time and energy, has its attraction. I noticed in my own children at a very early age a distinct pleasure in hitting a nail into a piece of wood. The proof of personal achievement is immediate if the nail is truly hit. One of the worst things about machine-made boots is that the process deprives a number of men of an occupation which is perpetually encouraged by a succession of small nail-driving achievements. These men and unemployed riveters might find consolation in rock-climbing as practised by the Munich school.

It is easy to see the ludicrous side of this development of 'artificial aids.' Let us not forget that the material view of life, with the disillusionment on the spiritual side that accompanies it, often leaves the contemplative view of life a rather drab affair, from which escape is possible by absorption in rapid or violent action and in an emotional excitement akin to intoxication. And on the higher grade climbs the temporary escape from the 'wretchedness of humanity' must be very complete. If you can imagine yourself on the path cut out of the solid rock called the Steinerne Rinne, which runs along the base of the most famous climbs of the Wilde Kaiser, you will get a glimpse of an expert party at work. The cost of pitons and ropes is still borne by the climbers themselves, and there is no turnstile yet to defray the expenses of the show. You will find a restaurant on the shelf, and can sip your beer as you watch or drink to the health—which is often in jeopardy—of the party literally 'hanging on' far above you. The cliffs are about a thousand feet high.

A party of two starts for the Fiechtl-Weinberger route, one of the dearly beloved 'direct' routes leading almost in a straight line to the north peak of the Predigtstuhl. Provisions and warm clothes hardly enter into the equipment of an expert cragsman. *Kletterschuhe* of course, a couple of long ropes, a liberal supply of pitons and clasp-rings, and a couple of hammers. Two caves close to one another in the face of the cliff indicate the way, which lies just to the left of them. An overhanging crack with some good holds is a nice mild beginning; then comes a small, slanting crack of about twenty feet leading to the famous overhang. Some parties have a way of removing their pitons after use, and have been known to remove those left by previous parties. A certain amount of hammering may be done here and the leader ties on to both ropes, the object of this being to ease the work of the leader by letting the second man help to haul him up the overhang on the rope passed through a ring clasped to a piton slightly above and to the side. On one occasion the actual godfather of the climb spent half an hour struggling to pass the overhang and had to give it up. For these sixth-grade tests a man must not only be an expert rock gymnast, he must be feeling perfectly fit and in the right mood! The second man was keen to try, but the leader discouraged the suggestion on the ground that it would be even more difficult for him to come up second.

Next day this crack is climbed in a few minutes, the balcony of the hut and the Steinerne Rinne itself being black with spectators. Whether the effect of being watched by many pairs of wondering eyes is to give increased confidence or to diminish caution is an interesting point. Now comes the overhang. Numerous pitons give excellent security, but it is an awkward place, only possible by a delicate adjustment of the feet against a concavity in the rock to maintain the balance, while the body is raised on the bulge, and by getting some help from a very thin crack that rises vertically above it. One of the most brilliant of the experts spent one and a half hours at the place.

A still greater effort is needed for the crack that follows! It is holdless and too narrow to get into. The only grip obtainable is on some smooth, rib-like irregularities in the rock running parallel to the crack. There is no place where it is possible to relax the effort. It is described as 'one of those places where the only salvation lies in continuous movement. One reaches the top with the hands more dead than alive and the heart racing.'

The rest is comparatively easy, a traverse on the face, followed by a succession of vertical cracks and ribs and a long chimney at the end. And when they get back they are welcomed with mugs of beer held out by admirers in the watching crowd. Supper is all ready for them, and they eat it surrounded by a wondering crowd, 'as elephants are watched eating at the Zoo.'

Another climb that is considered a necessary prelude to admittance to the highest class of experts is the south-east wall of the Fleischbank. This time the second man on the last climb described has his chance of leading up, and it is his first ascent of the route. This is a climb that demands less extreme effort than the Fiechtl-Weinberger route, but very delicate movements, 'similar to those of an acrobat on the top of a pile of objects balanced on the top of one another.' Except for the first hundred and fifty feet the climb presents continuous and extreme difficulties right up to the top of the huge wall. Spectators for this performance are scattered about the slopes of a neighbouring peak, the Goinger Halt, and on the col called the Ellmauer Tor, now made easy of access by the construction of the path called the Steinerne Rinne.

Good time, little over an hour, is made over the first half. A typical bit is where the leader, having made a traverse by means of

19. HUMAN FLIES

pitons, securing himself as he goes by passing the rope through clasp-rings, arrives at the last piton.   After attaching a clasp-ring and threading the rope he has to go back a short distance and use the rope held tight by the second man to pull himself up.   Half-way is one of the crucial points, named the Rossi overhang in honour of one of the two makers of the climb.   Pitons in abundance have made a fall unlikely, but the final approach under the overhang is a delicate operation.   From the last possible holding-place to the actual edge of the overhang is rather more than twenty feet, of which the last dozen feet are of smooth rock that is impenetrable to a piton.   The leader knows it is a place where it makes all the difference to have been there before, but, as he says himself, 'the holding was more than good and double, and there was nothing much to knock one's head against'—a nice way of expressing the super-vertical angle of the rock!

The second man shouts to the spectators to warn them that the most exciting moment has arrived, and the leader moves off the stance. His own words will best describe the exciting moments that follow, and that well repay the spectators for any trouble they have had in reaching their 'seats.'

My mistake was in threading the middle finger of my left hand through an idiotic first piton about five feet to my left, which inevitably upset the whole balance of the body.   While my right hand, holding a clasp-ring, was barely a couple of inches from the good second piton, some fellow on the Goinger Halt broke the general silence with the remark: 'He's up!'   The last syllable was barely out of his mouth when I found myself twenty feet below, on a level with my second man, hanging head downwards.   While he was getting me back to an upright and safe position, no light feat either, my hat rotating in mid-air floated serenely down till it reached the Steinerne Rinne!

The second man modestly suggests that the leader try again, but the wrenching of the finger from the piton has damaged the latter's wrist and he lets the second take the lead.   The overhang is climbed like other overhangs, with the help of a pull by the second man on the rope, passed through a piton somewhat above, and such help as can be got from the soles of the shoes planted against the rock.   The final overhang is of a similar nature but requiring rather less strength and more technical skill than the famous one on the Fiechtl-Weinberger route.   They certainly deserved their mugs of beer.

It is easy to believe that, as one of these young men says, these climbs are only possible if a man is 'liberated from all fear and giddiness.'   It is also terribly easy to believe what another of them confesses, that 'if they are still alive at twenty-seven years of age they are incapable of doing anything more,' so great is the strain on the nervous system.

Here we have the excitement of rock-climbing carried to the point of intoxication. But the doings of intoxicated people are followed with far more amusement and interest than those of the sober, and to some the state of intoxication is the aim of drink. The habit is spreading. It is fully established in parts of the Julian Alps. The 'Matterhorn' of these Alps is Il Montasio, offering magnificent precipices, that of the north face being 2,500 feet in height. The Grand Old Man of the Julian Alps, Dr. Julius Kugy, made the mountaineering ascent of this face in 1902. Latterly it has become a happy hunting ground for the rash young men of all nationalities who live within easy reach of its excitements.

The methods employed and the situations encountered are somewhat similar to those found on the Wilde Kaiser. There is more ice to provide danger from stones, and more rotten rock to keep the nerves stretched on the Montasio climbs. It is worth while spending a few moments with a party on the face. National rivalry has begun to play no small part in these feats of daring, and the Italian party we shall look at is endeavouring to deprive a trio of Bavarian experts of the honour of being the only conquerors of the Cresta dei Draghi. This route winds among terrific towers and provides plenty of difficult climbing before the final wall is reached. At the foot of this, two alternatives present themselves. On the right the precipice is covered with grass tufts of uninviting appearance; in front a slanting crack runs up under a huge block of rock. This looked the better way. The leader tells us:

I attacked the crack, climbing 'à la Dülfer' for about thirty feet, till I reached a point under the great rock which bulged slightly over the crack. Between my legs I looked down at the Stuparich hut. With a big effort I got up the overhang by desperate contortions on the rock, regardless of all the laws of technique, and reached the foot of a wall that rose vertically above me. A great mass of rock of most reassuring appearance protruded from the wall. I got astride of it and secured the second man as he climbed the crack. While he was wrestling with the roof, I became conscious of a disagreeable sensation as if the whole wall behind me was in motion, and I shall never forget the impression as of a cold clutch at my throat when I realized, to my horror, that the whole mass on which I was seated was slowly falling outwards. I yelled to the man below to take cover, I let go the rope, I gripped at the wall, making frantic efforts to get my finger into a providential crack, and by exerting all the strength in my legs I gradually got the huge rock back into its niche. My second was equal to the occasion, and calmly and safely, all the while under the threat of having both the great rock and his leader crash down upon his head, he got past the overhang.

The first two having traversed into a safe place, the third man came up by the wall covered with grass tufts and rejoined them with comparative ease!

Above this the angle eases off sufficiently for snow to lie in a steep couloir. Boots are put on and the party is presently engaged on the snow. Needless to say, there is not an axe among them. Holds for the hands are pecked out with the hammer brought for knocking in pitons, and the couloir is crossed successfully. A chimney, heavily glazed, is safely passed, and they emerge into an atmosphere of repose, of wonderful light, and of safety on the top of the mighty wall.

Some days later the direct route up the north wall is attempted. Here the danger is more continuous. The lower slabs are not very difficult, it is the showers of falling stones that keep the climber keyed up to the required pitch of excitement. The party has a lucky day, for the stones only begin to whistle past when they have reached a place where they are—for a time—out of danger. A broad ledge is reached whence more than one route leads to the top. No common-place ending will do for them. The leader moves along the ledge a short distance till a possible chimney takes his fancy, steep and difficult. Down it comes a considerable waterfall that numbs the fingers. Violent discharges of stones startle them at frequent intervals. 'The white missiles hissed close to us and provided us with the dangerous amusement of cowering beneath the overhanging rocks. We had the curious sensation of climbing the whole time in caves, though there was an interval of slithery chimney between each projecting roof.'

Difficult cracks are climbed to a kind of recess covered with grass and stones. 'It was most difficult ground; not a bit of firm rock could we find; everything crumbled and came away. We had to step as lightly as possible from rock to rock and in a row, for despite every precaution, stones flew about in profusion.' A short council of war was held on a ledge. The rope had become too dangerous to use, partly from the stones it dislodged, partly from the fact that a slip of any one would have meant certain death to the whole party. As they admitted themselves, that was hardly security worth mentioning! Taking each a separate line they went on, first over a most difficult and exposed wall, then up three separate chimneys

where the rock was all of the rottenest, till these united in a narrow
gully. Above this the ascent of a short wall proved the unexpected
ending of the climb. The weather, as it often does, obeyed the
decree of the fortune that favours the brave, waiting to deliver its dark
threats till a breakneck descent could be begun, and perhaps making
all three think, as the rain soaked to the skin, what their plight might
have been if it had caught them on the great wall.

The comments of one of the party on the two routes are instructive:

On the Cresta dei Draghi the route winds up from tower to tower, hiding
itself within the mountain. On the direct route to the summit there are no
offending détours, the way rises vertically up over smooth walls, the mountain
is conquered in the most perfect way. On the Cresta dei Draghi the rock, save
in a few places, is good and in the most exposed portions excellent—not so on
the north wall! Showers of stones came down the lower slabs; above these the
sheerness of the wall itself is a protection, but here the stones give way under our
feet and peril lurks in every hold. It is a continual battle of wits, with the nerves
at a stretch the whole time.

The writer's preference is implied in these comments.

The Scarlet Crag, Škrlatica, is another peak of the Julian Alps
whose dangerous attractions have been lately recognized. It rises
in dizzy perpendicular slabs from a secluded glen, the Velika Dnina.
Three men and a woman all set out in 1927 to see if the slight shadows
on the wall might prove to be climbable cracks and chimneys. The
type of climber will be recognized from their own admission: 'Certainly four is too many for a difficult climb, but the Škrlatica was the
stake, and none of us wanted to miss sharing the first ascent of the
north-west face.'

The path up the glen was hard to find; dense growth on either
side compelled them to follow the watercourse, and they had to
ascend some steep snow, without axes or crampons, before reaching
a ledge of rock where they spent the night. Every bit of wood had
to be climbed for, and, nice as it would have been to sit round the
fire, a precipice at their back and a big drop in front of their ledge
prevented it. Dawn came, and with it clouds that grew heavier
and began to condense in a drizzle as they prepared to start. The
lady of the party, horrified at the suggestion of devoting the day to
a mere reconnaissance of the face, produced a flask of brandy intended
for the celebration of victory on the summit and distributed its contents.

The lower part of the face was not very difficult, the early part
being climbed in boots. Chimneys, smooth, occasionally rotten,
ending in overhangs, were successfully attacked, and the rope had not

20. ŠKRLATICA

yet been uncoiled. Their progress was 'barred by a smooth slab inclined at an angle of over 70°. A foot-wide fissure led up it, and as its edges offered no apparent holds and the situation was very exposed, we roped.' The slab proved easier than it looked, as there were holds for the hands and wedging for the feet. Above them still rose the final wall. The distance of the summit was estimated by the climbers at three hundred feet, by the aneroid at a thousand feet, whereupon the bearer of the aneroid was advised to chuck it down the cliff 'to prevent it pulling their legs'! It was a fearsome problem ahead of them: to the left a precipice consisting of one huge slab, smooth and in places overhanging; to the right some chimneys suggested a possible way up, but they ended not far up in a rocky recess. The chimneys were successfully climbed, but the looseness of the rock and the overhangs that supported the possible resting-places made serious difficulties. An exposed traverse was crossed to a promontory, where a halt was made. It was already one o'clock. Climbers will get an idea of the 'atmosphere' of the place and of the party from the remark: 'Although we had eaten scarcely anything, we turned against food.'

It was the lady's turn to lead. She tried to ascend a chimney that slanted across the face above their heads by climbing straight up. Standing on a male shoulder, she found a hold within her reach and disappeared. After some time information came down that she was stuck and could barely cling to the rock. The owner of the shoulder again obliged, and enabled a second male to climb up to where he could support the lady's feet. In view of the fact that the face was vertical and the holds diminutive, the most conservative among us will forgive this second mere man for driving in a piton to hold on by. With increased support from him she passed the danger point, 'but her difficulties were not over, and her feet had to be supported with an axe.' Earlier in the climb on the steep snow the evening before the party were without axes, but it may be another instance of the miraculous bounty of the fortune that favours the brave. At last she reached a small ledge where she could get her breath after her efforts. She pulled up the male who had so well supported her, and, belayed by him, went on again up the cliff.

Needless to say, the pair in front had left their sacks with the two unhappy, anxious men below.

You, reader, who may have helped to make a complicated bundle of sacks 'down under' in what to you seemed wonderfully quick and to those above wonderfully slow time, will sympathize with these

K

last as they fumble over the knots. The last man, who remembered how his sack had parted from such a bundle on a former occasion, and fallen with his boots and food and all down a precipice, refused to be parted from it, and, as he insisted on climbing 'as if unroped,' his passage of the overhang 'on imaginary holds' must have severely taxed his strength and also the patience of the others.

It began to rain, an icy rain, a very serious thing on a *Kletterschuhe* climb. This modern climbing, where the sheer technical difficulty is the one great consideration, is apt to make a party blindly trustful of the weather. 'The rain took us absolutely by surprise. While climbing, we had not had time to notice the weather, all our attention being given to the rock.' Speed was now essential so that the rocks ahead might be climbed before sleet or snow should make them impossible. The four climbers were now huddled together in a recess on the face. The exit was a narrow ledge that ran out for a few yards on to the face and disappeared. A rounded, overhanging rock a dozen feet or so in height had then to be climbed. It was quite holdless. The lady again was given pride of place. Standing on the tallest man's shoulders she clawed about for a hold while the other two men held them, one each, as best they could from the recess. A bad moment came as she stretched for a hold and slipped, but she managed to subside astride of the shoulders of her human step-ladder, and from there to the nearest approach to terra firma to be found. Spurred on, rather than discouraged, by this failure, she mounted from her supporter's shoulders on to his head; a hold was reached, and with her feet supported she managed to climb up out of sight. Again she found herself with no holds, and one of the two men in the recess answered an appeal for help. Climbing 'like a cat' up the step-ladder and the overhanging rock he did his best to support her, but hold was so precarious that the step-ladder had to be brought up to assist.

Can you at all imagine the tangle of ropes produced by these manœuvres? The leader and the man supporting her feet were at opposite ends of a doubled rope held in the middle by the fourth man in the recess; with another rope he held the 'step-ladder.' Again, it is easy to be indulgent when we learn that this martyr in the recess drove in two pitons, connected them with a clasp-ring, and threaded the doubled rope through it. He had now six ropes in his hands, so tangled that only by giving a tug could he find out to whom each was attached. And the rain was now falling so that the rocks were streaming!

At last came a welcome shout that the leading pair were over the worst, and had found a place 150 feet above for the sacks. The man in the recess had held them in place by crushing them between his back and the rock. A couple were tied on and sent on their way, catching, as is their wont, on every possible protuberance they met. Impatience is only too apt to induce violence in the tug from above to get them past, and as they were half-way up one of the sacks hurtled through the air over their heads, each hoping it might not be his. One of the two men below climbed up to direct the remaining sacks on their way, but finding no safe stance he had to go on and join the pair above.

Once more the patient burden-bearer below is left, this time with two sacks to look after. An hour he had been there in the wet and cold. The overhang was this time climbed with feet against the face and hauling hand over hand on the rope. Climbing up the rocks above, where the angle had eased off slightly to 80°, with numbed fingers and water pouring down his sleeves on to his struggling body, with a double burden on his back, he at last reached the others like a drowned rat and gasping. The fallen rucksack was the lady's; not only her boots, but her money, her clothes, and her latchkey were in it!

Again it was 'ladies first.' A perpendicular step with really good holds was a promising start, but above she was confronted with another overhang. All her efforts combined with those of the largest pedestal in the party were unavailing. The sack-bearer, anxious for any excuse to get rid of his sacks, tried to pass in front, but the third man forestalled him and found a way up a little to one side. However, some small consolation was to come to the burden-bearer. The last two hundred feet were inclined at a less fearful angle; the three others started up some chimneys and found that the rain had made them very greasy and treacherous, so the last man had the satisfaction of finding a steep crack with good holds leading up out of all their anxieties to the summit ridge. The lady, having no boots to put on, made no halt, but hurried on. It is satisfactory to be able to picture them, in the Aljaž inn, which they reached in a couple of hours, forgetting the feel of cold, clinging garments in dry ones borrowed from the innkeeper and his wife, and in potations of mulled wine.

No mountaineer will refuse admiration of such a fine climb as that, and it is easy to appreciate the familiar nature of its difficulties and its triumphs. Our British climbs, while they are neither so long, nor, as a rule, so continuously severe, have provided innumerable days in which chimneys and overhangs, tangled ropes and human ladders, cold and wet—especially wet—and a convivial ending have played a similar part. The difficulties at times become so great that the margin of safety thins down to nothing; but that, too, has happened to the most classically orthodox of the great climbers, and it will continue to happen till the unknown and unexpected entirely cease to have any place in mountaineering. Retreat was always possible, the dangers of a kind that skill and stamina, resourcefulness and nerve could cause to disappear, and each successive bout with the adversary was won by loyal means.

It is with regret that within two years of this climb we find members of this gallant party indulging in an exhibition of steeplejack feats on the north face of Triglav. This face is nearly two miles broad and over three thousand feet high, a Lliwedd face multiplied by four, which has become a sort of climbing stadium where national as well as individual rivalries have introduced a dangerous element. One incident during the ascent of the great scar, called the Black Gully, that seams the face will show the type of work that is being introduced there. The incident occurred on the second day of the ascent, the first day of nearly twelve hours' continuous climbing ending in a bivouac on a narrow ledge, the party being tied together with their belts. The night was entirely sleepless for the man who was to lead next day. The heroine of the Škrlatica climb is not of the party. She made, later, with a single companion, an ascent close to the Black Gully, but deliberately distinct from it on an adjoining buttress, spending no less than *five nights* out on the face and escaping alive. But another Slovene lady is there to give to the leader, Jože Čop, the sort of support the latter had given the leading lady in the Škrlatica performance.

The party has climbed out of the gully and has reached a portion of the neighbouring buttress like the bows of a big barge, with over-hangs on each side, the edge of the buttress forming the sharp prow. On one side of this a narrow crack, interrupted half-way up by a ledge less than a foot broad, ran up obliquely into a smooth slab below the overhang. Let us quote the lady's own words:

This is how we got up the place: Čop led up to the crack and at once fixed an iron piton at the foot of it. Making use of a few sound holds he got on to the narrow ledge. It was very hard work and needed very great care. Above the ledge he fixed another piton to secure first himself and then me when I followed him. Then getting close to him I stepped on to the ledge and stood with legs wide apart. My left hand found a small hold to cling to; my right, grasping the rope with which I held Čop, was in the crack and I leaned my head against the rock. In this way I had firm anchorage, and Čop then climbed over me, and with his feet on my shoulders looked for a suitable place to drive in a piton, but found none. He therefore mounted on to my head, and after another short search began to hammer in a piton. He hammered and hammered, till my legs began to tremble under the strain and we both swayed over the abyss. The piton was firm at last and the rope was passed through the clasp-ring. Čop raised himself up off my head, but failed to find a fresh foot-hold and had to step down again. Again he started up, and this time got a hand-hold and a precarious foot-hold that got him safely up the remaining four metres of the crack and on to a safe stance. There he was obliged to rest. He drove in a piton, using it first as a hand-hold, then as a step to stand on while he drove in the next piton, which enabled him to get up a little higher under the overhang.

This achievement of Čop's made as great a demand on his strength as on his nerve, and if I had not seen it myself I would not have believed a man could do so much. Meanwhile Čop proceeded with every precaution, driving in a piton wherever he could—he used more than ten! Several times he called out to me to hold his rope, as he might fall at any moment. And desperately I clung on to the slender link on which the lives of all three of us depended.

But Čop did not fall. On the contrary, he gained height, inch by inch. Below the projecting eave he turned off a yard to the left to rest again on a bit of safe ground, so as to gather new strength to conquer the overhang, which was extremely difficult, with small, inadequate holds. He did it splendidly. Above this he drove in yet another piton, holding on with two fingers of his left hand. Finally he tackled the last and very severe difficulty, an overhanging crack, and reached a good, safe anchorage, where he drove in three pitons close together, so as to belay me as I climbed up.

Now, in regard to the use of pitons, it has been said: 'If you cut a step in ice to secure a hold, why not a hold cut out of or hammered into the rock?' Well, the extent of the difference depends on the way you look at mountains. If you regard them, as most men who have spent some time alone with them regard them, as something more than a mere lump of matter, as things that have a sort of personality of their own, ready to give you the things that you prize most; if, in fact, you feel towards them anything of what Kim's lama felt, that 'Who goes to the Hills, goes to his mother,' then there is something altogether abhorrent in this method of getting your own way by driving in nails. If you wrestle with a friend, the whole essence of the thing is spoiled if you use sharp claws to get a hold. Ice is but a sort of grease the mountain puts upon his body to make him more elusive; its removal is no violation of any sporting instinct; loose stones, too, are but portions of his scaly skin that are dead; the piton must be driven into the living rock to make it fast. This attitude may appear fanciful; it is the simple truth as I look at it.

This craze for hammering a way through, regardless of natural obstacles, is a form of climbing suggestive of the larger wild beasts which crash through by force. The 'lord-of-the-jungle' route, the most direct and often the worst possible from every mountaineering point of view, is being glorified in foreign publications. It is the expression in mountaineering of the thirst for displaying dominance, the gospel of force which was thought to have received a set-back in the Great War, but which nothing but a scale of values unknown in the material world can supersede.

These are the words in which a modern expert expresses his philosophy: 'The value of an extremely difficult undertaking lies not so much in the hopeless endurance of adverse circumstances, as in the difficulties created by our own volition and overcome by our own efforts, far transcending any form of mountaineering which has a utilitarian foundation, such as exploration, scientific research, aesthetic enjoyment, or any other.'

It would seem, then, that the supreme value of mountaineering is to be won if I scramble up the wall of a tall house by driving pitons into the mortar, and by exacting and dangerous movements reach a window-ledge overhanging the street. There I can spend the night, and proceed next morning to overcome the remaining wall and overhanging gutter, having taken care to increase the emotional thrills by having some of the bricks loosened and sacks of coals poured from the roof at intervals. I admit the adventure would be thrilling, it would be entirely due to my own volition, and the satisfaction of arriving on the roof acute, but is it as simple as that to create what has a value far transcending the ascents of Saussure, of the Duke of the Abruzzi, and others, even of some of yours and mine?

It is the apotheosis of egoism. If self-satisfaction be the aim of climbing, then it must be admitted that the modern expert achieves it in a degree which Bernard Shaw himself might envy. 'This transcendent quality has no need of explanation or justification, because precisely by the very essence of its nature, which goes far beyond the feelings or the actions of normal life, it must be seen and realized itself. It is a kind of lyrical and heroic state . . . it is not a thing that can be known, but a possibility which is a matter of experience and realization.' A state induced by drink or drugs appears to satisfy the definition. The heads of these young men are turned, not by any terrors of the vertical, but by the adulation of those

upon the horizontal plane. It is a youthful excess, a state of happy inebriation where the faculty of self-criticism is suppressed, deserving of indulgence in the young, but reprehensible in those who have had time to form a more considered judgment. Is it quite fair for the old to encourage the recklessness of youth in words like this, spoken in a panegyric of daring climbing that has ended in death?

'Then up again, to the assault of the rock and of the summit, to commemorate the fallen one in a victory yet higher and more difficult. This is the supreme reward of mountaineering, that forges characters of steel and wills before which things quail, and which finds in torment, in struggle, in peril envisaged every hour, the joy and beauty of life.' And again: 'Plunge yourselves into fatigue and danger.'

As if youth needed encouragement to take risks of this kind! Much may be needed to make it see adventure in a life of service, or to risk material possessions; none at all is required to attract it to the obvious dangers of flying, of fast driving, and of difficult mountaineering. Already the pursuit of danger is becoming a cult among a few young climbers. Fear is one of the strongest of all the emotions, and when the loss of faith and ideals has left as mere blocks of matter things in which a spirit lived before, emotional excitement is more eagerly sought after than ever, and a mind inclined towards introspection can find in fear an excitement that stimulates it like a drug. Lammer is one of the most suitable examples among climbers, the supreme egoist, the one who went off to drink himself drunk with the good wine of mountaineering, who tells us that 'without fear life would not be worth living.'

Is it the fear of being afraid that induces this glorification of recklessness, and the belief, based on this fear, that perpetual exposure to the fear of death will breed courage? The history of mountaineering shows us only too clearly that constant exposure to danger destroys the delicacy of sensibility and the appreciation of real danger. It is lack of sensibility to a particular danger that enables window-cleaners and steeplejacks to carry on their work without the nervous strain that would be put on others unaccustomed to positions attended by such fearsome possibilities. Courage is a moral quality that is ready to support the will, either to meet a physical strain or to meet the slings and arrows of outrageous fortune. It is a kind of elasticity a man has in the fibre of his being, so that his nerves will stretch without breaking. Constant stretching will destroy that elasticity in the end; there were thousands of such cases in the war. And can we have any better evidence of this effect of constant strain than the admission mentioned above, that if the modern cragsman lives till twenty-seven he is good for nothing more?

It is an illusion to suppose that the possible emotions of mountaineering or of life can be crammed into a few years. Those who believe they have exhausted its thrills before they are thirty have done so in the sort of way that an American tourist does England in a short visit, every possible hour of which is charged with new impressions, giving him a rich satisfaction of possession and achievement, while the deeper significance of what he sees may not even be suspected.

A brief account of the adventure of two young Frenchmen on the Charmoz will show how little the cult of danger needs encouragement. They had planned for the last four days of their holiday something that might redeem by a brilliant success the bad season of 1926 that was coming to a close; a first traverse from the Col du Dru to the Aiguille Verte, to be followed immediately by a first ascent of the north face of the Charmoz. That was their modest plan: not a bad double to bring off in four days of a bad season!

On the Mer de Glace the view of good snow on the great ice-slope that might be called a hanging glacier on the face of the Charmoz suggested the advisability of making sure of getting the latter safely bagged first, so they turned back, and before midday were well engaged on the big wall of rocks below the ice-slope. It proved difficult, compelling some abandonment of the direct line and constraining them to a more devious route. Night fell as they were close to the lower edge of the ice-slope. The situation was sufficiently grim to inspire some uneasiness, even in these very bold young men. No illusion was possible as to the angle of the slope that rose above them, and on which they must adventure themselves when morning came, and the couloir above it looked even more repellent. Something not very different from fear entered their hearts, and there were other sources for it than the precipice above. Disquieting signs of bad weather had appeared, and there was the prospect of a bivouac anticipated with mingled feelings of fear and excitement, a bivouac high up on a big mountain being in their eyes the consecration of the great mountaineer. 'Side by side, with our feet in our sacks and our bodies thinly wrapped in newspapers we lay and waited, as if for a mysterious revelation that never came.'

It is the early hours of a night out that pass with the most despairing slowness. Expecting dawn they see far below a luminous caterpillar crawling up the valley, the 11.30 train at Vallorcine! Lightning begins to flicker in the early morning hours, confirming the signs of bad weather on the way.   So clear are these signs to parties down below that not a single light reveals the departure of a party for a climb.   How easy it is for our subconscious inclinations to read encouragement or discouragement into weather signs!   In this case we have the admission, 'The violence of our desires drew a veil across our eyes'!

At six o'clock crampons are put on as they leave the last islands of rock straight below the couloir far above, that has its origin in a notch of the north-east *arête* close to the summit.   The direct line, as far as it is possible, is still the one preferred.

There is some lingering over this fastening of crampons, the tightening of puttees and of belts, moments full of the thrill of expectation as of a runner waiting on the mark.   And why is it that this gesture of tightening the belt is symbolical of a bracing of the will?   Is it a sort of final repression of softer and more carnal cravings?

Hard snow, ideal for giving hold to the crampon points, carries them rapidly up the slope, whose steepness increases as the drop below grows longer and the couloir comes nearer.   And what a couloir! A cataract of ice pouring down between walls of smooth slabs! Making for the rocks to the right of it they find themselves at once in the greatest possible difficulties.   Streamlets of hard ice run between the holdless rocks.   The only possible line of progress seems to be towards the couloir, a waterfall of ice.   Eighty feet of rope run out as the leader chips notches for the points of the crampons, then the spare rope is used and the second man has to follow before there is any secure holding for either.   As he reaches the notches and turns face to the ice to stand up in them, his ice-axe slips from his hand. An instinctive effort to turn and clutch it is checked just in time to prevent a loss of his precarious balance, and as he regains his equilibrium he has a glimpse of it disappearing into the gulf below.   A pocket-knife is tried and barely scratches the surface of the hard ice. So near the vertical is the angle that the greatest delicacy of movement is required to free the knee-joint from the slope as the leg pivots on a crampon point.   At last an edge of rock appears, emerging from the glassy surface; its coat of ice is hacked off and the pair can enjoy a moment's rest, after four hours of unceasing toil and strain.

And in that moment the catastrophic ending of the adventure descends upon them.   The clouds that had hung threateningly below suddenly rush up and envelop them.   Through the mist they see the monstrous spike of the Aiguille de la République, its point almost on their level, and then the grey walls of mist shut out everything but a few square yards of slab and ice. They judge the gap in the north-east ridge at the top of the couloir to be about three hundred feet above them.

The first flakes of snow fall and the slabs begin to whiten. A look down the wall they have come up tells them that to struggle up that three hundred feet is the only way of safety. The portion of the couloir immediately above them is a sheet of ice that appears to overhang; it is like transparent armour, through which they could see, in places, the rock beneath. The rocks at the edge are unclimb-able slabs. The rock wall to the right is ice-covered. An attempt to force a passage there proves it to be utterly impossible. A nearer survey of the couloir confirms the hopelessness of looking for a way out there. The descent has to be faced.

Somewhere among the inhospitable slabs a projection is found, enough for a belay. Other projections are found below, and by a series of descents on the doubled rope the horrible couloir is gradually left behind and the great ice-slope reached. Only a portion of it is visible and it lies at a fearful angle. The newly fallen snow slips off at the lightest touch, while the layer that bore them up so securely in the morning has become soft and treacherous. Without an axe to hold or steady him, his arms buried in the unstable layer of snow resting on the ice, the first man leads off down the slope, certain that sooner or later the slip must come. And not far down the slope it comes, the support of hands and feet sliding away simultaneously beneath him. 'An awful pang of fear; sudden and quick as a flash, and then at once a calm, and with it a surprising presence of mind and lucidity of thought.'

A desperate effort to arrest the slide ensues, the arms plunging into a new patch of soft snow, the crampons clawing wildly at the exposed ice and skidding over it. Then he feels the rope tighten round him and thinks 'he has been pulled off by the shock; it must all be over quickly now.' And then the moment of surprise and of sudden relief as he realizes that the man above has held on, and looks up to see him actually smiling! 'I smile too; perhaps it is not, after all, so hard to die, we had got over the worst.'

A new confidence comes: 'I no longer felt that vague disquietude that had been brooding over our fate for all those past hours. From that moment I was sure that our hour had come and passed, and that, whatever might happen, we should emerge victorious from our trial.'

Gradually the angle of the slope diminished while the danger of

22. AIGUILLE DES CHARMOZ – NORTH FACE

an avalanche increased. As far as possible they hugged the rocks at the edge of the ice, taking whatever cover was afforded by protruding rocks. A point was reached where a traverse of the slope had to be made. The ice-axe changed hands and its owner went on across the slope without it, while his friend held him. Over sixty feet of rope were out when a large piece of snow slipped and carried the leader down. The rope ran out, the axe bent and quivered under the strain—and axe and snow both held!

Soaked to the skin, their hands raw from the constant friction of ropes and snow, their nerves exhausted by these constant shocks, they badly needed food but had not time or inclination for it. A drink of brandy was too much for one of them, and he had just been violently sick when a sound like an explosion above made him look up to see an avalanche bearing straight down upon him. Luckily it broke against a rock just before it reached him. A foaming torrent of snow poured over him, but he stuck to the slope in grim desperation and found himself still firm when it had passed. Only a few splashes reached his friend. It was the last trial on the slope, and a few minutes later they had reached the haven of rocks, the scene of the previous night's bivouac. It was already six o'clock, and it was dark before they reached the glacier of La Thendia. No matches had escaped the general soaking to light either lantern or boiling apparatus; the *bergschrund* was passed in darkness. Gradually the ice became less broken and a quicker pace was made. The moraine was only a short distance away when the last shock came.

The leading man, axeless, slipped into a crevasse in crossing a bridge which proved to be ice and not snow. For a moment he lost consciousness, and regained it to find himself up to the armpits in a great mass of soft snow that plugged the crevasse, and the rope half-strangling him. Instant demands, in the strongest of language, for his companion to relax the tension only produced demands from him, in similar language, to do the same. The sudden pull of the first man's fall had carried the man behind in one great bound right over the crevasse to a point some eighty feet below, where the tension of the rope held him almost paralysed. Once more they managed to recover a stable position on their feet and staggered on towards the path to Montenvers, which they entered in the light of another day, forty-five hours after leaving it.

To the credit of these two adventurers, they expect reproval and admit that reproval is justified. And older men who know anything of the young will feel no surprise at their remaining unrepentant or at their reason for so remaining. 'What base ingratitude should we show if we abjured these hard lessons offered by the mountains and should turn aside from these dangerous pastimes in which, hand in hand with death, we have had revelations of a life ardent and free, such as we have dreamed of without daring to believe it to be a possible reality!' What ought we to say to them, reader? Shall it be like the Frenchman's comment on Balaclava? Magnificent! But it is not mountaineering! or shall it be: Quite right, do it again!

If any one was guilty of giving this latter advice, it was not taken. It was left for climbing robots with ice and rock pitons to complete an ascent by this face. After an attempt by the rock wall to the right of the couloir had reached a point on the north-west *arête* and resulted in two nights out upon the mountain, another attempt was made by the rocks to the left or east side of the couloir, and a notch was reached high on the north-east *arête*. There bad weather came on and *three nights were spent there* in a Zdarsky sack. Descent being then impossible, the ascent of the remainder of the ridge was faced, and the party succeeded in escaping with their lives over the summit and down the ordinary route by the Charmoz–Grépon couloir!

Looking across the Mer de Glace from the Charmoz or from Montenvers, the climbing robot will see another north face that offers him a superb test of his efficiency as a climbing machine, and as an engineer, and also of his lack of sensibility to danger, that of the Grandes Jorasses. The recent history of attempts upon this face shows the tragic rivalry in folly into which climbing can degenerate.

Two young Bavarians start a climbing holiday in the western Alps with this *pièce de résistance,* fearing, probably, that one of the other parties, greedy for this tit-bit among first ascents, should forestall them. On the very first attempt the rope is cut and the head of an axe carried in a belt smashed by falling stones. Most of the attempts do not reach the huge wall of slabs that forms the upper part of the face. After almost unbelievable feats of endurance in climbing, in bicycling, and generally existing on the slenderest resources, they return five weeks later to the Leschaux bivouac for yet another attempt upon the face. In the bivouac they find a diary left by a rival German party of similar habit of climbing. It reads: 'We are standing at the base of the north face. It appears quite harmless. If it wasn't snowing we should try the climb at once.' And there is a last entry for the next day: 'We are expecting H. and K. [our bicyclist friends], our strongest competitors!' Storms keep these latter in the hut for four days, picturing their rivals in the pride of victory braving the weather in their tent-sack somewhere on the summit ridge. At last the weather clears, and they go to the foot of the face to see if the snow has frozen hard on to the great slabs. It has not; it lies loose on ice, making an attempt too obviously suicidal even for them, and then suddenly in a snowy recess they see the mangled bodies of the rival party. A piton hanging loose in the doubled rope shows the possible cause of the accident. One almost wishes that this face could be put entirely 'out of bounds' by the French authorities.

This chapter, like others that have preceded it, shall close upon the Matterhorn. This giant also has his north face. Till the last few years every mountaineer has avoided it, despite the immense attraction it must have for men who are either insensible to consequences for themselves and others, or crazy for the fearful thrill that danger, certain and unavoidable, can bring.

Attempts on this face in 1928 and 1930 had confirmed the dangerous character of any route upon it. In 1931 the party of two killed on the north face of the Grandes Jorasses had intended to make an assault upon this north face of the Matterhorn, but were just anticipated by Franz and Toni Schmid of Munich. These two brothers bivouac at eight thousand feet, having previously reconnoitred the route to the foot of the face. Leaving at midnight, they reach the Hörnli hut at two o'clock, and tell the hut-keeper to warn all parties that they will be on the north face. Then they descend on to the Matterhorn Glacier and cross the *bergschrund* at four o'clock on to an ice slope a thousand feet high at an angle of 60° that leads far up into the face. Steps on such a slope are a luxury for which they cannot afford either time or energy. A piton driven into the ice while the second man comes up is the utmost concession they can make to safety. From the top of the slope a well-marked curving gully slopes up for a great distance in the rocks. It is shown in the diagram on p. 144. It is shallow, extremely steep, 'streaming with water and raked by stones and icicles,' and vanishes in the rocks of the final precipice. Glazed rocks made the entry into this death-trap extremely difficult. Security was non-existent during almost the whole climb. At one point only a *standing-place* was discovered, where a short rest was possible. The climbing above this was up nearly vertical bits of crumbling rock and the narrow chimneys between, ice adding much to the difficulty. It was dusk when they reached the level of the Solvay hut. A small boss of rock was found above this when it became too dark to see; pitons were driven in and they tied themselves on for the night. A standing position was the only one possible!

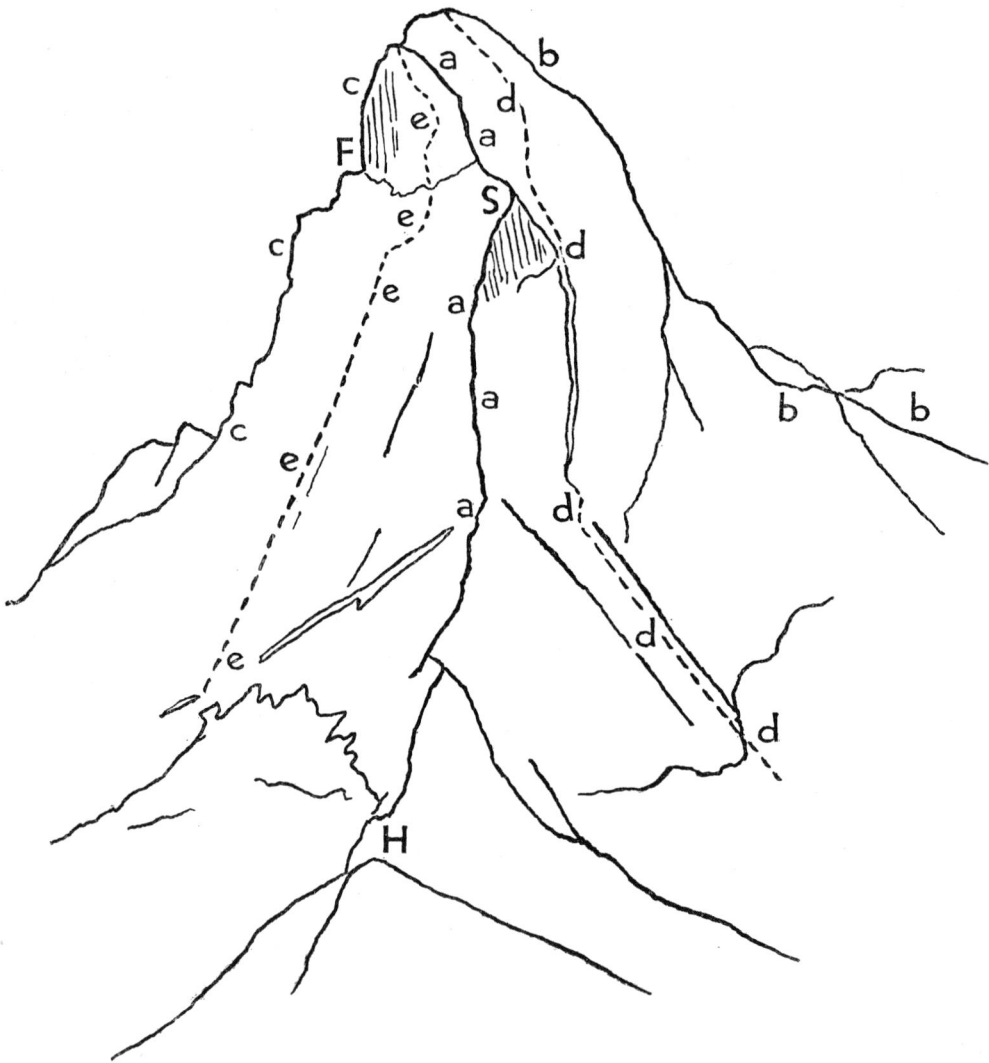

North (right) and East (left) faces divided by the Hörnli ridge

a a Hörnli ridge, route of Whymper's ascent

d d⎫ Bad routes on North and East
e e⎭   faces referred to in the text

b b Zmutt ridge

F Furggen shoulder

c c Furggen ridge

H Hörnli

S Shoulder

23. THE MATTERHORN—NORTH AND EAST FACES

The sun rose, and by seven o'clock had thawed their limbs suffi-ciently to let them move, but the sky was threatening as they renewed the crawl up the face. The worst difficulties of all confronted them before they had advanced two hundred feet. The slabs were com-pletely iced up, so that pitons could not be used; only a thicker coat of ice on some yellow rocks nearer the Zmutt ridge enabled them to fashion sufficient hold to pass this difficulty. Traverses of the most hazardous nature had to be made above, till some threads of snow winding up among the precipitous rock were reached, and afforded what seemed an almost easy way to the Italian summit. A storm broke on the summit, and they waited, huddled together in the tent-sack, just below the ridge. Another storm broke as they reached the ropes on the Swiss face above the shoulder, and again they crouched under shelter while it spent its fury. Heavy snow and small avalanches poured down on them. It took them another three and a half hours to reach the Solvay hut. All that evening and *the next day* the snow fell, and only on the day after that could they fight their way through fresh snow, knee-deep, down to the Hörnli hut.

Is it possible to imagine a party more utterly at the mercy of the weather? Nothing could have prevented a disaster if the weather had broken a few hours earlier, or if the climb had taken, as it well might, a few hours more. Their success may have saved them from death the following week. They arrived at the foot of the north face of the Grandes Jorasses only a day or two later than the two Bavarian cyclists mentioned above. The satisfaction of their Matterhorn victory, and the fate of the other German party may have made them feel: 'For this time, it is enough'! Toni Schmid was killed the next year, attempting a very difficult ice-climb, the north-west face of the Gross Wiesbachhorn. It was an accident due to a slip. Such an accident is far more likely to occur to climbers who habitually attempt what is barely within the capacity of the greatest skill, but it is a risk which all mountaineers have been prepared to accept. It is in a different category from the risks deliberately taken on routes swept by stones or ice, or on expeditions undertaken in doubtful weather where bad weather means almost certain death.

It is no exaggeration to say that the methods recently introduced into modern climbing, and the utter recklessness that sacrifices all regard for safety to the satisfaction of personal achievement, have disgusted many mountaineers whose record is sufficient proof of their love of adventure, their skill and courage, and their intense love of every sort of mountaineering that does not contain a lie in the soul.

To deny any aim beyond the assertion of self is a lie in the soul, if we allow the existence of anything that can be called a soul. If we do not, then, I agree, we must regard self-satisfaction as sufficient, and apply to mountaineering and all other activities the principle of living to eat and not eating to live. Eating will be indulged more dangerously, but not as pleasantly or refreshingly as before, and appetite will fail. Our last remaining satisfaction will then be to revile the quality of the food. Not even a climbing Heinz's 'piton sauce' will be able to give it relish.

CHAPTER IX

THE HIGHEST MOUNTAINS OF THE WORLD

As I write this, at the close of 1934, Everest is still unclimbed. That it can be climbed by men, with or without oxygen, was proved on the second Everest expedition in 1922. The actual accomplishment of the ascent still awaits the conjunction of the right men, the right use of previous experience, good organization and equipment, and good conditions. But for the absence of the last, it is possible that either of the 1924 or 1933 expeditions would have reached the summit.

On every one of the four expeditions, of 1921, 1922, 1924, and 1933, there were men capable of reaching it. The actual difficulties presented by the rocks of the still unclimbed stages were proved, first by Mallory and Norton in 1924 and later by members of the 1933 expedition, to be more formidable than had been expected. It will be interesting to see whether pitons, as well as gas, will be used to bring about the conquest of Everest. But let us go back to the beginning.

The Everest expeditions differ in an important respect from previous mountaineering enterprises. They are not the result of individual enterprise, the selection of the climbers and the payment of the cost being the responsibility of men of whom few take part in the actual climbing of the mountain. The Himalayan expeditions referred to in Chapter VI, as well as others more recently made by Dr. Longstaff, Mr. C. F. Meade, Dr. A. M. Kellas, and others, were carried out on the climbers' own initiative and at a cost often ludicrously small in comparison with that of the elaborate expeditions organized by the Everest Committee, composed of members of the Alpine Club and of the Royal Geographical Society. The public know practically nothing of these private expeditions. They were undertaken for pleasure and with a view to mountain exploration rather than to the accomplishment of a single great feat.

Now this system of selecting climbers, and paying for them by what almost amounts to public subscription, if we include the proceeds of newspaper articles, lectures, and cinematograph shows, introduces a new element of responsibility in the men chosen. However much

L

the selectors may endeavour to impress upon the men picked for the struggle the need for caution, they cannot relieve them entirely of the feeling that they are being selected and sent out to accomplish a particular feat. Failure to achieve that object must bring disappointment to others besides themselves. And with every succeeding expedition in which a man takes part that feeling grows.

So far only one man, George Leigh Mallory, has taken a leading part in more than two Everest expeditions. He was one of the first party to explore that mountain's mysteries and proved that there is only one route which offers any hope of success to men of the present generation. He was one of the party that proved that the effects of altitude, even at twenty-seven thousand feet, where the density of the air is little more than one-third of the normal, are not sufficient to prevent resolute men from making their limbs obey the will that urges them to keep moving upwards.

He was one of the two who, on the third expedition, left on a last attempt to turn failure into success. Whether he did so or not is still a mystery; he was never seen again. No matter when and how Everest may be climbed, Mallory's name is inseparably associated with the great struggle to win the highest point of earth for those whose idea of possession is limited to what has been trodden on or handled.

It is tempting to say of a mountaineer so famous as Mallory, so admirably built by Nature for mastering her own obstacles, and endowed with a knightly soul that was always striving towards a high ideal, that it was inevitable he should climb mountains. Unfortunately there is nothing inevitable about the discovery of a man's latent possibilities, and this was especially the case with mountaineering, which, thirty years ago, had hardly begun to enjoy, or, should I say, to suffer from the publicity accorded to other sports and arts. Most active children climb walls and trees, and Mallory made use of the opportunities to do so afforded by a country rectory, but at the age of eighteen he had climbed nothing bigger than the Malvern Hills, nor had he shown any interest in the few books of mountain adventure in the library at Winchester. He was a good enough all-round athlete to play for Magdalene College, Cambridge, at both sorts of football and to row for it in its first eight, and the new Mallory Court recently added to it is a fitting memorial to the man who not only became one of its most famous sons on Everest, but who did much to help the Master, Mr. A. C. Benson, in raising Magdalene from comparative obscurity towards the very high position it now holds among Cambridge colleges. He developed many interests there, and it is quite possible that mountains might have meant almost nothing in his life. It was just chance that I took out to the Alps in 1904 a boy destined to become so famous upon Everest.

I had ceased to climb with guides; the only colleague at Winchester who was a climber died, and my love of solitary climbing did not blind me to the folly of attempting big glacier expeditions alone. I was looking for recruits.

My first I discovered developing photographs in forbidden hours. Subsequent conversation revealed the fact that he had climbed, or rather walked up, the gentle slopes of the Cima di Jazzi. He was a gymnast. Here was my first recruit. Mallory was a friend of his and an even better gymnast. He was my second. He obtained permission from home to come with me to the Alps, I hope not entirely on his undertaking to follow faithfully the 'guide,' who had been given a professional halo by his parents. It is interesting to remember that on the first mountain on which I took him in the Alps, the easy Mont Vélan, he was incapacitated by mountain sickness at under twelve thousand feet!

He was a beautiful climber, with such good balance that any movement was made with the least possible effort. What Mr. G. W. Young has said in a great tribute to that acknowledged prince among guides, Franz Lochmatter, 'I never saw him "struggle," ' might have been said of Mallory. Climbing with him was inseparable from artistry. No man living has a better knowledge of the Everest expedition than Colonel E. F. Norton, and in his opinion Mallory was the greatest antagonist Everest has had—or is likely to have.

At the risk of damaging the reputation of Winchester for producing 'safe' men, I have to record that the share taken by Wykehamists in this Everest adventure was disproportionately large. A Wykehamist viceroy, Lord Chelmsford, gave the permission to approach the Dalai Lama, which had hitherto been refused; another Wykehamist, Mr. Bell (afterwards Sir Charles Bell), the resident in Sikkim, was on such good terms with the lama that he had only to ask for leave to obtain it; the two climbers upon whom devolved the exploration of Everest and the discovery of a route were both Wykehamists, Mallory and Bullock. The latter has been described in a biography of Mallory as a man 'of fine physique but very limited experience.' The truth is that, when Bullock was elected to the Alpine Club in 1908, Captain Farrar, a good judge, described his qualification as one of the best that had ever come before the committee. He continued climbing in the Alps till 1912, after which his duties in the consular service, mainly in tropical places, gave him only rare opportunities for climbing and must have somewhat diminished his great staying powers. But he was certainly, in 1921, as he still was in 1929, an admirably safe man at the end of a rope. It was right of him, however, to consider Mallory as the leader of the climbing-party and to leave the initiative to him; and Mallory was a man who, as Norton says, 'jumped into the lead' when difficulties arose.

I sometimes wonder whether, if the future had been shown me, I would have asked him to come to the Alps. He is the only one of all the young men whom I have introduced to climbing who has had a serious accident on a mountain. When I think of all that mountains meant to Mallory, the answer must be yes, and I have no doubt whatever what his own choice would have been.

The first expedition suffered from the purely climbing point of view in being rather a voyage of discovery than a serious attempt to reach the highest point. In fact, it is known as the Reconnaissance. Colonel Howard-Bury, its leader, was not a climber, and the mountaineering party suffered serious losses before the foot of Everest was reached. Dr. Kellas, a Scotsman, who had carried out with coolies alone more ascents of peaks over twenty thousand feet than any man living, died of heart-failure after suffering for several days from enteritis on the journey through Tibet. Mr. Raeburn, one of the best known of British guideless climbers, proved too old to stand the strain that Tibet puts upon the heart, the lungs, and the digestive organs. The only remaining men who might share in the assault on Everest were Morshead and Wheeler, two officers engaged on the survey, of whom only Morshead had had even a limited experience of real mountaineering.

But if Mallory and Bullock can have had small hopes of reaching the summit of Everest, when the route was discovered, the weeks of discovery and exploration that preceded their one hopeless attempt were enough to make this first expedition the most interesting of all.

No climber, previous to 1921, had been within fifty miles of Everest or had ever seen more than the upper portion of the south-east face and the long north-east ridge rising at a comparatively gentle angle that invited an attack along its crest. Seen from a distance of a hundred miles, Everest offered a far simpler climbing problem than either of the two magnificent peaks that approach within a thousand feet of it: one of them, the gloriously inaccessible giant that towers above the Baltoro Glacier, and whose name, K 2, is a warning against the terrible effect of a military mathematical education; the other,

Kanchenjunga (Kangchenjunga for those who fear to clip their *g*'s), upon which Dr. Bauer and his gallant men have accomplished the greatest mountaineering feats that have ever been recorded. Now the climbers were about to approach under the walls of Everest and see whether other difficulties beyond those due to mere height above its neighbours would defend access to its highest point.

As the expedition enters the bleak uplands of Tibet the very name of the mountain changes. The Tibetan passport supplied to it gives permission to explore the region of Chomolungma, the 'Goddess Mother of the Snows.' Such a name already existing makes us deplore the name of Everest almost as much as that of K 2. Whenever India receives its measure of self-government, can we not for once indulge in a *beau geste* and restore with all possible publicity this beautiful name to the highest summit of Nepal, of Tibet, and of the whole world, a foretaste of what the contribution of Asia to the world may be? There is a good deal to learn from people who can baptize their mountains in this way.

No climbers can ever have had or can ever have again the same thrill of expectation as came to Mallory and Bullock as they approached near to Everest after a first dim sight of it near Kampa Dzong. Mont Blanc was familiar to Saussure many years before he climbed it. The Matterhorn had exposed all its grim features to the men of Zermatt and of Valtournanche long before it occurred to them that it was possible or desirable to climb it. But the highest mountain of the world had reserved the disclosure of its features to the men who came to climb it.

And that disclosure was made in a fitting manner. They crossed the Yalu and followed the gorge along its western bank under rocky summits that hid the exciting possibilities in the direction of Everest, till they emerged on the edge of a sandy plain. A steep hill was climbed to a crest overlooking the gorge. And Mallory has told us what they saw from there.

We were able to make out almost exactly where Everest should be; but the clouds were dark in that direction. We gazed at them intently through field-glasses as though by some miracle we might pierce the veil. Presently the miracle happened. We caught the gleam of snow behind the grey mists. A whole group of mountains began to appear in gigantic fragments. Mountain shapes are often fantastic seen through a mist; these were like the wildest creation of a dream. A preposterous triangular lump rose out of the depths; its edge came leaping up at an angle of about seventy degrees and ended nowhere. To the left a black, serrated crest was hanging in the sky incredibly. Gradually, very gradually, we saw the great mountain-sides and glaciers and *arêtes,* now one fragment and then another through the floating rifts, until far higher in the sky than imagination had dared to suggest, the white summit of Everest appeared. And in this series of partial glimpses we had seen a whole; we were able to piece together the fragments, to interpret the dream. However much might remain to be understood, the centre had a clear meaning as one mountain shape, the shape of Everest.

And in the evening of the same day they came up with the coolies and donkeys sheltering from the pitiless wind of Tibet on a grassy bank beside a spring.

We also sought shelter. But a short while after sunset the wind subsided. We all came forth and proceeded to a little eminence near at hand; and as we looked down the valley there was Everest, calm in the stillness of evening and clear in the evening light. I have dwelt upon this episode at some length because in our travels before we reached the mountain it is for me beyond other adventures unforgettable.

And when they pitched their tents near the end of the Rongbuk Glacier, ready to come to grips with the mountain, it still held many mysteries behind a screen of intervening peaks higher than any they had seen before, but yet not high enough to hide the central mass that towered several thousand feet above them.

From where they were encamped, the glacier running northwards at a gentle angle offered a road through these screening mountains to the lovely cwms hidden under the last great walls of Everest. The ridge above the camp that continued northwards and rose in the peak of Chang Tse (North Peak) to over 24,700 feet completely obscured the junction with the north-east ridge, whose upper part was expected to provide the easiest route.

The days that followed were filled with discovery and wonder. Glacier work at eighteen thousand feet is hard work, and they had reached altitudes where descent no longer brings the relief from lassitude that may be expected at fifteen thousand feet. But there was not the extreme fatigue and the monotonous struggle for breath which Mallory found so deadening to the faculties at the higher altitudes reached in the later expeditions. It is easy for journalists to write of the wonders seen from heights of over twenty-five thousand feet, and the reading public expect it. Mallory was certainly one of the sincerest men I have known, as well as one of the most sensitive to beauty, and I will take his word as to what men really feel and what they can really appreciate at the highest points reached, rather than anything I may read which is written to give an impression of wonder or romance, or the sort of caption that might introduce a piece of cinema film.   This is what he wrote of the great ascent to nearly twenty-seven thousand feet in 1922:

> It must be remembered that the mind is not easily interested under such con-
> ditions.   The intelligence is gradually numbed as the supply of oxygen diminishes
> and the body comes nearer to exhaustion. . . . The view, for instance—and as
> a rule I'm keen enough about the view—did not interest me; I was not 'taking
> notice.'   Wonderful as such an experience would be I had not even the desire
> to look over the north-east ridge; I would have gladly got to the north-east
> shoulder as being the sort of place one ought to reach, but I had no strong desire
> to get there, and none at all for the wonder of being there.

During the early weeks of reconnaissance on the West Rongbuk Glacier we find them tired in the evening, more so than after a normal day's climbing in the Alps, but with interest keenly alive and the capacity for observation and appreciation hardly diminished.   The glacier which Alpine experience had led them to regard as an easy road to steeper things was covered with great pinnacles, standing as much as fifty feet high on solid bases, the result of melting.   Occa-sionally a trough in the midst of these spires of white, glittering ice gave them a reasonable stretch of good going; generally the easiest way was in the stream beds at the glacier side.   On the glacier itself something malignant and enervating in the atmosphere robbed them of their strength.   Mallory says: 'I might feel as fit and fresh as I could wish on the moraine at the side, but only once succeeded in crossing a glacier without feeling a despairing lassitude.'   One is reminded of the accounts of many early ascents of Mont Blanc, when snowy valleys seemed to produce a similar effect.   Perhaps the change from dry to moister air accounts for it.

It was late in June before the reconnaissance up the West Rongbuk Glacier began.   The south-east monsoon appears to vary considerably, not only in the date of its arrival but in the type of weather it brings to this district that is near the limit of its advance.   Opportunities for obser-vation have not yet been frequent enough to show what are the best conditions possible on Everest.   Was 1921 a particularly good year?   Were 1924 and 1933 particularly bad years?   It is still largely guess-work.   Mallory and Bullock carried out all their reconnaissance work and the one attempt to reach a great height upon the mountain in July, August, and September, that is to say, entirely in the period of the monsoon.   But the precipitation of snow, though generally not many inches in a day, was enough to turn Everest into a white mountain. At levels near twenty thousand feet the snow would disappear quickly, but on the higher parts of Everest no melting occurred, and the north-west wind, checked by the opposing monsoon currents, was not enough to sweep the rock clean and black.

The element of exploration was most refreshingly important in this 1921 expedition. So accurate and detailed are the maps and Climbers' Guides on which the modern expert relies to lead him to his climb, that the joys of solving the problem of approach are almost unimaginable, at least to men whose aim is the satisfaction of achieving a performance of notorious difficulty. To the first two who approached Everest, the reconnaissance offered a most exciting and at the same time baffling problem.

From a camp in the Rongbuk valley at sixteen thousand feet they could look southward straight up between the containing mountain walls to Everest. And from this northern side Everest is simply and grandly pre-eminent. The West Rongbuk Glacier runs almost level towards the foot of its immense wall. Five miles up above its foot Lingtren, a broad mountain with graceful peaks rising three thousand feet above the ice to over twenty-one thousand feet, divides it into two ice-streams, which disappear to right and left behind the sides of the glacier trough. Far above the peaks of Lingtren rises the north wall of Everest. The crest of the wall, rising gradually from a high shoulder to the east, the now familiar north-east shoulder, well over twenty-seven thousand feet, is the long ridge, conspicuous in distant views of Everest from the south-east, which had offered a hopeful line of ascent. The highest peak is a final cone of six or seven hundred feet at the western end, and from it a ridge falls, a little north of west, in a grand sweep of steep rocks, something like the east ridge of the Grandes Jorasses magnified threefold, to a saddle more than five thousand feet below the summit, where this ridge runs nearly level before descending behind Lingtren.

From the north-east shoulder a spur came north towards them, presumably connected by a snow col with the North Peak (Chang Tse) and the chain that contained the glacier on the east. This col was entirely hidden; the nature of its west slopes was a riddle that must be solved, for the col, if accessible, was the most obvious starting-point for the final climb. Two other riddles must also be solved before a reconnaissance of the northern approach could be considered complete, the possibility of reaching the saddle on the north-west ridge and the mystery that lay behind that ridge.

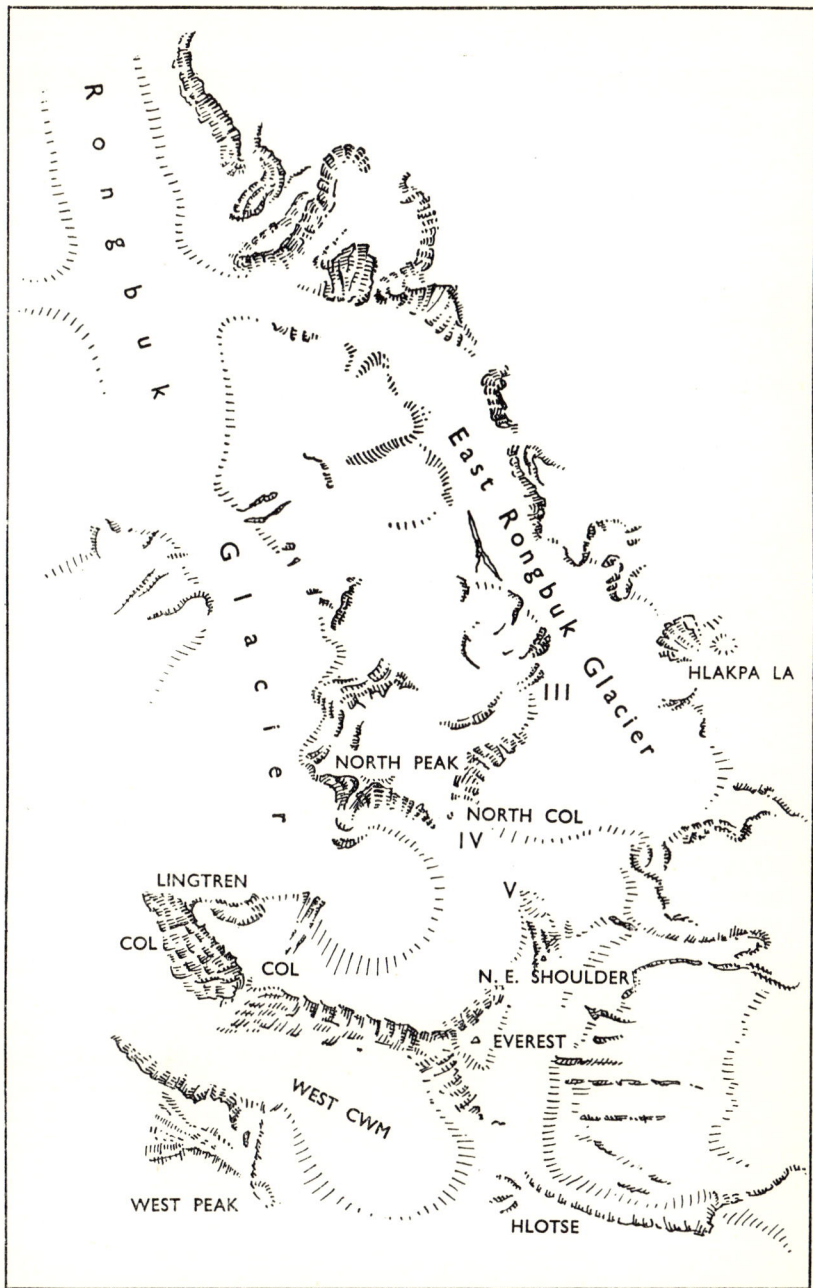

Rongbuk

East Rongbuk Glacier

Glacier

HLAKPA LA

III

NORTH PEAK

NORTH COL

IV

V

LINGTREN

COL

COL

N. E. SHOULDER

EVEREST

WEST CWM

WEST PEAK

HLOTSE

24. MAP OF THE EVEREST RIDGES

An ascent of a peak 22,500 feet high to the west of the camp, involving a rise of over five thousand feet, tested their condition and gave them some valuable information. Much of the slope connecting the north-east shoulder with the hidden col below it was visible and lay back at a comparatively easy angle. A crinkled summit to the west of Everest seemed to lie behind the frontier ridge and to be connected, not with the summit, but with a rocky south peak of Everest (Hlotse), implying a deep cwm under the west face lying entirely in Nepal. From the North Peak a ridge appeared to run eastward, an impression which helped to keep hidden the existence of a glacier, the East Rongbuk Glacier, descending from the north col on the east but actually bending north and discharging into the lower West Rongbuk Glacier. This was the highest peak either had ever ascended, and Mallory's comments on their condition and on the weather are of interest: 'The ascent had come very near to exhausting our strength; for my part I felt distinctly mountain-sick.' . . . Thunderclouds had come up from the north and were so threatening that they dared not halt long. 'After fifteen minutes we started down at three o'clock. Fortune favoured us. The wind was no more than a breeze; a few flakes of snow were unnoticed in our flight; the temperature was mild; the storm's malice was somehow dissipated with no harm done. We rejoined our coolies at five o'clock and were back in camp at 7.15.' It sounds like a useful and instructive day rather than one of great enjoyment.

A higher camp beside the western glacier was the starting-point for attempts to enter the mysterious cwm.

From it they could look across to the right of Lingtren at Pumori and the fantastic peaks beside it on the narrow crest of the frontier ridge. Some unforgettable evenings were spent here watching them.

This group of mountains, always beautiful and often in the highest degree impressive, was now to figure for our eyes as the principal in that oft-repeated drama which seems always to be a first night, fresh and full of wonder whenever we are present to watch it. The clinging curtains were rent and swirled aside and closed again, lifted and lowered and flung wide at last; sunlight broke through with sharp shadows and clean edges revealed—and we were there to witness the amazing spectacle. Below the terrible mountains, one white smooth island rose from the quiet sea of ice and was bathed in the full light of the western sun before the splendour failed.

After more than one attempt frustrated by unexpected obstacles on the glacier, or by misty weather, they rounded the western slopes of Lingtren and reached the col between it and Pumori and could look at last into the western cwm. It must have been a great day, for any one to whom impressions count as well as achievement. Mallory's diary tells us:

It was an exciting walk. I so much feared the cloud would spoil all. It was just light enough to get on without lanterns after the moon went down. At dawn everything was covered, but not by heavy clouds. Like guilty creatures of darkness surprised by the light, they went scattering away as we came up, and the whole scene opened out. The north ridge of Everest was clear and bright even before sunrise. We reached the col at 5 a.m., a fantastically beautiful scene; and we looked across into the west cwm at last, terribly cold and forbidding under the shadow of Everest. It was nearly an hour after sunrise before the sun hit the west peak.

If I were offered just for a few minutes the use of a magic carpet that would take me to any part of the Himalayas, it is not to the top of Everest that I should bid it take me. It would be to the head of that lonely western cwm between the buttresses of Everest and Hlotse when the evening sun was pouring its warm light on the curtain that falls thousands of feet between them. The challenge to the spirit would not be new. It would be the same that came when I sat with Mallory and others below the buttresses of Chamber Court at Winchester, following them up to the patch of starry sky above, and changing them to other buttresses, it might be the Crestone Rey which we had climbed the summer before to the crest of Monte Rosa, to the ridge whence one looks through the gaps in the sea of cloud to the meadows of Macugnaga eleven thousand feet below. But the challenge, though still the same, would be given by the highest mountain in the world.

They could not enter the cwm; a hopeless precipice cut them off from it. They saw that the glacier born in the cwm was steep and difficult, approachable only from Nepal, and that the great precipices below the col between Everest and Hlotse were almost certainly beyond the power of men to climb. From a negative point of view what they saw was decisive.

There remained the exploration of the North Col from the west. In the last days of their stay by the West Rongbuk Glacier, Bullock ascended to the bay under the north wall of Everest and confirmed the earlier impression of a cloudy day that the approach to the col on this side was so steep, long, and difficult that it was essential to find out if the east side did not afford an easier way.

The reconnaissance from the north was all but ended. A couple of days were to be given to the exploration of what looked a quite

unimportant glacier, which discharged a meagre stream into the West
Rongbuk Glacier on the east side a couple of miles above its foot.
Luck was against them, for news came that the plates Mallory had
exposed had been put in back to front, and the two days were spent
in retrieving this disastrous mistake. The apparently unimportant
glacier was left unexplored, with the result that the direct route it
afforded to the east side of the North Col was not discovered till some
weeks later by a very roundabout approach from a base in the Kharta
valley, away to the east. Yet this latter approach gave a much-
needed refreshment to the eye after the week of solitude and savage
grandeur by the West Rongbuk Glacier. The Kama valley is overlooked by Everest and Hlotse, and also by Makalu, perhaps the most
spectacular of all the great mountains of the world; and at the same
time it is full of softer beauties, moving Mallory to say:

When all is said about Chomolungma, the Goddess Mother of the Snows,
and about Chomo Uri, the Goddess of the Turquoise Mountain, I come back
to the valley bed itself, the broad pastures, where our tents lay, where cattle grazed
and where butter was made, the little stream we followed up to the valley head,
wandering along its well-turfed banks under the high moraine, the few rare
plants, saxifrage, gentians, and primulas, so well watered there, and a soft, familiar
blueness in the air which even here may charm us. Though I bow to the
goddesses, I cannot forget at their feet a gentler spirit than theirs, a little shy
perhaps, but constant in the changing winds and variable moods of mountains
and always friendly.

There speaks a mountaineer who loved his mountain wholly,
unreservedly, not one who would separate the contemplative from
the acrobatic, the spiritual from the physical. And we may catch
with the words the gentle sigh of a man who is a little tired. For
nearly six weeks they had been living a strenuous life at heights
between 16,000 and 22,500 feet, and men accustomed to civilized
life at sea-level do not do that without experiencing a general strain
that calls for relaxation.

The view of the *arête* that falls nearly due east from the north-east
shoulder was sufficient to rule it out as a possible route to the summit.

The riddle of the approach to the North Col was still unsolved.
The Kama valley and the glacier at its head led up to the utterly
impossible east face of Everest, the North Col being hidden behind
the great north-east ridge. From a high point in the ridge separating
the upper Kama valley from the upper part of the Kharta Glacier,
they saw enough to confirm the fears that had been increasing in their
minds that it did not lead up to the North Col.

Disappointed, but too interested to be discouraged, they moved all the tents and baggage down the Kama valley and into the Kharta valley, for from the head of this valley some pass must lead over to the glacier below the elusive North Col.

It was on this day that Mallory describes himself as being conscious of unusual lack of condition. 'I felt for the first time a symptom of weariness beyond muscular fatigue and beyond the vague lassitude of mountain-sickness.'

When, a few days later, the camp was established high up the Kharta valley at 16,500 feet, Mallory was temporarily *hors de combat*.

The following comment on the situation by Mallory will show how he and Bullock had worked together.

The mystery must surely now be penetrated and the most important discovery of all be made. A competition with my companion for the honour of being first was, I hope, as far from my thoughts as ever it had been. From the start Bullock and I had shared the whole campaign and worked and made our plans together, and neither for a moment had envied the other the monopoly of a particular adventure. I confess that not to be in at the death after leading the hunt so long was a bitter expectation. But the hunt must not be stopped; and from the un-grateful comfort of my sleeping-bag, I waved farewell to Bullock.

Bullock went on up the main glacier to a col at its head, and returned still baffled. Major Morshead having joined the party and Mallory having recovered, the three of them went up a tributary glacier almost due east, and, after a most exhausting ascent in the hot glare of a thin mist, at last reached the gap called the Hlakpa La and looked across a level glacier floor towards the North Col. The ridge running east from the North Peak and shutting off the col from a northern approach was seen to be a myth; it was but a buttress of the North Peak. The glacier below them, the East Rongbuk Glacier, must, after all, find an exit into the Rongbuk valley.

The whole expedition is a most interesting example of Nature's use of the unexpected in her designing of mountains.

A route to the North Col and the only ridge of Everest that was humanly possible was now clear. Three weeks were spent at the base camp in the Kharta valley making preparation for an assault. The contrast between the effects on men's condition of several weeks of Himalayan and Alpine climbing is becoming clearer. In the Alps a man who gives himself a reasonable number of rest days between his expeditions becomes progressively fitter. This was far from being the case with the 1921 party, though none had yet reached an altitude of twenty-three thousand feet.

Three of our strongest coolies were ill at this camp; others seemed to be tired more easily than they should be. And what of the *sahibs*? At least it must be said that several of them were not looking their best. Bullock, though he never complained, seemed to be no longer the fit man he was at the end of July. And for my part I began to experience a certain lack of exuberance when going uphill . . . my reserve of strength had somehow diminished. The whole machine, in fact, was running down.

Those last words put the case exactly and later expeditions confirm them. While acclimatization proceeds at varying rates with different individuals, and as a rule more rapidly with men who have already been at high altitudes, there is a steady, slow, general deterioration which overtakes acclimatization after some weeks, and which seems to retard a man's recovery from big ascents to over twenty-seven thousand feet.

The one attempt on Everest was made as late as 24th September. The party had pushed up to the Hlakpa La on the 22nd, but the condition of the coolies and the difficulty of transport obliged all, except Mallory, Bullock, and Wheeler, to wait there or return to the Kharta valley. These three, with a few coolies, spent the night on the upper East Rongbuk Glacier, and reached the North Col next morning. The conditions of this slope of a thousand feet vary to a surprising extent. In 1921 the party go straight up, finding 'only one passage shortly below the col that caused either anxiety or trouble.' This consisted of deep snow lying at a very steep angle, in which they had to plough five hundred steps. In no other year has the col been reached in this simple fashion; Mallory himself had slept well, and felt capable of going a considerable distance up the easy rock and snow of the rounded ridge that rose to the north-east shoulder. Bullock, though tired, was by no means at the end of his tether. Wheeler was ready to try, but had no feeling in his feet. For a moment or two they faced the wind on the col, and what they saw, as much as what they felt, was decisive. The whole face above was covered in a rushing cloud of fine snow, driven across the ridge by a terrific wind and pouring down the leeward side. It would have been criminal folly to attempt to go on.

The wind, strong from the north-west, indicated that the monsoon conditions were ending; if those conditions temporarily returned, a snowfall might be expected. For this year Everest had shut the door to all visitors but wind and snow. The reconnaissance was over. To no future parties could the mountain offer the first wonderful revelation of its features and its character, and the secret of the approach.

Photography and the publication of the story of such expeditions spread interest and knowledge to thousands, but remove the peculiar attraction of the unknown which made this first expedition unique in the experience of its members.

The next year's expedition was a different story. Its whole aim was concentrated on one thing, the assault on Everest from the North Col. And though Everest had exposed her character, with her strength and her weakness, one great secret was still unsolved: could man climb at all at the height of that long ridge that rises from the north-east shoulder? No climber had ever yet reached twenty-five thousand feet. Experiments had shown men to be capable, when at rest, of supporting pressures corresponding to greater heights. Were they capable of prolonged exertion at greater heights? This was the great problem to be solved: if men were proved to be able to climb at all under such conditions, then sooner or later Everest would certainly be climbed.

Every Everest expedition stands on the shoulders of the one before. The problem is not to find better men, but to bring the picked men to the final assault, fresher, and provided with greater comfort and, if possible, nearer to the last day's work than before. The 1922 party was chosen with a view to the assault on the mountain, and it was worthy of the big thing it was attempting.

General Bruce was in command. His appearance alone was enough to warm the blood of any man, climber or coolie; he knew the Himalayas from many years spent among them; he had a great gift for getting the best out of a native, and, above all, he was a climber himself and could be trusted to see that the assaulting party had every possible assistance. His age made possible a self-denying ordinance which forbade him to advance beyond the base camp. His second-in-command in charge of the advanced base was Colonel Strutt, an experienced climber himself, and a man with great experience in dealing with all sorts and conditions of climbers. T. G. Longstaff combined in his person three valuable personalities: Himalayan expert, doctor, and naturalist. There were two other doctors in the party—not in their medical capacity—Somervell, whose Alpine record indicated him as a man likely to be a formidable antagonist for Everest, and Wakefield, who for some years held the Cumberland fell-walking record. Mallory was clearly a first choice for the final climbing-party. Bullock, who had never failed to produce any effort demanded in the Reconnaissance, had to resume his duties in the consular service, but George Finch, who was not quite fit to go in

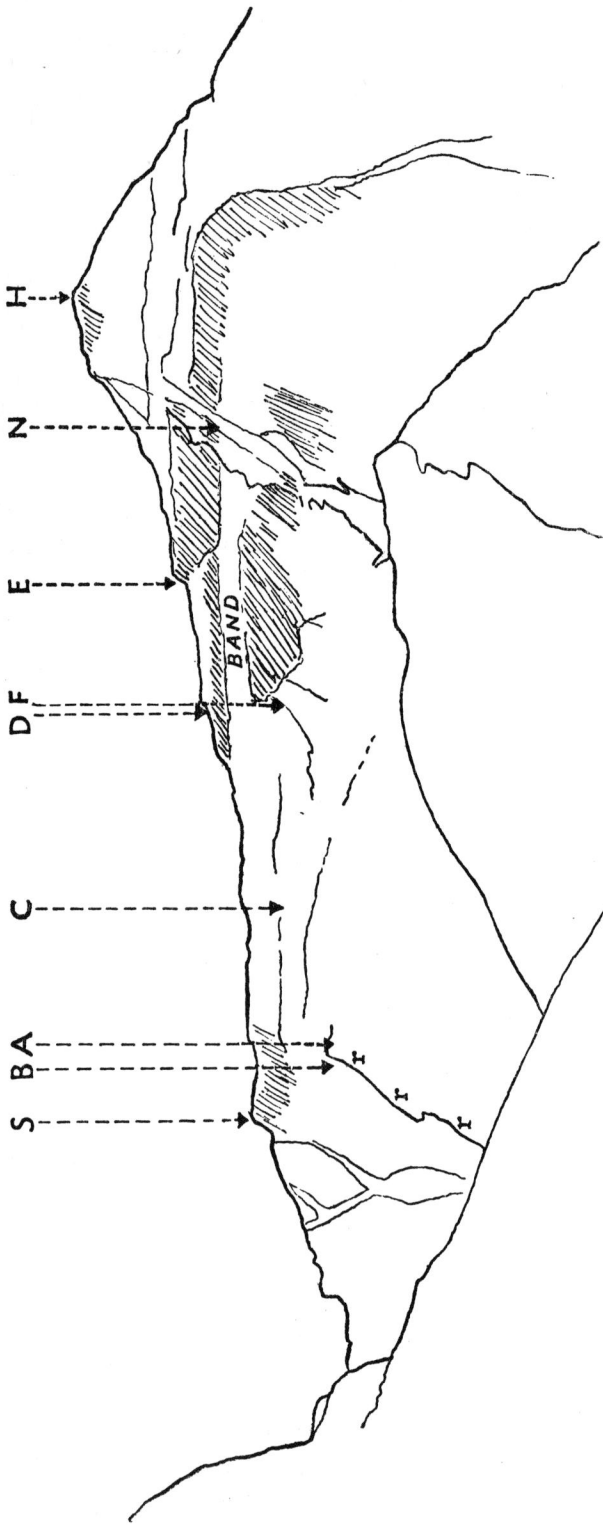

S North-east Shoulder.

r r r Route from North Col.

Various positions of Camp V near 25,500 ft. just out of sight below start of r r r.

A Point reached by Mallory, Norton, Somervell in 1922.

B Camp VI (1924) at about 26,700 feet.

C Camp VI (1933) at about 27,400 feet.

D First Step.

E Second Step.

F Point reached by Finch, Bruce in 1922.

N Point reached by Norton in 1924 and by Wyn Harris, Wager, Smythe in 1933.

H Highest Point of Everest.

BAND is the band of rock between the steep (shaded) cliffs followed by all who have reached N.

1921, was able to come, and he was the oxygen expert of the party. The Indian services provided some splendid material. Colonel E. F. Norton, a tall, slim climber with a specially slow pulse, who proved to be a first-rate choice; C. G. Crawford, an Indian civilian, who took part also in the 1933 expedition; and Major Morshead, who was in charge of the survey party in 1921 and who joined the 1922 party as a climber. One of the transport officers, Captain Geoffrey Bruce, without climbing experience, took part in one of the attempts on the mountain with oxygen.

The use of oxygen was a much-debated point. How far the great weight of the apparatus, over thirty pounds, would cancel the benefit derived from inhaling the contents; how far a sudden interruption of the oxygen supply might endanger a man's life at low pressures, and how far its use might affect his subsequent condition, these were questions that only actual experience could answer. That it might prove a valuable stimulant or restorative was an undeniable possibility, and it was therefore taken. Objections to its use as being against the true spirit of mountaineering were offered, but, as was to be expected in an undertaking of this kind, they were set aside. The excitement of a scientific experiment was added to the other attractions of climbing Everest.

Those who may sympathize with Mallory and others, who objected to the use of oxygen as being destructive of the objects for which men climb mountains, must remember that the business of the Everest Committee was to do everything to get climbers to the summit as easily and as safely as possible. When the conquest of Everest is the final end in view the only question we have to consider about the use of oxygen is: 'Will it help, or not?' There is quite a different question to settle if the climbing of a mountain is a means to some ulterior, less material end.

As was expected, the way up the East Rongbuk Glacier was found to provide a quick, direct approach to the North Col. Neither this 1922 expedition nor any of the succeeding ones have found the thousand-foot slope below the col as simple an undertaking as did the men of 1921, who climbed it late in September. Whatever the conditions, there can be little doubt that it must always be chosen in preference to the steep slope, over three thousand feet high, that falls on the western side.

The lower part of the slope was climbed by a steep fissure in the ice, where a rope was fixed to assist the porters. Tents were set up, well sheltered from the north-west wind, on a shelf below the col,

M

but the ice conditions are curiously variable here, and half an hour of climbing by a somewhat intricate route separated this camp from the point on the col where the ascent of the north-east ridge begins.

The oxygen apparatus was not in working order when this camp was ready on 19th May. A non-oxygen party went up to it on that day for the first great assault on Everest: Mallory, Norton, Somervell, and Morshead, with nine porters. Everything promised well. Here was a strong party, all fit and in excellent spirits, almost as snug at twenty-three thousand feet as they might have been in an Alpine hut. The weather omens were good; the day had been almost windless and the stars shone above them out of a black sky.

If only one could start refreshed with sleep, and as eager in spirit as when one goes to bed! Alas! it is never so a few hours later. To pass from a cosy bed to the chilly discomforts of dressing and the packing of food into one's inside or one's rucksack can be distasteful to us in the Alps; imagine what it must be before the sun has appeared on a snowy shelf at twenty-three thousand feet! The porters, having shut all the openings through which air could enter in the night, were nearly all ill, and all disinclined to move. Mallory tried to stimulate these inert, unhappy beings into activity while Norton prepared breakfast. Boots had been cuddled in the sleeping-bags, but not so the tins of spaghetti, whose contents had frozen hard enough to defy an axe. Precious time and precious hot water were consumed in thawing them.

Four porters only were sufficiently restored by breakfast to go on, and in a couple of hours the party was under way. In half an hour they were on the actual col and saw the ridge of Everest close at hand, offering an easy route towards the north-east shoulder. Along an edge of stones, at first loose, and higher up bound together with snow, they made good progress. The wind was giving them a respite; for once the air was calm. Then, when they had risen about twelve hundred feet, the respite ended. They halted, and all but Morshead put on their spare clothes. In jerking free the rope Mallory moved Norton's rucksack, which fell, carrying spare clothes and Mallory's pyjama legs down to the Rongbuk Glacier.

Soon the sun hid behind a grey cloud, and they were battling with the horrible wind that swept over the north face. It cut through everything, and to get some shelter Mallory turned to the left across a slope of hard snow. Crampons would have been ideal here for rapid progress, but they had not been brought; their use would have meant certain frostbite. The wind was such that it was essential to get away from its full force quickly. Cutting steps at twenty-five thousand feet, at any but the most deliberate rate, is exhausting, and after a three-hundred-foot staircase had been made and the party lay on the rocks, out of the wind, Mallory admits he was very tired.

Should they push on higher and try and reach twenty-six thousand feet before camping? The porters had to be sent down, and in the threatening weather there was danger in taking them higher, thus giving them greater height and less time for the descent. The necessity of ensuring their safety under the menace of a rising wind enforced a decision to pitch the tent in the best place they could find at their present height. And they were no longer the men they had been at the start. That terrible wind had made it certain that the summit could not be reached. Deadly cold, like a breath from the awful solitudes of space that surround the earth, it came down like a barrage to hold them off. Its effects were not realized till some hours later. Norton had an ear frostbitten that prevented his lying on that side. Morshead was severely chilled, and the serious frostbites in his fingers were due to its effects; even Mallory, who had been cutting steps at the greatest possible speed, had three finger-tips affected, simply from having exchanged a lined leather glove for a woollen one to get a better hold on his axe. Subsequent events have proved that the last four thousand feet of Everest are utterly beyond man's power to accomplish in a single day. Two camps between the North Col and the summit were regarded as the minimum in 1924 and 1933.

There is no good level place anywhere at this height to accommodate two tents comfortably. They were set up, some distance apart, Norton and Mallory in one, Somervell and Morshead in the other, one half of the floor on sloping rock, the other half on such a platform as could be built up with stones by weary men. It was an unrefreshing night. Sleeping-bags called double are pleasantly roomy for one, and mean confinement and the sharing of every movement for two. Deliberate hard breathing was necessary, and a sharp boulder pushed up deeper and deeper between Mallory's shoulder-blades. 'How under these circumstances we achieved sleep, and I believe that both of us were sometimes unconscious in a sort of light, intermittent slumber, I cannot attempt to explain.'

There was plenty to keep less tired men awake! The night before a big climb is often a wakeful one for a climber in the Alps. These four men were actually passing a night at a height greater than man had ever reached on foot, and were to attack the last defences of the highest mountain in the world. Providence has, after all, been kind in dulling man's mental faculties at such heights, otherwise sleep for the imaginative would be impossible. For they would be dull souls indeed who could feel no exultation at what had already been achieved; and the greatness of the immediate past, the present, and the hours to come were not entirely obliterated by the dulling lack of oxygen. ' "Hang it all," we cooed, "it's not so bad," ' is Norton's way of expressing it.

As objects became discernible in the light of morning, they saw that a thick mist had come around them, and that the rocks were white under a covering of fresh snow. At half-past six, surprisingly, a break in the right quarter appeared, and with it came the necessity for action. The start from the North Col had been bad; that they started at all from this higher camp is a testimony to the determina-tion of the men who spent the night there. They rose as tired as when they lay down, stiff and cramped with cold. As Mallory stumbled across with a load from one tent to another he asked himself: ' "Is it possible for me to go on?" Judging from physical evidence, No; I hadn't the power to lift my weight step after step. And yet from experience I knew that I should go on for a time at all events; something would set the machinery going and somehow I should be able to keep it at work.'

Another rucksack escaped from cold, fumbling fingers and was caught up on a rocky ledge a hundred feet below. It contained the day's provisions, more vital than spare clothes, and Morshead spent his last remaining strength in recovering it. Roping-up gave, as it rarely fails to give, the feeling of contact with bigger issues, of unfailing loyalty, and of a common aim which braces and unites a party who have learned to know each other well.

After only a few paces Morshead stopped and said quietly: 'I think I won't come with you any farther. I should only keep you back.' He assured them he could look after himself, and only needed rest, so they left him at the camp. The ridge was not difficult, no gymnastic feats were needed, no pulling up, no wedging in cracks; such efforts would have produced exhaustion immediately. A slow, steady pace, economizing every ounce of remaining strength, was the only way of maintaining progress. If the will kept the lungs working hard, the limbs almost automatically did what was required to lift the body and transfer the weight. Mallory got a foot dangerously cold from wearing four socks instead of three inside the boot; it was rubbed back to warmth by Norton, and with the circulation eased by the removal of a sock it remained warm throughout the day.

The soft snow, from four to eight inches deep, was not a serious hindrance; the rate of progress was nearly four hundred feet an hour. It was soon realized that even if this rate was kept up the summit was unattainable that day. Without discussion, the idea of getting back to Morshead in time to take him down to camp on the North Col was accepted as governing the limit of time they could allow themselves before turning back. It is just one more instance of the example this splendid party gave of the considerations that should determine such decisions. Half-past two was the limit fixed, and at quarter past two, having just surmounted a steeper pitch and emerged on to easier ground, they halted to rest and try to eat before facing the descent.

They were not at the end of their tether; any climber who goes on till he reaches that condition high up on Everest is inviting disaster. They were able to take in something of the view. The North Peak had become an insignificant fellow almost beneath notice, the great Chö Uyo to the west only touched the horizon, and told them they must be at nearly twenty-seven thousand feet. The dinner courses, swallowed with difficulty by parched throats, were sugar in various forms or raisins and prunes. There was no trickle from the dry powdery snow that overlay the stones. Medical opinion had uttered stern warnings against the use of alcohol, whence Mallory concluded that the nips of brandy they took can have contained no alcohol, for its effects were altogether good, giving just the fillip needed for the long descent.

They reached Morshead in an hour and a half. Another descent of two thousand feet, free from difficulty, would take them to the North Col, and they had still three hours of daylight left. But they were tiring, and Morshead was a sick man, almost exhausted. These slopes of the north ridge are easy enough to a fit, experienced climber, and yet steep enough to make an unchecked slip fatal. Mallory was leading down the upper edge of a snow slope on the eastern side of the ridge. The third man on the rope slipped while the last man was unprepared for a shock, and both began sliding down the face. The second man was pulled off when the rope tightened. Mallory was moving when the slip occurred; he heard enough to realize what had happened and in a moment had driven the pick into the snow and passed the rope over it. Holding the rope behind the axe in his right hand while he pressed on the pick, he waited for the shock. The second man was checked on some rocks, and the full weight of the three men falling did not come on the rope in one shock. The bodies, swinging round, tightened the rope in the critical instant, and pick, rope, and Mallory held firm. It must have been a very near thing. From one of the bodies came a violent expression of disgust at the prospect of having to climb up again!

A little lower Morshead's strength gave out. Supported by Norton's shoulder and an arm round his waist he dragged himself along somehow towards the col. Darkness had fallen, for the pace could only be terribly slow. An edge of stones showing against the snow gave them a line to follow almost to the col, and the wind, as if in breathless admiration of what was done that day, made no attempt to hinder them, even letting them light a candle with a Japanese match. Below them on the ledge, within a couple of hundred yards, were the tents where they pictured all possible comforts for tired bodies and craving appetites. And those two hundred yards among crevasses and ice-cliffs kept them groping their way with weary limbs and frozen fingers till half-past eleven, when they could say at last 'Thank God' at the entrance to the tents.

Alas! the boilers had been taken down that day; there was nothing in which to melt snow, and without a drink nothing solid could be swallowed. A sickly mess of frozen condensed milk and jam was hacked out and passed for strawberry ice. A very few hours later the weary descent was continued to the haven of Camp III.

The great remaining problem of Everest had been solved. Men had climbed without oxygen almost to twenty-seven thousand feet, and they were men who deserved success. Great mountaineers, and greatest of all in the spirit in thich they carried out their climb.

At the foot of the North Col they met Finch preparing to start with Geoffrey Bruce for a second attempt, this time with oxygen. Their highest camp was pitched about five hundred feet higher than that of the first party, but still, as we now know, not high enough to give them a chance of reaching the summit. The wind blew very hard, and all next day they stayed in their tent. In the afternoon the wind had fallen, and porters arrived, bringing thermos flasks of hot drink sent by Captain Noel, whose enthusiasm for photography kept him for four days on the North Col. Though it was six o'clock when these men arrived, they went down the same evening unescorted to the col; it sounds a risky performance in view of the experiences of the first party descending from the peak.

During the second night in the high camp, Bruce, Finch, and Tejbir, a particularly good porter who was to carry oxygen next day, took oxygen, and by Finch's account derived great benefit from it. Next morning Tejbir, carrying reserves of oxygen, collapsed at twenty-six thousand feet and was sent back to the high camp visible only a few hundred feet below.   Finch and Bruce struggled on up the ridge another five hundred feet and then began to traverse the north face, hoping to find more shelter from the icy blasts, a hope that seems unduly optimistic in view of Finch's own reason for pitching his camp on the ridge itself, that 'a wind is felt more severely on the windward side of a ridge than on the crest.'   The fact is that on a mountain more than elsewhere the wind 'bloweth where it listeth,' and a spot that is sheltered one minute may be detestable with whirling snow-particles the next.

The rocks of the north face slope outwards, forming a series of sloping ledges and steeper pitches separating them, which in most places are easily climbed or circumvented.   Bruce, the inexperienced, gave to his expert leader reassuring evidence of his security upon them and they went unroped.   After traversing the face, making height very slowly, they began to climb up more directly towards the ridge. An accident to Bruce's apparatus cut off his supply of oxygen.   None of the dire results predicted in England followed.   He climbed up to meet Finch and the latter was equal to the emergency, connecting Bruce to his own cylinders while repairs were carried out.

Chö Uyo was now well below them; only the peak of Everest itself rose less than half a mile away and some seventeen hundred feet above them.   But they had reached their limit.   After two nights and a day in the storm-swept tent, they had shown wonderful courage to start at all.   By two o'clock they had reached the north-east ridge again, taking a higher line than in ascending, and there they dumped four cylinders.   A blessed relief it must have been when one of these five-pound weights could be sent clattering down the face.   The wind had fallen when they found Tejbir fast asleep in all three sleeping-bags at the high camp.   Porters could be heard coming up from the camp below to bring down the party, so Tejbir was left to descend with them.   Finch and Bruce came on as fast as they could and reached the comforts of Camp III on the level glacier the same night.

The case for oxygen was helped, but not proved.   The height climbed from the highest camp was about the same in each attempt, the degree of exhaustion we may assume to have been greater rather than less, for the oxygen party turned back because they could go no farther, not because they had reached the extreme limit of time. It is true that Finch and Bruce experienced a bad wind at their high camp.   We know that it moderated sufficiently for porters to come up and descend again on the day that was spent in that camp, and

Finch himself tells us that on the second night, after taking oxygen, they 'slept well and warmly.' Their condition at starting for the final climb after such a night would compare favourably with that of the non-oxygen party. If Morshead had been well and had needed no assistance in descending, the non-oxygen party might have maintained their rate of descent and reached Camp IV or even Camp III before dark.

The subsequent condition of the climbers, too, is interesting. Norton's heart was strained, and he was frostbitten, though not severely. Morshead, owing to failure to put on spare clothes, was severely frostbitten and Bruce rather severely. Finch made a bad recovery, and was quite unfit for a second attempt after a week's rest. Only Mallory and Somervell of the men who had been high on the mountain were fit for another try. They and Crawford started with fourteen porters for the North Col on 7th June, more than a fortnight after the previous attempts. Much snow had fallen and the going was very heavy. The three climbers took turns in treading out the deep track up the slopes below the North Col to ease the work for the laden porters. When Mallory's turn came he tells us: 'I found the effort at each step so great that no method of breathing I had formerly employed was adequate; it was necessary to pause after each lifting movement for a whole series of breaths.'

And then, six hundred feet below the camp, on the easy slope of a corridor that slanted up towards it, with the sun shining and the air calm, the catastrophe happened. A sound 'like that of untamped gunpowder' startled them, the nature of which was unfamiliar but only too easily guessed, and in a moment the snow began to crumple and seethe about them, and they were carried down. The experiences of men who survive such avalanches are very similar. Mallory says: 'I began to move slowly downwards, inevitably carried on the whole moving surface by a force I was utterly powerless to resist. For a second or two I seemed hardly to be in danger as I went quietly sliding down with the snow. Then the rope at my waist tightened and held me back. A wave of snow came over me and I was buried. I supposed that the matter was settled.'

The avalanche slowed down and stopped without producing great pressure; he found his arms free and his legs near the surface and he had little difficulty in extricating himself. Somervell, Crawford, and the porter next Mallory emerged also, all of them unhurt. Not so all the roped parties of porters. Four had been carried farther and had had the same wonderful escape. They had extricated themselves and were pointing to where the others had been carried over an ice-cliff. The survivors hurried round below it and did all that was possible to rescue the buried men. Two were dug out, one of them after being buried head downwards for forty minutes, and both lived, in fact were able to walk down to Camp III. The fate of the others was only too plain. It was a genuine accident; none of the three climbers in charge, with their considerable experience of snow conditions, had reason to expect danger on such a slope.

It was a tragic ending to the expedition of 1922.

In spite of this calamity, regarded by Tibetans as a vengeance of the gods for the violation of their sacred abodes, porters were found ready to 'go high' again in 1924. Mallory was to take up a new post at Cambridge that promised to give him just the sort of work he wanted. He was pressed to go on this third expedition, and he went. I am sure that he would have been well content if Everest had been left alone. The thrilling voyage of discovery in 1921 had removed the attraction of mystery from the adventure. The great climb to twenty-seven thousand feet in 1922 had solved the question whether Everest was too high for men to climb. It remained only to be seen whether another intense effort would be sufficiently helped by a combination of favourable circumstances, a reasonably late monsoon, greater comforts, especially in the camps, the possibility of getting porters to a still higher camp, to make it possible to finish off the last two thousand feet. Men hate to refuse an appeal to share adventure, and the climbing of Everest was a thing to which Mallory had put his hand, and which he was exceptionally fitted to carry through. The one who would suffer most by his going knew what mountains meant to him and had too great a heart to hold him back.

Somervell was there again, his vigour only just less wonderful than in 1922 after working in a medical mission in the heat of Travancore. Norton, too, was able to come, and when General Bruce came under the doctor's ban on the journey through Tibet, he knew how fortunate he was in having such a man to take over the command. Beetham, Somervell's companion in Alpine campaigns crowded with victories, Hazard, and Odell, all splendid goers on a mountain, joined the party for their first call on Everest. Geoffrey Bruce and Sandy Irvine, officially staff officer and handyman, were unofficially men to be specially chosen to climb at the highest altitudes.

The demons of Everest were roused by this third expedition to special fury. Very low temperatures with wind and snow made the conditions at the lower camps so severe that, when the way to Camp

IV by the North Col was established, the strength of the assaulting party had been grievously taxed. Nevertheless, more elaborate provision for the climbers' comfort, more doses of firmness and persuasion to the porters to get them to carry up equipment for a higher camp, produced their expected effect, and the assault was pushed many hundred feet nearer to the summit. Indeed, we do not know certainly, we may never know, whether the cross of victory our hearts have raised to Mallory and Irvine should be placed by materialists at twenty-eight thousand or twenty-nine thousand feet. Does it really matter?

On the 1924 expedition it was decided that the final assaults, from a camp placed as high as twenty-seven thousand feet or over, should be delivered by parties of only two climbers. For the purpose of getting at least one climber to the top of Everest, it is clearly the plan that offers most prospect of success, for it means that the rate of progress may be that of the fastest man, if we accept the idea that a climber is to be trusted to return to camp by himself when symptoms of exhaustion show themselves. There is no need to dwell on the extra risks involved, which are very different for men at twenty-eight thousand feet near the limits of endurance and for men on a holiday rock-climb in the Alps. The only fatal accident to a climbing-party on the upper part of Everest has happened to a party of two. The accounts of the 1924 and 1933 expeditions show the risks run by exhausted men returning unsupported by one or more companions.

The first attempt, when the weather fiends ceased from their worst cruelties at the end of May, was made by Mallory and Geoffrey Bruce, and was stopped at the camp at twenty-five thousand feet by the impossibility of getting the porters to go higher with the tents for the camp above, though Bruce had much of his namesake's influence over them. The wind had been very bad indeed, and had taken the heart out of them. Norton and Somervell followed, and nothing shows better Norton's exceptional qualifications to direct as well as carry out these assaults upon the mountain than his success, on the chill early morning of 3rd June, when he persuaded the unwilling native porters to go higher still with the tents and set them up at a height of very nearly twenty-seven thousand feet. Once they have gone to that height and been spared by the ill-tempered gods, they will go again. It is terror of the unknown as much as physical distress that holds them back.

And now Everest produced his last and unexpected line of defences in bands of rock offering serious difficulties, even to climbers full of oxygen. Nothing is easier than to underestimate the difficulty of a small portion of a generally easy face, especially when it is looked at from below and at a distance which disguises the difference of level. It is, on the other hand, common to overestimate difficulties from above, and this would be done by the airmen, even when they did not mistake Makalu for Everest.

The nature of the final climbing difficulties to be surmounted by a party starting from the North Col are easily understood. The features of the upper part of the mountain that matter most are:

(1) The small final pyramid of six or seven hundred feet, which will, I believe, prove more difficult to climb than has hitherto been supposed. Photographs show that it should be climbable, either by a traverse of its north face at about 28,400 feet and an ascent to the very last portion of the north-west ridge, or by its east ridge, which is steep enough to make heavy demands on a leader if he prefers the snow to the rocks just north of it.

(2) The bands of rock that prevent easy access to the foot of the final pyramid. Two bands of dark rock run across the north face at about twenty-eight thousand feet, just above a broad belt of less steep yellowish rock that provides ledges where progress is hampered by the condition of the climber rather than by the difficulties he encounters. These dark bands meet the long north-east ridge at the two steep rises known as the First and Second Steps; the latter, which is the section of the broader band, is now known to be a very formidable obstacle.

(3) A long, shallow couloir formed where the whole upper part of the north face (of the final pyramid and the face below it) is thrust forward. The couloir is very well marked in all views of Everest from the north. Where it cuts across the above-mentioned bands of dark rock, these latter are interrupted, and here is the obvious place to try to pass them. It will be seen, however, that the couloir runs almost straight up the face, and that in consequence its wall, facing nearly east between the interrupted portions of the north face, is at a high angle, much higher than that of the north face below the bands, so that climbing becomes far more dangerous directly the axis of the couloir is passed. Hence the arrest of Norton in 1924, and of Wyn Harris, Wager, and Smythe in 1933, just at this point.

The human machine, like a child of independent character, likes to show it knows its business better than those who study it most. The physiologists had doubted whether man could exist at all for hours at twenty-five thousand feet, and at the camp near twenty-seven thousand feet Norton, without any breathing apparatus except that supplied by Nature, records: 'Spent the best night I have had since Camp I.'

Of the alternative routes to the foot of the final pyramid, by the ridge or by a traverse below the dark rock bands to the couloir, Norton chose the latter, and as regards the avoidance of extreme difficulty he was probably right. At a height of twenty-eight thousand feet, close to the couloir, Somervell, racked by a cough caused by the extreme dryness of the air, had to stop. Norton went on alone, the difficulties increasing as he got farther west, and entered the couloir, where he was stopped on its farther wall. Apart from the snow that lay loose upon the rocks, the climbing had become dangerous, and it is sufficient proof of the strain upon a man climbing alone on such ground that Norton called to Somervell for a rope to assure his return over ground that he had traversed with ease just after leaving him. The climbing of the far wall of this couloir alone, where the ledges take a wicked downward slope, where a man is lost if his balance or nerve fail him for an instant, is a test to which I should be sorry to challenge any friend of mine, when I know he cannot rely on the normal sources of energy that are mysteriously directed into action by the mind. The will may force the nerves to bear the strain up to their limit, but it cannot make them do more, and the will itself, as Norton and Mallory have both told us, is lessened at this height. Whether will and nerves are really one or mutually dependent on each other are questions the psychologists and the physiologists can try to settle for themselves. The combined effect of strain and altitude actually shown in a man's altered power to control his movements is what concerns us here.

In spite of a cough that threatened at times to choke Somervell, the North Col was reached that night. From the tents below they were seen and heard on the col, and when oxygen was sent up, Norton shouted down: 'We don't want the d—d oxygen, we want drink!' Both he and Somervell had a dose of oxygen and say they found little benefit from it, but were quite fit to go on without it, and reached Camp IV at 9.30. Next day Norton was led back to Camp III suffering from snow-blindness.

These two having failed, though failing gloriously, Mallory decided to try once more. Two men were now thoroughly fit and able to go with him, Odell and Irvine. He chose Irvine on the ground that they were to carry oxygen, and that, besides having a thorough knowledge of its workings, he had great confidence in its utility; and this Odell had not, having himself derived little benefit from its use. And if a boundless enthusiasm and unselfishness, and a wonderful supply of vital energy, were a claim to a place in the assaulting party, then Irvine had more than made good his claim. I cannot banish a regret that Odell, a first-rate man from every mountaineering point of view, was not with Mallory, but the serious climbing difficulties of Everest were not realized. Mallory has pulled novices up slabs on Lliwedd which they were quite unable to climb unaided, where there was good security against any strain and the need for saving time was absent. On Everest it is different.

Mallory and Irvine never returned. It is very unlikely that they died from exhaustion and exposure, for both would not succumb to exhaustion simultaneously, and the only hope for the exhausted man would be for the other to descend for help. It is far more likely that a slip occurred. Mallory knew from Norton that the lower route presented serious difficulties after reaching the couloir; it would confirm his own natural preference for the ridge. What happened is a secret that may one day be disclosed, if they fell down the north face on to the West Rongbuk Glacier. If they perished of exposure, it will not be known till the north-east ridge is climbed, and that may well be neither the first nor the second time men reach the summit.

They spent the night of 6th June with porters at Camp V, whence they dispatched a note saying: 'There is no wind here, and things look promising.' On the 7th they went on up to Camp VI, and Odell followed up to Camp V. In the evening the porters descending from Camp VI brought a note from Mallory apologizing for the mess left at Camp V, telling Odell to be sure of getting back to Camp IV in time to leave it next night, as they hoped to do themselves, and ending with the words: 'We'll probably go on two cylinders, but it's a —— —— load for climbing. Perfect weather for the job!'

Next day Odell strolled—there is no other word for it—up to Camp VI, a feat accomplished with such ease that it is hard to appreciate the significance it has on the possibilities of acclimatization in special individuals. The early morning was clear, but mist gathered before midday. From a crag about half-way between Camp V and Camp VI he got a view, during a temporary clearance, of the ridge and final pyramid. On a snow slope below a rocky step a tiny dark object moved up towards the step. A second object followed. The first object climbed to the top of the step, then the curtain of cloud hid them from view.

The height and difficulty of the Second Step, seen from close at hand by members of the 1933 expedition and described as 'rising smooth and unbroken for a hundred feet like the bows of a battle-cruiser,' dispose of the possibility of its being the rocky step Odell saw climbed so quickly. I have no doubt at all that what Odell saw was the two climbers and not, as was actually suggested, a couple of birds. They seem to have been climbing one at a time, and the presumption therefore is that they were roped. The lateness of the hour, 12.50, indicates a delayed start due to defects in the apparatus or to unexpected difficulties on the rocks. These two are the only men who may have reached the crest of the ridge above the First Step. Wyn Harris and Shipton reached its foot in 1933, and, from the view they had of the Second Step, they concluded it was so formidable as to rule out any attempt before trying the lower route. On their return after being stopped in the couloir, they again came to the First Step and had not strength left to attempt it.

I can well picture Mallory, even in that thin air that barely keeps the fires of energy aglow, responding to the challenge of the Second Step. Were there ever so many voices urging a man to accept that challenge? This is the last chance of carrying out what you came these thousands of miles to do. Once above this step, the way is open to the final pyramid. Few places are more likely to drive a man to the extreme limit of what he can climb than a difficult step upon what is regarded as an easy mountain. Mallory's balance was so good that he was accustomed to move on slabs, where the slightest mistake would mean a fall, as if they were level ground; he seemed to have no consciousness how small the margin of safety was.

Of all the possibilities, two are more likely than others: either that he fell in a supreme effort to pass this Second Step, or that Irvine slipped on the slabs before they reached it. An inexperienced climber is either too timid or over-confident, so that he does not know when he is insecure. A man like Sandy Irvine, eager to do everything to help and nothing to hinder or to delay his leader, is loath to answer the question: 'Are you all right there?' with anything but an emphatic affirmative. A slip, even supposing a man is ready for it, is a serious thing on outward-sloping rocks, and it must be borne in mind that the saving of time had become essential to success and would urge them to move as far as possible together. You cannot send men upon a great adventure and expect them, when the goal is almost won, to turn back from the risks that must be taken to achieve success. You cannot escape all responsibility for a tragic ending to an

exhausting and dangerous undertaking by telling them to be careful.
It is true, literally, that Mallory was never *asked* to make this last attempt,
just as a man brought up for organizing cock-fighting might truly say
after putting a particularly game bird in the pit: 'I never induced
it to fight.'

By all means let us encourage men to go on their own responsibility
to climb the Himalayas and any other mountains, but do not let us
set the ring for them as we have begun to do. Our great footballers,
our great cricketers, have become public entertainers, and we must
accept the fact. Mountaineering is altogether unfitted to follow such
a trend. This is what my personal feeling has always been, and now
the sense of personal loss by Mallory's death has strengthened the
feeling. Forgive me, reader, if its expression offends you. If the
climbing of the last thousand feet of Everest will confer the benefits
upon humanity that are claimed, then the measure of responsibility
which falls on those who initiate these expeditions, with their inevitable
dangers to the health and life of the men who lead the attack, is an
honourable burden.

The temptation to any climber to go on one of these expeditions is
immense. Self-abnegation must have won a hard victory over desire
when Odell declined the invitation of the Everest Committee in
1933. The results of that expedition may have softened his regrets.
It was admirably organized and led by Mr. Hugh Ruttledge. The
men to climb the last stage, and the equipment, were as good as it
was possible to obtain. Bad weather, as in 1924, delayed the establishment of camps and, but for careful husbanding of their energies,
would have seriously diminished the powers of the leading climbers.

Two parties were able to make a start from a camp at 27,400 feet
about 400 yards east of the First Step. That such a camp could be
established at all and used as a starting-point would have seemed an
impossible dream to the members of the first expedition in 1921.
It is a result, not of the increased capacity of the climbers, but of the
greater supply and wise use of human and other material and of
experience. The porters who had carried up the equipment were
escorted back by Longland, whose achievement in bringing them
safely down to the North Col in a blizzard is alone sufficient to mark
him as a great mountaineer as well as a very expert climber.

Wyn Harris and Wager, having decided after a close inspection
of the Second Step against the ridge route, traversed almost horizontally into the couloir and were stopped at the point reached by
Norton and already described. It was not exhaustion; it was the

difficult nature of the rocks and lack of time to allow of a safe return from the summit, supposing it could be reached, that turned them back. The difficulty of the rock may be inferred from the need they felt to assure themselves once more of the greater difficulty of the ridge route.

During a fresh reconnoitring of the ridge route on their way back to Camp VI, an ice-axe was found lying loose on a sloping slab. It is no proof that its owner, either Mallory or Irvine, fell with it, for a climber at such a height, to whom every economy of strength is necessary, would have no inducement to recover it in order to follow a leader along a rocky ridge.

An attempt to climb the First Step was now beyond their severely taxed energies, though Wager managed to drag himself up to the ridge below it and look down the terrible precipices of the south-east face.

Next day Smythe and Shipton, who had come up to Camp VI, were held prisoners there by a snowfall, and after a second night decided to go straight for the couloir. Shipton had had a poor night, and was forced to turn back while he still had strength to reach camp. Between Camp VI and Camp V he almost fell, letting himself down from a ledge on to snow that slipped from under him, and later, when a sudden wind sprang up, it must have been by the narrowest margin that he escaped alive. Smythe reached the difficult ground in the couloir at ten o'clock, and an hour later he had covered fifty feet of rock. The extra danger of fresh snow, on rocks that would need most careful climbing when dry, was an emphatic warning of the folly of going on, and he went back to spend a third night at Camp VI. He passed an excellent night, he tells us, slept for thirteen hours in spite of a wind strong enough to pile snow against his tent, and later strong enough to blow him off his feet coming down to Camp V. Great virtue is there in a slow pulse when it comes to passing a night at over twenty-seven thousand feet. Smythe and Norton are walking and sleeping examples of it!

The monsoon had announced its approach. A coat of white that thickened every day covered the only climbable rocks of Everest, and watching it the expedition had no choice but to accept defeat. It was a most gallant attempt, well planned and carried out by great mountaineers whose splendid co-operation, thoroughness, and wonderful endurance were worthy of a great success. Almost all of them suffered from the strain with temporarily dilated hearts or frostbite in varying degrees, and recovery is slow. Ruttledge himself says, even

after several days given to recuperating at lower altitudes in hope that the weather would still permit another attempt:

We soon discovered that it is difficult to stage 'come-backs' on Everest; for Wager, Harris, and Longland suffered from sleeplessness at Camp III, and would not have been really fit for action even had the opportunity arisen. Smythe and Shipton seemed pretty fit, but it was obvious that every one had lost a good deal of weight, and I think that even these two would have suffered severely had they gone really high again.

If the expedition did not succeed in pushing the attack beyond the point reached in 1924, it has done much to prove what is the most favourable line for the next attack, and to show more clearly the difficulties it will have to face. The traverse and couloir is indicated as the route on which to concentrate, for the north-east ridge is far narrower and more difficult than was supposed. Photographs of the ground where the final attack was stopped show that a traverse lower down will provide an easier way of reaching a steep subsidiary couloir filled in almost any weather conditions with continuous snow. The ascent of this snow—and from the lower traverse it will be quite four hundred feet before easy ground is reached—will be laborious and dangerous, for the snow lies at a high angle and it can have no sure adhesion to the rock, a hard surface on the snow here being due not to melting but to wind, and underneath it may be incoherent powder. Even when this bad place is passed, Everest may have a difficult pitch of fifty feet to hold off invaders from the very highest crest.

If the climbing of Everest is, as we have been told, an important stage in the victory of mind over matter, then let every conceivable method be adopted to ensure success. Let dynamite be taken to excavate a better platform for the tents at the highest camps; let the climbers be in sufficient numbers to be always at hand to help an exhausted man; let pitons be taken, cables fixed, and oxygen dumped at various points. It is by these mechanical inventions that the superstitious terrors of the natives will be destroyed, far more than by any sacrifice of life or health. And let everything possible be done to facilitate the ascent of future parties; otherwise there will be an appearance of withholding from others the benefits that an ascent of Everest confers.

I have to admit that I am less optimistic than the initiators of the Everest expeditions as to the benefits that will accrue when the object of the committee is attained, and the first ascent of the highest mountain in the world is an accomplished fact. The most obvious good, we

N

are told, is an increased knowledge of our own capacities. Our own? Certainly those that did not know the men before will have an increased knowledge of the capacities of Mallory, Norton, Smythe, and other splendid champions of mountaineering. But my experience as a schoolmaster has made me less sure of the benefit of this vicarious glory won by champions. The winning of laurels by one or two specially gifted performers may, I am afraid, be an induce-ment to others to rest upon them, and not to go and win new laurels for themselves. When a man in a comfortable arm-chair reads of these heroic feats on Everest, he may simply assert his own confidence in the superiority of mind over matter by ordering a glass of distilled liquor or by turning on an electric stove, with the reflection: 'Well! It's not my fancy,' or: 'By Jove! What fine fellows we Englishmen are!' Or he may—and let us hope it is a frequent case—regard it as a call to be up and doing something—something that means long and strenuous effort. I am doubtful, however, whether the actual ac-complishment of the last thousand feet, with its sense of completion of a long and difficult job, will stir him to the latter alternative more than any heroic attempt that fails.

And do we destroy nothing by using all this mass of men and material to conquer Everest? Mallory, after a catalogue extending to some forty lines of the various items in the vast collection of stores and equipment carried across Tibet, concludes:

When I call to mind the whole begoggled crowd moving with slow determina-tion over the snow and up the mountain slopes, and with such remarkable persistence bearing up the formidable loads; when after the lapse of months I envisage the whole prodigious evidences of this vast intention, how can I help rejoicing in the yet undimmed splendour, the undiminished glory, the unconquered supremacy of Mount Everest?

That sentiment, savouring of heresy to certainly one past member of the Everest Committee, expresses such a fundamental attitude to mountains and is so exactly what I have always felt myself, that the manner of Mallory's introduction to the Alps may be, in part at least, responsible. When Saussure climbed Mont Blanc, hardly a peak of the Alps had been measured or ascended; the pleasures to be found above the snowline were unsuspected and only slowly realized. There have been many expeditions to the Himalayas that have revealed its beauties; there is no mountain scenery in the world more impressive than that which Conway and Sella pictured for us after their expeditions to the Karakoram range. The conquest of a famous peak that has cost men dearly and won them fame is often a proof of the finish of a great age of growth rather than its beginning. The conquest of the Matterhorn is of that kind.

Everest will be conquered by just the very thing in which the present age excels, the skill to use the material things that Nature has provided. And the importance attached to the actual subjuga-tion of the peak is an indication of the extent to which men have come to measure all progress by material results, and have temporarily discarded any spiritual determination of values. They may be right in doing so, and those may be wrong who refuse to do so. There is a moral value discernible in any great persistent effort, and the men who climb Everest are the very men who already possess the moral virtues that mountaineering fosters. They have stood the severest of tests magnificently. Men will always love to see a great test, especially when the instrument may break under the strain, but when men's lives are at stake and when we are dealing with what is, in the very best sense, a recreation, the testing had better be left entirely to the individuals themselves.

In 1929 and 1931, while permission for another Everest expedition was withheld, a Bavarian party under Dr. Bauer performed on the great ice ridge of Kanchenjunga what is certainly the greatest feat, as regards technical achievement, in the history of mountaineering. These expeditions also were subsidized, more than half the cost being paid by the German and Austrian and the Munich Academic Alpine Clubs.

Kanchenjunga does not, like Everest, reserve its beauties for those who have toiled over high passes and wind-swept plateaux to reach it. In clear weather it unveils its splendours to any strollers in the crowd that is carried up to Darjeeling. And it makes no secret of the fact that none but the very brave can hope to conquer it. As in the case of Everest, a long ridge running north from the summit at a small general angle suggests the line for the final attack. But whereas the north ridge of Everest is reached in a single day from the level glacier below, to reach the ridge of Kanchenjunga is one of the biggest problems that have ever faced a climber. Dr. Bauer's party chose the only route that can commend itself to good mountaineers, and weeks of hard, dangerous work were done upon it before a successful solution of the problem was in sight. This route lies up a great spur, which leaves the main north ridge at a little over twenty-six thousand feet and runs down in a snowy crest, where powdery snow and altitude are the climber's worst adversaries, for four thousand feet, then plunges, first in a sharp, steep, broken edge for three thousand feet, and then in furrowed stone-swept precipices to the upper level of the Zemu Glacier.

One good look at this spur would have ruled it out at once as a route if any other had been possible. There is no other for men whose judgment is sound. Only one serious attempt by another route has been tried. This was in 1930, when an expedition of international character, which included Mr. F. S. Smythe, as climber and photographer and correspondent of *The Times,* having received permission to enter Nepal, attacked the mountain from the north-west. A great wall of hanging glacier, rock, and ice, on which the danger of avalanches is written in fearful and unmistakable signs, rose above the party encamped on the upper part of the Kanchenjunga Glacier. On the wall were three terraces. To reach the lowest of these, ice-work of the most exacting kind, with ice-pitons, was necessary, and was carried out with great skill and reckless daring under constant menace from above. Porters were being brought up in the hope of establishing a camp on the terrace, when the inevitable avalanche fell. By a miracle only one of the party, a porter, Chetin, perhaps the best who ever carried a load in the Himalayas, was crushed and killed. It is indefensible to take porters into an obvious death-trap of this kind.

This 1930 expedition then tried the north-west ridge itself. A first step, a pinnacle three hundred feet high, showed the brilliant crags-manship of one of the German climbers and the futility of continuing the attempt. It was unfortunate that M. Kurz, a Swiss member of the party, was detained by illness in the base camp, so that the party were deprived of his counsel on the spot.

To return to the Bavarians in 1929. From the advanced base, Camp VI, at over sixteen thousand feet, a way was forced through the ice-fall to the upper snow basin, and the serious difficulties began. Camp VII, called 'the Eyrie,' was reached by climbing in which judgment and skill could minimize but not avoid perpetual dangers from falling rocks. Only in the early mornings was it possible to traverse the slopes below in comparative safety.

It came about two or three times that a descending party was still on the march at midday. On these occasions it was like being under shell-fire. Boulders a cubic metre in size whistled, roared, and thundered down, bursting as they struck, like glass, into a thousand pieces. Any one who failed to keep absolutely cool, recognizing by the sound what was going to hit him and what was going wide, was lost indeed.

Despite most careful planning of the route, Dr. Bauer admits: 'It was just the wings of chance that enabled us to traverse these slopes without accident.'

Above the Eyrie for three thousand feet the ridge presented such a succession of new and fearful obstacles that it is amazing its ascent was even attempted. Any party of experienced climbers looking at it would have said: 'It would take weeks to cut up it.' And they would have been perfectly right; it did take weeks, but Bauer and his men did it.

A section of the ridge would have given a triangle with sides nearly double the base; you need not be a geometrical genius to infer that the slopes that fell from the crest were of appalling steepness. The edge was broken into a series of vertical steps, some of them 250 feet in height. There were no bare ice slopes, the core of rock was everywhere buried under fantastic formations, built of icicles and *névé*, towers piled one on another, vertical flutings, entire curtains of ice hanging from the cornices, pinnacles which could only be passed by tunnelling, and enormous growths like mushrooms. Many hundreds of cubic metres of ice were hacked away before the porters could pass these strange monsters of the air that had settled on the ridge. It took thirteen days of the hardest work, from 13th to 25th September, to push a track up past Camp VIII at 20,700 feet to Camp IX at 21,700 feet. Above Camp IX the angle eased off and the few towers were easier. Camp X at over 23,000 feet was reached, and a cave excavated to accommodate several men; it meant the removal of from thirteen to sixteen cubic metres of ice. From there, on 3rd October, two of the party went up the ridge to reconnoitre and tread out the track, judging the way to be now clear to the junction with the main north ridge and along this to the top of Kanchenjunga. They returned to Camp X at noon to rest for the big effort next day, never dreaming that the German height record of 24,200 feet made that morning was to stand for two years more.

Black clouds came with the dawn next day, a cold wind blew, and snow began to fall. It fell continuously for forty-eight hours. On the morning of 6th October the sky cleared. In the new snow, lightly crusted by wind-pressure and letting them in to their thighs when weight was put upon it, Bauer, Allwein, and two porters struggled up a thousand feet before they had to give in and return to Camp X in order to give the snow time to consolidate. The rest of the party went down to attempt a reconnaissance of the north-west face of the mountain, permission to enter Nepal having at last reached them. That afternoon clouds piled up in the south to an immense height, and the peculiar sea-green colour came over the sky which sometimes heralds the most terrible storms in the Alps as well as in the Himalayas. Seven feet of snow fell before the next day ended, and still they hung on till the issue changed from the possibility of advance to that of escaping alive.

Roped at long intervals, they pushed through the masses of new snow, leaving a trench behind them so deep that their heads barely rose above the sides. Often the snow on the steeper slopes avalanched as the leader put his foot upon it. Once it gave when three men were on it, and only a desperate effort held them up. Camp IX was reached and dug out. The descent of the steep steps below this was terrible. Half the packs had to be thrown over the precipices before an advance seemed possible. Beigel and a companion, in trying to clear a way here for the porters on the worst day of all, 7th October, had passed some terrible hours. Whichever of them led was swept off his feet by masses of snow that poured down the pitches. On one of the traverses the leader was only saved by the second man leaping over the precipice on the other side, and in their fall the sacks with provisions and equipment were lost. The night was spent without any shelter under a cornice. Beigel's feet were so badly frostbitten that all the efforts of his friends, rubbing them for two days, could not save them.

All the way down to Lachen, far below the glacier, they had to fight their way down, carrying the helpless Beigel wherever possible, through all the obstacles that snow and rain, pouring relentlessly down, can produce in a high mountain valley. It was midnight of 20th October when Bauer arrived with Beigel at Lachen. 'Dishevelled, dead-beat, our nerves worn out with the wild struggle against Nature, with unkempt beards and covered with mud,' they entered the lighted dining-room of a bungalow where a gentleman, whose nationality I leave as a puzzle to the reader, got up and shook their hands with the simple greeting: 'Oh, welcome! Will you have tea or whisky?'

In 1931 the Eyrie at 18,500 feet was once more established on 19th July. The storms of two years had placed upon the ridge above, where the way had been hacked out in 1929, new monsters of snow and ice. In three days a long stretch of track was made, and then a spell of weather came, warm enough, even at this height, to melt the supports on which the track was laid. If ever a 'permanent way' is laid to the top of Kanchenjunga, it will not pass along this ridge.

The damper weather affected the health of both natives and Europeans, and on 9th August came the fatal accident to Schaller and a porter.

Schaller was one of the two daring climbers who, in the previous August, with the aid of innumerable pitons fixed by previous parties and themselves, made the ascent of the south-west ridge of the Aiguille Noire de Péteret, described in the *Alpine Journal* as 'one of the most terrible expeditions ever accomplished.' Schaller's companion on that climb had been killed soon after on a similar type of climb on the Predigtstuhl.

Bauer was a close witness of the accident. Schaller had followed the groove cut in the flank of the ridge, and disappeared behind a rib into the steep gully by which the crest was regained. The porter, a steady climber, followed past the rib into the gully. The third man stood by the rib with the rope belayed. Suddenly the porter shot down the groove and Schaller flew through the air over him in a great curve, and snow poured down the gully. The rope broke, as it was bound to do, on the edge of the rib, and they fell thousands of feet on to the glacier. The shock affected the porters even more than the Europeans. 'For us,' Bauer says, 'the continuance of the attack on Kanchenjunga was a foregone conclusion and a duty.'

A week later the scene of the tragedy was passed once more. Eight days were spent in making the last very difficult portion up to Camp VIII as safe as possible for heavily laden men.

On the crest towered successive mushroom-shaped pinnacles one above the other; at least five of these, twenty to thirty feet high, had to be entirely demolished. . . . Every blow had to be carefully struck, each required its special technique. We were poised like wild animals, crouching before the cornices, balancing between earth and sky, sometimes on the party's respective heads in the endeavour to avoid a simultaneous fall when the overhangs collapsed.

Yet another eight days were spent in hewing a way up the great towers and across the ferocious gaps of the next thousand feet to Camp IX. Continuous snow for five days did not stop the work, and on 10th September Camp X, above the difficulties and slightly higher than in 1929, at over twenty-three thousand feet was at last dug out and occupied. Plodding forward, in snow knee-deep, height was slowly won. Camp XI was ready for occupation on 15th September, at about twenty-five thousand feet. The temperature at night in this camp fell to −22° F., and on a fine day at noon did not rise above 12° F. In the ice-caves made by the party the temperature fell very little below the freezing-point.

On 17th September Hartmann and Wien pushed on to the top of
the north-east spur, over twenty-six thousand feet, where it dropped
slightly before running into a steep slope of four hundred feet, whose
edge was part of the main north ridge. This slope they reported to
be in a dangerous condition, eighteen inches of powdery snow lying
upon it. Next day Allwein, Pirchner, and Wien started again, still
hoping to pass the place and dig out a last Camp XII at about
twenty-seven thousand feet on the final ridge, which they judged
would lead them to the summit without offering any serious difficulties.
They confirmed the report of the previous day that the slope leading
to the north ridge was, in its present state, not fit to climb. Snow had
begun to fall daily and there was reason to expect worse, not better,
weather. The achievements of this Bavarian party show to what
standards of courage, of endurance, and of every type of mountaineering
technique it is possible to attain; the decision to retreat is perhaps as
great a testimony to their judgment.

Was the prize as nearly within their grasp as they believed? It
is permissible to doubt it. For it is so easy for experienced men, as
we know in the case of Everest, to underestimate the difficulties of
the slopes seen above them, but at a considerable distance. Those
difficulties cannot, in any case, equal those which the party overcame
on the north-east spur, but slopes of dangerous snow or slabs of rock
cannot be cut away as can the crest of a ridge, and, more important
than all, such difficulties as occur will be at from twenty-six to twenty-
eight thousand feet, where the experiences of all the Everest climbers
show that the capacity for violent and prolonged effort is sadly diminished from what it is at five or six thousand feet lower. The men
who follow the route of Dr. Bauer's parties will indeed be brave men.
What a prospect the descent of that long spur offers to an exhausted
man! The thought of that awful staircase thousands of feet high, as
the only link remaining with the world below, must grow grimmer and
harder to banish with every advance won along the final ridge. The
men who pursue the attack on Kanchenjunga will be men whose
courage needs no testing.

I had hoped to be able to record at the end of this chapter the
successful completion of Herr Merkl's second attempt to climb
Nanga Parbat. It ended, in July of 1934, in the worst disaster that
has yet happened to Himalayan climbers, three Europeans and seven
porters being overwhelmed in a blizzard after a very high camp had
been established, probably within a few hours' climbing from the
summit.

27. A HIGH CAMP ON NANGA PARBAT

Though in actual height above sea-level Nanga Parbat is nearly three thousand feet less than Everest, on the north side it presents the greatest mountain face in the whole world. Professor Norman Collie, who accompanied Mummery and Hastings in their attack on the peak in 1895, describes it as 'rising without break from the scorching sands of the Bunji plain, first to the cool pine-woods and fertile valleys five thousand feet above, next to the glaciers, and farther back and higher to the ice-clad avalanche-swept precipices which ring round the topmost snows of Nanga Parbat itself, whose summit towers twenty-three thousand feet above the Indus at its base.' And it rivals Kanchenjunga and K 2 in difficulty of access, the upper snows being approachable only by many thousands of feet of most arduous and often dangerous climbing.

Mummery with a single native made a magnificent effort to scale the precipices of the face above the Diamirai Glacier on the west, and then agreed that a less difficult route must be sought. He started for the Diama pass north of the peak with two natives and was never seen again. Either they were killed attempting to descend the fearful precipices they had not yet seen on the far side of the pass, or on the way up by an avalanche falling from the face of Nanga Parbat.

Herr Merkl's party was an extremely strong one, its members being well known for daring exploits in the Alps. Merkl and Welzenbach, who both perished on the mountain, were the two who spent five days and four nights on the north face of the Charmoz in 1931, the last three nights being passed close to the summit in a series of snow-storms that left a foot and a half of snow upon the rocks. It may be that after surviving an experience like that men feel that they can face any risks of weather, even a blizzard at twenty-five thousand feet. And when the greatest difficulties have been passed, and a camp at last established within striking distance of the goal, there is every temptation to hang on in the hope of seizing any chance of victory the conditions and the weather may concede.

The route Herr Merkl showed me in February 1934 seemed to be the most possible; it could not be called a good route. It passed under the north-east face of the great mountain, hung with glaciers that might pour huge avalanches across it at any moment. As in the previous expedition in 1932, the slopes, involving difficult ice-work, were traversed below this face, and the east ridge reached at about twenty-three thousand feet. Herr Merkl seemed confident that there were no very serious difficulties between this point and the summit. From the photographs he showed me it was clear that his standard of what he considered difficult was high.

One of the 1934 party, Drexel, died of pneumonia early in June, but no serious accident from avalanches occurred in pushing up to the higher camps. On 6th July Aschenbrenner and Schneider, from Camp VII at a little over twenty-three thousand feet, reached a height of nearly twenty-six thousand feet, and estimated that the summit was not more than four hours distant. They were going well, and only stopped because they had reached the point where they were to be joined by Merkl, Welzenbach, and Wieland, with porters, bringing up Camp VIII.

This point proved to be too high for the porters to reach that day, so Aschenbrenner and Schneider went down to meet the others, and Camp VIII was established at 24,900 feet. All day Nanga Parbat had risen clear above an immense sea of cloud which covered every-thing below twenty-two thousand feet. No serious obstacle, such as had stopped the climbers on Everest and Kanchenjunga at their highest point, lay in front of them. It seemed as if they had only to walk up on the morrow to collect the prize of all their efforts.

That very night a terrible change in the weather pinned them in Camp VIII, till hopes of victory turned to doubts of the possibility of escape. All 7th July and the following night the conditions grew worse. Nothing kept out the powdery snow driven by a raging wind; the tent-poles broke, and it was impossible to make the cookers work.

On 8th July the retreat began. Aschenbrenner and Schneider, with three porters, set off first to make a track down to Camp VII in the deep new snow. The rest followed, but owing to exhaustion and the death of a porter they failed to reach Camp VII, where a tent was still standing, and had to pass the night in the open in the most terrible conditions it is possible to imagine. Wieland died next day on the way to Camp VII, Welzenbach soon after reaching it. Merkl could eat nothing, yet his amazing vitality enabled him to live till 13th July and on that day crawl down to the site of Camp VI, only to find it either buried or carried away. Two porters were still with him. One managed to reach the rest at Camp IV in spite of fearful injuries from frostbite, the other, Gay-Lay, stayed to die with Merkl. If the credit of a first ascent is the great reward to be won on Nanga Parbat, the successful party can hope for little more than to collect a prize on which the names of Merkl and his friends are already written.

The Europeans in this party were very experienced and capable climbers; they knew the risks involved in reaching the high camps and in having to retreat from them in bad weather, and they took them deliberately. It is difficult to justify the practice of persuading native porters to share dangers which are incurred to satisfy what is, it must be admitted, a personal ambition.

These mighty struggles in the Himalayas have shown to the world the growth and development of mountaineering. The press, the loud-speaker, and the cinema have made known the names of the principals, and have given to thousands who have no knowledge of mountaineer-ing their share of excitement over the achievement of results and records. These achievements are the latest, biggest blooms that have appeared on the hardy stock of mountaineering. They need, as blooms grown for exhibition do, expert skill and all the costly aids that science can produce; larger and more striking to the eye, they are not more exquisite in quality and perhaps less fragrant than some whose names are never printed in the catalogues of fame, but they are grand blooms. Shall we cease to grow for exhibition purposes when the first and second prizes are won? That may not be yet awhile; Everest and Kanchenjunga make us compete in a class in which it is difficult to win. And when the story of the victory is told, it will be the inevitable sequel to the epic of those glorious first attempts.

CHAPTER X

MOUNTAINEERING is the least national of all sports; it will exist, if it does not exist already, wherever there are mountains that offer adventure in the climbing of them, and the appeal it makes is one that has been heard and answered already by men in all quarters of the globe. No attempt is made here to trace its history in different countries, beyond what has been done in previous chapters, nor to make comparisons that would be odious. All that I hope to do is to indicate by a few examples from their literature, and by the help of what I have observed in actual meetings with climbing-parties of other nations, what seem to be some of the national characteristics in their habit and in their view of mountaineering.

Let it be clear from the start that there is no suggestion that any of these characteristics are the property of any one nation. If I suggest acquisitiveness in connection with one nation, remember that there are peak-baggers to be found in all; if any is picked out as exuberant, it does not mean that boisterous gaiety is unknown elsewhere, even on the rain-swept hills of Scotland, though you might fairly imply that it is less common there than on the southern faces of the Alps.

Above all, I shall try to avoid measuring values by comparisons of climbing achievements. In an appreciation of mountaineering, or any other sport, let us bear in mind the principle on which its value must be judged in any large community from a great country down to a university or school; what matters is not single individual perform-ances or records, but the proportion of its members who have felt in themselves the delight in intelligent effort that sport affords, who have assimilated the spirit of fair play which finds no value in victory won by unsporting methods, and who see in the ultimate purpose pursued something that cannot be measured by any numerical standard.

The first country in which mountaineering was at all extensively practised was Switzerland. At all events my reason for mentioning it first is what I believe to be a good chronological one. So large a part of the country is covered by mountains with good climbing on them, such lovely large patches denoting regions of perpetual snow appear on the Swiss pages of our atlas, that it could hardly fail to be the home of mountaineering.

It is the country in which climbing is a national habit as it is nowhere else. There is no other country whose inhabitants climb so much for pure enjoyment and with less thought of the statistical results brought home. Climbing for many Swiss, male or female, is a natural way of spending the week-end holiday. For parties that visit the Alps from other countries, a climbing holiday has often the character of an expedition whose success depends on the tale of peaks that can be counted or recounted on returning; their time for acquisition is limited; it will be a year before they can make good the losses through bad weather or errors in judgment, or add to their gains. For the Swiss climber, the week-ends follow one another so frequently that he is not burdened with that necessity of filling the time profitably which is such a detriment to the enjoyment of leisure.

The Swiss are not a wealthy nation. That has been a great help to the cause of guideless climbing. Almost all the early English climbers would have been counted men of wealth in Switzerland; they could afford the services of the great guides who led them to their victories. Occasionally a first-rate climber, like Mr. Frederick Morshead, gave up all big expeditions in the Alps because he could no longer afford the expenses involved in employing guides, and refused to impose on those he loved the apprehension which in his day was aroused by dispensing with professional aid. It is the Swiss who have done most to bring their greatest national pastime within reach of poorer men by showing that its pleasures can be safely enjoyed without guides, and also by the provision of huts which are used by many parties, especially by those of the large Alpine clubs in the country, as cheap hotels in which a stay of several days can be made at very small expense.

They show great sense and an intimate knowledge of mountains in the choice of climbs they make, rarely choosing an ascent that is not safely within the limits of the party's powers, and recognizing that difficulty is not the measure of enjoyment. The meets of sections of the Swiss Alpine Club and of the various Academic clubs and of other associations supply in Swiss life the same sort of thing as country-house and village cricket do in England, partly sporting, partly social, whose aim is enjoyment shared more than victory achieved. The proceedings of these meets might with appropriate alterations be found in the verses that describe the ascent of the Stock-horn above Lucerne in 1536, already referred to in Chapter II.

The Swiss in the Alps is *chez lui.* Mountaineering is deeply rooted in his nature; it shows with him little evidence of the dangerous growths of mechanization and competitive rivalry, and unmistakable signs of vigour and endurance and understanding of what it can give to life, at any rate outside the ranks of the experts and the professional guides.

Even with these last, among whom some of the rivalry of business competition is inevitable, the best have won and maintained a wonderful reputation for the simple integrity of their character, their mastery of technique, and their feeling for mountains: there have been men among them, like Franz Lochmatter, in whom all bitterness of rivalry and envy has disappeared in complete devotion to their calling. It is remarkable how Swiss guides as a class can banish all idea of a business transaction from the companionship and from the help they give their employers on a mountain, and what courtesy they nearly always show to guideless climbers, whom they may fairly regard as men who have helped to take the bread out of their mouths. The prejudices and suspicions that always accompany a restricted outlook are still found among them, though they are changing as simplicity and rugged individuality disappear in contact with civilized life. Your expert guide at a fashionable climbing centre drives his car and poses before the cinema. He is entering the exalted ranks of our public entertainers.

Winter sports have been a great resource to set against the diminishing opportunities for earning money by guiding in the summer. This diminution is bound to continue. The best men will get employment with climbers who come to do the biggest things; Mont Blanc and the Matterhorn will continue to tempt visitors to get taken up by guides till the *téléférique* transports them there with less demand upon their time and energies and even upon their pocket; otherwise the guideless among summer climbers must increase and the guided decrease.

This increase is not only a matter of preference. The growing popularity of climbing, and the discovery that it can be enjoyed at comparatively small expense, has brought in enormous numbers of climbers who simply cannot afford to pay a guide. And while there is a pleasant prospect of real poverty disappearing as methods of distribution become capable of dealing with improvements in methods of production, there is no reason to expect an increase in the number of those who can afford to double the expenses of a summer holiday in the Alps by taking guides. The glamour of fashion has long passed from the Alps in August for the English. Those that are found there at that time have come thither for simpler and more enduring reasons; but fashion means money and employ- ment for the local entertainers, and in the Alps this used to mean the guides.

The instructor who looks after those who come for winter sports is more polished than the old mountain guide. He practises a more standardized form of sport and deals with a more standardized type of person, especially the female type. Many of the expeditions are in the nature of exercises in well-marked tracks, on which he will be less often called upon to face the responsibility and danger which have made his calling so honourable. Not all, however; the invading crowd of winter visitors contains a good number to whom the peaks make more appeal than the technical side of ski-ing, to whom skis are a pleasant aid in what would otherwise be an impossibly laborious approach. With those who mountaineer with skis the guide finds himself again.

This digression on the guide needs no excuse when we are speaking of Swiss mountaineering. The words 'Swiss guide' conjure up the whole story of mountain exploration. They have certainly been used to describe men who are not of Swiss nationality. And when we come to prove this matter of racial origin among men whose whole lives are passed in the sunshine and shadow of the Alps, we see what an upstart is this modern nationality. Has Croz more in common with a Normandy peasant, or Emile Rey with a Neapolitan, than they have with one another? Are we to think of men who live on different slopes of the same mountain, with centuries of similar habits, surroundings, and traditions behind them, as being of different races, because the politicians have drawn a frontier line between?

A country may well be proud of having drawn within its political boundaries a district which nurtures the kind of men from whom the great guides have come; it would be ludicrous if it took credit for the stoutness of heart and limb, and the familiarity with rock and snow, that have come from generations that lived among mountains which have only recently become its own. Does Italy or France claim to have bred Jacques Balmat and Croz? Chamonix belonged to the House of Savoy when they were born. We can be content to thank the Alps themselves for the great deeds of the local heroes, at any rate in the last century, on whichever side of a great mountain they happen to have been born and bred.

With such abundance and variety of climbing close at hand, and with a scarcity of men of leisure, it is not surprising that Swiss climbers have taken little part in the exploration of distant ranges except as professionals.

As guides, however, they have led exploring parties in the great ranges of the world. Their names occur over and over again in the story of mountain adventure in the Caucasus, the Himalayas, and the ranges in both the American continents. They have shown qualities which it is easy to associate with their home mountains; for they have been loyal, courageous, enduring, and yet it is difficult to picture them happily settled anywhere but in the land of their birth.

There is all the evidence of a home-grown product in the character of Swiss mountaineering. It is that of men who have known mountains in all their various moods, their weaknesses and their dangers, almost as a child knows its parents; indeed, so completely as a child that they were apt to judge all mountains by their own Alps, even the famous Melchior Anderegg being guilty of overestimating nearly sevenfold the time required for the traverse of the ridge from Crib Goch to Snowdon on a winter's day. For him the hollow of Cwm Glas should have provided alps for great herds of cattle and sites for villages. Having quoted that well-known story against Melchior, I must in fairness add the equally well-known example of the extraordinary keenness of observation which a good guide almost unconsciously brings to bear on the path he follows in strange surroundings; he retraced an intricate route through the streets of London.

The Swiss stand for the cardinal virtues in mountaineering which will enable a man to make high expeditions in safety. They know their mountains, they love them, they enjoy climbing them. They combine courage with prudence and knowledge, and they keep abreast of any technical developments in methods of equipment which do not endanger the purpose which their climbing serves. Mountaineering took early root among them, and among them it shows all the signs of vigorous life with no traces of decay.

Here is a typical case of a climb easily possible in a week-end from Geneva or Lausanne, a newly taken route up the Dent de l'Est, the peak that towers above the Rhône valley near St. Maurice, from whose precipices descend avalanches which in very bad weather may produce a cataract of mud and rocks that spreads across the valley and sometimes cuts the railway line. Some tiny chalets in a wild spot on the south-east flank, where the spring avalanches rush past but do not touch them, gave shelter for the night. The hosts are two young boys who look after a small herd that manages to find some pasture hanging on the slopes; their hospitality a bit of fire and a strip of the plank bed that carries a sparse covering of straw.

There is moonlight at the start. Traces of sheep-tracks and then steep shale lead up to a col on an eastern shoulder of the peak. Below comes into view the small, steep Petit Plan Névé Glacier, and in front, rising from it in its whole height, the east wall of the peak. This is the terrific wall you crane your neck to see as you pass it in the train below. The peak is black, as the moon has gone behind it, and the climber gropes his way along the first of the ledges that are the feature of the climb. Easy and broad at first, he follows it to a couloir, full of hard snow stuck all over with stones like the sweets on a sugar cake; a place to hurry through. The ground becomes steeper, and the hands are needed more.

The rising sun shows up a sky of dappled cloud driven by a strong west wind; the threat it contains is not enough to cause retreat. Just above the climber now is the beginning of the great, clear-cut, rocky ledge that runs horizontally to his right across the face and is the key to the passage of the cliffs. A short wall of rock bars access to it. Generously the story-teller refuses to deprive any followers of the pleasure of discovering how it may be climbed.

The ledge is broad and steeply sloping; it runs along a brown wall, very exposed and sensational. For the first few yards the way is obvious. Sufficient is the joy of being on good rock and letting oneself soar up on the wings of enthusiasm. A short flight! The wings shut up as the ledge slopes and the way is hard to see, and arresting when it is seen. The ledge can be seen above leading on, but between is a wall of grey limestone, with a fearful drop below. Few holds, small and firm, rock that is slippery and cold, the pitch all but vertical, sixty feet or more, and all the time the climber is conscious of the void below. Not a place to descend without a doubled rope!

The ledge above is reached. It is less cleanly chiselled than the one below, and grows broken and easy as it opens on to the shoulder of the Jorat *arête* above the last great drop save for the final wall. The south-east face is now visible to the climber, and is pleasantly warm and inviting to look at in comparison with the cold walls left behind. It is bare and built up of grey, polished slabs like the side of a great battleship. He pictures with what a gay clatter the stones and empty tins hurled from the summit would bound down these slabs. One might be on the cliffs below the summit of Snowdon or Ben Nevis.

Only two more difficulties are still to be faced before he can join

o

the frequented route that leads up shifting shale to the west ridge. One is a small, sharp rock with a roof, on which the limits of friction are used, and almost passed, before the hand closes thankfully on the topmost tile; rubber shoes would make it easier. The other is an overhang some ten feet high, which demands a strenuous pull up on the arms.

A broad and reassuring ledge leads across the foot of the final south wall to the scree; the only danger now is the missiles aforesaid, launched by happy tourists on the peak over the tempting wall. A warning shout reveals his presence to them, and he can pursue his way at leisure to the summit.

That might almost be an English, certainly a Scotch climb, slightly enlarged. How similar these rock-climbs seem to those who have not done them! And how different to those who have!

One can pass without difficulty from such a climb to British rocks, and in these days it is hard to believe that British climbing did not start on British rocks.

British mountaineering had its origin in a natural love of adventure responding to a love of nature in her untouched solitudes, which woke to new life in England in the earlier part of the last century. Its early traditions and its character were formed in the Alps under Swiss guides. Great national games with no parallel in other countries have given a meaning to the word sport which is not yet fully understood outside Britain—at least that is the conclusion we must come to if we judge from the significance attached to the word elsewhere.

This existing tradition of sport has permeated our mountaineering. Fixed ropes were distasteful; pitons were, and with most of us still are, anathema, that is to say, unsporting, as bad as digging heels into the pitch. And it is awful to think of the number of pitches that are so damaged now in the Bavarian, the Julian, and the eastern Italian Alps!

Discovery was a very strong element in British mountaineering. Our share of first ascents of the great peaks of the Alps, of the Caucasus, the Himalayas, the Rockies, and the Andes really demands an apology, now we know what value some other nations attach to being first. If I gave figures I might be accused of boasting, and that is an accusation which we particularly dread, for we like to keep the nakedness of our pride decently covered. The importance of the element of discovery and exploration is shown by the incident already referred to in a previous chapter, when a prominent climber suggested that the *raison d'être* of the Alpine Club ceased with the completion of important first ascents.

In the eighties came the discovery that in Britain there were rocks to climb as steep and difficult as any climbed in the Alps. This discovery not only opened up a great new field of activity, it presented a somewhat different view of the objects of mountaineering. There is clearly a difference that goes deep between ascending a peak which challenges you to find and then win your way deliberately to its summit, and taking a difficult route to a point which you know to be easily accessible by slopes where you can descend with your hands in your pockets.

The sporting element—that which stimulates interest in technique and leads to classification and competition—exists in both cases. The peak has lost something of its appeal to the emotions, and the element of mystery and discovery has become less important, often it has gone altogether. At the same time we know well that British climbers linger on British summits to enjoy the fruits of victory. Are those fruits less sweet, or the purples of the rock-hollows less rich, or the distant scene less full of mystery, because there is no shade of anxiety over the way of their return? With the Alpine peak it is a case of love at first sight, with the British hill-top it is a discovery of charm by close association.

It is difficult to see what is distinctive in the attitude of one's own countrymen to mountaineering, for it is impossible to view them from the outside. Two characteristics occur to me—independence is one, and the other is the habit of shielding the natural play of the emotions from prying eyes, under a veil of humour or a mask of impassivity.

Independence is a privilege of assurance. We hold an assured position in the history of mountaineering and in the world of sport. As in many other places, we got there first, to some extent because we had no anxiety for the security of our homes, and because we had men with the leisure and the means to devote to this most attractive adventure, as well as because the love of adventure is in our blood. The advantage of the prestige, which our fortunate situation and the enterprise of our early mountain explorers have won for us, is that we can enjoy our mountaineering without feeling the burden of international competition. You cannot read foreign Alpine publications without feeling that this burden is felt elsewhere.

We are pleased at being among the first to open up this attractive realm of mountaineering, and in such a convincing fashion that there is no need to advertise the fact. And here, as in many parts of the world, we like to point out the benefits that our taking possession has conferred. Think of all the little cairns that mark the spread of our dominion over the cliffs round Wastdale and Pen y Gwryd! How well they mark the line of victorious progress, and warn you against deviation from it! Our history repeats itself whenever an Englishman establishes his claim to a new ascent and invites others to follow, making it easy for them to do so by cairn-building on the spot and by publicity. In climbing, the commission he takes as original occupier is, of course, of a psychological, not a material kind. This useful type of new ascent is now hard to find. The fashion is coming back to precipices that flaunted their inaccessibility to the early explorers, and are now yielding to artificial aids coupled with our acceptance of a diminished prospect of survival. This type of climb appeals to us less than to some other nations, but a good sound climb that carries the title-deeds of ownership has always excited our desires.

The early struggles for Mont Blanc, the Matterhorn, and the giants of the Caucasus and Himalayas had been open; the men who had the initiative, the courage, and the means to go in and win them were few. Already by 1894 we might read in an excellent German guide to the eastern Alps: 'The discovery of a new route is kept secret; problems are no longer set to the world and trumpeted abroad; it has become harder to find a route than to follow it when found.' The idea of mountaineering as a pure matter of achievement has now made this later comment out of date. The north face of the Grandes Jorasses for many modern experts is a 'problem set to the world.' Everest and Kanchenjunga are so to us all.

The English have so far retained their sanity of outlook in regard to such climbs. Mr. Young's attempt on this face of the Grandes Jorasses is regarded even by himself as that of a boy trying to steal apples, not an undertaking which authority will bless.

If we take a look at the Englishman extending his claims into this last hostile portion of the field of new ascents, it shall be in England —the part of it called Wales. Clogwyn dur Arddu is hard enough to get the tongue round, it is worse still to take the panting body up, the blackest, steepest cliff, with the largest unscratched patches of any rock-face that we have. The west buttress remained 'the last great problem in Wales.'

We Englishmen are, on the whole, a kindly, generous race. Had it been a case of one remaining egg at a breakfast-table of hungry men—a good comparison in this chapter, for no other nation in

28. A FAVOURITE SWISS PLAYGROUND

Europe eats eggs at breakfast—it might have remained uneaten. It might have been desired, it would have been renounced; the west buttress was looked at and not renounced. In fact a party, having looked, returned one day to find another about to help itself, that is to say, looking up the 250-foot slab that constitutes the main flesh-raising portion of this appetizing morsel.

The first party had established a claim by leaving a rope ring some way up the slab, the second by getting twenty feet beyond this, but the piton they had then endeavoured to drive in, unlike Gibraltar and others which secure our trade routes, had become dislodged. The two parties agreed to share.

It was not at all a typical day for British climbing; it was warm, and the rocks were dry. They retained, however, a characteristic that provides the Englishman with an opportunity of showing his passion for cleanliness. Lucky Britain to have such turf upon its cliffs, for that is not all it does for us, as you will see. It adds something to the laurels of a new ascent that nothing can take away, and at the same time it supplies a grievance such as a man bred in Britain loves. On the first attempt 'one advanced a foot or so at a time, digging for holds and removing turf piecemeal . . . in a year or so ladies will climb the west buttress of Clogwyn dur Arddu and marvel at the difficulties we encountered.' On the second we find:

The climb was unrecognizable; where previously we had grasped substantial masses of turf there was now smooth and uncompromising rock. 'How on earth do you get up this?' was asked by one in difficulties on a portion of the slab. 'Well, you'll have to use that tuft,' was the answer, indicating a turf beard of grass that hung over above. 'Glad you've left something,' was the growling acknowledgment.

The conclusion is clear, is it not? Tufts are a help or a hindrance according to the need of elevation of the male pioneer in the physical or mental sense, and their removal clears the difficulties for the ladies who are to follow. This much is certain; they show our gallantry.

The Englishman is a handy man; a couple of stones had been carried up and were pressed into the crack that ran up between the great slab and its overhanging wall, and gave a hint of security to the ascent. They performed the office of pitons without their brazen or rather iron admission of iniquity. Appearances were observed.

Somehow or other the leader contrived to replace his boots by rubber shoes, and in these to overcome the smoothest, most repellent pitch. This comes at the top of a chimney that overhangs and widens where a step across is needed. 'It is a long stride, the balance is uncertain, the hand-holds mere finger-scrapes, the exposure and the precipice beneath terrific.' 'The Faith and Friction slab' is the name that Mr. Smythe suggests for it.

And above it a *piton* is driven in. Yes, a real piton this time, and pitons do not grow on Welsh rocks; someone must have carried it up.

That does not end the difficulties. There is a section which has to be climbed quickly, because the strain of supporting the body on finger-tips alone is severe. There is an overhang of turf, and beyond all that 'the solitary piece of pure gymnastics on the climb,' an overhang of fifteen feet.

Faith and Friction! When Mr. Smythe has to rely on these we need no further assurance that the standards of British climbs are as high as any to be found in the 'one piton' class. New surfaces of rock on which nature has provided no means of support for the higher mammals can be trodden, though it becomes doubtful if one can say *under* foot of man, by mechanical aids; they can hardly make greater demands on his strength of nerve or natural capacity. 'Après cela,' or 'après lui, il faut tirer l'échelle!' That is the PS. we feel inclined to write; perhaps it is the one we are meant to write when we read the accounts of modern rock climbs.

Despite the fact that the last great problem in Wales is solved, it would not be surprising if another positively last made its appearance there before long; at any rate plenty will be found elsewhere. The independent quality of British climbing will always be coming upon new problems, because we climb in the spirit of individual caprice rather than in groups that follow a fashion; we stray farther from the beaten track; some of us wander about till we find something that takes our fancy, and we do not care very much whether it is other people's fancy. A Frenchman likes to be doing the correct thing; a German likes to be given a line to follow. You will see wider variations—more eccentricities—if you prefer that word—in the Englishman's costume and equipment on a mountain, as well as in his manner of enjoying himself. He may, like Conway, distribute the activities of a single season along 'the Alps from end to end,' or he may concentrate, like Dr. Graham Brown, on showing that it is still possible to trace new lines of ascent up the most frowning faces of Mont Blanc, even alongside those which he and Mr. Smythe had already so courageously marked.

He may also, after tasting all the thrills of new and exciting adventure, find pleasure still in expeditions which to a French

29. CLOGWYN DUR ARDDU

expert would present all the repellent lack of elegance which he expresses in the word *plat*.

This love of independence makes it less easy to be genial. The Englishman joins a London club more to escape society than to find it. I must not exaggerate or impute to my countrymen an attitude towards other parties on a mountain, like my own, which is often abominable, and for which a mathematical education and a habit of solitary climbing are not entirely responsible. All I mean is that if the privilege of having a hut to himself and his party, or the privilege of declining the honour of representing his country at an Alpine international conference, could be honourably purchased, the Englishman's offer would be the highest. Less dependence on himself in his education and amusements and closer contact with the affairs of other nations are now making him a better mixer.

The second characteristic of our climbing, a characteristic often noted by foreign writers, is humour. It is proverbial that we take our pleasures sadly; it is quite as true that we take our difficulties humorously. These traits are the two leading-strings we employ to restrain the violent sway of deep emotions and keep them near the line of impassivity.

This is how Mummery describes the descent on a doubled rope of a pitch on the Grépon.

I found the first twenty feet very easy, then I began to think that the Alpine Club rope is too thin for this sort of work, and I noted a curious and inexplicable increase in my weight. To add to these various troubles the axe, which was held by a loop round my arm, caught in a crack and snapped the string. Luckily, by a convulsive jerk, I just managed to catch it in my left hand. This performance, however, greatly excited Burgener, who, unable to see what had happened, thought his Herr and not merely the ice-axe was contemplating a rapid descent on to the Mer de Glace. Having restored our spirits by a quiet consideration of the contents of a certain flask, we set off in pursuit of Venetz, who had carried away our only remaining rope.

To Guido Rey it seems

a flying panic in a dream, as if I were flying through the air and suddenly fell and saw the ground rise up towards me without ever coming within reach. Supported on the rope with hands that were bleeding and weary with the effort, I swung restlessly to and fro, vainly groping for solid ground. My body felt horribly heavy, the rope was tight round my chest, and I could hardly breathe. My companions, who were already down below, called up to me to hasten, pointing out holds I could not find. It seemed as if they mocked me. I cursed and swore! At last, exhausted and angry, I let myself slide heavily down the rope, almost like a falling body. I noticed on the rope some fine blood-red stains, and I came to earth. I had awakened from my dream. Forthwith I drew out my pocket-book and made a few notes.

There you have different presentations of the same incident.

An expedition which the solitary climber will not repeat if he can help it, as soon as he becomes conscious of the inconvenience his disappearance will cause to others, is that of finding himself cut off by apparently impassable cliffs with a long stretch of climbing, not free from difficulty, behind him, and evening coming on. It happened to Leslie Stephen.

Tempted by an apparently easy route, I made a diversion towards the valley, and, after some complicated scramblings, found myself at the edge of some tremendous cliffs, invisible from above, but, so far as I could see, impassable. There is a pleasure in these accidental discoveries which is some reward to the guideless traveller for his unnecessary wanderings. I was probably the first person who ever reached a place which is totally out of the proper route from any given point to any other, and it is probable enough that my performance may never be repeated. I might therefore flatter myself that I alone of the human race can enjoy the memory of one particular view—not, it is true, more striking in itself than many other views, but having the incalculable merit of being in a sense my own personal property. At such places, too, one feels the true mountain charm of solitude. If my grasp had suddenly given way as I was craning over those ghastly crags, I should have been consigned to a grave far wilder than that 'in the arms of Helvellyn,' and which might as likely as not remain undiscovered till there was little left to reward the discoverer. A skeleton, a few rags, the tattered relics of certain more coherent rags which just passed themselves off for clothes at Primiero, and perhaps the mangled remains of a watch and an ice-axe, would hardly be worth the trouble of a prolonged search. These cheerful reflections passed through my mind, and added considerably to the influence of the strangely wild scenery.

That shows how we laugh away the deeper feelings such a situation arouses in us. It gives little idea of the reality of those feelings at the time. It is written to amuse us. It would be eccentric, even in an Englishman, to be amused in such a predicament. The French have adopted with the new cult of sport something of this cult of imper-turbability. As a rule, they are nearer the reality than we dare to be. There is neither exaggeration nor concealment in this description of a scene thrilling in that anticipation of danger which is worse than its arrival. It is the north face of the Fletschhorn.

Below the face balls of snow encrusted with stones are piled into a great cone. The sharp edges and corners of fragments of fallen *séracs* show amongst them.

Half-way up a belt of black rocks breaks the sparkling whiteness of the precipice. *Séracs* pushed down by the ice above overhang its upper edge. Higher up still a wall of ice stretches right across the face from the north-east to the north-west ridge.

Just to the right of the direct line below the summit a wall of blue ice, vertical everywhere save in this one place, is broken by an inclined plane slashed all over with crevasses. This inclined plane provides the only possible link between the lower and upper portions of the face. Beyond, the angle of the slope diminishes, there is snow resting on it. Two straight, black, parallel furrows run down from a pyramid of dark rock that emerges from the ice and lifts its profile in the north ridge against the sky. It stays the gleaming snowy point, so slender and light it seems to float like a vapour in the air. A couloir of ice, overlaid with snow, falls, broad and precipitous, from the north-west ridge. A huge sea-green bulge forms the upper part of its western side.

We stood there rooted to the spot in admiration, and with our admiration there mingled a respect that was akin to fear. Oscar brings his telescope to bear upon it. The rocky band, half-way up, magnified by the lens, becomes a source of more anxiety than the *séracs* that hang threateningly above it. The sight of those smooth slabs, disposed like the tiles of a roof, is enough to chill to pessimism our leader's fiery ardour.

It may be the more realistic and passionate descriptions of foreign climbers, it may be a growing need for more genuine expressions of the emotions aroused by high adventure, besides the obvious differences of temperament, that have given a warmer tone to some later descriptions by Englishmen. Mr. Young can give us a share of the emotions of his party. There are comparisons and tricks of language that touch up the picture for presentation to the public which must be done in the studio, but he takes you to the spot and lets you feel its effect. His descriptions will be familiar to most of those who will read these pages.

Alpine literature in England shows less national characteristics in this generation, but the Englishman is so easily frightened by sentiment that he will not easily put off his armour of restraint and humour. He will blame a national limitation of expression, and then complain of sentimentality when the feelings are expressed more freely. In our attitude to such a good thing as mountaineering we need not be afraid of reality. The camera has shown us that in the pictorial representation of men climbing peaks. I wonder if there is any one who, as a small boy, heard and saw Albert Smith making known the Alps with his panorama to Londoners after his ascent of Mont Blanc in 1851, and as an old man also heard and saw Mr. F. S. Smythe doing the same for the Himalayas with his film—after his ascent of Kamet in 1931. It would be interesting to see both perform-ances on the same day and note the advance these eighty years have seen in mountaineering. The difference in methods and effectiveness is as wonderful in the illustrations as in the climbers! The camera has come into its own with mountain photography. After seeing the snow-scenes brilliantly lit upon the screen, the infinite variety of tone, the beauty of form and delicacy of shadow, we must agree, whatever our views on other face-treatment, that in the portrayal of mountains truth is stranger and more attractive than fiction.

The Frenchman in our early Alpine literature is characterized on the mountain, as he has been upon our stage, by an excitable nature and a habit of expressing himself by gesture as well as by word of mouth, a tempting figure to portray beside the imperturbable Englishman!

Reynaud, 'a flying figure' in mid-air below the lip of a great *bergschrund*, with a boot 'which might have belonged to Moore' as a factor in persuading him to take the plunge, is the French climber portrayed by Whymper. Apart from references to engineers and surveyors, and a mention in a footnote of a second ascent of Les Ecrins by M. Vincent, he gives us no other description of a French climber on a mountain. It is true that Whymper's scrambles do not go beyond 1869, when climbing had taken little hold on French-men, the French Alpine Club being founded in 1874. The fact remains that Whymper's picture is the one that for many years would be accepted in the minds of his readers till their own experience had corrected it.

For Tartarin we are not responsible. I was once told that Daudet's model for this glorious, inimitable creation was Reynaud himself. I have no reason whatever to think it true. The nearest I have been to this excitable, ludicrous type was in Dauphiné. An English climber came down to La Bérarde one evening, having met on the Pic Coolidge a Frenchman who refused dramatically to complete the final portion of the ascent; he was then within a few minutes of the top. After referring to previous acts of valour—I cannot say whether African lions were mentioned—he pointed to the summit and exclaimed: 'Mais ces rochers! Jamais!'

An Englishman whom I know well has told me how he made the same great refusal. It was on the Piz Corvatsch, a snow peak above Pontresina that is by no means difficult. The snow ridge narrows as you near the highest point. My friend is a man who knows his own mind, and he there and then decided that the ridge had ceased to provide the attraction that he sought and found in sport. He stopped. The guide applied the usual persuasion of the rope. Whereupon my friend whipped out his knife—he is a handy man with his tools, and I have no doubts of the keenness of its edge—and made it clear by pantomime if not by word of mouth what would happen to the guide's rope if another step was taken towards the summit.

It is hard to see any relationship between the Tartarinesque type of climber and a representative member of the Groupe de Haute Montagne, founded three years after the war. The names of Jacques and Tom de Lépiney will always be associated with this new outburst of climbing activity. The Petit Clocher de Planereuse shall provide an example of the sort of thing they like.

It is a steep tower in view of the Saleinaz hut. The ascent by the west face is difficult enough to provide a *pièce de résistance* for most appetites. For the brothers de Lépiney the drop over the south wall of over three hundred feet to the col connecting it with the Grand Clocher was to give the requisite flavouring to the expedition. Some parties find a full day's occupation in the ascent by the west face. I remember seeing a party—it was neither English nor French—start for it, and, after I had returned from a good day on the Grand and Petit Darrey, watching them from the hut descending in the late evening.

The two de Lépineys did not begin their ascent till near midday. They have reached the place where the south wall drops, vertical or overhanging, towards the col. The absence of any careful study of the face lends additional excitement to the immediate future. The descent has been done before, that is about all they know of it. 'Nous avons une longue corde, nous passerons toujours' is their attitude.

A rope ring is fixed. They drop down into the unknown. Jacques lands on something and Tom follows. A few feet above his brother he is told to halt on small holds where it is not easy to maintain himself at all. His protest is stopped by seeing that Jacques is in little better case. It is a ticklish manœuvre to extract a bit of rope for another ring and replace the sack. If you have climbed steep rocks you will know the sort of place. You cannot move hand or foot or shift your position an inch, you cannot touch a single thing or lay it down, without being aware of the void below waiting for anything it can swallow. These two are in the middle of a cliff that an eagle might have chosen for its eyrie if the ledge had been reasonably flat.

Then the rope above sticks. They pull and pull and it does not move. 'A slight anxiety grips us: right or left, up or down, there is not a hope of escape if the rope does not come loose.' A slight anxiety! We might be reading Mummery; his influence is much seen in the attitude and in the writings of this school of French climbers.

At last a more violent jerk gets it free. It is forty minutes before Tom can start to follow the leader down the next bit. Waiting can be the most trying form of service on a mountain. How far the forty minutes of inaction are different from repose can be gathered from Tom's comment: 'When at last I gripped the doubled rope with both hands to begin the drop, I had a delicious feeling of repose and well-being!'

It was not a simple descent. It was necessary to edge away across the face, the utmost care being taken to secure enough hold on projections in the wall to prevent a pendulum-like swing back into a position that would have had no possible issue. Half-way across, the rope has to be fixed again. The only nick has rounded edges. Fortunately Jacques reaches a good stance before Tom has to follow. Despite all his care the rope works off, first one side of the notch, then the other, but the holds become sufficient near the end. They have come upon an old rope-ring, and are in view of the easier route they might have followed. On the col they rejoin their boots, and the route that has for them now become almost a promenade leads on to the top of the Grand Clocher, and it is only five o'clock.

If there is an unseen dispenser of such enterprises we can imagine him going to the French section for the ingredients labelled *élan,* a touch of *crânerie* too, perhaps, to make it tasty.

The cleavage between the competitive and the contemplative attitude to mountaineering is more marked in France than in England; across the Channel they are more logically minded, less inclined to compromise. For instance, a man is regarded there as having no religion if he is outside the fold of the Church, and they are sceptical of the sincerity of other views. For the school of climbing represented by the Groupe de Haute Montagne mountaineering is a sport on a competitive basis, its aim being attainment of a victory that is hard to win. Mummery stands high in their esteem. Their acceptance of danger, their defence against the accusation of indifference to aesthetic consideration, is very reminiscent of his views on 'the Pleasures and Penalties of Mountaineering': 'The most difficult walls are often the most beautiful, and they must be seen from close at hand—the impression of beauty a mountain gives is closely related to the efforts we have made to win it.'

30. RAISED TO THE ALPINE PEERAGE

Mummery was certainly a champion of the combative side of mountaineering, but he had a foot or more than that in the other camp. The recreative side of sport, the side whose results are long in showing, which provides no regular copy for the daily paper, and which is the indispensable link between the physical and the contemplative aspects of mountaineering, has not yet received full recognition outside England. Difficulty and excitement are the characteristics of sport that count.

The Groupe de Haute Montagne is fairly representative of the development of French mountaineering that now occupies the pages of French and other journals. Let us not forget Javelle, and let us be sure that there are still Frenchmen who enjoy the peace as well as the more exciting pleasures, even if they do not win the fame, or its modern form, publicity, which mountains give.

It is a pleasing feature of French climbing that it has so far shown little desire to follow some schools of climbing in other countries in the exaggerated use of mechanical aids. One or two exploits with rockets and lassos on rocky needles do not affect the general truth of this. Before we leave the consideration of specially French mountaineering, let us have one more look at a French party on what remains, despite its crowds of victors from all over the world, the 'home ground,' the Chamonix Aiguilles. Mummery has been canonized there, and there is no need to point the attraction for his admirers of an enterprise in which he had failed—failed gloriously, after 'two days on an iceslope'—the ascent of the north face of the Aiguille du Plan.

A few glimpses are all you can have; you must read the account in *Les Crêtes du Mont Blanc*, by Jacques and Tom de Lépiney. An icewall is the only possible approach to what one might call the firstfloor landing, the upper part of the small Blaitière Glacier. A joint in the adversary's armour shows between the icewall and the rock. Hand and footholds enable them to creep up till a human ladder, whose top step is Ségogne's shoulder, which takes the point of the crampons fairly well, enables the leader, Jacques de Lépiney, to reach the edge of a crevasse where the front of the wall scales off.

The landing has only been reached twice before. To leave it is a worse problem than to reach it. The wall above demands the extreme limit of effort. In trying a desperate pullup the leader drops his axe into a deep fissure and Ségogne has to pass up his. A moment of illhumour shows the stress upon the nerves. Another try in a crack with an overhanging exit, then a slab smooth and steep enough to give exquisite relief when the fingers clutch round a sharp edge above, and the worst pitch is passed. The party pushes on, keyed up to its finest form. It takes a peculiarly awkward corner in its stride, such a stride too, with the body leaning over nothing at all, a bulging rock at the stomach and a pull-up at the end. 'Lagarde, phlegmatic, monocle in eye, scores full marks and sends us into fits of laughter.' The phlegmatic, with a monocle! Surely this is a stage Englishman, not a Frenchman. Perhaps the fact that he raises a laugh betrays it. I know Englishmen who would find no humour in it. One up to the Frenchmen!

It is already five o'clock when they come on to the main ridge at the Brèche du Caïman. 'Bivouac now, or shall we climb the Caïman first?' Despite a protest from Ségogne, a mountaineer with a contempt for mere gymnastics, they go to add the Caïman to the bag—and in the failing light, close to the top, they have to give it up. After all, what is the Caïman compared to the Plan, which has beaten Baumann, Mummery, and Emile Rey? Back at the Brèche du Caïman they bivouac. A form of sleep begins to come, and suddenly a flash; not from the electric railway in the valley, but lightning, a herald of elemental forces that can cut off all retreat. Instant escape is the only course. They look over the south side of the Brèche. A succession of drops on the doubled rope there might lead to safety; it is too desperate a venture in the dark. Darkness forbids also the retracing of the way of ascent or the traverse of the ridge over the Crocodile to the Plan. A traverse under the Crocodile will be snow, and the darkness less of a hindrance. They decide on this: it is a nightmare flight. The snow thins out and de Lépiney has to cut the ice. Ségogne has no axe: the steps are invisible, and the two behind must grope for them on the dark, slippery surface. Soon all three are on the slope. Ségogne brings out his knife and tries to help his balance with the point against the ice. The worst passage is where they descend into a deep furrow, close to where the buttress of the Crocodile rises out of the slope. To Ségogne it seems a descent into hell: never has existence seemed to hang on so slender a thread. Hours have passed before the base of the Crocodile is reached. The worst is over. The threat of the storm is further off and with the turning of a corner of rock safety and victory lie before them. In the wan light of a grey dawn the ridge is gained again at the Brèche du Crocodile and the last rocks of the Plan are climbed with the strength that still remains.

This is a grand climb, where man is fairly matched against mountain, and a climb suited to the nation of whom another of her sons wrote: 'Ce sont des émotions d'âme que ce peuple demande, les plus fortes sont les meilleures. Ce ne sont pourtant pas les choses cruelles qu'il aime, il en a peur au contraire, mais il aime l'effroi qu'elles lui donnent.' To turn from de Lépiney's own description of it to open my copy of *La Montagne* for April 1934 and read: 'The Committee' (of the French Alpine Club) 'has voted a Himalayan expedition "qui doit revêtir le caractère d'une entreprise nationale et consacrer le prestige de l'alpinisme français,"' is something of an anti-climax. It sounds like an announcement of the painting of the lily, and a very fair French lily too!

The contribution of German and Austrian climbers in the develop-ment of mountaineering, in anything measured by quantitative standards, is enormous, perhaps greater than that of all other nations put together. When a German adopts an idea he follows it up further and with greater industry and patience than any one else. You have only to meet a typical German party in the Swiss Alps, carrying huge, heavy rucksacks, and see the completeness of their preparations and equipment, and listen to them discussing their programme, worked out to the last detail, to know that this people takes its pleasures seriously, if not sadly. There is a methodical precision about their expeditions which would rob them of their attraction for many Englishmen and for all Frenchmen. I think the German finds pleasure in this minute working-out of the end in view, perhaps because his end is not quite the same. Mountaineering being a means to an end, it is approached and used in different ways according to what that end is.

The unexpected, anything that may alter the programme, upsets him. For instance, two English girls visiting the Harz Mountains with a German lady vexed her by wishing to view the landscape from other places than the indicated *Aussichtspunkt*. Again, on the Grivola, in 1931, on the ordinary ascent by one of the broad rock-buttresses from the Trajo Glacier, my party was surprised to see small scarlet patches on the rock. On coming up to these we saw they were pieces of paper, and soon afterwards we came up with a couple of German climbers. This device for marking the route so that it is at once found on the descent is old and excellent. I had often thought of adopting it but never done so, nor have I seen it used by parties of any other nation. The two Germans had stopped, in doubt if they were on the correct route. We also doubted, but one can go almost anywhere on this face, and we climbed a crack which

led to easier ground and signs of previous ascent. We found no
great difficulty in the crack, nor do I think the Germans would
have done so. They did not climb it simply because they were
determined to follow the correct route. We met them later in the
day near the summit as we were coming down.

That is typical of German thoroughness and precision, not of
German ability to climb. The Alpine clubs of Austria, founded
in 1862, and of Germany, founded in 1869, united in 1874 to form
the great D.u.Ö.A.V., the Deutscher und Österreichischer Alpen-
verein. Its membership in 1907 was already over seventy thousand,
and among so many thousands there are necessarily many who have
little natural aptitude for climbing and who nevertheless convey
themselves safely to the summits of the Alps by patient effort and
careful attention to everything that will help to get them there. The
short description in the previous chapter of Dr. Paul Bauer's attempts
on Kanchenjunga, if it has enabled you to form at all a true judgment
of those achievements, is sufficient proof that in the execution of the
greatest climbs German mountain-craft and German endurance and
courage are second to none. Every climbing journal that records
the great deeds of the year in the mountaineering world supplies
further evidence.

This book deals with the character of the changes in the general
development of mountaineering more than with their extent or their
statistical analysis. The main change of this kind that has come
from German sources, the application of mechanical aids in climbing,
has been already noticed. Apart from this, it is the amount and the
methodical nature of their work, rather than the discovery of new
possibilities in the world of mountaineering, that impresses us in the
records of German and Austrian achievement. The volume of their
labours in the matter of maps, guide-books, and records of mountain
travel and exploration is astonishing.

Herr Merzbacher's two volumes on the Caucasus, published in
1901, are typical. Nearly two thousand pages filled with the results
of careful observation. You need a Teuton stomach to retain an
appetite for detail through such a colossal feast. If a guide-book is
written in German, you may be sure that it is more detailed and
probably more accurate than if in any other language—unless we
except translations from the German. As far as it is possible to
remove the element of the unexpected and the enjoyment of discovery
from mountaineering, it is done. To say that a peak 'has been climbed
from the col by the south ridge in two and a half hours and is not

31. EXALTATION

particularly difficult' is sufficient information for a party that is capable of finding its way upon a mountain and enjoys doing so, while it leaves almost all the pleasure of discovery, as well as execution. A German seems to like to be told exactly where the difficulties occur and the exact method of overcoming them.

Daring and method are closely allied in their mountaineering enterprises. The number of those who have found themselves on the pitiless upper ice-slopes of the Brenva face of Mont Blanc is still comparatively small. More than one of them may have felt, like Dr. Paul Güssfeldt, that the situation seemed desperate. I doubt whether any but he has actually taken out his note-book and written 'situation desperate,' at the time. It is mainly the Munich school of climbing with its wonderful gymnasium of the Wilde Kaiser close at hand that has carried out the classification of climbing in grades, under leaders like Rudatis, who regard the sport of climbing as a competition between man and man.

Technically Germans are carrying out the idea of applying mechanical aids, especially pitons and *Karabiner*, to the ascent of rock-walls more thoroughly and to a further logical conclusion than others: their great achievements lend force to their example. Spiritually they have gone back to the pagan ideas and the legendary heroes that stand for the ideal of self-exaltation. This ideal is liable to ugly distortion. This is how Trenker, a Tyrolese who seems to have adopted it, in a book which has been considered worth translation into English, describes the sentiment inspired by a mountain summit in a companion: 'Come up here, you louts and slackers, come up here, you greedy guts, the devil 'll take you. I can look down on all of you, on you who despise me down in the valley, just because I'm a poor boy.' It is nice to take away the taste of that by thinking of the hunchback porter, Luc Meynet, in an ecstasy of gratitude upon the Matterhorn.

Where mountaineering is accepted as a great sport, as it is in Germany and Austria, there is bound to be some vulgarizing of it in exploitation by commercial enterprise. Trenker tells us that the 'Fight for the Matterhorn,' with the relish of a love story added, was 'the second best commercial success of the year.' The superficialities of mountaineering, sometimes its more malignant growths, catch the eye of the public that does not know mountains, just as the clothes or a disfigurement on the face of a stranger may be all that we notice about him.

The growth of nationalism is being forced hard in Germany at

P

present. There is no need for the assertion of this national prestige in mountaineering, for no one denies to Germany her place in that sun. Some of her climbers may show a desire to oust others from such places as they have there. It is a German Alpine author who has made the most extravagant and exclusive claims for the achievements of his countrymen. On the other hand, Dr. Kugy, of Austrian birth, is never tired of pointing out that mountains are the property of all who love them and have climbed them. And the best of German climbers show no such envious desires. I can find no national assertiveness in the accounts of Dr. Bauer's expedition to Kanchen- junga or in that of Herr Merkl to Nanga Parbat. These thrilling tales are models of modest records of great achievement.

Let us cross the border into Italy. It is easier at present to do it with the pen than with the ice-axe. There we have another country whose nationalism is being encouraged, and by a very great man indeed. I do not know whether the Duce has read Guido Rey. If he has I am sure that this passage would find a response in his heart: 'Too often has the stale old fable of *dolce far niente* resounded in our ears, uttered by those who do not know the virtues of our race, for it not to be henceforth the bounden duty of every good Italian to refute it on every occasion, according to his powers.'

The nature of that response is indicated by the appeals to undertake arduous and dangerous climbs which have been appearing in Italian climbing journals. These are typical:

A climber has fallen. Let a hundred others arise for the morrow. Let other youths strew edelweiss and alpenrose upon the body of the fallen comrade; and lay it with trembling devotion face upturned under the soft turf. Then up, once more to the assault of the rocks and of the summit, to commemorate the fallen one in the highest and most difficult of victories!

The medal for valour in sport, the highest distinction accorded by the Duce to exceptional athletes who break world records or are victors in international contests, will be awarded to climbers who vanquish mountains by new ascents of the sixth standard.

All Italians ought to know how to live in mountainous country. All our wars will always take place in the mountains, and the cult of mountaineering passionately pursued, and spreading more and more among our young men, will contribute to the military preparedness of the young generation.

It is easy to read an aggressively competitive purpose into such appeals. And it would evidently be easy to turn the spirit they arouse to such a purpose. Italy herself has already shown us that early and hasty judgment of her new spirit may be wrong. Many things that had an aggressive beginning and a still more aggressive appearance in the new *risorgimento* have turned out to be the early exuberances of a nation in whom a great leader has seen the primary need of a consciousness of its own possibilities. Employers who welcomed and employees who feared it as a weapon against the workers, have both learned their mistake and found that a common interest was the goal to which they were directed. Those who carry out the details of a plan, especially one on a national scale, will not see the picture of the design all at once.

It is early to judge the real effects of the new spirit on Italian moun-taineering. A spirited child becoming conscious of the powers in its legs will often see how near the edge it can go without falling off. It is one of the characteristics of childhood that age does not part with readily. It is indeed not in itself a desire born of rivalry or envy. The latest feats of Italian climbers may be regarded, as a young Italian climber vehemently tells us they should be regarded, as a 'struggle of the will against the baseness of fear and instinct; a proof and consciousness of our spiritual power; an affirmation of faith in ourselves and in our life.'

The spirit of rivalry is easily awakened; if the youth who lives next door claims to be able to go nearer the edge, is it likely that his claim will pass unchallenged by young Italy of the present day?

And so we may read: 'The conquest of the north wall of the Cima Grande di Lavaredo, achieved by three guides of Cortina and Misurina, has struck the whole Alpine world with amazement, and has given to Italian climbers one of the most coveted of victories in which the Austro-Germans have been our special rivals.'

In such a rivalry how should the Matterhorn escape being a subject of dispute? As one of the participants in the latest battles upon it says:

The history of the Matterhorn is that of a long and passionate struggle such as no other mountain has known. To every victory from the north, Italians always replied by a success to match it, and in the list of the great conquerors, Whymper, Carrel, Mummery, Penhall, Guido Rey, Piacenza, one out of every two names is Italian. Up to 1928, however, the four faces were still unclimbed. The exploits of Hermann and the brothers Schmid on the west and north faces appeared at first to have given a definite preponderance to one side. But, once more, the gap was first lessened, then filled up by two Italian parties. The ascent of the south face and that of the east face, with its terrific overhang, definitely confirmed Italian rights over the half of the Matterhorn that is lit by the sun.

Yes, the four walls were left alone up till 1929. It is hard to say which of them provides the worst route. Every single one presents the very dangers which it is a first principle of mountaincraft to avoid. Perhaps the east face may be considered the worst of all, because, until it reaches the actual head of the peak, it lies over rock whose main difficulty is its bad quality. A party that ascends by this route can claim to have been under fire from falling stones more continuously than on any other route made upon the Matterhorn. A motorist who dashed at top speed along a side-road that crossed a succession of busy main roads might make a similar claim; the temerity of the proceeding will not be disputed.

A long traverse of the upper edge of the Furggen Glacier brought the party directly under the Swiss summit. As far as possible the route is to be the shortest line, the line of greatest slope up the face, the *direttissima* so dear to Italian enthusiasts. It was not long before the stones came at them. One sings past, the whistle of another is stopped by a thud, and Maurice Bich is hit; his white woollen helmet turns red, but luckily the stone was small and he does not even stop. A second discharge all but catches them as they cross a small couloir. The wall grows steeper, and they use a thin ridge of snow that crowns a rib of rock, nearly on a level with the shoulder on the Hörnli route.

At half-past nine they are safely on the ledge that runs below the final wall, less than seven hundred feet below the top. The victory seems likely to be too easily won. At eight o'clock that evening they are but three hundred feet higher. The difficulties of the ten and a half hours' climb can be imagined, the desperate struggles on tiny holds, the breathless seconds where the friction of rough cloth is the only upward force as the fingers clutch on some sort of edge, or when the safety of the party hangs on a piton that may or may not continue to do its duty, and between the efforts the long waits on ledges where stalactites of ice hang overhead.

Pitons supply the hold when the Matterhorn offers none. A big rock comes down on Louis Carrel, tearing his clothes and damaging his foot. 'I sent down a rock,' is his quiet comment.

A projecting rock on the cliff, in profile like a human face, demands long and complicated manœuvres. A rope is thrown and at last passed between the lips and under the chin of this monstrous face. Hours pass before the last man has to brace himself to face the difficulties that lie between him and the men now perched upon the profile. A block of rock comes away under his left hand, the piton comes out, tinkles against the rock, and rests against his chest; the hold he grips with his right hand crumbles. He holds himself up with his two hands open on the sloping ledge. Carrel throws across another rope and one arm after another is passed through the noose. He fights his way inch by inch, holding desperately to the rope and finally to the boot that appears above his head, till a hand can seize him by the wrist and pull him on to a place where he can rest.

It is six o'clock and snow is beginning to fall, first melting on the rock, then adhering, so that the fingers are numbed as they search for holds beneath. Louis Carrel and the other guides force their way up, till darkness falls completely. Benedetti and two of the guides are under the actual cornice of the summit; Mazzotti, with the other two, is lower down on a ledge so narrow and overhung that they cannot stand. A second piton is hammered in with an axe, the hammer having been lost, close to a bright, new piton, which had been put in a crack by Carrel and had worked loose. Tied to these two pitons they pass the night.

Occasional short nightmares show that fitful sleep visits them, and they wake up to find the rope holding them over the abyss. At half-past three they begin to climb past the overhanging rock above, which in the night has become covered with snow and ice. Louis Carrel, when they reach the three above, has already begun to break through the cornice, and at half-past eight 'the ascent of the east face of the Matterhorn is an accomplished fact.' And now we can say: 'Requiescat in pace,' or in such peace as the crash of falling rocks allows.

International rivalry is a noxious element to introduce into the atmosphere of the Matterhorn. Rivalry becomes an ugly thing in sport when it is more than an encouragement to men to do their best. Whymper is at his worst when calling upon Croz 'in the name of friendship' to prise away the crags and hurl them down near the Italians to make them realize their defeat; so are those who, according to the Tyrolese writer Trenker, reproached Carrel for the help he had given Whymper in his attempts upon the peak. 'Human nature' is the reason accepted by the dismal Johnnies who accept every misdirection of instinct into which men drift as being subject to some immutable law. The reality of an ideal such as mountains set before us in our best moments, which can give a right direction to our instincts, does not exist for them, because they choose to regard reality as ending where the mists upon the mountain-side begin.

Mountaineering is good enough to flourish without this ugly rivalry. Men will pursue research work for sheer love of it, just as diligently and with a clearer perception of the aim in view, whether they share their discoveries with other workers or work alone without any heed of rival enthusiasts. And a party can climb with no less pleasure, often with more pleasure, and with no less development of strength and skill and knowledge, if there is no idea of human rivalry whatever. Sport pursued for enjoyment is the best field there is for bringing men together in a perfectly natural way and abolishing pre-judices. The big man of the place and his boot-boy face the fast bowler on the village pitch with feelings dependent only on what nature has supplied; they receive much the same sympathy if run out by their partner, and the same applause if they lift the ball over the hedge, and they feel equally foolish returning for a duck and equally elated at reaching fifty or a hundred. So, too, in mountaineering, the struggle is with elemental forces that are no respecters of persons. The chance of a stone hitting a German, a Frenchman, or an Italian on the east face of the Matterhorn is quite independent of their nationality, and I do not think that even Mussolini or Hitler could give his countrymen any special advantage in their own Alps. Ice is just as slippery to all, and snow-conditions as difficult to learn.

Nowhere does Nature try to write the word 'generosity' for her children in such enormous letters as in her mountain exercise-book. Every foot we go up is a widening of our horizon. And the most general characteristic of mountain folk is their natural hospitality. In season and out of season, especially the latter, along the chains of high mountains that form political boundaries in western Europe, you can depend on a delightful, natural hospitality that suggests a sort of brotherly alliance against the forces of the mountain and the weather, provided always—and it is rather a big proviso—that there is no official interference of political authority.

Mountaineering has enabled us to see, as we never did before, that a great range is not a barrier but an invitation to those who have hitherto so regarded it to meet upon its crest. A few expeditions on high frontier peaks would be an excellent preparation for those who have to discuss and *settle* affairs between nations. Not the best-known peaks, for large hotels, obsequious hotel-keepers, and press photo-graphers would ruin the plan. The representative of country B (you see I have avoided A) would employ a guide belonging to country C with which there was matter to discuss; the representative of C would have a guide from B. Any delicacies taken in the way of food or drink would be in sealed bags carried by each party, to be opened only when the two parties met upon the ridge, climbing up from their own sides. Each would be required to descend, unannounced beforehand, to seek hospitality from peasants living on the slopes beyond their own political boundary. If possible, doubtful weather with probable storms should be chosen to heighten the appreciation of that simple hospitality. On the frontier ridge the two parties would proceed roped together over some steep, loose rocks and an ice-slope or two, to the summit. Each of the two guides would afterwards send in a report of the behaviour of both men. If this test was satisfactorily survived as to bodily safety and mental equanimity, the two representatives might well be trusted to negotiate. The fact that there are now two men in Europe capable of instituting and enforcing such a test makes one long to see it tried; but I am afraid it might not appeal to either of them.

To make these glorious peaks of the Alps in any sense whatever an instrument for sowing discord, envy, or jealousy between man and man is a degradation of the great purpose which the last century discovered in them; it is a wilful attempt to restrict the riches that are there in abundance for all to share. The very best a mountain gives is what is obtainable by all who climb. Those who attempt to take it for themselves are by that very action changing it to something of lower value. Men will go on climbing by routes that demand all they can honourably give of strength and intelligence and admiration —the union of man and mountain is not complete until they have done that—and without any need of the spur of national, or even of human rivalry. This is what sets the value of mountaineering above price, that, at its best, no rivalry can make a scarcity that raises value, and no abundance can lower that value. The easiest snow peak and the hardest pinnacle have something that is free to all to find, that scoffs at prices fixed by human estimates. The labourers who start at the eleventh hour *are* sometimes rewarded equally with those who start at one.

To set a very high value on priority and difficulty in mountaineering is to introduce into it the same stupid contentions and questions of precedence that exist in the lower spheres of human activity. Instead of debasing the ideals of mountaineering to the level of values current in the plain, why not keep them at their highest as a refreshing exception to contemplate, one that will encourage us to believe that we may pursue the common purpose suggested by the peaks themselves? For on whatever side we stand, the higher they invite us to fix our eyes upon them, the more nearly will the directions of our purpose coincide.

The peculiarly controversial character which these struggles on the Matterhorn have assumed from the very start is sufficient excuse for the above digression.

There are climbers of many other nations to which no special reference can be made here. There are the Belgians, who can look with a pride in which all mountaineers have a special share, on the record of their great King Albert, the only reigning sovereign who has been devoted to our sport. There are the Japanese, who have found a device which expresses the ideal and the practical as well as it can be done in words: 'May our six senses be pure and may the weather on the honourable mountain be fine.' That is, if possible, freer from any suggestion of rivalry than 'Excelsior' on the 'banner with a strange device,' and it is incomparably better in its recognition of the practical difficulties of carrying out the climbers' purpose than that of Longfellow's hero, who seems to have been one of the worst-equipped solitary climbers that ever deserved to come to grief. The Japanese motto dates from the days long before Japan became one of the great powers. They may now have something more on the lines of the French: 'Pour la Patrie, par la Montagne.'

The Dutch number among many fine climbers a 'Flying Dutch-man' in the Alps, and P. C. Visser and his wife, the explorers of the Hunza-Karakorams. Of all these other nations who have shared in the growth of mountaineering there is one of which I must make more than a mere mention—the Americans; for here also, as in all inter-national affairs, however slight their interest may be, it seems impossible to leave them out.

'Slight interest' may raise a cry of protest from any American who reads it. Yet I maintain that for such a nation the words are justified. I know that the great lexicographer of the Alps, Dr. W. A. B. Coolidge, was American-born; that great feats have been performed in the Alps by climbers like Mr. Underhill, in the Selkirks by Mr. Howard Palmer, in the desolate Polar ranges of Alaska by Allen Carpe, William Ladd, Terriss Moore, and others, and that adventurous exploration by Americans has extended to the ranges of India and Tibet. I know that the climbing playground of North Wales and of the Lake District might be put into one of the national parks of the U.S.A. and never noticed, that the glacier area of the North American Rockies is greater than that of the Alps, and that the U.S.A. contains sixty peaks of over fourteen thousand feet. That is not what matters.

How does the proportion of keen mountaineers, that is to say, of men who choose a climbing holiday in preference to any other, in

Chicago or San Francisco, compare with the numbers in Manchester, Lyons, Munich, or Turin, and what is the attitude to mountains of those Americans who climb them? That is the point, and judged by such tests I think many Americans would agree with me that the great contribution of their country has been insignificant in the past and must lie in the future. I want to try, very briefly, to suggest one or two reasons why this is so.

The opinion of the mass, if it is a mass of Americans, sways a man's opinion more in the U.S.A. than in any other country, so that his opinions come to him ready-made. This standardization makes for progress in the material world, progress towards greater comfort for the body, which is a definite aim. In the world of contemplative thought and perception, America has not yet shown creative power. She has bought thousands of Europe's best pictures, the greatest masterpieces of European musicians are performed in America with bigger orchestras and better European artists than anywhere in the world. And she has so far produced nothing in the way of pictures or music to be compared to these works in quality.

How could it be otherwise? Her past is a history of great achievement in the conquest of material resources. The pioneering spirit that has pushed that tide of victory farther and farther west still loves to add more and more treasures to an enormous store of possessions, and the quicker the better. It is in a spirit of acquisition that most Americans come to climb. The Matterhorn and Mont Blanc have been worth putting in the bag to carry home. It may be the first great peak they have been on. They put themselves into the hands of a competent guide and are taken up—in good weather the danger is very small. I have met such parties. A guide confided to me that one of a couple of young Americans must have slipped a hundred times on the Swiss side of the Matterhorn; he looked exhausted and rather frightened, as any man might on a big mountain entirely beyond his own powers. However, he got his peak, and I dare say he will never climb another. And I do not think that that was an exceptional case.

Even in the American records of big mountaineering adventure, there is rarely any indication of anything beyond the satisfaction of dominating a natural obstacle. Quantity per hour increased by more and more taylorized methods has been so often for the American the aim in his own country and in his visits to Europe that it would be strange if it was not noticeable in his mountaineering too.

He has not had time to take a long look at anything, and the appreciation of quality outside material things is a slow growth. The things that endure and are always around us, enveloping human life, show so little change and movement that in the hustle of life they do not challenge notice, and least of all where the battle of life is fought at highest speed. The American is very quick to absorb informa' tion. He is far more likely to be able to tell you the size of Winchester Cathedral compared with St. Peter's at Rome and other churches, the date of its older portions, and the most famous mutilations of its sculptures by the Puritans, than most inhabitants of Winchester. He hardly knows it at all as it is known by one who has lived his life beside it, who drops in at odd moments, to sit or walk in its aisles and transepts, for no reason that could be gathered from a guide'book, to whom it is not the actual age of what surrounds him that matters so much as the suggestion it conveys of things where time does not matter at all.

Veneration, which implies some humbling of the spirit, seems to be required, and that is not common in America. Veneration for anything like material success or worldly position is abject; veneration akin to worship of some worthy object is necessary for the production of great work that can lift men up. Real inspiration dies out with the capacity for objective worship. The pioneer is apt to regard every' thing he sees as an invitation to conquest, and you cannot venerate what you can regard as conquered.

The feats of Americans in mountaineering have been such as one would expect from such an enterprising, vigorous young nation. Their achievements are less numerous because their life is still so full of excitement and adventure that the physical side of mountaineering could not have appealed to many of them as it did to those who lived more settled lives in Victorian times in England.

Yet America is the nation, beyond all others, that has most to learn from mountaineering on the contemplative side, the side to which she has been most blind. And if Nature had left her without the means of cultivating the pleasures that bring refreshment and repose and new adventures in the spiritual world, she would be in a sorry case. It is not so. America has no old cathedrals, to develop that capacity for worship which is the priceless treasure we have not yet lost in western Europe, and which can remain with us though every picture in our museums should cross the Atlantic. But she has got something older, more beautiful, and more instructive still in her snow mountains. Much depends on what she asks of them and what she will let them teach her. Her sons and daughters may make new records on them; they may climb them by hazardous routes and in amazingly short times. That will make exciting reading and will show, what we all knew already, that there is a great store of vitality and courage in Americans. It will show no increase of what is lacking of that which mountains can so well supply.

When I hear of a party in America that has climbed no peaks well known in climbing circles, that on some of their days they halted longer on the summit and on the way down than any party in America has been known to do, then I shall think that the era of new adventure in American mountaineering has begun. Such news could only reach me by private information, for I cannot imagine any American editor allowing a thing of this sort in any publication.

It is the removal of the need for hurry that opens the door of the mind to all sorts of impressions that cannot force their way through the surrounding hustle of everyday life. And it is the displacement of other thoughts in the mind by the need for the easy and constant direction of physical effort that leaves it delightfully free for the reception of those impressions when physical effort ceases. On a climb time often passes extraordinarily quickly, and that generally means on a mountain that the mind has been going slow though the body may have been strenuously employed. That is why the kind of healthy fatigue that produces perfect sleep may come at the end of a day's climbing; it is a benefit which the most restless of peoples will not despise. In mere walking the action of the body is so mechanical that the mind is free to work; some of the hardest thinking is done by solitary walkers in preparing sermons and speeches. In climbing, even where there is no strain upon the nerves, there is generally enough attention required for the placing of hands and feet to keep the mind from working at anything but low pressure. When we halt, the mind may be peculiarly ready to receive impressions, and these are taken in, as it were, with the whole being, and without any conscious effort at all. This is the perfect use of leisure, that time when we can, if we choose, take in with no expenditure of effort what the bountiful hand of Providence supplies through the peaks around us. From them we may draw the motive and the inspiration for what we call our working hours, and acquire knowledge of the immeasurable realities of life of which nothing can ever rob us.

'Time is money.' This Anglo-Saxon maxim is much honoured in America. It is a valuable idea in material development and in our hours of work. Time and money are therefore just the ideas that we should endeavour to banish from leisure, which is meant to remind us of the things in which time and money cease to have importance. The more our leisure is occupied with things which banish these two ideas, the more profitable it will be to mind and body. Now mountains are the least changing, the most timeless things of earth, and you cannot go into their more intimate recesses without finding out that money may cease to have any value at all.

I once heard a very distinguished professor lecture on social conditions a hundred years hence, when the problem of the struggle for material existence would have been solved by increase of production, and the more difficult problem of the use of leisure would confront the world. He said that America was the country which had most opportunities of using leisure but was also the country which had the least idea of how to do it. Perhaps America will let her mountains help to refute that professor, and it may be her women who will give the lead. It has been written by a learned observer of American habits that 'the women are accustomed to leisure, and do not fear or despise it, for the men have passed it on to them, not knowing what to do with it themselves.'

It is rather curious to observe how similar in the different countries of Europe the growth of mountaineering has been among women. Here and there in the very early days a Mademoiselle d'Angeville, and later a Miss Walker, would climb great peaks from a desire which the greatest physical discomforts could not quench. Then the rapid spread of sporting activity among women occurred in the present century, and in a few years we find women of all nationalities climbing after and sometimes leading their countrymen. As we should expect, women climbers tend to follow the latest fashions in climbing more obediently than men, standards of technical proficiency being more esteemed in women's climbing clubs than in men's. That is the natural result of a desire to eliminate a sort of physical inferiority complex; the mere description of an ascent as 'manless' is quite informative. This inferiority complex can hardly survive the accounts of climbs like those of Miss Gertrude Bell on the north-east face of the Finsteraarhorn, and of other more modern lady climbers who have thoroughly absorbed the competitive spirit, shortening the time taken over the most difficult routes made by famous men on the Grandes Jorasses, and adopting still more hazardous and more lavishly pitoned routes on the precipices of the Julian Alps. Indeed, it looks as if a few 'womanless' ascents might be required in the future in the qualification for some of the more exclusive men's clubs.

A lady is the author of a delightful story called *The Enchanted April,* in which four women, jaded by the monotony of their lives and by all the little cares that occupy the time of people in civilized communities, break loose and go off at a venture to a villa in Italy. There the beauty of nature and the right use of leisure rejuvenate them. Enchanted months, that may have almost any name from January to December, and are no dreams of fiction, are awaiting innumerable parties of Americans who are young enough and eager enough to desire them. It is tempting, especially to a schoolmaster, to fall into the snare of prescribing a recipe for enchantment. All the books in the world will not procure it. Experience cannot do more than help to avoid adverse influences, and experience suggests: Avoid a crowd, and choose your place for the beauty of its peaks. Make no attempt to find out what has been climbed and take no Climbers' Guide with you. Climb what attracts you, and by a ridge rather than a face, and make your choice on the principle that beauty is more important than opportunities for the testing of technique. Make sure that many hours are spent in high places in doing nothing that can be recorded. Choose your resting-place, camp, hut, or hotel, so that it combines beauty of position with the utmost possible independence and detachment from community life, and the minimum expenditure of time on supplying what is needed for physical well-being.

America has already an advantage in possessing one requirement. She has still a child's capacity for enchantment. In Europe it is almost a mark of intelligence to have lost it, as you can read in countless European novels. Nevertheless, if you want to find a European of mature age who still retains this privilege of childhood, look for him first among men who love mountains.

It may be that, even among such, enchantment will fail. Then America is our hope, for Americans are great missionaries. When they have learned the mountain secrets of enchantment, and when we have had them stolen from us by rivalry and mechanization, perhaps they will come over to us and help us to get them back.

This is not quite groundless optimism, for America has produced John Muir, of all men who have written about mountains the most eager, the most childlike, and the most ready for enchantment. He is the Saussure of American mountaineering, an enthusiastic naturalist and geologist, whose studies are directed by a great and generous love of mountains. He has not lost the imagination that may have come to him through his ancestors from the misty hills of Scotland, and he

has the sunny, youthful exuberance of young America. The spon-
taneousness of his enthusiasm is remarkable if we consider that his
book on the mountains of California was published in 1894, more
than twenty years after the appearance of Clarence King's *Mountaineering
in the Sierra Nevada.* If Muir is the Saussure of America, King might
be described as its Sanger Davies, whose book on the Dolomites
was considered to have been not untruthfully, though indiscreetly,
announced in a weekly review under the heading 'Fiction.'

It is a pity that King climbed before the age of the cinema had
dawned. His ascent of Mount Tyndall as portrayed by him would
have made a grand film. The start could hardly be bettered. 'Our
friends helped us on with our packs in silence, and as we shook
hands there was not a dry eye in the party.' The bivouac on a shelf
of granite is nearly as good:

We ate our supper of cold venison and bread, and whittled from the sides of
the wooden barometer-case shavings enough to warm water for a cup of miser-
ably tepid tea, and then—rolled ourselves in our blankets and lay down to enjoy
the view. . . . A sudden chill enveloped us. Stars in a moment crowded
through the dark heaven, flashing with a frosty splendour. The snow con-
gealed, the brooks ceased to flow, and, under the powerful sudden leverage of
frost, immense blocks were dislodged all along the mountain summits and came
thundering down the slopes, booming upon the ice, dashing wildly upon rocks.
Under the lee of our shelf we felt quite safe, but neither Cotter nor I could help
being startled, and jumping just a little, as these missiles, weighing often many
tons, struck the ledge over our heads and whizzed down the gorge.'

There is the climb up the cliff, of which the following is but one
among many incidents:

About thirty feet directly over our heads was another shelf, which, if we could
reach, seemed to offer at least a temporary way upward. On its edge were two
or three spikes of granite; whether firmly connected with the cliff, or merely
blocks of débris, we could not tell from below. I said to Cotter, I thought of
but one possible plan; it was to lasso one of these blocks and to climb, sailor-
fashion, hand over hand, up the rope. In the lasso I had perfect confidence,
for I had seen more than one Spanish bull throw his whole weight against it
without parting a strand. The shelf was so narrow that throwing the coil of
rope was a very difficult undertaking. I tried three times, and Cotter spent five
minutes vainly whirling the loop at the granite spikes. At last I made a lucky
throw, and it tightened upon one of the smaller protuberances. I drew the noose
close, and very gradually threw my hundred and fifty pounds upon the rope;
then Cotter joined me, and, for a moment, we both hung our united weight
upon it. Whether the rock moved slightly or whether the lasso stretched a little

we were unable to decide, but the trial must be made, and I began to climb slowly. The smooth precipice face against which my body swung offered no foothold, and the whole climb had therefore to be done by the arms, an effort requiring all one's determination. When about half-way up I was obliged to rest, and, curling my feet in the rope, managed to relieve my arms for a moment. In this position I could not resist the fascinating temptation of a survey downward.

It was Mr. King himself who had led into temptation.
Then the glissade:

Without untying the lasso which bound us together, we sprang upon the snow with a shout, and glissaded down splendidly, turning now and then a somersault, and shooting out like cannon-balls almost to the middle of the frozen lake, I upon my back and Cotter feet first, in a swimming position. The ice cracked in all directions. It was only a thin, transparent film, through which we could see deep into the lake. Untying ourselves, we hurried ashore in different directions, lest our combined weight should be too great a strain upon any point.

That is merely on the approach to the peak. Reluctantly I must cut out large, exciting bits. Once King acknowledges:

We were now in a dangerous position: to fall into the crevice upon one side was to be wedged to death between rock and ice; to make a slip was to be shot down five hundred feet, and then hurled over the brink of a precipice. In the friendly seat which this wedge gave me I stopped to take wet and dry observations with the thermometer—this being an absolute preventive of a scare—and to enjoy the view.

The ascent of the final peak is worthy of the approach.
A smooth granite wall ran right round the summit, and a pillar of snow and ice resting in a niche of the precipice provided a sufficiently sensational finish.

At last, in order to prevent myself from falling over backwards, I was obliged to thrust my hand into the crack between the ice and the wall, and the spire became so narrow that I could do this on both sides, so that the climb was made as upon a tree, cutting mere toe-holes and embracing the whole column of ice in my arms. At last I reached the top, and, with the greatest caution, wormed my body over the brink, and, rolling out upon the smooth surface of the granite, looked over and watched Cotter make his climb. He came steadily up, with no sense of nervousness, until he got to the narrow part of the ice, and here he stopped and looked up with a forlorn face to me; but as he climbed up over the edge the broad smile came back to his face, and he asked me if it had occurred to me that we had, by and by, to go down again.
We had now an easy slope to the summit, and hurried up over rocks and ice,

reaching the crest at exactly twelve o'clock. I rang my hammer upon the topmost rock; and we grasped hands, and I reverently named the grand peak Mount Tyndall.

I doubt if Hollywood could improve on that.

John Muir is entirely different. In his book, *The Mountains of California,* we find no attempt to draw attention to the temerity of his exploits. It is the attempt of a simple, enthusiastic soul to let us share his delight in what he saw and did in the course of years of wandering, generally alone in the mountains and especially in the snowy Sierra, which to him was above all others 'the Range of Light, the most divinely beautiful of all the mountains I have ever seen.' He used to winter in a small cabin in Yosemite Valley, which he describes as 'that sublime Sierra temple where every day we may see the grandest sights.' If the following was a good sample of his day, it is safe to say that John Muir knew how to enjoy his mountains in a way that could never lose its intensity.

I had long been anxious to study some points in the structure of the ice-cone that is formed every winter at the foot of the upper Yosemite fall, but the blinding spray by which it is invested had hitherto prevented me from making a sufficiently near approach. This morning the entire body of the fall was torn into gauzy shreds, and thrown horizontally along the face of the cliff, leaving the cone dry; and while making my way to the top of an overlooking ledge to seize so favourable an opportunity to examine the interior of the cone, the peaks of the Merced group came in sight over the shoulder of the South Dome, each waving a resplendent banner against the blue sky, as regular in form, and as firm in texture, as if of woven silk. So rare and splendid a phenomenon, of course, overbore all other considerations, and I at once let the ice-cone go, and began to force my way out of the valley to some dome or ridge sufficiently lofty to command a general view of the main summits, feeling assured that I should find them bannered still more gloriously; nor was I in the least disappointed. Indian Cañon, through which I climbed, was choked with snow that had been shot down in avalanches from the high cliffs on either side, rendering the ascent difficult, but, inspired by the roaring storm, the tedious wallowing brought no fatigue, and in four hours I joined the top of a ridge above the valley, eight thousand feet high. And there in bold relief, like a clear painting, appeared a most imposing scene. Innumerable peaks, black and sharp, rose grandly into the dark blue sky, their bases set in solid white, their sides streaked and splashed with snow like ocean rocks with foam; and from every summit, all free and unconfused, was streaming a beautiful, silky, silvery banner, from half a mile to a mile in length, slender at the point of attachment, then widening gradually as it extended from the peak until it was about a thousand or fifteen hundred feet in breadth, as near as I could estimate.

Muir revels in the high pasture as a good mountaineer should do.

After the lapse of an hour or two, vertical bars of sunshine are seen ahead between the brown shafts of the pines, showing that you are approaching an open space, and then you suddenly emerge from the forest shadows upon a delightful purple lawn lying smooth and free in the light like a lake. This is a glacier meadow. It is about a mile and a half long by a quarter of a mile wide. The trees come pressing forward all around in close serried ranks, planting their feet exactly on its margin, and holding themselves erect, strict and orderly like soldiers on parade; thus bounding the meadow with exquisite precision, yet with free curving lines such as Nature alone can draw. With inexpressible delight you wade out into the grassy sunlake, feeling yourself contained in one of Nature's most sacred chambers, withdrawn from the sterner influences of the mountains, secure from all intrusion, secure from yourself, free in the universal beauty. And notwithstanding the scene is so impressively spiritual, and you seem dissolved in it, yet everything about you is beating with warm, terrestrial human love and life delightfully substantial and familiar.

I do not think you will want to skip the description of this glacier meadow if you ever come across it, and if you have memories of your own that help to bring it up before you. He is quite simple and sincere in his wish to make you share his ecstasies over these things, that are seen in their perfect setting among high mountains. The midday storms are among them:

When the glorious pearl and alabaster clouds of the noonday storms are being built, I never give attention to anything else. No mountain or mountain-range, however divinely clothed with light, has a more enduring charm than those fleeting mountains of the sky.

He sees that birds and beasts, as well as human beings, respond to mountain influences in different ways.

I also noticed one solitary grey eagle braving the storm on the top of a tall pine-stump just outside the main grove. He was standing bolt upright with his back to the wind, a tuft of snow piled on his square shoulders, a monument of passive endurance. Thus every snow-bound bird seemed more or less uncomfortable, if not in positive distress. The storm was reflected in every gesture, and not one cheerful note, not to say song, came from a single bill; their cowering, joyless endurance offering a striking contrast to the spontaneous, irrepressible gladness of the ouzel, who could no more help exhaling sweet song than a rose sweet fragrance. He *must* sing though the heavens fall. . . . Once I was snow-bound on Mount Shasta for three days, a little below the timber line. It was a dark and stormy time, well calculated to test the skill and endurance of mountaineers. The snow-laden gale drove on night and day in hissing, blinding floods, and when at length it began to abate, I found that a small band of wild

Q

sheep had weathered the storm in the lee of a clump of dwarf pines a few yards above my storm-nest, where the snow was eight or ten feet deep. I was warm, back of a rock, with blankets, bread, and fire. My brave companions lay in the snow, without food, and with only the partial shelter of the short trees, yet they made no sign of suffering or faint-heartedness.

Like Saussure in his eagerness to know the secrets of high mountains, Muir is far more strenuous and independent in his efforts to climb them. He rarely carried an axe, and his methods in more than one respect seem to have been unconventional.

On the southern shore of a frozen lake I encountered an extensive field of hard, granular snow, up which I scampered in fine tone, intending to follow it to its head, and cross the rocky spur against which it leans, hoping thus to come direct upon the base of the Ritter peak. The surface was pitted with oval hollows, made by stones and drifted pine-needles that had melted themselves into the mass by the radiation of absorbed sun-heat. These afforded good footholds, but the surface curved more and more steeply at the head, and the pits became shallower and less abundant, until I found myself in danger of being shed off like avalanching snow. I persisted, however, creeping on all fours, and shuffling up the smoothest places on my back, as I had often done on burnished granite, until, after slipping several times, I was compelled to retrace my course to the bottom, and make my way round the west end of the lake, and thence up to the summit of the divide.

It was a short day of autumn, and when he reached the foot of the final peak of Ritter, prudence counselled a visit of inspection only. But, as Muir says, 'we little know until tried how much of the uncontrollable there is in us, urging across glacier and torrents and up dangerous heights, let the judgment forbid as it may.' He saw in front of him some snow which had fallen in an avalanche and proceeded up it,

intending to follow it as far as possible, and at least obtain some fine wild views for my pains. . . . I thus made my way into a wilderness of crumbling spires and battlements, built together in bewildering combinations, and glazed in many places with a thin coating of ice, which I had to hammer off with stones. The situation was becoming gradually more perilous; but having passed several dangerous spots, I dared not think of descending; for, so steep was the entire ascent, one would inevitably fall to the glacier in case a single misstep was made. At length, after attaining an elevation of about 12,800 feet, I found myself at the foot of a sheer drop in the bed of the avalanche channel I was tracing, which seemed absolutely to bar further progress. It was only about forty-five or fifty feet high and somewhat roughened by fissures and projections, but these seemed so slight and insecure as footholds, that I tried hard to avoid the precipice altogether by scaling the wall of the channel on either side. But though less steep, the walls were smoother than the obstructing rock, and repeated efforts only showed that I must either go right ahead or turn back. The tried dangers beneath seemed even greater than that of the cliff in front; therefore, after scanning its face again and again, I began to scale it, picking my holds with intense caution. After gaining a point about half-way to the top, I was suddenly brought to a dead stop, with arms outspread, clinging close to the face of rock, unable to move hand or foot either up or down. My doom appeared fixed. I *must* fall. There would be a moment of bewilderment and then a lifeless rumble down the one general precipice to the glacier below.

When the final danger flashed upon me, I became nerve-shaken for the first time since setting foot on the mountains, and my mind seemed to fill with a stifling smoke. But this terrible eclipse lasted only a moment, when life blazed forth again with preternatural clearness. I seemed certainly to become possessed of a new sense. The other self, bygone experiences, instinct, or guardian angel —call it what you will—came forward and assumed control. Then my trembling muscles became firm again, every rift and flaw in the rock was seen as through a microscope, and my limbs moved with a positiveness and precision with which I seemed to have nothing to do. Had I been borne aloft upon wings, my deliverance could not have been more complete.

A very unsophisticated mountaineer, John Muir! Yes, and because of it the doors of the palace of enchantment open for him as they will not do for others who can place his ascent of Mount Ritter in the first or second grade, or among the easy moderates.

America has produced Muir. That does not mean that Americans approach mountains as he did. It would be as untrue to say so as to say that Englishmen are free from insularity and prejudice because England has produced Shelley. If thousands of Americans can learn to climb and look at mountains as John Muir did, allowing themselves an ice-axe and a map, but taking care not to take his book or any other climbing book with them, or to think that they can experience his emotions by reading him before they have dis- covered them for themselves, then they will have begun to refute any allegations made about their inability to use leisure, and will have begun training for the missionary work of rejuvenating the old countries. Perhaps I have been unjust in my judgments of American mountaineering in the past; at least I have tried to draw a happy picture of its future.

BOOK III
PERPETUAL YOUTH

CHAPTER XI

Is mountaineering already beginning to show signs of old age? Are sophistication and the increasing use of artificial aids symptoms of a maturity that is a prelude to decrepitude? Or does it possess within itself some *elixir vitae* that will keep it attractive enough to win the hearts of succeeding generations? Is the recent emphasizing of danger and difficulty an attempt to disguise a loss of youthful bloom and excite desire by the use of meretricious charms, or does mountaineering possess the secret of perpetual youth? To know that the romance of mountaineering will continue far into the future would be even better than to know the greatness of its story in the past and present.

Now, in considering the union of a man with the object of his affections, the selection he makes is of vital importance if the element of romance is to endure.

When mountains win a man's heart, it is generally a case of love at first sight. If he has not become an ardent climber after his first introduction to the Alps, it is unlikely that he will ever become so. The manner of his introduction is therefore all-important.

Let us see how this all-important introduction to mountains was made in the case of some of those who have been in every sense of the word ardent mountaineers.

Saussure says: 'I have had from childhood the most positive passion for the pleasures of the mountains. I still remember the sensation I felt when, for the first time, my hands touched the rocks of the Salève and my eyes enjoyed its points of view.' Considering that the scientific aim of ascending mountains was the only one admitted as reasonable in his day, the suggestion of the physical as well as the contemplative aspect is remarkable.

A century later a great climber of a very different type to Saussure thus describes the introduction that inspired him: 'At the age of fifteen the crags of the Via Mala and the snows of the Théodule roused a passion within me that has grown with years, and has to

233

no small extent moulded my life and thought.' The snows of the Théodule; and it is Mummery who writes! There is a width of outlook in Mummery which shows that it was mountains and not the sport of climbing only which held his devotion. 'No sooner have I ascended a peak than it becomes a friend, and delightful as it may be to seek "fresh woods and pastures new," in my heart of hearts I long for the slopes of which I know every wrinkle, for which each way awakens memories of mirth and laughter, and of the friends of long ago.'

The technical obstacles of a climb are the obvious attraction that no young climber can miss. They are the superficial charms displayed for all to admire. But if his head is first turned by them, the snows of the Théodule may seem so plain as to be repellent.

Conway is a man to whom mountains have appealed in every mood and under every clime. His first ascent is the Worcestershire Beacon.

To go inland instead of to the seashore had seemed a poor sort of expedition till I had climbed this hill, and then I had no further use for the sea. . . . The view was the great revelation. I had never beheld so much of the world at once. Names were nothing to me, nor counties and far-away towns and tiny dots of cathedrals; I remember little of all that, but can recall as though it was yesterday the great, flat, extending world that spread away and away on this side and on that, and called to be wandered over and possessed by wandering. Wide outstretching vistas, thank Heaven, still retain for me the same mysterious charm that belonged to that one.

And perhaps that early experience explains why Conway is ever a wanderer, pursuing, and never quite reaching, the perfect place among distant ranges of the world.

This was an experience of much greater importance than the epoch-making discovery that a stretch and a kick would get him up the back of the Toad Rock at Tunbridge Wells. 'It was my first experience of the joy of rock-climbing—the concrete pleasure of solving a gymnastic problem. I have never been a great rock-climber, but from that day the cragsman's delight has been comprehensible.'

The first real mountain he ascended was Snowdon. He describes the ascent as 'a mere uphill walk along a mule road,' and remembers nothing of it till 'to my inexpressible delight, we came into clouds.' Later he is justly indignant at being made to complete his first mountain ascent astride a horse, with his arms round an aunt's waist. He pleads guilty to the pride of achievement, as we all must if we are honest. 'The fact that I had been up Snowdon, the highest mountain in

England and Wales, and that I had been in the clouds, overwhelmed all other memories and induced a sense of childish importance which I trust no one ever discovered. . . . In the upshot, this adventure set me on the road I was to follow.'

Earlier chapters have shown him on the highest portion of that road. It is impossible to resist following him beyond its early stages to his first view of the Alps from Zimmerwald.

At last came a morning when the sun shone through my window, and I looked unexpectedly forth—lo! there were the snow-mountains, radiant, over-whelming, the whole row of them, from Blümlisalp to Finsteraarhorn, glittering in a sun-mantle of new-fallen snow. They were not in the least like clouds, nor like anything I had ever beheld or dreamed of. Had they been built of transparent crystal they could not have been more brilliant. I felt them as no part of this earth, or in any way belonging to the world of experience. Here at least was the other world, visible, inaccessible, no doubt, but authentically there; actual yet incredible, veritably solid, with an aspect of eternal endurance, yet also ethereal; overwhelmingly magnificent, but attractive too. No dimmest idea of climbing them entered my mind; I gazed and gazed, and all day long returned to gaze again with a formless, inarticulate, intoxicating emotion that, alas! can never return. They were not individual to me—Jungfrau and Eiger and the rest. I resented being bothered with their names. They were just the walls of heaven.

It is like Mr. Belloc's wonderful first vision of the Alps on his path to Rome. Many climbers may be glad that a closer approach changed this formless emotion into a less reverent attitude; otherwise they might not have had Conway and Coolidge's Climbers' Guides, which reduce the traverse of a great Zermatt peak to so many 'hours' walking.'

It is with diffidence that I try to give you a glimpse of Mr. Geoffrey Young's approach to mountains. To see just what he really feels is harder than with most writers, though he makes us willing enough to do so. Touring with his father as quite a young boy, he laid the foundation of a special intimacy with the Welsh hills, long before he made any contact with that face of Lliwedd, whose sternest features he has made familiar to so many Easter parties. It was the discovery of Whymper's *Scrambles* in the library at Marlborough that made him long to climb great peaks. His first snow expedition was made with a Cambridge friend—a modest guideless adventure. 'There was no more than a hard snowfield on the Col du Palet, and a wilted and dingy one at that! But never a glacier has since seemed so noble. We made the most of its non-existent terrors under a grey dawn; and plodded afterwards down the spring alps to Val d'Isère, with the gravity becoming to proven mountaineers.' Humble and childlike beginnings for one who was to be the hero of so many thrilling episodes on high hills, and who was to give us such masses of accumulated wisdom under the name of *Mountain Craft*. But though when he became a man he put away many childish things, it seems to me he has not discarded the best of them.

Guido Rey was taken out on the hills when a young lad, by Quintino Sella. His cousins were more experienced, and he had a struggle to keep up with them; and of these early days he says: 'I rather think emulation played a large part in my longing for moun-tains.' There was, in his case, a certain disappointment in the reality he found there compared with the idea that pictures of the Alps had given him. He was taken up slopes too arduous, and rocks too difficult for his powers. Prohibition, albeit of clear waters, was in force for him as it was for Mr. Young before he reached years of discretion. Both of them regret the wasted opportunities of slaking the magnificent thirst that hill-sides offered them in boyhood.

In Rey's performances with knotted ropes and ladders on the Furggen ridge of the Matterhorn there are traces of a childish petulance and will to dominate, which may have been encouraged by the spirit of emulation aroused on his first expeditions. Fortunately there is another Rey that responded ardently to the appeal of high places. Up on the ridges

I found a mountain world that had never been painted, that no book had ever described, more wonderful and new than the dream of any fairy-tale. Feelings were mine that I had never felt before; the instinctive joy at rising above every-thing that was mean and low, the sensuous delight of great fatigue, and the deep sleep that follows on it. The bread I ate up there tasted as it never did before. And I discovered the new, strange happiness of arriving on the highest point, the very summit where the mountain ceases to go up, where the mind ceases to desire; an almost perfect form of simple satisfaction such as a philosopher might feel who, after long researches, reaches a truth in which his spirit finds contentment and repose.

It is this latter Guido Rey who has wrapped the Matterhorn in such a golden light of adoration that what he does upon it is of comparatively small importance.

To guides, the Alps are the home of their childhood and their source of livelihood. We expect them to have their interest centred in their craft and to be inarticulate in the expression of their feelings. One, however, has written his experiences, who was also a con-summate master in his profession, Christian Klucker. It is interesting to see what was his first approach to mountains, and how he thinks men should regard them.

On a beautiful Sunday in July, after leaving the cattle in the care of my younger brother, I set off in the direction of the Fex Glacier with my companion, a seventeen-year-old seminary student from Fex, and reached the top of the pass after a pleasant walk over the unbroken glacier. The only crevasse we met with was the *bergschrund* below the pass, and we turned it without danger. This magnificent tour, and especially the view from the high pass into Val Malenco as far as Sondrio in the Valtelline, left an unforgettable impression on my mind.

Klucker was then nine years old.

And later on: 'Every summer we visited the beautiful pyramid of Piz Ot, which commands such splendid views, and likewise Piz Languard.' Depression and disappointments were his portion about the time young Englishmen go to the university, and he found solace in climbing the mountains round Sils. There were no good guides in the commune, and Klucker was occasionally engaged to act as one. He tells us the curious incident that was 'the main motive, and indeed the basis of his career as a guide.' The young Countess von Reichenbach, one of two ladies whom he had piloted on the hills near Sils, presented him with a picture, underneath which was a dedication containing the words from Psalm cxxi: 'I will lift up mine eyes unto the hills, from whence cometh my help.' 'Down in the valley,' thought Klucker, 'there will be no help, either material or moral, for me.'

He gave up his trade of wheelwright and became a guide—to be later nicknamed 'the infallible' by Captain J. P. Farrar, the greatest mountaineer among many famous men who employed him.

In a letter to the guide Walter Risch, Klucker says:

You write about aiming higher all the time, so as to keep pace with cultural development. Let us omit *Kultur* in connection with the ideal, free-hearted mountaineer, because too much of a good thing will drive us, in mountaineering also, into the arms of 'sheer sport.' The younger generation in particular should hold strictly and strongly to the rule that the ideal conception of mountain-climbing is not to be supplanted by sport and competitive rivalry. I despise mechanical mountain-climbing, when it becomes a general practice.

One more name must not be omitted among the few famous mountaineers whose manner of approach to mountains I have mentioned: that of Whymper. His *Scrambles Amongst the Alps* has fired more boys with a desire to climb than any other book. It is a tale of adventure well told, and the illustrations have been helped by an imagination that was far more elastic and more powerful than any camera, however tilted.

Whymper was, moreover, a sort of Homer of modern moun-taineering. Axes, ropes, chimneys, *arêtes,* couloirs, ice-slopes, and *bergschrunds,* guides like Croz and Carrel, to say nothing of the Alpine porter, were things that could be launched with all the novelty of Homer's epithets on a public that was just ready to take interest in a great new sport. And beside all that, there was the epic struggle with the Matterhorn, and the final drama of its conquest.

Whymper was sent out to make sketches of the Alps, and in particular Mont Pelvoux in Dauphiné. The Englishman whose victory the sketches were to illustrate failed to climb the peak. An agreeable Frenchman persuaded Whymper to join him in a fresh attack. They conquered, and the story of the *Scrambles* was begun.

The Matterhorn attracted Whymper by its grandeur and its in-accessibility. What rivalries and jealousies have risen about its cliffs since then! The early years of Whymper's climbing career give the impression of a genuine enthusiasm, but no one who has followed the story of his travels subsequent to the year 1865 can fail to see a lowering of enjoyment and of aim. The great recreations of life often lose their joyousness when they have to provide the material means of subsistence, and their highest restorative virtues can be destroyed by constant use. And sincerity, which is vital to the preservation of ideals, may be sorely tried by perpetual demands for a profession of faith.

If men write to sell, they must sometimes paint the expression of their feelings in colours that too easily rub off and leave them less sensitive than before. When they confine themselves to facts and a technique they know, they are on surer foundations. It is when a man begins to trade with what he holds most dear that he is bound to lose. I think all the great mountaineers whom I have quoted earlier in this chapter wrote because they had a precious thing to share with others, something that was above the thought of barter. We can sometimes share the best things in life; we cannot traffic with them, for they are above price.

What conclusion can we draw from the first experiences of the great mountaineers I have quoted? The physical side takes its proper place as an essential part of the whole idea of mountaineering. They wanted to climb peaks because the peaks made them long to do so, not because they hoped to measure themselves with other climbers with results gratifying to their pride. They did not ask themselves: 'Shall

I be able to do what X has done or go one better?' or, in more modern phraseology: 'Can I hope to be a sixth-grade climber or even start a seventh?'

No doubt it is highly gratifying to youthful pride to reach the sixth form of a gymnastic school of mountaineering. At the same time a man may be learning more of the real values of life if he is an unclassed but active member of a mountaineering university of all the faculties.

After a few visits to the Alps I began leading others, even younger and less experienced than myself, to that source of health and beauty and adventure, to see if they would drink those life-giving waters. Some of them did. There is no more certain method of retaining and adding to the enthusiasm and the raptures of one's own youth. Mallory became the best-known of these best of all companions. He himself has left no record of his early impressions of snow mountains beyond a single entry in the minutes that we kept. As he had never known any real mountain at all before that first introduction to the Alps, the nature of that introduction may be of some general interest as well as another illustration for the purpose of this chapter.

We started a party of three. We failed on our first peak, the Vélan, either to reach the top or to obtain the hoped-for view. Mountain-sickness and the weather robbed us of what might have been a magnificent presentation to the Alps. Two days later we crossed the Grand Combin. Then we took the passes in a long day from Chanrion to Zermatt, traversed Monte Rosa to Gressoney, and came back over the Felikjoch. Mallory and I went on to Chamonix, with some adventures in descending the Trient ice-fall, crossed the Col du Géant, and finally Mont Blanc from the Dôme hut to Chamonix. The routes up our peaks mattered comparatively little. I know there was a chimney going up the Combin that we all enjoyed, and there was a short, steep ice-slope descending near the top that I approached with apprehension; I remember going our hardest on a terrace below the ice-cliffs. I can still see some lovely rough orange rocks that we scaled by mistake in reaching a niche in the ridge south of Les Bouquetins, which we thought was the North Col du Mont Brûlé, and which was not. Of the Crestone Rey I remember nothing except that it was the way we chose up the Dufourspitze. I can still almost taste the cream we ate at an alp on the way to the Sella hut, and still almost feel the finger of the old man who served us as he poked it into a hole in my knickerbockers and said: 'Ah! je vois que vous êtes Anglais!' The Dôme hut on Mont Blanc gives me a picture of an atmosphere full of flying particles of dry snow, apparently blown by the storm through the good wooden walls; of ice on the floor unmelted through the night, and of a lump of very ancient cheese discovered on a shelf and toasted to try and appease our terrible hunger. I remember an undignified descent of the last bit of the Mur de la Côte, when I tired of cutting steps and believed that the nails in my companion's boots would be to him as crampons; perhaps he too was reminded of it by a similar descent of the last bit of the North Col on Everest, but there was no Finch with a camera to chaff us.

But far eclipsing all is the memory of our state of mind after the first success on the Combin, as we approached the Panossière hut, and later the inn at Mauvoisin; the blessed certainty in all of us that we had spent the best day of our lives, not counting the treasures we had seen and made our own, but knowing them to be beyond price. The supremacy of that great day was shaken by the experiences of the one spent on the high-level route to Zermatt. We felt it had definitely passed on with us as we descended into Italy from the peak of Monte Rosa. And as we trudged through the woods by the paths above the Bossons Glacier that do eventually lead to Couttet's, we realized that Mont Blanc could displace even Monte Rosa as a promoter of ultimate satisfactions.

The climbing, with all the excitements and the problems it offered, had been glorious, but it was only part of a much bigger thing. It might be compared to a good dinner given by a wonderful host, a joy to eat, but at the same time not by any means all you had expected or received from him.

Arolla has been the scene of many a climber's first introduction to the Alps, and there is no better place. A simple snow peak is the only one that bears its name, the Pigne d'Arolla. It is hard for me to imagine how any one can look up at the Pigne, whether it be an hour when its long white crest carries one's eye up into unfathomable depths of blue sky, or when it sheds the light of another world upon the darkening valley, and not long to share its outlook on the world.

There are plenty of climbers who have not felt at all like that. *A chacun son goût!* I asked a boy who had been taken on his first Alpine holiday to Arolla whether he went up the Pigne. 'Oh, no!' he said. 'They told me it was nothing but a snow grind!' I thought of another who has done many climbs with me and gets full enjoyment out of the sporting side of mountaineering, and for whom the very best of such days has never surpassed the day upon the Pigne; not her first day on a high mountain, either.

In mountaineering the issue is between man and mountain, not man and man. The mountain does not change, and man has nearly reached the limit of his natural climbing powers; hence the pursuit of difficulty must end in a *reductio ad absurdum* if the climber makes increased use of mechanical aids to remove the very difficulties he creates. There will come a time when the line of ropes and pitons by which he climbs his precipice will be indistinguishable from a *téléférique*.

The climbers who regard competition as the basis of their sport will be wise to make more and more rules to enable them to measure their powers and allot the proper pride of place to the best performers. We may, on the analogy of golf, come to a handicap system where a party is allowed only so many pitons, either as bisques to be used at will or in certain cracks. Perhaps on the analogy of cricket the dimensions of the implements may be defined, and the number of spikes on the crampons be controlled, or the type of nails in a boot. Some of the modern climbs would be still more exciting if rubber-barred. We might even see something like body-line bowling if a climb is included in the Olympic Games, and one of the parties may send men ahead to hurl missiles on the other!

How good it is to know that some higher wisdom has arranged that, as men drift further away from the purpose of sport that brings most benefit, they find less and less enjoyment in it, and are induced to consider again what sport is for. The living force in sport is recreation, and that implies amusement and enjoyment. County cricket, and still more Test Match cricket, is hard work in the sphere of public entertainment, almost as hard work, though not yet as dangerous, as that of the gladiators. Even in schools the increasingly elaborate organization and over-emphasis on the discipline of games is sapping the capacity for enjoyment in them. And there is a danger that this invaluable source of healthy amusement and pleasure will dry up and leave us to look for them in other, and perhaps less profitable ways.

It is not the case that keenness over sports is entirely dependent on competition, or only present when victory is the only aim to be considered. Let me give just one example of the type of thing I mean, and I make no apology for taking it from cricket. Cricket is an older sport than modern mountaineering, and sports have much to learn from one another.

There is a field near a famous fishing-stream, where an annual match is played. The portion chosen for the pitch has had no special preparation; but it has been weeded, cut, and rolled so often that a shooter or a bumping ball is becoming almost rare enough to cause surprise. The village rector has got up the local side, the visiting team is a mixed lot from an ancient seat of learning.

It is a perfect summer day, when the shadows are short and dark; there are summer smells of hay and warm green life, and in the sky big white clouds that form and disappear without delivering a threat of stopping the game. A local gardener is batting. A famous cricketer is bowling at him with the same intensity of purpose, the same complete mastery of pitch and flight that has worried great batsmen in England and Australia. The gardener is beaten once or twice; he blocks a few balls and then lets fly. The ball soars over the head of the outfield, as he stumbles in the tussocks near the boundary, and falls beyond the fence into a swampy patch, where it needs a search-party to find it. And the applause is led by—the bowler! He and his side are as delighted as the spectators.

One thing the many grades of cricketer on the visiting side have in common: a belief that there is no cricket that gives purer enjoyment than this; and when the game is over, whichever side has won is genuinely sorry that the other side has lost. Men grow tired of the competitive element in sport, and recognize that refreshment and enjoyment are what keep it young and life-giving.

At the end of a summer day spent like that in keen activity and the best kind of fellowship, there comes an assurance, indefinable but convincing, that an end has been pursued, vaguer and more distant, yet better and more lasting than any satisfaction obtainable from a competition. This is the only type of cricket I have played which seemed to lead towards the same ultimate goal as mountaineering, the goal I have tried to show in a later chapter. It is the sort of cricket that will be played longest, when all but those who are paid to play will have recognized that sport is, after all, a medium for the enjoyable exercise of the faculties, rather than an instrument for measuring them.

Mountaineering has not yet reached the climax of the competitive and organizing stage, which climbers, especially some foreign climbers, seem to regard as the basis on which it rests. The phase of specialization has only begun, but specialization is an inevitable consequence of assigning an exaggerated importance to the competitive aspect. It is a particularly stupid mistake in sports like running or climbing; for it is only at the expense of restricted development in more important ways that human beings will ever run as fast as hares or climb walls like cats. If the attainment of a higher standard of performance is to be the aim of mountaineering, there will be an increasing inducement for the less expert to sit complacently by the fire and read about the exploits of the star performers, instead of using their own faculties in the pursuit of an ideal which is none the less real and approachable for being impossible to measure by physical standards.

There are limits that are not distant to the measurable progress of mountaineering. When we read in our club journal that the exploration of some district is complete, that the last big climb has been done in Wales, that the limits of human possibilities have once more been reached, the limits of the measurable progress of mountaineering are clearly in sight, however far beyond the span of our own life.

That inimitable artist, Samivel, has admirably shown us the limits of the development of the competitive side of climbing in his work *Sous l'Œil des Choucas*. For me his cartoons represent the action of a kindly Providence in process of eliminating what is harmful to the children of men, with gentle but irresistible insistence forcing them back to what is for their health and enjoyment.

A time is coming when club journals will be harder to fill with what is highly flavoured with the spice of danger. The competitive spirit will weaken like the germ of scarlet fever till it finds some future generation to infect. Meanwhile men will climb in increasing measure for enjoyment.

The climber who may have seen little beyond the sporting side of mountaineering, may eventually succumb to the subtler joys offered by a mountain that enables him to take his ease upon it, to listen to **its** pleasant voice, and to enjoy the quiet assurance of its presence; laying aside for a time the burden of maintaining a position in the club lists of new ascents. Whereas the man who merely walks in contemplative paths will find in middle age that Providence has given a marked preference to youth in planning the strenuous side of mountaineering. It is exceptional for a man to be able to learn the delight of strenuous climbing after fifty; and it is not only the muscles and the heart and lungs, it is desire that fails.

We notice, too, both in the purely sporting and in the purely contemplative type, the increasing tendency to a rigid and narrow outlook, to a lack of perspective, that is often noticeable in bachelors and old maids. Ruskin is quite old-maidish in his lack of understanding of the early enthusiasts of mountaineering. It is true that some of them, like Mummery, were so ardent in their defence of the sport, and made such efforts to conceal a weakness for the spiritual

R

(a) In A.D. 2000 (b) In A.D. 3000

33. THE FUTURE OF MECHANIZED CLIMBING

Plates from 'Sous l'Œil des Choucas,' by Samivel, pub. by Delagrave, Paris

appeal of mountains, that in their case the union of the physical and spiritual might almost be regarded as a sort of clandestine affair that had not received the blessing of authority.

And there is often a diminution of delight that may be a warning. There grows in the mere performance of difficult feats a competitive spirit that checks spontaneous enjoyment. We cannot enjoy our mountain to the full if we are keeping an eye, and it may be a very jealous eye, on the doings of others. And if the object of our effort is an achievement whose value is to be measured by comparison with the performances of others, if it is to secure for ourselves a special claim to one of a limited number of routes not yet taken, then our success must be won at some loss to others, and the prizes available must diminish with every year that passes. There is no ultimate satisfaction in such success. On the other hand, there is developed in those who adopt a purely contemplative attitude to mountains a passivity which resists the challenge to action they throw down. And it is in the accepting of that challenge that we learn how much we must give of physical endeavour to bring our aspirations to fruition. The doctrinaires never get there.

Men have to learn, and they prefer to learn, the things that matter, by the heuristic method, finding out their mistakes by making them. Each generation likes to have its lesson from that stern educator experience, rather than at second hand from the generation to which its parents belong. This older generation must accept the position, viewing the mistakes of the younger with regret, but at the same time with hope, seeing in them not the finger of decadence, but the methods of a stern teacher that will eventually bring them back to the right way. Samivel places the final cleaning of the mountaineering slate as late as A.D. 3000. It will hardly take as long as that.

Meanwhile the wise man will pursue his romance. For him the mountain is enough; he cares not whether other men have desired her. Each year he finds new charms revealed to him, and on the old familiar features there is a wealth of association, like the rich patina that time spreads upon the walls of old buildings when they are not begrimed with smoke.

The way we approach a mountain must depend on what we think it offers us. It may be just a few hours of excitement, or it may be a very short stage upon an adventurous journey to some mysterious and distant goal. In the first case we shall approach it as we should a day's trip on an excursion steamer, and try to cram all the excite-ment into it we can. In the second case it will be to us like a day on a ship that is bearing us on a long voyage to look for hidden treasure; the mere fact of being on such a quest is excitement enough; no obstructing storms are needed to make the hours pass eventfully.

A man can only appreciate the attractions of a great mountain that come within the limits of his own perceptions, he can never know them all. Nor do two men ever find quite the same delight in a mountain, or pursue mountaineering with the same intent. It is particularly hard for experience to justify general conclusions about mountains. Nevertheless, the records which I have read of great climbers who are lovers of the mountains, the evidence of personal observation of many who have first climbed and loved them before my eyes, do show that mountaineering has the best prospect of retaining the charm of perpetual youth, if it is presented as a newly discovered treasure and not as a matter of personal achievement. Hands and feet are most willing instruments in the pursuit of that treasure; every clutch and pull and thrust is glad with the thrill of great endeavour. That endeavour may be visualized as the summit till we get there, but then, if not before, there should be something beyond all that hands and feet or the performances of other men can measure.

There is a discovery to be made. This is how it was made by Professor A. D. Godley, in appearance the most melancholy, with his pen the most humorous, and in heart the most devoted of mountain-lovers.

I do not suppose that a more crassly ignorant amateur than I was ever walked in a pair of improperly nailed boots. However, having been somehow imported into Switzerland, as I heard people talking about the so-called pastime of climbing, I thought I would demonstrate the futility of the thing *ambulando*. I therefore took to myself professionals and an alpenstock 'like the mast of some tall ammiral' —the possession of an ice-axe then implied some pretensions to being what is called an expert—and thus equipped I set out to walk over the Adler pass from Zermatt to Mattmark. This seemed to be a good test, as Baedeker said it was wild and hazardous. We scaled those dizzy precipices, or rather we walked and waded over leagues of very bad snow, which was naturally much more embarrassing to me than to the rest of the party.

It was a misty day, and we saw no view. When we got to Mattmark my face felt a little hot after some eight hours' exposure to fresh snow, and I cooled it with very cold water (lanoline was not invented then). Over the agonies which my complexion endured some hours afterwards I can only draw a veil—and I remember wishing that I had drawn that veil before I started. Looking back on the cold details of that expedition, I can find nothing in it that a properly constituted mind could call enjoyable; yet I knew very well that I seemed to myself to have discovered an entirely new and unmixed pleasure, and to have merely wasted all the years which I had spent outside Switzerland. I am almost ashamed to say how little I have changed my mind since then!

Once such a discovery is made, once this vision has come which may expose you to being labelled a mystic by those whose delight is in attaching labels, you may indulge without fear all the interest you are pleased to find in mountain-craft and in the performance of other climbers. The vision of that immeasurable object of desire and source of happiness, however vague and intangible it may become in ordinary times, will be sufficient to keep you from straying far away into the paths of personal rivalry or of mechanized mountaineering.

If an individual is so made that steep mountains give him a taste of ultimate good that nothing else supplies so well, then it does not greatly matter where he sees them and climbs them first. Let him avoid places like Zermatt or Montenvers, or the frequented centres of the Dolomites, where the babel of competitive achievement is so overwhelming that the voices of the peaks themselves are barely audible. Let him choose a place where the essential elements of great height and beauty of snow are present, and where he can often find the intimacy of nature unbroken. Such a choice is still easy and will always be easy in the Alps; nor is there any need to avoid the best places, allowing the word best to be dependent on a widely varied individual taste. You will agree that a best place implies beauty in the valley and good climbing of varied character close at hand.

Three names come into my mind at once, and the fact that a good meal and a good bed are waiting for the climber at the end of his day to prepare him for the next, is no reason for exclusion from the best. I am comparing them with no other places, nor with each other; they are chosen as typical of the best places. I know them all well from many visits to them: the Lötschental, Cogne, Arolla.

The Lötschental is one of the comparatively small number of valleys that run parallel to the main chain of the Swiss Alps east and west, and in so directing them Nature seems to have conferred special beauty upon them. The Bietschhorn, and to a less extent the Lauter-brunnen Breithorn, are the peaks that give distinction and fame to the valley, and on the Bietschhorn you will rarely be the only party on the mountain or have the hut to yourselves in fine weather. There are many other peaks, shorter, easier, longer, or more difficult than either of those, and I have rarely seen any other party upon them.

And there is not a peak on either side of the valley on which I should fear to disappoint a novice, if he have the root of the matter in him, and if he be privileged to see from it the sun rise or set upon the line of the Pennines from the Saas peaks to Mont Blanc, with the perfect snow point of the Weisshorn to catch his eye first and keep it last beyond the great sleeping shadow of the Rhône valley.

Discovery, rather than rivalry, may be your portion here. Close to the best-placed hotel is an attractive little rock peak, the first traverse of whose five points was only made in 1923, and the second by the same party plus a daughter in 1929. And if you wish for something harder, and have the strength of mind to let the Climbers' Guide remain unread, you may enjoy all the pleasures of exploration on ridges of the Schienhorn, or the Grosshorn, or the Breitlauihorn. Now that the fashion has come to accomplish bad routes on famous peaks, there is little danger of the Lötschental coming under the spoiling hands of competition and sophistication.

Cogne is another valley that in its upper reaches runs east and west. The Gran Paradiso and the Herbetet and the Grivola are the notables that draw off nearly all the climbers that come. Besides the beautiful Valnontey, whose western wall is the ridge of these great three, many other valleys radiate from the main valley. With the excellent map of the district issued by the Italian Alpine Club and no other literature you may have weeks of undisturbed discovery and adventure. If you want something that is completely new, a climb that no one claims to have robbed of its virginity in any Climbers' Guide or club journal, the quickest and most certain way of finding it would be to ask Mr. Yeld, who was for many years editor of the *Alpine Journal,* and who, after a long mountaineering life spent mainly in exploration of this district, was still picking up new things when close on the allotted span of three-score years and ten. That was in 1912, so it is well not to delay too long. In that year two young Englishmen—I am now old enough to call them both young—accidentally provided him with a small addition to the long list of *premières* which he had searched out and made his own.

He himself, from Cogne, had pointed out the prominent small peak that appeared to close the main valley to the east as the Tour de Ponton, a peak already fully labelled and put away in the Climbers' Guide. Now the two young men, having bivouacked high up the valley in a delectable place called the Chavanis pastures, had climbed two or three miles of hitherto unclimbed ridges. The amount of

Eritrichium nanum found upon them was proof enough—at any rate in the western Alps—that they were off the beaten track. The ridges have names, but not fame, so the former do not matter; they are mentioned because in the late afternoon, the first of two perfect days, they found themselves at the foot of the supposed Tour de Ponton, and, behold, it was the Punta Nera!

Next evening Mr. Yeld was told of it. Most fortunately the two young men had left alone the side of the peak which gave it, in Mr. Yeld's eyes, the attraction of virginity, and before the night was over he was on his way up the valley on a mule, and next evening he came back happy in possession.

Even the three well-known peaks of Cogne which I have mentioned are not crowded as are the Chamonix or Oberland or Zermatt peaks. In the course of several days—not, I am glad to say, within the space of twenty-four hours like those toughest, soundest, and best beloved of companions, Captain Farrar and Daniel Maquignaz—I have visited every point of the ridge from the Gran Paradiso to the Col de l'Herbetet without meeting a single climber. Competition, when it is found at Cogne—in what climbing centre is it not found? —is in discovery as much as in audacity.

Arolla is my third and best-known place. Experts complain of the paucity and quality of the rock climbs, and let us therefore bless the reputation that keeps these blasé folk away. The rocks of the Collon are loose, the Pigne is accessible over easy snow, the Za is too small to be considered a great peak. No matter! All these have personality and of a different kind; any one of them can give a man or girl whose sensibility is fresh a day of life that will never be forgotten.

And in Arolla, which few lovers of the Alps have not visited, which has been a popular centre for more than half a century, the climber may easily add the element of discovery to his pleasures if he does not allow himself to be pushed into the groove of fashion. Take, for example, the Za. The Za is a very prominent spike, big enough even in the earliest days of mountaineering to be considered a peak, which, but for points of the Perroc, a long way north, is the culminating point of the long ridge of Les Dents, above Arolla on the east.

It is more interesting to regard it as a mountaineering problem than as an exercise in gymnastics. The obvious key to the solution is to reach the ridge on either side of the final spike by a good route. On the far, east side, easy snow slopes come up to the rocks, and the white edge of these slopes can be seen in the small depressions on either side. The rock on the face of this long wall of Les Dents is in many places loose. Apart from a very few well-defined buttresses there is not a route up to the ridge that is safe from falling stones. The popular climb up the face of the Za is certainly not so. Alas! I have proved it, and in doing so nearly slew a future minister of the colonies, a vice-president of the Alpine Club. We were three young men, going quickly to join the rest of our party at the Bertol hut on the way over to Zermatt. At the foot of the west face of the Za we overtook two parties, one of two guides with the above-mentioned English climber, another of a clumsy climber of another nation with a rather indifferent guide. To avoid being delayed by these parties, and also to avoid delaying them in case we took long to climb one of the lower pitches, we took a route higher than the usual well-scratched one, and got on to some extremely loose rocks. The second man embraced a big one, which immediately tried to make off with him for the lower regions. We had closed up on the bad rock and I was firmly placed, so that beyond some spiteful scratching of his face and head for the liberty taken by our second, we had no physical damage. But we passed some dreadful moments as the boulder leaped over the cliff below, bursting into many fragments, each capable of dealing death. Then reassuring curses reached us from below.

There are plenty of missiles ready above the regular route, which the slightest disturbance from melting snow or rain can bring down. There is evidence enough on the lower rocks, and in the changes that take place above, to show that they come down frequently. However, the face climb is firmly established in popular favour, and if you are prepared to pay the toll of some hours' sleep, of a cold halt for food when the faculty of enjoyment is benumbed, and of the discomfort of cold rocks, you can make the face climb with only a small chance of being knocked out. By the directest possible ascent you are paying your homage to fashion and are giving those proofs of physical courage which seem to be considered so necessary in the post-war generation by some sections of the Alpine community.

The climb up the Za by the east face above the snowfield, good as it is, is very short, less than half an hour, and the approach by the Bertol hut is very roundabout. Flank attacks, when possible, appeal to the intelligence in mountaineering as in more sanguinary struggles, and in the case of the Za there are two excellent methods of approach on either side of the west face, by buttresses which are entirely safe from falling stones, and so permit several indulgences; a start at an hour but little in advance of that at which Leslie Stephen considered Christian morality to become binding, a leisured halt under conditions where the faculties of appreciation are fully awake; warm, inviting rocks to climb, and a pleasantly late return as the sunlight on the peaks around takes on the warmth of a farewell. Is that a too hedonistic view of climbing? I think not; it is just the expression of a preference for the interesting, the recreative, and the spiritual in it, rather than for the technical and moral satisfaction it affords.

On one of these buttresses you may take your first long halt on the edge of a small snowfield under the Douves Blanches, and you may reach it simultaneously with the sun. There is not a trace of a previous ascent; the Za, now close at hand, has become something far more than a spike, and you can look at him as long as you like, adoring and unchilled. Higher up, a splendid short pitch up a sharp edge of rock takes you to the north summit of the Douves Blanches. This pitch is so solidly built that it will be unchanged centuries hence. Then a short stretch on the ridge, or a little below it, where you may think you have missed the best way, and are nevertheless sure you are in the right place, and you find yourself at the foot of the east face, and at some time after midday, when all the other parties have gone, you are basking on the summit.

The other flank approach is by the long buttress that runs up on the north of the west face. It is a longer climb than the face, nearly two thousand feet; no falling stone can come near you on it, and from the very start you must keep your route-finding faculties awake if the difficulties are not to become great. The rock is exceptionally good for this face of Les Dents. You will not be able to resist the spiral finish up the minaret in which the buttress ends, before crossing the few yards of snow that separate you from the foot of the Za slab on the east face.

It is the unanimous opinion of all who have done both climbs (for, as far as I know, all are one) that this is a better climb than the west face. For a training climb it has provided much more than enough, and, as far as I know, five hours is the shortest time on the buttress for a party of two. That is surely sufficient temptation to you to halve that time, and even that will not prevent appreciation of its merits.

I know of no climbs I would undertake with more certainty of enjoyment than these two flank approaches to the Za. It is true that in each case a minor summit is reached first. Is that a drawback?

Is not the respectful and proper way to treat the highest in the land to approach them through lesser greatnesses attendant on them? The more you respect your peak, the more you will obtain from audience with it.

I have chosen the Za that it may suggest to climbers the similar examples their own experience can recall of the unlimited possibilities of freshness and discovery about peaks that pass for being thoroughly known. For every man now and in the future, the most satisfying period of mountaineering will begin, and may be continued indefinitely, when he approaches mountains in the right spirit. Do you approach a peak as a purveyor of goods that are labelled and priced, which have a definite quality and marked value, and hoping to get as much or more than other men have done? Or do you approach it as a friend with whom you have been longing to spend a day, knowing that he always calls out the best in you, whether it be in physical effort or in use of mountaineering craft, or in arousing new appetite for knowledge and for beauty and the impulse to share its bounty?

This last benefit, the desire to share, is the best of all assurances that mountaineering will enjoy perpetual youth. All Alpine publications, especially those of European clubs with large membership, are full of encouragement and exhortation for youth to climb. And as though it were admitted that the future of mountaineering depends on a union of the physical and the spiritual, the journals that are at present most eager in adjuring their young nationals to outdo all previous deeds of daring, still contain reminders of the calmer, aesthetic appeal made by the most challenging of peaks. Some instinct is still alive that is a warning of the sterility of the competitive or acquisitive habit.

Advice is given in abundance, and most of it is good; and for some there remains what is, to them, a more excellent way. The man who would keep his old impressions fresh and go on adding new ones to them to the very end may do so by re-creating his enthusiasms in others. In a single day, filled with intense and delightful stress on ridge or glacier, with sunshine and laughter, with thrills of anxiety and the perfect repose of realization, and with its moments of new vision, he may see those enthusiasms born again in youth with a new vitality and a new soul; and it has cost him nothing that it is not pure joy to give.

What sacrifice does the taking of young, inexperienced climbers impose upon an experienced man? Clemenceau's view was that 'tout se paye,' a philosophy natural to a cynic and a pagan, and quite untrue in this case. He renounces a few of what may be regarded as the bachelor rewards of climbing; he might have acquired a few collector's pieces in the matter of notable expeditions, a longer list of four-thousand-metre peaks, a few more mentions in Climbers' Guides. The value of difficult ascents measured by competitive standards depreciates rapidly. I wonder, too, how many men, as old age comes to them, have so lost the sense of real values as to think any collector's piece, any feat of Alpine prowess, comparable to a person in whom they see their own life reborn, the love of mountains growing and blossoming with a freshness and beauty that is enhanced to them by their own appreciation of what only years of learning and affection can procure. There is no shadow of finality over the old age of one to whom the mountains themselves have given these living pledges of perpetual youth.

Does he pay in added risk? Not if the expeditions he undertakes are chosen with a view to those who are learning. This means that, except for a year or two before the first generation of four- or five-year-olds have passed out of his hands, the climbs he makes are not of great severity. The price is negligible if account is taken of the very large share of planning and of leading, and the constant need for taking decisions which falls to the lot of the more experienced members of guideless parties.

By using professional assistance most parties, certainly those that contain novices, can undertake expeditions of a greater standard of difficulty than would be justifiable without. The approach to moun-tains is not the same for the novice, nor is there the same creative joy for the experienced amateur. The tendency will be to use the services of the guides to do more difficult expeditions, in which the opportunities for any but a very experienced amateur to lead or to make a decision may be said hardly to exist. I try to think of occa-sions when I have met a party with guides ascending a peak when the amateur has been leading, and my memory will not supply one, though I know it happens. Moreover, for the novice the idea of achievement, of getting something of tariffed quality, is emphasized. There is something in the employment of professionals that will not let me consider it the ideal approach to mountains. I cannot help it. It is not for lack of admiration of guides; you have only to turn back to previous pages of this book to see Mummery with Burgener, Young and Ryan with Knubel and the Lochmatters, in situations where the relationships of guides and amateurs are perfect. Among them are men who are complete masters of their craft, and if the object of mountaineering is to be difficult accomplishment, there are no men that will enable it to be attained so surely. The best of amateurs may employ them as experts in the execution of ambitious enterprise. Admitting all this, there remains with me the same difficulty in regarding the professional expert as essential for the attainment of the best in mountaineering as in religion. Some men will always find easiest the direct, individual approach. It is not that they lack admiration for those who offer to guide them in these upward and difficult paths; it is that experience has shown them that the most gladdening assurance of the reality they pursue is that which comes when they feel themselves to be in most intimate and direct contact with it, and know that what it gives is far better than anything they can take from it. That assurance may come on the easiest as well as on the most difficult of summits.

The mountaineer who 'begets' other mountaineers, keeps few of them within his family circle; independent fathers do not expect to have other than independent children. Lucky indeed is the man who can still climb with one of his first mountaineering progeny when both have passed into middle age and both can live and climb with all the memories of youth as well as with youth itself; that great fortune has been mine.

The desire to beget enthusiasm is likely to reproduce itself in the next generation. One of my first family, Mallory, asked me to come and do a climb in Wales with a couple of what he called my grand-children. It was fitting on this occasion that grandfather should refuse to lead, and before the climb was over—it was one of what were then recently discovered routes on Clogwyn y Person—other considerations than courtesy had made me glad of my refusal. Not that grandfather disgraced himself—there was no shameful tension of the rope at his waist—but it was the first occasion on which he had watched a leader in preference to—as well as with less anxiety than—being one. As he had expected, it was too difficult a climb for grandchildren at birth. Indeed, I believe that as mountaineers they did not long survive birth. The exposure suffered on that climb was Spartan in its severity!

Other cases I know in which the desire to implant and share the love of mountaineering for the priceless well-being of body and soul which it confers has, at a quite early stage in a climber's development, begun to supplant the desire for competitive achievement.

There will always be plenty of climbers to pursue this last. Their

34. THE RIGHT PLACE

feats can be admired without envy by those who regard this branch as a remarkable lateral offshoot of the well-rooted tree of mountaineering, whose true habit of growth is upward. There is a danger that in order to show the blossoms upon it more easily to men standing on the flat, it will be pulled down till it breaks. That would be a pity, but it would not kill the tree.

CHAPTER XII

ALL women, and those men who observe such things, know the rejuvenating effect of a new dress. Its effect upon a mountain differs from its effect upon other objects of men's devotion in making it more *difficile*. High mountains always choose white; nothing suits them so well, and they will have nothing to do with fabrics that never wear out or are unaffected by the sun. A new dress is often worn only for a few hours before being discarded and sent to be used in other forms to clothe the humble fields.

In winter much longer dresses are worn, and the whole appearance is more chastely beautiful. Quite early in the history of mountaineering A. W. Moore discovered and proclaimed this fresh new beauty that was created by a mere change of season. Moore was a man likely to make such a discovery. In their attitude to mountains, none of the famous climbers who exhausted the rich vein of first ascents in the age of gold were more adventurous and appreciative than he, or more devoted to mountains in all their aspects.

At the present day there is hardly a single famous peak of the Alps that has not been climbed in winter, rock peaks as well as snow peaks. The Matterhorn was climbed in March 1882 by Vittorio Sella, well known as a mountaineer, and still better known for the portraits, admirably posed and brilliant in contrast, which he has brought back from nearly all the famous mountains of the world. In the spring of 1934 he told me he was hoping to climb the Matterhorn once more! On this winter ascent more than half a century ago the party left Breuil an hour before midnight and reached the Col du Lion, walking mostly by lantern light, at 6 a.m. The rocks of the final peak were free from snow, and the summit was gained at 2 p.m. 'The air was perfectly still and the view cloudless.' The main difficulties were found on the descent below the shoulder, the usually easy broken rocks of the east face and the ridge being frozen up into a dangerously slippery slope.

The Meije was climbed in March 1926, by MM. Armand Delille and P. Dalloz. The afternoon was far advanced when they won their peak; the long bivouac that followed near the Pas du Chat, not far below the summit, is described as 'no colder than a summer bivouac.' The start up the great wall and the head of the great couloir were glazed and difficult, but otherwise the rocks of this warm south face were in good condition.

The Grépon had to yield to the extraordinary skill and daring of Armand Charlet at almost the same time, and the still more exacting winter course, the traverse of the Drus, was accomplished in February 1928. Armand Charlet was again the leader of this great winter climb, with a single companion, Camille Dévouassaud, who was making his first acquaintance with the Dru.

The route taken up the Petit Dru was the same as in summer, except that at one point a parallel couloir was taken instead of the usual one, and on the final 150 feet, where the couloir, smothered in ice, was abandoned for the steep rocks at the side. 'Most of the chimneys of the Petit Dru were full of ice, and the holds glazed, but as we were in good form our progress was always rapid.' We can judge that the party had a pretty high standard when we read that they were on the top of the Petit Dru at 10.15, and on the Grand Dru at 11.20! Charlet describes the conditions generally as exceptionally good, much better than those met with on his ascent of the Grépon, which would have made the traverse of the Drus impossible in his view, and few will dispute that what was impossible to Charlet was impossible by present standards. The climb up to the Grand Dru was easier than expected, 'only the first traverse leading to the Z was really difficult; the Z itself quite dry, and the final chimney was climbed without having fully to extend myself'!

They took their one halt of the day, three-quarters of an hour on the Grand Dru, before descending. The nature of the descent may be inferred from the short description that follows, if we remember it is Charlet who speaks. 'The descent of the Grand Dru to the glacier was one of the most difficult and dangerous I have ever had to make; all the holds were glazed; the smallest cracks were blocked with frozen snow. Twenty descents on the doubled rope had to be made; in the climbing season only seven are employed if required. At last, after three hours of very difficult work, we reached the glacier, and at 3.15 p.m. the hut itself.' Only ten hours from leaving to re-entering the hut! On the Mer de Glace skis are put on; darkness falls soon after, and it is with skis over the shoulder that the descent to Argentière is made.

I think we may fairly say that such winter climbs are still *tours de force.* It is not simply the actual obstacles in the form of strange growths of ice and snow that make them so. Snow slopes and ridges, and even rocks, are often in good condition high up, for the snow that falls upon them remains dry and is blown off by the wind. Skis have made the ascent of the lower slopes possible, and have given to their descent a thrill of speed which has drawn many into the high mountains for no other reason than to enjoy the run down. Cold, and the shortness of the days, with the increased danger of failing to read the warnings of the sky, are what make big ascents few and far between. Moore's comments on winter climbing have not lost their truth:

> Fine weather is, of course, even more essential than in summer, but the chances of it are at least as good at one season as at the other, if my experience in two successive winters in widely separated districts can be relied on. The shortness of the days is an obstacle to any very considerable excursion, except when there happens to be a moon, so that it is advisable to study an almanac before fixing the date of starting. But to my mind, one of the great advantages of the winter is that a mountaineer who wishes for a little excitement is not compelled to seek it in expeditions of the first class; a mantle of snow wonderfully exaggerates the height of the lower peaks and passes, and many of these, which in summer a man is apt to look upon as 'grinds,' and comparatively void of interest, become very agreeable climbs, and can mostly be accomplished between 7 a.m. and 5 p.m., no slight merit in the eyes of those who, like myself, consider the perpetual business of getting up in the middle of the night a considerable drawback to the pleasures of a summer tour. That long and fairly difficult expeditions are feasible I have shown, and I do not believe that they involve appreciable risk beyond what must be run in the same excursions in summer.

Moore's expeditions were mainly passes on which the danger of frostbite in the fingers from snow-covered rocks, and in the feet from waiting in steps on long steep slopes, was less than in later winter ascents. Theodore Cornish climbed the Schreckhorn in January 1889. He says:

> In going up a great snow couloir we were unpleasantly reminded of unseen dangers by two snow avalanches at no great distance off. The next day another party had one, I believe, in still more dangerous proximity. The cold all this while was intense, and that great bugbear to winter climbers, frostbite, seemed at times inevitable. In my case, however, I think it was effectually staved off by watching the vigorous measures which the guides adopted with my friend. I concealed my feelings, and, like the late Lord Derby, 'I preferred the gout'!

Precautions of dry stockings, extra socks, and boots roomy enough to avoid any sort of compression, can do much to avoid the danger

35. A WINTER TRANSFORMATION

of frostbite; it will, nevertheless, always be a danger on slopes involving step-cutting, and the wearing of crampons, unless it does away with the need for steps, increases the danger. At Grindelwald, in March 1900, a Swiss climber made the ascent of the Eiger with Jossi. The weather was fine, but they found a good deal of ice; and several weeks in hospital at Berne with frozen toes was the price paid. In the same month a pupil of mine and I were in a party of eight, four of them guides, who climbed the Wetterhorn—that was before I had any sort of responsibility for the choice or conduct of any but my own solitary expeditions. The danger and labour was all in getting to the Gleckstein hut. In the early morning the snow in the couloir high up was hard, and steps were cut all the way up, and when we emerged on to the level snow at its head, our fingers and toes gave us painful reminders of the cold waits they had had to endure, all of us save my pupil, who suffered not at all. That was at sunrise; we had a grand day, and it was from heat rather than cold that we suffered on the way down. Only on taking off his boots in the evening in the Bear Hotel did my pupil discover that his toes were a horrid pale green. He was in bed for some weeks, but only lost two or three millimetres of his big toe, having, by good luck rather than foresight, refrained from warming them to restore the circulation!

Winter mountaineering is mainly on snow. The fathers of moun-taineering were far better on snow than on rock. It was natural that they should accomplish winter ascents which even now strike us as notable feats; for those among them who were prepared for the toil over the lower slopes, and the acute discomforts of January nights in huts whose roofs leaked more and more icy drips as the atmosphere within grew less intolerably cold, the Alps in winter dress brought fresh enthusiasm. Such men were never numerous. Now in certain centres the crowds that collect under the shadow of the high peaks to eat, drink, and be merry, to dress, to dance, to play bridge, and to worship speed, are hardly less numerous than in the days past, when it was quite the thing to go to Switzerland in August. And among these crowds are to be found a considerable number of people of both sexes, and of ages from ten to sixty, who make high expeditions.

This book deals with mountaineering, not with winter sports as the term is popularly understood. Skis represent a valuable addition to equipment for spring or winter mountaineering. They have made it a comparatively easy matter to accomplish snow expeditions which the time and labour required made impossible before, save under exceptional conditions of weather. They have given to those who

S

use them a new study of technique that provides them with an interest comparable to that which cricket enthusiasts find in batting. Demonstrations by experts on the screen and before the study fire can fill many an hour.

Facility of access is one of the recognized signs of advance in the standard of living for climbers. The motor car and the mountain railways, funicular and *téléférique,* have also played their part, but, as a rule, these must be left some distance lower down than the point at which we must leave skis.

Have I uttered blasphemy? Has that idea of facility of access carried me too far into an odious comparison? I think it has. The motor and the *téléférique,* with one or two notable exceptions like the Jungfrau railway, do not take us where we could go on foot. Skis can take us into the recesses of the high mountains at times when they would otherwise be inaccessible.

Is ski-ing among high mountains mountaineering? The point has been debated with a heat unsuitable to the best conditions for the sport. To draw the line where ski-ing becomes mountaineering is like drawing the line on the earth where night ends and day begins; it depends entirely on your own position! The ski seems to me to take the same sort of position in regard to snow that lets us in too deep as the crampon does in regard to ice that offers no depth of penetration at all to finger or toe. Some hold to the one and despise the other; some love both; in a few neither stirs desire. Both are definitely established as growths of modern mountaineering; rather like a newly developed muscle that enables you to perform some new and pleasurable feat; not essential to contentment, and certainly not to life.

I believe the employment of ski will tend, as do the crampon and the piton, to direct attention to the more technical side of mountaineering as a sport, causing its development to proceed along more standardized lines. Skis are a restriction as well as a convenience and a pleasure, just as a bicycle is; there are a great many places where you cannot wear them. They must be left or carried, being difficult things to put into a rucksack, and if you shorten them to the dimensions of the rock-climber's ice-axe you have taken away the speed which is their charm; you cannot fly with clipped wings. If skis are taken, the route will generally be chosen with a view to the run it will afford; it must be remembered on the side of the skiers that a descent on skis can be repeated more than once at short intervals without danger of staleness, the opportunities for observation of the surroundings and the duration of monotonous stretches being both far less.

Ski-ing must generally end where climbing begins, that is to say, where the hands are needed or where steps must be made, as well as on any ground bare of snow. That does not imply that ski-ing and mountaineering are two different things. It would be absurd to refuse the name of mountaineering to a *raid à skis* like that described by Monsieur L. Zwingelstein, which took him from Grenoble to Nice, and from there to the Tyrol via Zermatt and back again via the Oberland. Such a tour brings out the pleasures and the penalties attaching to the use of skis. The forest zone in winter is apt to be a difficult one for skiers. The path through, if there is one, is often, as it was found on this tour, covered with powdery snow on which you 'sink up to the knees and have to drive the skis forwards without seeing them. In these conditions progress is slow and laborious.' Those who have attempted to go through such snow on foot can imagine what it would have been without skis!

The following passage in Zwingelstein's description must be typical of long tours:

With this sticky, powdery snow the valley seemed endless. . . . Then the descent began. Soon tracks appear in which I slide along in great comfort. . . . I come upon a number of skiers, I pass a hotel and descend towards Tignes on a veritable skating-rink, a most tiring descent with the heavy sack I am carrying. A thick covering of snow on the road enables me to keep on my skis as far as Sainte-Foy; that still leaves five or six miles to be done before my day ends!

The skier's ideal is to motor to the point where skis are put on, and to find a motor waiting where they are taken off. Alas! it is not always realized, and sometimes because the brotherhood between mountaineers and skiers is not always what it should be. 'Motors all but empty, containing one or two skiers, pass me, and show no wish to stop in answer to my gestures. Quelle belle solidarité! Mais au fait, je n'ai affaire qu'à des sportsmen et non à des montagnards.' The last words are left untranslated because the French word *sportsmen* is untranslatable into English for the reasons given in Chapter VIII.

When climbing begins skis become an encumbrance far worse than crampons when they are not in use. They may be an intolerable nuisance on difficult rocks, though it is conceivable that in a cleft too wide for back- and knee-work a special ski-bridging technique might be invented, with the points turned downwards for utilizing small holds. On steep snow or ice they are seldom a blessing. We can assume that any one who can successfully carry out a tour from Nice to the Tyrol through the High Alps, knows where and how to use his skis, and that the following incidents of the passage of the Col du Chardonnet may be taken as an illustration of the limitations of skis in mountaineering.

In cloudy weather the party, now two, leave Lognan and push their way up slowly through deep, fresh snow, reaching the foot of the col at midday. 'The mist is all round us and snow begins to fall; soon a cold wind springs up. *Rien ne manque plus!* It is only as daylight is failing that we reach the col.' On the far side,

the slope is ice covered with eight inches of loose snow, and we have to put on crampons; and as darkness is increasing we rope up. I descend first, making my skis, tied together with the spare rope, slide down beneath me. In this way they sweep off the fresh snow and allow the crampons to bite into the ice; moreover, their dark mass gives me an idea of what the angle is. This descent in the dark is very, very slow. An avalanche of powdery snow goes past a dozen yards away on our left. As the angle increases the skis put a greater downward drag upon me; in fact, they are such a hindrance that I let them down at the end of the rope, keeping them thus attached to my waist. Presently they feel to me as if they were falling, then I feel nothing at all, and the rope remains slack. Can it be the *bergschrund*?

I begin to grope my way down again, but the slope steepens till it is hard to stand upon it. Below me I can just make out the dark mass of the skis. We are at the *bergschrund*, then? But how high is it? I am let down over a ten-foot wall, at the bottom of which I plunge up to the thigh in soft snow.

My friend rejoins me on the rope doubled over an ice-axe. The cold is terrible; seeing nothing, we continue on foot, sinking into two feet of fresh snow. The slope eases off and we decide to bivouac. It is nine o'clock.

They were carrying nearly fifty pounds apiece, in view of such emergencies, and a reasonably warm night is passed. In the morning skis are put on again, but, even so, they sink in a foot and are a long time reaching the final slope leading to the Fenêtre de Saleinaz.

There is so much fresh snow that to reach the pass there can be no thought of zigzagging up on skis; we have to go on foot, making tracks straight up the line of greatest slope. It is terribly hard work, for I sink in up to the waist. I try various devices, using my skis placed horizontally like the rungs of a ladder, sticking them up on end and pulling up on them, and so forth. . . . Under such conditions it takes three hours to reach the pass!

Having got there at last, roped together and steering by compass, they reach the very welcome comforts of the Cabane Dupuis. It has taken them seven hours to cover the distance from the bivouac on the Saleinaz Glacier, three times as long as to cover the distance on foot in summer!

No use can be made of splendid weather next day for fear of
avalanches, and a guided party comes up to the hut. Together they
all cross the Fenêtre du Chamois to Champex, the last slope up the
pass being so dangerous that they pass it 'one by one, sinking deep
into the snow.' At the foot of the couloir, on the Champex side,
skis are put on once more. 'We let our companions dash on ahead,
as our heavy sacks forbid any great speed.' In the woods great humps
like the take-off for a jump cause a constant loss of balance and a few
tumbles. Orsières is reached for lunch, and left in the rain, and they
tramp up the great St. Bernard road carrying the skis. Snow is falling
at Rive-Haute; beyond Liddes they are obliged to put on skis; soaked
through, they reach Bourg St. Pierre after night has fallen.

Mountaineering on skis in winter is far from being the succession
of effortless glidings, as on wings, which the artists employed by the
hotels and railways would have us believe it to be. Skis have made
winter mountaineering more possible; they have not, be it said to
their credit, done away with the effort that is an essential feature of it.
It is surprising how small a part of the tales of mountaineering on skis
is occupied with what is supposed to be its greatest glory, the run
down; surprising till we reflect that the time occupied in the run
down is short, and that in the course of it all the faculties are concentrated, even more than those of the driver of a car, on the guidance
and management of the skis. Apart from that, the sensation of
speed is one of the least possible to describe.

To refer to winter mountaineering at all as being out of season may
appear strange at the present day, at any rate to those who have not
made their first acquaintance with mountains in the summer. To
those who have, it has brought a renewal of the spirit of discovery in
which that acquaintance was made. And even to those who have
made some winter ascents, and who are more familiar with British
hills under winter than under summer conditions, a winter ascent
of any peak near the ten-thousand-foot level brings the satisfaction
of having won something by special enterprise and by a refusal to
accept anything like a one-month climbing year. Winter limitations remain, for all that. No hotel proprietor has yet succeeded in
inducing the sun to stay up late on winter evenings, and the high
peaks are just as capable as ever of lowering looks and terribly stern
and frigid moods that last for many days. Conditions are less familiar,
and the penalties for mistakes more certain than in summer, and all
rock peaks are more difficult. This sort of incident on a winter
ascent of the Jalouc, related by Kugy, has happened to not a few

other climbers. Soft snow had given place to a stretch of slabs, where ice covered the rocks and only small steps could be cut. The third man descending in front of Kugy turned to him and asked if he was safe. Kugy replied: 'Yes!' and held the rope, when he saw him slip, with a confident laugh in his own security.

Suddenly the whole steep ice-slab, on which I was standing, broke under the weight. I lost my balance, my feet flew up, and I fell on my back. In a few seconds the weight of our fall would have dragged the whole party down. The thought flashed across my mind that we were all lost. Then, at this moment of crisis in our lives, I felt a jerk from above. Jože was standing in crampons on dry rock, and had anchored himself with all his strength.

Winter spreads dangers in all sorts of places that we can safely trust in summer. It is the transformation of the lower slopes, the decoration of the banks of earth, the rocks, and the branches of the trees with fairy-like formations of sparkling snow, that give most new beauty to winter mountaineering. The enchantment of the upper snows descends upon stretches of the path along which we plod wearily down on a hot summer's evening till Kugy can write thus of them: 'The moon, high in the heavens, shone on our path and kindled a thousand lamps among the icy slopes on either side, now dancing like will-o'-the-wisps, now seeming to move in solemn procession.'

Few and well remembered are the days when the winter mountaineer sees these new beauties; on many duller days he turns his steps homeward to the warm hotel in the Alps, or to the cosy parlours of Pen y Gwryd and Pen y Pass, with a reminder from the mountains which sometimes amounts to a dismissal, that winter is the season which shows us more than any other our need for human comforts and human companionship.

The season that is more out of season than any other among snow mountains is the early spring. It has been to me such an altogether wonderful time in my climbing life that I want to say something of its pleasures, and it is therefore a disappointment to find in Alpine history so little that bears upon it.

If material existed in any quantity, it would be found in that greatest and most complete record of mountaineering adventure, the *Alpine Journal*. Volume after volume was opened, and the contents scanned. Winter ascents there were, but nothing that declared its spring origin caught my attention till I came to Vol. XXV and found 'The Ligurian Alps in Early Spring.' Vol. XXVII offered me 'An

Easter Tour in the Bergamasque Alps,' Vol. XXIX, 'Corsica in
May'; then nothing more till I came to 'April Days' in Vol. XLIII.
It was a great surprise, for all these articles, except that on Corsica by
V. H. Gatty, were my own. And they were not written because
I thought I had discovered something new; my first introduction to
the Pyrenees was at Easter, and made long before I possessed an
Alpine Journal, and my first spring introduction to the Alps was
made even earlier. They were written simply because April has given
me more unforgettable days on mountains than any other month;
indeed, no April among high mountains has ever failed to give me
at least one day of complete and utter contentment, of rejuvenation
of mind and of my attitude to mountains, however impossible
rejuvenation of body has become.

There is some excuse, then, if this chapter of mountaineering history
is more personal than others; there is too little material from better
sources. Ski-ing at Easter is becoming more popular, but it is actually
diminishing what I regard as the real perfect type of April mountaineering, that is to say, on peaks barely high enough to carry glaciers,
where hard snow may often be found by looking for it, and above all
on slopes over which one may walk, as Kugy describes it, 'where
the warm breath of earth has stripped the garment of snow, revealing
the brown earth beneath, through the gardens of crocus, soldanella,
and Christmas rose, born as by magic overnight.'

In April you climb day after day without meeting a soul, and
indeed it is in this month that most of the real red-letter days of solitary
climbers may be found. It may be that in winter the mountains are
too stern companions; in summer it is the glaciers that seem to be
specially left there to refresh us after summer heat. Crossing glaciers
alone is not the best form of satisfaction we can get from climbing.

Most of my own spring mountaineering has been done alone. It was
often difficult to get companions for this additional climbing holiday
of the year, and there is some influence which I gratefully acknowledge and have no wish to analyse, that makes early spring the
season when mountains are peculiarly communicative to a man
alone. Change only a word or two in a passage of Lord Grey's book
about fly-fishing in spring and you will get some explanation of
this influence. Fly-fishing is a sport akin to mountaineering, in that
it attracts you by a material goal and leads you into contemplative
pleasures, blending the exercise of a craft with the refreshment of the
spirit, so that one is not complete without the other. This is the
passage:

April is not a warm month, but it has some warm days, and if an angler who cannot fish all through the month happens to choose these days for fishing, he ought to count himself a fortunate man. Such days may come at any time of the month, in the beginning, middle, or end, but in the north, at any rate before the end of April, trees will be still brown and bare. That does not matter. There will be a spirit in the air, an appeal, a promise, a prophecy, to make a man's heart leap up within him. . . . On such a day in early April the birds will sing as if this were the day for which they had longed and waited, as if the highest bliss had come. Though some of our feeling about the conscious enjoyment of birds and other forms of life may be mere fancy, it is altogether true that there is an ecstasy about the first warm days of spring which cannot be resisted, and we cannot tell how much comes from within and how much from without us. There is a spirit stirring abroad. We know that we share it, and that it is not ours alone.

Mountains as well as birds share the climber's enjoyment of such a day, as the following passage of Dr. Kugy's will show you. He has chosen May instead of April because winter takes a firmer hold among the hills.

Nothing in all the world can be compared with the beauty which God's mercy scatters over the foothills when spring begins its upward journey; when the sombre meadow-land beneath the forest border sheds its covering of snow, and now rested, warm, and ready for each new marvel, looks forth upon the day; when the thrush sings in the forest, and primroses hang fragrant on every cliff.

How has this come? Last time, the floating veils of winter lay over the beech-wood hangers far down into the valley, still, cold, silver-grey. And to-day there is a stirring, a smile, the divine smile of a happy awakening. . . . And one fine Sunday you will find the beech-forest in fullest splendour, clothed in the most festal colours of this festal earth. Laughter and speech alike fail you; as in the overwhelming happiness of a dream, you stand regarding the hill-sides covered with the robe of May, and every mountain as a bride adorned with her jewels.

The return to the first high pastures in summer is very good at the end of a long day on the snow. It does not give quite the same thrill of pleasure as the soft gurgling laugh of water under the snow, that tells us of the stream that is born again and of the preparation of the summer beauties, so that we can quote for it as aptly as Lord Grey has quoted for the sap that rises to the buds:

> Sending little rhythmic floods
> Of fairy sound in fairy ears.
> Thus all beauty that appears
> Has birth as sound to finer sense,
> And lighter clad intelligence.

36. A SPRING AWAKENING

In Britain Easter is, as much as any other, a climbing season. Rocks are not often glazed, or wetter than in summer; the days are long enough, and snow, where it lies, is better than at any other time. If I had to choose between the rival attractions our island offers at this season, my choice would be the Coolins, if it was not Ben Nevis or Glencoe.   All these have given me April days that were incomparable.

It is in higher ranges that April climbing is out of season, and it is best of all where you are reminded, every time you come off your mountain, that summer is very nigh.   The Pyrenees can be at their very best; snow conditions can vary from execrable to admirable, and the spring sun is fiercer there than in the other ranges of western Europe.   There I have been so smitten by the sun in my first few days that a friend who joined me asked if I had mumps.   The Maritime Alps have never failed to pour sunshine into my life.   Time after time I have come off the snow and had the same warmth of welcome from the ground that I had a quarter of a century ago on my first descent of the southern slopes of the seaward alps.   The wintry feeling had gone from the air, and down in the glen the primroses and violets were coming out in profusion, though the height was still more than three thousand feet above the sea.

And every time I have seen it I have been struck with new wonder at the sight which I saw first on reaching the ridge of the Ligurian Alps, where you look northward and right across the plain of Italy to the Pennine Alps.   Far off and dim, but unmistakable, stretches the line of giant sentinels that watch over the Italian plain.   Their immense distance, their ethereal look, the knowledge of their actual size and splendour, and above all the feeling of their great living friendship, are overwhelming.   I did not stop to examine them or pick out individuals, but all the way along the ridge I felt they were there.   Mountaineers belong to that fortunate class of men who have friends whose mere presence satisfies their wants.   No need to talk, even to look; something there is in their presence alone which is enough for happiness.

The top may be altogether shrouded in mist, as it was the only time I have been on the Marguareis, the highest of the Ligurian Alps.   The April magic will still in some way hover about it. And what should a man think of, having realized this dream of isolation?   Why, of that which holds him with the strongest and tenderest ties to earth; to each man his own and happiest thoughts, of these let us talk to our mountain host and win his blessing.

The promise of summer to come is rendered all the more precious by the reminders of winter that has hardly yet begun to relax its hold. A long, desolate valley, like Val Daone in the Alps, north of Lago di Garda, can be a grim place in April, when the havoc wrought by avalanches appears appalling. I remember how the path was con-stantly crossing openings in the wood where the descending masses had opened a wide lane strewn with mangled trunks and branches. And the manner in which this artillery of Nature was loaded was being shown me at the moment. Out of the still mists tiny flakes were coming noiselessly down, so gently that the open spaces seemed to be growing white, instead of being overlaid with a covering, while the dark foliage of the pines turned to a silvery grey. I am sure I could not spend a winter in Val Daone without becoming super-stitious by prolonged contemplation of a power which works in such a ghostly calm, and strikes with such awful suddenness and force.

In April a peak of over ten thousand feet has been, for me at any rate, a high ambition. Sometimes it has been hardly won after more than one attempt, and then there is something about such an occa-sional spring day of high success that moves us as summer victories of greater feats may not. One such day the Cima Tosa vouchsafed me, an April day before the Great War. It must have been a specially good day, for I could not have invented the complete contentment and the gratitude you may see struggling for articulate expression in these words which I wrote on my return:

In the woods all was peace. The absorbing struggle with the details of the way was over, and with the trees and streams the lower world came back; but not as I had left it in the morning; a spell had fallen on it. It is at the close of such a day that the climber may be rewarded with one of those enchanted hours when he realizes the consummation of all his hopes, and the mountain's acceptance of his love; when the flood of golden light that comes out of the west enriches the fields in which he has toiled with a wealth too great for him to comprehend. And though the commonplace comes back, and the futilities of modern life close over our heads like cold grey clouds, so that we no longer see the sunshine of life undimmed as in that hour, we know it was no vain illusion we pursued, but a fruitful blessing that will one day fall on us again.

Few of our visits to the mountain can have a perfect ending. Each time he leaves the plains there is the beginning of a possible romance in the climber's life. But it is only the beginning over which he has control. Climbers are shockingly businesslike in the planning of their romances. Once the vague 'besoin de la montagne' has entered into them, they will seek out the beloved, each, without exception, with a sublime confidence that, for him at least, her mood will always be a smiling one. The end is beyond our schemes. A few of these romances may end suddenly, a few with disappointment, many with feasting in the secular and the ecclesiastical sense. Each year brings nearer the age when we shall see with envious eyes the favours of the hills reserved for younger men, or, it may be, in ourselves 'desire shall fail.' And, therefore, even in youth, we should treasure most those hours in which, after the snow and rocks have drawn the passion from our blood, we get a foretaste of a pleasure which the years are powerless to destroy. 'S'être donné, être encore à elle.' As I lingered on the path, delaying my farewell to the queen of the Brenta, I knew that it is the realiza- tion of this and not satiety that brings content, the renewal of our affections and beliefs which mark the attainment of our quest, and that will bring us a message of good tidings from the hills when the last climb is ended and we are looking for the final rest:

'The rest ungrudged by duty or desire.'

Many times has that impression of an April day in 1912 been confirmed. It might well have been written of a long day on the Basodino in April 1933, which ended with a long, lovely valley walk in bright moonlight, weary, but in a great contentment that filled the mind to the exclusion of all else. There must be a double portion of perpetual youth about April climbs that resists all the attacks of disillusionment.

Moreover, from a climbing point of view, there is no doubt that mountains have the power, not given to man, of adding some thousand cubits to their stature. Real difficulties may begin upon the path that affords a pleasant stroll in summer. I remember a typical obstacle stopping me at less than five thousand feet near Bignasco. Frost had worked the trickles of water from the cliff into a curtain that had fallen right over the path. With the sun shining through the varying thickness of the ice, it was good indeed to look at, and best left alone, for an attempt to open a way through it with the axe might have brought innumerable tons of it upon my head.

There are sometimes real compensations. Only a few weeks before beginning this chapter I had the best glissade of my life. I had ascended steep slopes which the sun had stripped bare up to seven thousand feet, hoping to find a small pass through some limestone precipices near the Col des Aravis. They would always be rather dangerous slopes for ski-ing, steep turf with many small interruptions of rock and long, dead grass, providing a sliding surface for snow inclined to avalanche. There was no sort of reason to start a roll down, but if one had done so near the top nothing would have stopped it for two thousand feet. The pass disclosed itself obligingly, a perfect gap between high rocks, and on the far side a most alluring snow slope, neither hard nor too soft, and at just the right angle. It ran down for twelve hundred feet at least, to a small level basin beyond the edge of which I could see nothing. There a few trees, showing near the edge, convinced me that the fears of being cut off by cliffs, which grow upon solitary climbers as they advance in age, were fears that were liars. I let myself go. No skier ever enjoyed more ease of movement; the slightest effort regulated the speed, as fast or as slow as one could wish, and I closed my eyes to get the perfection of dreaming flight. You may not believe me, but it was really the possibility of going to sleep that made me open them again. A short stretch of heavy walking took me across the small snow basin to its edge, and behold! as I looked over, another perfect slope! It took me without any effort at all close to where the level fields of the valley began. And there were no skis to shoulder as I walked along the paths to join the road.

No! it is not often like that; far from it, and we forget all but the worst of the other times! Snow is often bad, and seldom good, in April. On slopes below those that are very high and windswept, it is generally so bad for walking that the choice of a locality has an important bearing on the point. Weather conditions being similar, snow on slopes that are between four and eight thousand feet is best within the influence of a sea-climate; the snowline is higher, and the snow itself has more melting and subsequent consolidation than in colder regions. And where can we find a sea-climate better than in Corsica?

Corsica alone among the lands of high mountains can be said to have tempted the early generation of mountaineers to climb in spring. Its snowy peaks, seen from the foothills behind the Riviera coast under a hot sun, must capture the heart of any mountaineer. The Reverend W. H. Hawker, one of the first visitors to find the attraction of its peaks, has expressed the opinion of other followers when he says: 'It was natural that the frequent sight of this lovely vision acted with powerful attraction upon myself and some of my friends who were passing the winter at Mentone.' In March 1866, in his first visit, he did no climbing, unless the crossing on mules of the snows of the Col de Vergio, now a road pass just over five thousand feet, can be so described. But at the end of April he was back again and climbed Monte Rotondo, or rather its eastern summit. He was more fortunate than a French gentleman, who was credited with an ascent in which the snow slopes had been so hard and slippery that steps had to be cut with a large stone. Monte d'Oro was also climbed, the local man acting as a guide, showing excellent form on rock and a strong disinclination to have anything to do with snow.

In January 1881 Mr. Seton Karr left Corte 'with two hunters, two donkeys, a piece of rope, hatchet, large sack of bread and smaller necessaries.' The hunters need not be included among the greater necessaries, seeing that one had to be pulled up the harder snow and that the party was led on to the wrong peak, a good deal lower and a mile away.

It was impossible that a jewel like Corsica should be overlooked by such a connoisseur as Dr. Freshfield. He took François Dévouassoud with him, but did little notable climbing on his visits; in fact, this conqueror of Caucasian and Himalayan heights was a little too disdainful, and Monte Rotondo, one of the most easy-going of the Corsican peaks, was obliged to remind him of their claim to his respect.

The ascent of the opposite crags cost me some pain. There is one easy way to the right. François despised it, attracted by a granite staircase nearer us, the last flight of which proved incomplete. I soon found myself clutching the crag above my head with 'hooked hands,' and moving my feet about vainly for foothold, while François, having relieved me of my umbrella, remarked with more than his usual calmness: 'Ça va bien.' For a second I had one of those direct visions said to be given to drowning men; only it was prospective, which is, I believe, unusual. I saw the present editor of the *Alpine Journal* revising the proof of an 'obituary notice,' in which, after recounting with his habitual accuracy the fractured condition in which his predecessor had been found, he proceeded to demonstrate that in climbing even the easiest rock-peak with an umbrella, but without a rope, it was undesirable to attempt short cuts, and wound up with a judiciously qualified congratulation to climbers in general that a life spent in preaching 'rules and regulations' should have been crowned by so useful an example of the result of their breach!

Those who have memories of Freshfield and Coolidge will, perhaps, have them pleasantly revived by the quotation.

It is not Freshfield's climbing in Corsica that is notable; it is the impression its beauty makes upon him. 'I, at any rate, know of no such combination of sea and mountains—no region where within so small a space Nature takes so many different and sublime or exquisite aspects as she does in Corsica.' Coming from Freshfield, that is as good an advertisement as a place could wish to have. Corsica has charmed every climber who has gone there. It remains sufficiently free from the statistical inventory of its charms in Climbers' Guides to be almost an undiscovered country for the man who visits its mountains. The attractions of Calvi and other parts of its magnificent coast are now fully advertised in France. The group of splendid peaks that culminate in Paglia Orba round the head of the Viro glen are well known, and the Grotte des Anges, which was a roomy shelter for most parties till a few years ago, will soon have to be replaced by a hotel or a provisioned hut.

There is climbing of great difficulty to be had in Corsica. The north face of Paglia Orba, climbed by George Finch, is a great climb in summer and a very big undertaking indeed in normal April conditions. If you can climb Tafonato on a fine April day and descend from it dissatisfied, you are in pitiable case. The rock is of grand quality, and though it is not hard climbing up the face to the stupendous hole in the middle of the peak, the angle is very high, and you will need good, firm snow. The hole is three hundred feet at least below the summit ridge, and about thirty feet through, so that even if you take the width of the crest as negligible you have less than 6° of deviation from the vertical to share between the two opposite faces of the peak that rise from the hole! The last part of the ascent that lies on the north-west face will always need care when it is covered with snow and ice, and that will generally be the case in April.

Reading what has been written of Corsican mountaineering in the Alpine periodicals of different countries, in the pages of George Finch, and in the climbing chronicles of Eton, one is struck by the peculiar fascination of this wonderful island. The peaks that offer most obvious attraction to a climber in height and form have now been climbed, and in order to supply new material for a Climbers' Guide to Corsica, it will soon be as necessary as in the Alps to do it by exceptional technical achievements rather than by discovery of what is still unknown.

I say soon, for it is not quite necessary yet. You may find, as I have done, the Capo Trovatore. This peak is so rich in the element of discovery and enchantment that is found in April climbing that I must share the secret with you.

You may camp upon its actual foot; I dare not tell you how easily and quickly you may reach that camp and transport your impedi-menta thither, and how perfect is the dining-and-smoking-room provided by an enormous overhanging rock. In April you are sure to have a cold touch from winter to make you purr with delight at the first warm caress of summer; in other words, you will have to creep over several inches of snow into your tent at night, a day or two before bathing and basking in the late afternoon on the rocks beside the stream that runs past your door. The light bag that is your mattress may be quickly filled with the springy heath that is blooming on bushes which grow to ten feet in height; the cyclamen will be coming out in abundance if it is late in April; round you are more unclimbed rocky peaks, red and steep and reminiscent of the Dru, than you could have imagined possible; I say unclimbed only because I have no evidence whatever to the contrary. Sitting outside the cave while the wood (which there is no need to spare) is burning down to a nice red fire, you look up a narrow valley to a snow peak on the backbone of the island, and try to establish its identity. I remember we thought how pleasant it would be to reach it by the ridge that formed one of the valley walls. We got half-way up to the near end of that ridge, the easy half, before being turned back by the weather and by the increase of the angle beyond our expectations. Later we saw that our route would probably have taken days where we had reckoned hours!

Let me get back to Capo Trovatore. Twice I have tried to climb it and twice failed, and never has failure been more enjoyable! The peak is like the Aiguille Noire de Péteret on a small scale; not very small, for from the Englishmen's Arm-chair—a much smaller but pleasanter place than the Fauteuil des Allemands—the peak rises nearly three thousand feet.

If you spot the path through the *maquis* you may reach the Arm-chair in about an hour or an hour and a half; for there are no slabs to climb before you have to take to the bed of the stream, between a very steep rock buttress on your right, and an almost equally steep slope of rock and grass and trees on your left, and the great boulders are no serious obstacle when you reach them. The Arm-chair, where you must make your choice of route, is at the foot of a first slabby step, over which the water falls. Here the stream-bed begins to bear more steeply up under the face of the peak.

Our first attempt in 1929 was meant to provide a good short day, and it was a luncheon rather than a breakfast that we ate in the Arm-chair. The face of the peak rose in steep slabs, and there was plenty of snow lying even at our level of about three thousand feet, for there had been a heavy fall recently. In any case we felt the direct route up the face must be left for braver men. The two ridges that ran down from the peak on either side of the face were very steep in the highest thousand feet, and showed big steps that were nearly, if not quite, vertical. The first thing to be done was to get on to one of these ridges before that last sharp rise, just as one does on the Aiguille Noire. We chose the left-hand ridge (which wise men do not do on that Aiguille), because the slopes immediately above us were open and more inviting.

The ascent was as varied as a Corsican ascent can be. Trees there have a value that only the rock purist or the bearer of artificial aids will despise. We were a party of three, and we climbed without a halt for three hours before we reached the ridge at a height of nearly five thousand feet. It was three o'clock, and we hardly looked at the great pitch at whose foot we had arrived. There was not too much time to get back to camp before dark. Thinking we saw an easier descent near the slabby, shallow valley where the stream started, we chose it. We were wrong, and twice had to double a rope to get down, for the angle was disagreeably steeper than it looked. The slabs close to the Arm-chair, which the snow had left wet, were steeper than we liked in nailed boots. There was very little daylight left when we got back.

The second attempt was made three years later, by the other ridge. The upper part looked more possible, though the ascent to it was less easy. The steep buttress that had towered above us as we came up the stream bed, was joined to the face at a niche which we could clearly reach by a gully filled with a terrible tangle of rock and prickly shrubs, set at a high angle. From the niche we hoped to be able to continue up some ledge of the face that would slope upwards till we joined the ridge.

A short and slightly bloody battle in the gully took us to the niche. The niche was a snare, for on the far side was an impossible drop of sixty feet or more to easier ground. Immediately above the niche the cliff was impossibly steep, so we descended our gully a short way till we could break out on to the face. Fifty feet up, a slab with hardly any hold at all for a few feet impressed the party, and I was glad to see a belay of sorts for doubling a rope if we had to come down the same way. There was climbing of varied character above; a chimney, to which access was obtainable by ignoring Longfellow's warning against the pine-tree's branch, was typically Corsican and unconventional; it was decidedly tricky for the heaviest of the party. The face became steeper the higher we rose; we had to make a very short descent on a doubled rope from the shelf we followed, to a broad, easier shelf below. Soon after we reached the ridge at about five thousand feet, at one of the gaps seen on the left-hand skyline of the

37. CAPO TROVATORE

illustration opposite, I think the one with trees near it above a huge, snow-covered slab. To reach this gap from the side shown, that is to say, opposite to that we had ascended from the Arm-chair, would be difficult.

We had had a long morning with plenty of incident, and it was after midday. Unfortunately a strong, cold wind met us at the gap, and after climbing some sixty feet up the steep pitch above us we had no doubt about the wisdom of returning. The pitch, as far as it was visible, is certainly climbable without extraordinary skill or artificial aids, but it would be best done in calm weather and in rubbers. We could see nothing of the ridge beyond.

On the descent we kept down the shelf to which we had dropped on the way up, and found much easier going till we were close to the niche mentioned above; we were on the wrong side of it, below the drop, and there was no apparent way of reaching it, the buttress which the niche connected with the face being impossible to climb on this side. Far away to our left we saw a stretch of slabs which we should have to pass in order to get down at all into the path a long way below the Arm-chair. At any rate we thought it worth while to try to climb round the buttress, and see if a descent could be made on some other side of it. A ledge took us with unexpected ease up above an increasing height of cliff to the ridge of the buttress, at its end above the Arm-chair. I peered over; the face there was apparently unclimbable, and doubled ropes are things I avoid if possible, especially if you are looking for a route of ascent. A vertical wall fell straight to the *maquis*-filled gully we had climbed to the niche. Progress was possible along a narrow recess that led back across the wall towards the upper part of the gully; I could not see how far it would be possible to continue. The recess was not more than a foot in height. Lying very flat, I wound my way along it to its end at a right-angled corner in the wall. To cross this to a reassuring stance on the farther wall was possible with the help of a small tree that grew exactly in the corner. It was not a very flourishing tree, but it had to serve. Carefully held by the others, who were out of sight—and, what is more exasperating, all but out of hearing— behind the ridge, I tested the tree and then trusted my weight to it enough to let me get a hand across on to the stance upon the rock beyond. Then I dragged my body, not without resistance from the branches, on to a comfortable ledge. There I unroped and went on across a shelf with sufficient holds till, to my great relief, I saw that we could reach the head of our gully without any further difficulty.

T

The others then came across, held from both ends, their faculty for considering several things at once enabling them to thread them-selves, after some hard thinking in awkward situations, between the same pair of branches as the rope.   No man could wear his sack in the recess; there were five sacks, and they were all tied together by the scout-expert who came last.   As they were dragged across the tree gave way.   It will be a difficult place without its aid.

Another failure.   We must have stopped at least seven or eight hundred feet below the top, and what a grand day it had been! Well! we said, as we cannot wait for the best conditions, we must climb it from behind by way of a slightly higher summit, which we knew to be easily accessible.   We had not seen the connecting ridge in profile.   We saw it a day or two after, when the photograph opposite page 275 was taken.   That will show you why we changed our minds.   Moreover, I have reason to think, from another photo-graph taken three years before, when Capo Trovatore was not more to me than a background for the view, that there is more than one jag to be passed.   The drop from the Aiguille Noire de Péteret to the Dames Anglaises has its counterpart in this third ridge.   Traces of white worn in winter and in early spring forbid my suggesting for these pinnacles the name Dames Corses; for true Corsican women never wear anything but black.

The peak is called Capo Trovatore for good reasons.   It is a beautiful name, suited to such a rock peak in its setting of spring green and sparkling snow.   Also, its charms have given rise to musical inspiration.   The youngest of the party, as befits a troubadour pondering at its feet, was moved to begin the composition, not of a simple air to the guitar, but of such fuller expression as the twentieth century has called forth from wind and strings.   Lastly and chiefly, it is a name which can give rise to none of those jealous disputes by climbers who claim possession.   To whom shall a peak belong, if not to him who finds it?   And there is nothing to prevent your finding it.   Provided only that you will leave it to be called the Capo Trovatore, I shall not dispute your claim.   For you cannot take it from me, whatever you do upon it.   Men may come with hammers and rings and bags of pitons; they may climb it by a Parson's Nose buttress, a *Schmittkamin*, a *couloir en Z,* or the *direttissima in I*; it will leave my possession of it untouched, as long as memory holds.

It is a climber's peak, too.   I would not ask you to take my opinion on its climbing attractions; my taste is too gross and plebeian; any hill can stir my appetite.   In our party was a young man who had recently re-edited Mr. Geoffrey Young's guide to the strictly vertical walls and buttresses favoured by what I may call the Cambridge group. (The aims of this group are, as the name will tell you, high, but more limited and practical than one would expect of Oxford.) No Cambridge man can resent my giving that name to those who have practised a cult of climbing whose tenets were first held in Trinity, and whose exploits are performed within hail of the master's and the porter's lodge. This young man fully shared the general satisfaction with our peak. It is not, therefore, merely an old man's fancy.

I should like to have another try to climb it. And yet, if I get up, the peak can hardly mean more to me than it does now, an assurance that the age of discovery in climbing will never close for those who choose the April climb that can make all things new.

However much the Capo Trovatore is mine, it may be yours. And if not the Capo Trovatore, then I am quite sure that a Cima, an Ago, a Pizzo Trovatore is waiting for you somewhere till you have learned to find it. And April is the month to look.

CHAPTER XIII

SOLITARY MOUNTAINEERING

THE early fathers of mountaineering condemned any number of less than three on a rope. Two was dangerous; to climb alone was lunacy. It is as clear a proof as we can have that the age of mountaineering in which Alpine journals and Alpine clubs were founded was primarily an age of snow climbing, when a glacier was the recognized route to nearly every peak.

Notwithstanding the invention of various devices for using a doubled rope to enable one man alone to extract a companion from the depths of a crevasse, three remains a better number than two on a glacier, in practice if not in theory, and one as the best number among crevasses has not yet commended itself to any but those who only really enjoy climbing when Death is taking particular notice of them. Mummery was perfectly right when he contended that with experience a man learns to detect almost any hidden crevasse if he keeps a careful watch. But that proviso about the incessant care needed is one of the strongest arguments against solitary climbing on a glacier. The increased vigilance necessary, the extraordinary care that must be taken in probing the snow to detect a crevasse and ascertain the strength of a snow bridge, where it begins and where it ends, if you are to avoid the probably fatal result of a moment's negligence, this is what makes a glacier a thoroughly objectionable place to a solitary man. It produces just the sort of tiresome, worrying, continual strain that robs mountaineering of its recreative quality, the best of all its qualities. To cross a crevassed glacier alone is a thing to be left for emergencies only; it is better to resist the temptation it affords to test your patience and your eyesight and to gratify your vanity and your desire for forbidden fruit. Personally I find that life away from mountains affords already more than ample opportunity for these things. There are times when it makes you feel as Mr. Belloc felt on his path to Rome, when he crossed the high railway bridge outside St. Ursanne, stepping from sleeper to sleeper and seeing the abyss between, imagining at every step what would happen if he missed his footing. And there are times when it is just wearisome.

It was this very obvious danger of a snow-covered glacier that was uppermost in the minds of those who condemned solitary climbing in general.   There were other objections, such as the risk of spraining an ankle.   Many years of experience of a weak ankle have taught me that it is not in places where movement is deliberate, such as steep slopes of rock or snow, that the ankle will turn over, but in places where the foot is thrown out at random, on an actual path or on very easy ground, the sort of places where no one would condemn a solitary walk.

Solitary mountaineering is the most splendid tonic ever offered to man.   The early climbers, with the best puritan motives, like pro-hibitionists, did not believe in the possibility of moderation.   And moderation is the word that the solitary climber needs to whisper to himself every time he sets out to visit that fascinating friend of his, the solitude that dwells among the snows and ministers to every pleasure of the sense as well as of the soul.   All sorts of motives tempt him to over-indulgence, to test the strength of his head, to be able to boast of the conquest he has made, to profit by the chance of drinking this *elixir vitae,* with the result that he often comes back like other victims of self-indulgence, boastful, or irritable, and less capable of sympathy or effort.   We shall see later, in speaking of Lammer, the effect of excessive self-indulgence in this stimulant. Restraint need not be deprivation of the best, or a playing for safety which is anathema to youth; it may be the restraint that is shown by a man in his handling of a thing that is infinitely precious, whose value depends greatly on the use he makes of it.   Watch a devout priest handling a chalice, and you will see the sort of restraint I mean.

If companions are with us, they rightly dominate our thoughts and actions.   There is no sport in which the movement of one affects the rest of the party more than in mountaineering.   Hours may be saved or lost by the way we help or hinder progress.   A quick step-cutter or a good route-finder can make the success of an expedition, a clumsy mover or a man without any flair for the best way on a mountain can mar it.   There is hardly any limit to what we can do to increase the enjoyment of others by the share of the burden we carry, by our management of the rope, and other ways familiar to every climber.   If we can rise to Mr. Geoffrey Young's ideal we may even consult our companion as to the selection of that portion of our clothes which is, for most of the day, to form a prominent object in his foreground.   And in every difficult passage on rock or ice the lives of a man's friends may be in his hands and his in theirs, though he and they may both at times be unconscious of the responsibility accepted. Mallory confesses to a small sin of omission in this respect, when he actually went to sleep for a few moments while supposed to be securing my rope as I led round a rather difficult corner on the frontier ridge of Mont Maudit. It was not till six years later that his article in the *Alpine Journal* made me aware of it.

When friends are with us, we are like small wireless sets in the neighbourhood of a powerful local broadcasting station to which we are always more or less tuned in; messages from distant non-human stations are barely perceptible. In the presence of other men and women mountains appear to be inanimate objects, immovable blocks of stone which may hinder or assist our human activities. To ascribe any sort of personality to them, and to attempt to make them live in the presence of active human companions, is like plunging straight into what Ruskin calls the pathetic fallacy. It is not always so when there is nothing to prevent the voice of mountains being heard. The man who has climbed much alone will come to ask himself: Is this perception of life in mountain form, after all, a fallacy, or a dimly perceived truth?

In a tableau on the stage, in which, though no word is spoken, action is taking place all the time, in which expressions alter, and costumes and lighting are constantly changing, is it a fallacy to ascribe personality to the actors if they are fulfilling the purpose of impressing ideas upon the minds of those that watch? Even in front of a picture, it is not fantastic to consider the forms the artist draws as possessing purpose, as transmitting the thoughts and passions he is trying to express. Indeed, we may be more moved to believe in the conscious action of these forms than in that of the human figures we meet when we go out into the street. The words and expressions of these last are often the result of outside influence making them agents for the expression of things external to themselves, such as the result of the three o'clock handicap, or the Test Match, or the rise or fall of specu-lative shares. Their reaction to joy or sorrow, to fear, wonder, or fashion, is almost as automatic as that of a mountain to a change of weather, or of season. Nearly every word and action is predetermined by the external influences that have preceded it.

In many ways human beings are, to a greater extent than mountains, machines for the recording of the obvious. We can tell exactly at what time So-and-so will appear at the club, where he will sit, and how he will be dressed; but it is seldom that we can be sure whether at a certain hour Mont Blanc will be visible, and whether he will greet us with a welcoming smile or sternly inform us of his preference for solitude.

This mood of the mountain is highly important, and particularly so to a solitary climber, for he has only his own observation and experience to guide him. And there are few things that bring home to us the small extent of our knowledge more than the matter of predicting the weather. Here is a thing which depends on movements of the earth and sun that are periodic. The weather at a given place at a given time might be foretold a hundred years ahead, and yet we cannot tell what it will be a fortnight hence. Our weather-forecasting is dependent on elementary observations made within a few days of the event. We have got as far as knowing that a depression will produce a rather gloomy sky, perhaps a shedding of tears, and that the satisfactory sense of repletion in the atmosphere which we call an anti-cyclone will result in a calm and probably smiling mood. We know, in fact, as much about the character of the clerk of the weather as to say that he will probably show the effects of depression and of a good dinner.

Mountaineering, and most of all solitary mountaineering, brings us right up against this extraordinary problem of weather. All this system of regular movement is so infinitely complex that the results of its working may be described as barely predictable at all. You may ascribe it to mere chance. If, as I hope is the case, you find it impossible to do that, then at once a mountain becomes an important actor in the carrying out of some great design; all the different dresses it puts on are worn with some object in view; the pleasures it gives you in wrestling with it, its calmness, its patience, its steadfastness, its varying beauty, the different moods with which it tests you and stimulates your curiosity and wonder, are all indications of the part it plays in that great design. Human beings regard themselves as such important figures in this design, they have such great apparent power of initiating thought and action for themselves, that they are often unconscious of being anything but uncontrolled individualities; they have, by discovering how to use the materials set ready to their hand, surrounded themselves with such elaborate and convincing proofs of their own power to control all forms of what we call matter, that the evidences of any intelligent controlling power other than human becomes exceedingly difficult to detect in the environment of civilized life.

Among mountains there are still places where every transmitting agency of human origin is cut off, and we can, if the mind be tuned aright, catch other messages and become conscious of a vastly bigger but far slower life. Movement among mountains is slow compared with that of a tree, almost imperceptible beside that of a human individual or an animal. Frost and sun may remove each year hundreds of tons from the face of a mountain without making it less recognizable a thousand years later. Nevertheless, the fall of a stone, the crash of a *sérac,* the low whisper of a stream may remind you of change and movement that are purposeful. The generous nature of that purpose is shown you by the smallest lake that nestles in a dimple of the mountain. Sun and wind will turn its drops of water into jewels as you stand beside it, and in the calmer moments necessary to reflection it reminds you how great a gift is receptivity to beauty. That receptivity, in the tarn or in yourself, may be due directly to the operation of scientific laws; but that, after all, is an explanation of *how* it happens, and merely puts off a small stage further the inquiry as to *why* it happens.

To say why anything happens, even to say why we climb, is so admittedly difficult that we feel inclined to exclaim at once as we do when asked a riddle: 'I give it up,' and without adding: 'Tell me'! Motives are seldom simple. Your solitary climber may climb in order to have the whole glory of achievement, he may dislike having to consider the wishes and feelings of others, he may merely wish to get away from his fellows; his may seem to be the supremely selfish form of mountaineering, and yet with these selfish motives there nearly always mingles a liberal admixture of curiosity, of love of adventure, and a longing to approach something that may bring revelation.

And if, in a mixture of motives, there is much of the desire to learn, climbing alone will teach you, as nothing else can, how to understand the forms and characters of mountains, their moods and their significance; above all, it will show you what are the things that give perpetual youth to mountaineering, something that is a never-failing source of vitality in it that will survive all the sophistication, the routine, and habit that are superficial marks of age.

Alpine periodicals contain few accounts of solitary climbs. They have always been in the main a record of achievement, and are necessarily becoming more so as they reflect the characteristics of an age of progress in technical development and of growing indifference to spiritual values. The strongest attractions of solitary climbing are of a peculiarly individual nature, and vary greatly, according to the sensibility and the beliefs of each climber, so that what has most vividly impressed one may be unimportant or unreal to another, while the actual accomplishments which can be measured by technical standards are generally insignificant compared with those of men acting in co-operation. That is sufficient to make it a subject unsuitable for the chronicles of mountaineering activity.

But in a book which attempts to take a view of the whole life-story of the winning of mountains by man, with its emotions as well as with its deeds, it would be strange to make no mention of the moments when these two have been alone together. It is no use trying to tell you what they say to one another at these moments; either you know it already far better than I can tell you, or you are quite indifferent to this aspect of the matter. All I will try to do is to point to occasional expressions in the written experiences of mountaineers which show that, when men are climbing alone, they seem to be nearer than at any other time to the sort of revelation that all men long for and to which they are rarely able to attain. As the climber's memory lengthens with every visit he makes to the mountains, among the hours that never lose their vividness and their importance in retrospect are those he has spent with them alone, now wrestling with them, now resting to get his breath and look at these great, beautiful, enigmatic creatures that always beckon him back to play with them, to love them, and to understand them more.

Freshfield, one of the very few of the early climbers who have lived into the present generation, and one who has climbed in many ranges, did all his big climbs with guides, and in a record of his long career there is little of purely climbing interest in the expeditions made among the foothills without them. Yet I believe that few adventures in this long mountaineering life left an impression that is as vivid and as entirely happy as a solitary ascent in early spring of the Cheiron, a foothill of the Alps less than six thousand feet high, that protects the French Riviera from the blasts of the north wind, and behind which the desolation of winter lies long before the sun can banish it.

At last I was up to the level of the base of the cliffs that form the crest of the Cheiron. To be able to use hands as well as feet was a delightful relief in the long uphill strain. I took the steepest rock I could find, and indulged my scrambling instinct. A short gully led up between two crags. As I reached the crest I was met by an icy blast which nearly knocked me back again. . . . It was late in the afternoon, and the sun was low in the western heavens. A wilder view I had never seen, even from the greatest heights. The sky was already deepening to a red winter sunset. . . . The overpowering effect of the vast weird landscape was due, not to any individual feature, but to its general expression. Placed in solitude under the influence of this lurid sunset on the high, desolate hill-top between the snows and the sea, the most matter-of-fact tourist could hardly think for long of such small things as hills and gulfs and cities. One felt brought face to face with a mighty struggle between the principalities and powers of nature, a strife in which night and winter were allied against day and summer and were on the point of gaining the mastery. As the sun sank in the west, the sea grew more and more grey; the flush died off the Corsican heights and left them wan ghosts on the edge of the world; the last gleams faded from the warm green shores and the red promontories beyond Nice; the icy blasts from the leagues of northern frost and snow shrieked past with an even fiercer howl of triumph, as if about to seize on the last strip of sun-protected land underfoot.

Notice that scramble to get up; it is important not to confuse solitary climbing with solitary roaming; the former has a completeness in the expression it gives to life which is absent from the contemplative walk.

Now take Whymper, a most practical climber, who turned his climbing almost too much to commercial purposes, and who is certainly not one who can ever be claimed as an apostle of contemplative mountaineering. Knowing how obstacles, such as a rock wall a few feet high, can stop the solitary climber, where a *courte échelle* of another human body would solve the difficulty, Whymper invented two devices to be used in default of other aids. One was a short rope attached to a grapnel about five inches long, rather like the hooks used for hanging pictures from a rail, which gives a good hold over an edge, so long as a steady pull downwards is maintained. It was stuck on the end of his alpenstock and dropped into a crack, or in emergencies 'was flung up till it attached itself to something,' and then Whymper pulled himself up on the bit of rope. His other device was to fix to one end of a rope a metal ring with a string tied to it; the other end of the rope was passed through the ring, and when the loop thus formed had been flung round a rock the loop was tightened by simply pulling the rope and letting the ring slide up. It gave security and nearly double length of rope for descents. Afterwards the string was pulled, the ring slipped down, the loop was loosened and 'was whipped off readily.' Well, perhaps! This second device sounds a good deal safer than the first.

One day, when neither Carrel nor Meynet were free to accompany him, Whymper started on a lonely reconnaissance of the Italian ridge of the Matterhorn; his experiences and his comments will help to show the intensification for a man alone of the usual sensations of a climb:

It is one of the few things which can be said in favour of mountaineering alone (a practice which has little besides to recommend it) that it awakens a man's faculties, and makes him observe. When one has no arms to help, and no head to guide him except his own, he must needs take note even of small things, for he cannot afford to throw away a chance; and so it came to pass, upon my solitary scramble, when above the snowline and beyond the ordinary limits of flowering plants, when peering about, noting angles and landmarks, that my eyes fell upon the tiny struggling plants—oftentimes a single flower on a single stalk—pioneers of vegetation, atoms of life in a world of desolation, which had found their way up—who can tell how?—from far below, and were obtaining bare sustenance from the scanty soil in protected nooks, and it gave a new interest to the well-known rocks to see what a gallant fight the survivors made (for many must have perished in the attempt) to ascend the great mountain.

So much for heightened observation alone. Now for a heightened thrill of climbing.

I have a vivid recollection of a gully of more than usual perplexity at the side of the Great Tower, with minute ledges and steep walls; of the ledges dwindling away and at last ceasing; and of finding myself, with arms and legs divergent, fixed as if crucified, pressing against the rock, and feeling each rise and fall of my chest as I breathed; of screwing my head round to look for hold, and not seeing any, and of jumping sideways on to the other side.

If you have sampled the position, reader, both alone and when roped to others, you will probably admit that the pains of crucifixion and the relief of escape were greater when you were alone!

Then read the impression the ridge makes upon him on this occasion:

In the whole range of my Alpine experience I have seen nothing more striking than this desolate, ruined, and shattered ridge at the back of the Great Tower. I have seen stranger shapes—rocks which mimic the human form, with monstrous leering faces, and isolated pinnacles, sharper and greater than any here; but I have never seen exhibited so impressively the tremendous effects which may be produced by frost, and by the long-continued action of forces whose individual effects are imperceptible.

The adventures of that day of solitary climbing were not over. Whymper had left his axe—an old navy boarding-axe—up in the tent near the Great Tower. The steps he had cut in the hard snow traversing round an angle of the cliff of the Tête du Lion were nearly melted away and icy; all he could do was to lean round the corner and prod the hard stuff into a step with the point of his alpenstock; it is not surprising (though he himself says he never could tell how it happened) that 'in attempting to pass the corner' he slipped and fell, and he actually fell two hundred feet and was miraculously stopped within a few feet of a great drop of eight hundred feet that must have been fatal. The solitary climber has no one to relieve him of the strain of making the way safe in such places. That is why long, difficult climbs concentrate the attention of a solitary man on the technical details to such an extent that he misses just the very things which he is in a unique position to observe and enjoy.

Mr. F. W. Bourdillon once wrote a delightful paper on the attractions of life in a chalet taken for the season in the Alps, which he contends is as much better than hotel life as owning books is better than getting them from a circulating library. And this is the supreme attraction:

Above all, you can enjoy what is certainly the most absolutely enjoyable form of climbing—climbing alone. I say this with fear and trembling, because I have been often warned by much better climbers than myself that one of the first and great commandments of the Alpine Club decalogue forbids to climb quite alone. But I have sometimes dared to wonder whether this law was not framed, or at least kept up, merely to heighten pleasure by the feeling of wrongdoing; as the famous citizen over his loin of roast pork expressed regret that he was not a Jew, to add a last epicurean zest of lawbreaking to his enjoyment of it.

You cannot read what Mr. Bourdillon writes about mountains without feeling that his devotion to them is absolutely wholehearted, and he too has his limitation clause for solitary climbing: 'Of course, it must be limited by obvious prudences.'

Mummery has something to say about it, the man to whom the great brown slabs bending over into immeasurable space were old and trusted friends, and the black, bulging ice of the gully was the very breath of his being. He too has a warning to add to his words of commendation. After defending the practice of climbing two on a rope he says:

The habit of climbing alone is open to far other and more serious objections. . . . It is certainly undesirable to push such solitary wanderings beyond very narrow limits. On the other hand, nothing develops a man's faculties so rapidly and completely. No one detects a crevasse so readily as the man who is accustomed to traverse snowfields by himself. No one takes such careful note of the line of ascent as the cragsman who has got to find his way back alone. The concentration of all responsibility and all the work on a single individual forces him to acquire an allround skill which is hardly to be gained in any other way.

And he adds, with a typical touch of cynical humour:

The fact that a man has been in the habit of climbing alone means that the law of the survival of the fittest has had full and ample opportunity of eliminating him, should he be, in any way, a careless or incapable mountaineer.

One man stands out for unrestrained indulgence in solitary climbing —Lammer. Lammer deserves more than a passing mention; he is an interesting phenomenon, an early example of the rather morbid growths that threaten the health of mountaineering at the present time. He is at pains in his writings to leave us in no doubt as to his attitude to mountains. 'My appeal is to you who are weary of the disorganization of modern life, and are giving yourselves utterly with your whole being and your whole energy to mountains.' It is made clear by all he says that the object of the giving is self-realization. For a long time this wild hermit of the precipices was regarded as the Ishmael of mountaineering. An embittered spirit runs through all his writing. He lashes himself into a feverish hatred of those who pursue their way among mountains after the fashion of most members of Alpine clubs, accusing all so-called 'reasonable' climbers of being cowards, Philistines, and hypocrites. 'Then the profound disgust that was in Nietzsche took possession of me, and I seized the whip . . . wherefore, every step I took and every word I wrote is a kick at these Philistines, these Pharisees.' And he admits he does it all 'pour épater le bourgeois.'

What is, for Lammer, the aim of mountaineering? 'It was the manner of my outward triumph over the peak and my inward pos-session of it. It was not the mountain that was the object of my effort, it was the passing, at whatever cost, between defeat and victory, the loyal struggle without human or mechanical aids, and danger in all its stark frightfulness.' He sees himself as a Wagnerian hero, or a 'hammer in the hands of God,' a God, be it said, made in the image of Lammer. He fights desperate battles against forces whose hostility is created by himself; the greater the terror with which he can clothe his mountain, the greater the self-exaltation of his victory. As he himself admits, there is not a trace of humour in him. This conjuring up of appalling forces to feed his lust for conquest is carried to an excess which makes Lammer's vision that of a drug-taker. The fascination that fear seems to have for some climbers of the present generation is prominent in Lammer's accounts. 'Do not take away my fear, and my brave fight against fear, for then existence would be but a sad, insipid thing, fitted only to give one a distaste for life.'

Lammer's adventures are intensely exciting and intensely egotistical. The difficulties and the dangers suffer none of the diminution paid as a due to modesty by convention or natural reserve, as in the accounts of British climbers. The heightening of the perils that surround him —and the reality is perilous enough—is the essence of the sport for Lammer, the drug on which depends his dream of heroism. For it is as a drug that his climbing acts on him, destroying all self-criticism and leading to a state in which true vision is lost. We may envy the exaltation and the delirious thrill of the drug-taker, not because it is better or more intense or more lasting than that which is given by reality, but because it can be called up at will; it is self-created, not received. And if the strength of an intoxicant is measured by the value of the self-exaltation it induces, then solitary climbing as practised by Lammer is a very powerful stimulant indeed, for under its influence he becomes a finer fellow than we can ever hope to be. 'To feel so completely oneself, what overwhelming grandeur is in that! . . . The joy of pride was seething in me. . . . Every time that at the end of efforts and of peril I have achieved a first ascent of a peak or discovered a new route, I have read in characters of flame: "Stronger art thou than the Almighty." '

What contempt he has for those who discovered that a convenient traverse would avoid the dangers of the jagged teeth of the Olperer-Fussstein ridge: 'Why, in doing thus, they are deceiving their own heart that longs for the joys of sport; only on these savage teeth open the red blooms of peril, the delights and varying fortunes of an aerial climb.' He runs on ahead of other parties, if there are any such on their way to the peak, 'that no one may reproach him with having profited by a foreign guide's experience.'

But let us for a moment forget his boastfulness and his morbidity, and admire his courage; he has given us plenty of occasion to do that. Picture him as he stands alone on the highest point of the Gross Venediger, after conquering the icy north-west wall, the very wall from which a gallant and solitary climber, Rohregger, was swept by an avalanche in 1820, trying to win the summit for whose conquest the Archduke John had conceived a fancy. A heavy fall of snow had increased the labour and danger of Lammer's ascent. Only fifty yards away, on the other point of the summit ridge, the deep steps of another party promised a safe and easy return to the refuge, but every step of the fifty yards of corniced ridge presented appalling possibilities of death. 'Were I to live ninety years,' he says (and the miracle has nearly been accomplished), 'the memory of that hour will make me shudder in my dreams. Let some other man, with no friend or rope to give assurance, pass over a cornice covered with a deep layer of powdery snow, thinking the while of the fall of many hundred feet he had there four years before—and feel no fear! *Homo sum!*' Lammer takes his fill of the terror it supplies—and then begins to cross!

On one side is the ragged edge of the wave where it curls over in the air, on the other a slope whose inclination Lammer tells us is 80°, from which the least touch will detach the coat of loose snow that hangs upon it. The only way is on the very crest. With infinite care he hollows out a step, and slowly advances into it his knee—a gentler pressure than that of the foot to put upon a snow bridge. Another scratching of the fragile structure, a thumping of the incoherent snow with the fist—you are fortunate, reader, in your dealing with loose steep snow if you have never had to use your fists—and the other leg comes over to a second step. For a moment the mist clears, and far below three dark points show him the party whose tracks he hopes to reach, walking with comfortable ease upon the level glacier. 'Lucky ones! Up here is a human creature, abandoned by all, trembling on his knees, on a balcony of frozen water, a thousand feet above the glacier—on his knees like some Gothic figure on the gable of this gallery appalling in its frailty!'

The slightest shock, any disturbance of the balance by a gust of wind, may be fatal. His heart beats as if it would burst, and strange words of flattery and appeal addressed to the mountain rise to his lips. A coating of ice forms on the handle of his axe and the thought of dropping it brings a new access of fear. The first gap is reached, the slope of the wave is less near the vertical, and he ventures to strike with the axe. A round piece, on which he was to put his foot, drops out and shows a dreadful hole through to the void below. He is walking on the thinnest and newest portion of the crest of ice. And with this his nerve almost goes; his breath is hard to get and his knees tremble; every step after this, though easier in reality, seems girt with deadly peril. Three-quarters of an hour the crossing of the fifty yards takes him, and it has added, so Lammer tells us, several years to his age!

There are times when the mountains play for Lammer a softer strain than this clamour of demons. 'Oh, wonder and mystery of silence! The fountains of the soul well up, the breath of life enters into me through every pore. Not only of the great mind of All do I think, in the smallest things there is a soul akin to mine.' The tiny spider flung by the wind to die upon the snow, the gentian that withers in his hat, excite his pity, a kind of real sympathy with dumb nature that is not common except in our countrymen, and he says well what is easy for the solitary climber to perceive: 'How near the surface beats the great heart of the universe.'

And then, like any drug-fiend, he is plunged into the depths of bitterness:

The August sun darts its red-hot needles into me, his friend. The wind brings no refreshing draught . . . the vile crowd of stunted firs bends beneath my foot and then returns to lash me from behind. Dripping with sweat, and with parched throat, I drag myself along. I rage because my thoughts will dwell on everything I hate, at all the horrible discords of the life below; I cannot shake off from my soul the dust of a civilization I abhor.

Well, most climbers have felt like that going up to a hut on a hot afternoon, and have made less fuss about it, at least in company. A man alone is less restrained; let those who climb alone take warning!

The inevitable fall into a crevasse comes to Lammer despite his boast of 'the special flair—incomprehensible even to himself' which he possesses for these hidden snares. The most dangerous place of all on a glacier is where the dry glacier is beginning to appear from under the covering of snow that lies over the upper slopes, and it was here that he fell through. 'I was weary with twelve hours' toil, I took a few steps carelessly, thinking of other things . . .'

Let any one who has climbed for as much as twenty years without taking a few steps carelessly throw the first stone! Thinking of other things, it may even be of your companions on the rope, that is the danger. Twice only have I fallen a serious distance into a crevasse; on both occasions it was on nearly level ground in the part of the glacier I have mentioned, and on both occasions my fall was due to the same cause. I had stopped and turned to my companions on the rope—once it was my young wife alone—to tell them of the need for care. The very next step, almost part of the act of turning round again, let me through, and the rope did not check me till I was a dozen feet below the surface. Both times I unconsciously kept tight hold of my axe and was able to get out, but it is an experience from which I would willingly save my bitterest enemy.

Lammer fell far, straight through a first floor of the crevasse to the bottom. He woke from the first stunning shock to find himself, as it were, in a dark fog, the only light coming through the two holes he had made, and the dim, cold walls of the crevasse pressing at his

38. TREASURIES OF THE SNOW

sides. His cheek-bone was broken in two places; blood poured from a deep cut above the eye, which made him fear, at first, his eye was gone. Death, a slow, inevitable death, seems to close its arms about him, and then he begins his fight for life. First he crawls to his axe, which has buried itself close by him in the snow; then he replaces his smashed glasses with a fresh pair, he takes his crampons off the sack and puts them on. By cutting steps on either wall, or by backing up as in a chimney with his crampon points pressed into the ice, he works his way up to the first ceiling of firm ice and puts his head through. A moment's relaxation of the muscles means a fall to the bottom. His shoulders catch; he has to come down to enlarge the hole; then his sack catches, and he has to descend again, and pass it through, before he emerges into the upper story of his icy prison. This is a higher and longer climb; the fear comes on him that his strength may fail and that he will fall, with no strength to rise again. At last the roof of snow is reached, a push with his head in the soft stuff sends him through, and he crawls out, to lie exhausted, but saved, outside its horrid walls.

How ludicrously illogical is this cult of fear! Lammer himself tells us that he would not for the world go through the experience again; he recoils from the concentrated terror it has so generously given him, the terror he professes to desire. These were his reflections an hour or two before: 'It was with a thrill of terror that I thought of the perils that would face me as I crossed the glacier in the full heat of the afternoon. . . . And yet I felt drawn towards it. "The horrible is what repels and attracts, the horrible is in my own heart," as Ibsen says.'

The peaks look down in calm indifference on him as on 'a gladiator flung into the arena among the famished tigers.' In the solitude of this white chaos of ice he sees what is frightful. In its silence he hears a trembling cry that never ends; he feels a hundred piercing eyes fixed upon him; the crevasses, like beasts of the Apocalypse, are waiting to snap him with their jaws; the avalanches hiss like serpents, the rocks roar as they crash down towards him. It is easy to see how men so obsessed with frightfulness and with Wagnerian heroism might use the former as an instrument of war, and regard themselves as the instruments for forging in violence a better world.

Lammer is obsessed with the desire for self-exaltation and nightmare terrors. He is like a child bravely venturing into the gloomy attics its fancy has peopled with all sorts of bogeys. It is the right frame of mind to cultivate if you climb for excitement and for the exultation of

U

victory. There is, fortunately, a quite different attitude that the solitary climber can adopt, which is to regard himself, as he enters the places where mountains alone are pursuing their mysterious existence, as a youth newly admitted to the company and conversation of those whom he has always looked up to and loved. These great presences with faces that are always attractive, whether they are grave or smiling, are not demons; the avalanches are not serpents, nor the crevasses malevolent beasts of prey, they are agents in a movement of infinite range that is of absorbing interest and difficult to understand. If he regards that movement as purposeful and generous, beauty, not horror, will predominate, and the comparative insignificance of his place in such a movement will only heighten the thrill of participation in it. If, on the other hand, there is nothing in all he sees beyond material forces aimlessly working themselves to a purposeless end, then there is nothing but bitterness and gloom in contemplation, and satisfaction must be sought as in Lammer's passionate assertion of himself in action.

And the solitary climber knows how good strenuous action is; whether he regards it as the necessary complement of a happy philosophy, or, as in Lammer's case, as an escape from pessimism. He will give Lammer full praise for these words: 'It is the meditations of the idle, the cold reasonings and broodings of the mind that have hatched out pessimism; action, which abandons itself to instincts that are free, kills it.' Only the future will show us all the beneficent energy that springs from games, from sport, and from art, when they are pursued with no other end in view. 'The weariness that your generation finds in life can only be vanquished by the eternal child that dwells within you.'

The need for action is in Lammer's case made the excuse for drugging himself with the excitement of danger. One of the sayings of Nietzsche, which he chooses to summarize his views, is: 'Build your houses on Vesuvius.' It is bad advice; for one of three things must happen: you and your house are destroyed in a way that may be dramatic but is extremely unpleasant, or your nerves go utterly to pieces from the strain, or you become callous to the danger and receive no more thrill from it than a window-cleaner who sits on the sill on the fourth story. The spirit of perpetual youth in mountaineer-ing is not to be found in either fear or danger, but in the light of pure enjoyment; moreover the full delight of adventure is lacking in the attack on some grim and famous wall like that of the Grandes Jorasses, which only the spirit of competition can make us regard as anything but a bad route to the summit. The element of the unexpected is too small. The absence or presence of a hand-hold on a slab may add much to the excitement of a climb, and such excitement may be obtained on any steep bit of mountain-side that invites us to spread ourselves upon it. But it is not as good, or as impressive, or as lasting as the sort of adventure that happens to any solitary climber who is wise enough to choose a modest peak that has no place in the outline drawings of any Climbers' Guide, or who is unfortunate or fortunate enough to have left his map at home. The kind of adventure that I mean, not to be exchanged for all the moments spent in groping for holds on slabby rocks, may be illustrated by one that happened near Gavarnie in the Pyrenees. If you go there in a fine April you will find the winter coat of snow wearing into holes that show patches of brown earth on the slopes around it, big enough to frighten away the skiers, and it is unlikely that you will meet other climbers. The snow may be horrible—I remember one spring when it took eight hours to reach the Port de Gavarnie, when for nearly a mile of the way progress was hardly possible except on all fours—or it may be good, as it was for a young man who came there, and was filled with wonder on seeing for the first time the range of peaks above, the mighty wall of the cirque.

In that range, not adjoining but near to the sharp jag, hundreds of feet deep, which Roland's sword has cut in the frontier ridge, rises the Taillon, a fine pyramidal peak whose importance measured by quantitative standards runs into five figures. Our young friend climbed it by a pleasant rock ridge, not occupied by forbidding gendarmes who tried to push him off, but by nicely made forms that gave a comforting assurance to finger or toe. A storm came on, as it is wont to do in these mountains, before he could descend along the frontier ridge to gain the Taillon Glacier. There is only one course to adopt when lightning is playing on a ridge: to leave it as soon as possible. To descend the northern precipice into France, judging by such small indications of the face as the clouds allowed him to see, was, at that point, impracticable. He came to a point where it was easy to reach, on the south side, a slope of snow that merged into the grey wall of mist and led down into Spain; altogether a beguiling slope, combining immediate safety with adventure. In a few minutes he was revelling in the long plunging strides that are almost effortless when the slope is sufficiently steep, and the snow less than knee-deep. In the mist the occasional rocks and inequalities, magnified to huge proportions, appeared so suddenly and vanished so quickly that he had the impression of flying down at enormous speed.

The slope continued to dip at an angle agreeable to tired legs; he seemed to have put leagues in distance and thousands of feet in height between himself and the frontier. The crashes of thunder grew fainter as the area of storm was left behind. The hail ceased. The slope became less steep, and under the snow a hidden stream began to make its stifled gurgles heard. Every moment he was expecting to reach the Val d'Arazas, which, he remembered from the map, ran parallel to the main range. His eyes were longing for some change in the small monotonous circle of mist and snow that clung round him as he moved. At last, with no more warning than a sudden infusion of warmer light into the greyness in front, the curtain of cloud passed up.

He found himself standing on the very brink of a cirque so wildly beautiful, so different in fantastic grandeur to what he had expected to see, that he felt his whole being caught and shaken by the wonder of it. The sudden vision of it literally took his breath away. On either side of him precipices of increasing depth ran out to two bastions of rock, which towered thousands of feet above the valley, the Val d'Arazas, lying far below across the opening of the cirque. But it was the colour, even more than the scale and form of what he saw, that held him spellbound. The vast amphitheatre was glowing with orange and crimson above, with dark velvety greens and purples below, as if all the passion of the south had surged up to melt the cold austerity of the snow. Colour is always vivid after storm, and its effect was intense upon eyes that had been resting for hours upon a monochrome of whitish grey.

Fatigue also may act strangely on a man's perceptions. Many times it produces mere peevishness and insensibility to beauty, to anything indeed but rest and food. There are times when it merely draws all restless desire for action from the limbs and mind, and leaves a man's whole being acutely sensitive to beauty, so that the senses yield unreasoning obedience to its spell.

Immediately in front, where the stream wriggled out of the snow and escaped over the rim of the cirque, the drop to practicable slopes was lower than elsewhere, but a single glance showed that drop to be unclimbable. This young man was not one of your fellows who know no fear. Anticipations of tragic possibilities were never far away in the hours before an arduous climb. And in these moments of intense feeling he saw the difficulty of escape. Yet the spell of the place was so strong upon him that he not only felt no fear, he felt the very will to escape weaken. He freed himself to look back towards the slopes he had descended, and followed them in imagination under the clouds up their long, weary length. Could he ever plod up there again to the frontier ridge in the few hours of daylight and with the diminished strength that were left him? He turned again and let his eyes rest upon the magical beauty of the glowing forms before him, which offered supreme contentment in just gazing at them, while they seemed to mock the possibility of action. It was a dangerous moment, when the presence of a friend was needed to supply a restorative to the will. And in that moment his eye was caught by something that looked like a piton in the rocks below the rim, some distance away to his right. You, reader, in your arm-chair, will know already that the explanation was simple; some chamois-hunter had had the piton put in there some years before to provide an exit from the cirque. Quite true, but none the less it was a miracle for that young man, alone in that great theatre, the most dramatic thing that had ever happened to him. It changed the whole character of what he saw; its beauty was no longer pagan; he saw in it something that restored his liberty of choice, and yet made him feel absurdly small and weak, rather like a child that sees the smile of forgiveness in its mother's face.

He made his way over to the piton, barely able to believe in its reality till he had touched it with his foot. It was a solid reality, the first of several that supplied what nature had omitted to provide for a descent, till pine-trees growing at all sorts of angles took the place of the steep rocks, now aiding, now obstructing progress. And as he descended, it was not only the unknown chamois-hunter that he thanked. That night he slept in an old house in Torla, served with delightful courtesy by a nobleman of Spain. Is not that a day of real adventure?

To encounter and escape a danger that is unsought and unexpected is far, far better than deliberately to seek dangers which are known and can be estimated before you start. It is impossible to climb on any big mountains, particularly at times when they are generally left alone, without occasionally getting into situations where it requires all a man's skill and experience to get him out. Such situations may arise where no technical difficulties exist, but they are nevertheless true tests of mountaineering craft.

Near the Col di Tenda there is a mountain called the Roccia dell' Abisso. It is an easy mountain, and it is accessible by its warm

southern slopes at times when a heavy snowfall may have made it
difficult otherwise to reach what must always be one of the main
objects of a visit to the Maritime or Ligurian Alps, a peak from which
may be seen the most wonderful view in Europe, without a rival for
extent and variety of beauty: the coast of the Riviera, with the sea
stretching away till it melts into the sky, save where the dim horizon
is broken by the peaks of Corsica, the plain of Northern Italy under
the lightest film of the mist, and beyond it, under the enchantment
of great distance, the chain of the Alps from Mont Blanc to Monte
Rosa.

Unfortunately, despite the fact that France and Italy fought side
by side in the greatest war of history, access to the Roccia dell' Abisso
is forbidden from every side, lest there should be discovery and
betrayal of some secret preparation for battle between these brothers-
in-arms.   More than one valley leads up to it from north and east.
The shortest and most obvious descent to Tenda was too likely to
lead to incarceration in an Italian lock-up.   And apart from the
difficulty caused by the confusing twist of the other northern valleys
as they merge into the final peak, the eye is apt to be a little blurred by
the contemplation of the view to which I have referred.   *Qui s'excuse,
s'accuse!* The man I have in mind, who had just left the summit, was
no longer a young man; he should have been above such weaknesses.
However, he made a wrong start.   When you have descended in
steep snow up to your thighs, even for ten minutes, the rectifying of
a mistake, which involves an immediate certainty of great labour in
re-ascent, inclines you to underestimate the risk of perishing in the
wrong valley.

There was no difficulty beyond the length of the valley and the
depth of the snow, and it was only as the afternoon wore on that he
became less and less sure that he would leave the valley alive.   The
problem of choosing the line over the snow that offered least fatigue
demanded as much care and as much knowledge, and was as vital
to safety, as the ascent of a steep rock face.   There was a greater
reality in the struggle with this tenacious opponent that held him by
the leg than in overcoming any obstacle which a deviation of route
could have avoided.   He was feeling that another half-mile would
be beyond his strength, when he turned a corner and saw the beginning
of the dark broken line that marks the thinning of the winter snow on
the edge of a well-made path.   To feel the hold of the snow slacken
and to see the good hard earth appear was a less sudden thrill, but as
exquisite as that of Lammer as he gasped beside the crevasse, from

whose pitiless jaws he had escaped. 'It is no dream, you are alive.' And he became aware of a world become more lovable.

Another thing enjoyed in perfection by the solitary climber is the sense of freedom. For him it is complete. He is like a boy going home for a long whole holiday; all the better if he has to travel to get there, and he knows there will always be a surprise waiting for him. There are no better moments of anticipation for a climber than when he sets off in the dawn of a day of promise to cross some pass or mountain that he does not know, at a season when he is likely to enjoy it entirely undisturbed. That moment, in particular, is super-latively good when he turns aside out of the valley where he slept, and enters a region where the snow still lies, where every evidence of human occupation is left behind. It has the thrill of a long private interview with someone who matters tremendously; he has just been shown into the big quiet room, and the door is shut. From this moment onwards his safety as well as his enjoyment will be increasingly dependent on what he does and how he does it, and the permanent results will depend on what his senses and his understanding can take in.

And, what is perhaps the best of all that this sense of freedom gives him, he can give full and natural expression to his feelings. For an Englishman, especially, that is a rare treat. Frenchmen like Maurois and Cazamian, who know us well, have seen that we are a people of strong emotions which we stifle, more or less successfully, under silence and stiffness, or which we mask with humour. By expressing our contempt for sentiment, we protect ourselves not only against merely superficial disturbances of feeling but against appeals to the emotions, which might stir them till they were beyond control.

Appreciation of beauty goes very deep in an Englishman when it is entirely natural, and not part of a veneer of culture. It is the appeal of beauty that brings up his tears in sorrow, and that blurs his vision as he watches the finish of a fine race. In any company it is difficult to express freely by look and word and gesture all the admiration we may feel for beauty; but alone on a mountain a man can be simply and entirely natural in his reaction to it. I am sure that at such times I have made sounds and movements that were nearer to song and dance than anything I have achieved at other times; and as for those attitudes of worship in which you may surprise a man alone upon a peak, following a sudden revelation of beauty more often than an escape from peril, they are natural attitudes, just the overflowing of the immense joy that permeates his whole being simply from having come to such a place.

At the end of a long day, when he comes down to eat his supper by some welcoming fire, the climber will realize alone, more clearly than in friendly company, that mountains beget hospitality and trust fulness in those that live among them, dependent on their moods. If your clothes are ragged, the mountain folk will want to mend them for you, and ask no payment in return; in places invaded by the so-called amenities of modern life they may refuse to take you in. I shall never forget the contrast between the faces of the hill people among whom I spent a night in the Ligurian Alps, and those of the passengers in the afternoon train to Monte Carlo and Nice; the former showed outward proofs of health, honesty, and kindliness, the latter of ruined health, avarice, and selfishness.

It is natural that the larger and more lasting adventures should make the deepest impressions upon the mind, but it would be a mistake to suppose that any solitary climber's day is without excitements of a technical kind. There is no one there to correct his mistakes; the choice of route is perpetually affording small problems which may demand a special solution. There are just a few routes which are safer for a man alone than for any party. One example will show the type I mean.

It is curious that it should be on the best known of all Alpine peaks, Mont Blanc, and on the side that is easiest of access. Neither of the well-known routes from Chamonix and from St. Gervais is free from dangers that exist for the most competent as well as for the least competent of parties. The number of stones that fall from the Aiguille du Midi, across a portion of the track that leads from the *station téléférique* of Pierre Pointue to the glacier, is so great that it is surprising that more casualties do not occur. And above, the route passes over the Petit Plateau, and may be swept by falls from the ice-cliffs of the Dôme du Goûter. On the St. Gervais route, in the couloir crossed by parties low down on the face of the Aiguille du Goûter, stones fall, not only in the afternoon, but, on a fine, clear morning, long before the sun is up. The convenience of these routes is so great that the danger is ignored; nevertheless, there are still a number of mountaineers who believe that the avoidance of such objective dangers is a thing to be desired, and to be achieved, if possible, by a reasonable modification of route. Such modification is offered by following in its entirety one of the ribs of the Aiguille. In its upper portion it has steep, narrow steps more difficult than anything on the broad, easy rib on the Bionassay side of the couloir. For a party the risk of detaching rocks is too great on the steepest of these steps, but for a solitary climber this route is more interesting, and entirely safe if he has experience in selecting safe holds among rocks of varying stability. Anything he detaches will not fall on the heads of parties in the couloir.

There are places now climbed where the use of the rope adds nothing to the safety of the individual, where the slip of one means the death of all, though such passages occur, as a rule, on climbs where the rope may be an invaluable assurance on other portions of the route. For the solitary climber, such climbs are most severe and exhausting tests of the human machine, which, like other machines, is not made to be tested but to give satisfactory service. It would be ridiculous to consider as more suitable for a solitary man those climbs which are so difficult and dangerous that the use of the rope increases the risk to life.

The strain of solitary climbing, both on the physical and the emotional side, is greater than climbing with friends, even though the latter be novices. After a long, strenuous day alone, Lammer would spend the night descending precipices in a succession of unrestful dreams, and his experience must have been shared by most men who have had to fight for life alone. It is far too strong a stimulant for regular use, and it is unique among all other stimulants in this, that the effect never quite wears off, and that the doses needed to produce results grow smaller and smaller with the use. Once a climber has come to know the mountains alone, face to face, he will understand what they say, even whether friends are there or not. And when he understands, he knows that the realization of self is the aim that will produce limitations and decay in mountaineering, just as it has done and will always do in sport, in art, and in religion. He has discovered something from them that he wants to share. And to take someone to these same mountain sages, and find that he too longs to share their secrets, is even better than the solitary climbs themselves.

Few have leisure now to spend months in exploration of distant unknown mountains; nor is there any need to go to the ends of the earth to find adventure and the emotional experiences that come to men in strange solitudes. If the sophistication of modern climbing begins to dull the edge of appetite, if the familiarity with famous peaks has left unsatisfied a longing for discovery, try solitary climbing if you have never experienced its delights. Are there no portions of the Sierra Nevada, of the Pyrenees, of the Bergamasque, the Ligurian, and other Alps with peaks of ten thousand feet that are unknown to you? When the snowline is below four thousand feet, it presents us with hundreds of snow peaks that the summer climber has never seen.

Read nothing that has ever been written about the district you select to visit, and it will be surprising if adventure does not come to you; and you will find also that the teaching of mountains that is given to you alone makes more impression than any other. All the great climbers who have written about solitary climbing have said this. And their writings leave us in little doubt of its appeal to the imagination. If you still doubt it, refresh your memory with the two accounts of solitary ascents made more than three thousand years ago, which prove it in a manner that will never be excelled in any literature. Has anything been written in appreciation of what mountains reveal to the imagination that can compare with the 'still, small voice' that spoke to Elijah on Horeb, or the effect of the revelation that came to Moses on Sinai? No tales in the Old Testament have pointed more clearly where direction may be found.

Both these great men learned that action is the fruit of contemplation, which without it remains barren. The monks went up into the mountains to nurse their souls in contemplation, and missed the truth that is found in climbing mountains, that action must follow aspiration. A profound wisdom underlies the natural desire of a child to convert suggestion into action. And it is to a man who is to mountains as a child that they reveal the secret of perpetual youth that is in them; so that he will, like Antaeus, return from every contact with them, stronger to wrestle with the difficulties of life, and quicker to catch the sunshine. In some of the quiet moments he spends alone with them he may learn small fragments of the boundless wisdom that is in them; and he may find that the difference between the vision of the solitary pilgrim and that which he can share with others has long ago been expressed as simply and clearly as is possible in words: 'He shewed his ways unto Moses, his works unto the children of Israel.'

CHAPTER XIV

SOLVITUR IN EXCELSIS

In the opening chapter of this book the personal note was prominent. In the other chapters it has not done more than help to bring some unity of design into the succession of varied and widely separated incidents that make the story. My views of the relative importance of events, and of the developments in the character and the aims of mountaineering, have affected my selection of the pictures put before you. Put this, at least, to my credit, that I have added nothing to the description of such climbs as are not already chronicled in Alpine history which can rob you of the pleasure of finding your own way upon a mountain. I hope there is not a single climb mentioned in this book which you will find easier or less attractive for my having done it. In this I have tried to act up to my views of what constitutes the joy of climbing.

My endeavour has been to return thanks for the glorious feast of good things which men have enjoyed upon mountains; and in spite of the omission of what you may think important, and in spite of shortcomings inevitable in one who takes a great subject for the first book he writes, I still hope that I have given the impression that ours is the greatest of all sports, and that it is something more than a sport.

And now, in these concluding words, the personal note will sound again. Perhaps there never has been a book of mountaineering experiences in which no boast was found. And this is my boast: that no one ever had his devotion to mountains rewarded with a greater measure of pure enjoyment. That use of the past tense does not mean that the sources of enjoyment have dried up and become a memory only. Mountaineering has shown me, as no other sport has, what a delusion is the belief that pleasure is the companion of youth and not of age. In youth we seldom realize our pleasures; we are too apt to look for results, and to judge by the misleading standards of quantity, so that the full rapture of the moment escapes us.　Men talk of the perfect happiness of schooldays.　What nonsense!　They were good, but we had not the knowledge to make the most of them. A boy who has hardly tasted wine does not enjoy a famous vintage as does your old connoisseur.　He may be able to drink more without suffering for it, just as he can climb more peaks and in less time; that is all.　The years bring better understanding and fuller knowledge of what matters most; of what use is life, if they do not?　At the age of fifty, on a modest peak of nine thousand feet, we can capture things that we missed upon the Matterhorn twenty-five years earlier.　The surprise and passionate exultation of those first big climbs of our youth, our coming-of-age as a mountaineer, will not recur.　But is it not as good to watch these emotions come, as you stand by the side of those who are making their *entrée* into the new world above the snowline?

In an age in which men's beliefs are shaken, when the ultimate end of life announced by mathematical philosophy is complete annihila- tion, the question why we climb is likely to be answered, and impatiently answered: 'Because we like it.'　There is something beyond that, however, which is worth considering, if there is any good in the pursuit of knowledge.　If it is worth while to assign true values to influences and events, then it is not altogether a vain thing for men to weigh their mountaineering experiences, and see what showing they make in the balance-sheet of life.　Let us take a very few examples from the men who have attempted in words to justify their faith.

These are the benefits which Mummery claims for the man who wrestles with gaunt bare slabs and icy gullies.　'Equally, whether he succeeds or fails, he delights in the fun and jollity of the struggle. . . . I do not pretend to be able to analyse this feeling, still less to be able to make it clear to unbelievers.　It must be felt to be understood, but it is potent to happiness and sends the blood tingling through the veins, destroying every trace of cynicism and striking at the very roots of pessimistic philosophy.'　Nor is he insensitive to the contemplative side.　'I should still wander among the upper snows, lured by the silent mists and the red blaze of the setting sun, even though physical or other infirmities, even though, in after aeons, the sprouting of wings and other angelic appendages may have sunk all thought of climbing and cragsmanship in the whelming past.'　You can see the man's real fierce love of mountains as things adorable in themselves behind the mask of humour.

This is Mr. Bourdillon's most conclusive reason for climbing mountains:

One reason is never given openly, rather is disguised and hidden and never even allowed in suggestion, and I venture to think it is because it is really the inmost moving impulse in all true mountain-lovers, a feeling so deep and so pure and so personal as to be almost sacred—too intimate for ordinary mention. That is, the ideal joy that only mountains give—the unreasoned, uncovetous, unworldly love of them, we know not why, we care not why, only because they are what they are; because they move us in some way which nothing else does; so that some moment in a smoke-grimed railway carriage, when in the pure morning air the far-off cloud of Mont Blanc suddenly hung above the mists as we rounded the curves beyond Vallorbe, or, still fairer, from the slopes near Neuchâtel, the whole Bernese range slept dreamlike in the lake at our feet, lives in our memories above a hundred more selfish, more poignant joys; and we feel that a world that can give such rapture must be a good world, a life capable of such feeling must be worth the living.

Yes, that is it; the assurance that what we see is good, and that life is good if we can realize it. There are no moments that stand out in our long hours of glorious experience like those in which we came to some high point, and, as we looked out over what was before us, we knew certainty, and doubt was impossible. Those moments are as great rocks to which the frail tabernacle of our mind is held fast, when the mists of doubt and the winds of fear come about it. We cannot help being shaken or having our vision darkened, but we know that we have had moments of clearer vision, and that in them we had certainty. A certainty of what? It is hard to put it into words. It was a certainty that beauty and truth and generosity were real things, that there was something embracing all of these that gave direction to life, and an assurance that their reality need not be doubted when we saw them as we generally do, as in a glass, darkly.

Regarding the beauty of mountains, the view of Ruskin has prevailed and still prevails over that of Dr. Johnson. Indeed, Alpine literature has suffered so much from over-production and standardization in the matter of sunrises and sunsets and summit views, that only the brave or the unsophisticated will dare to add their personal contribu-tion. That does not mean that dawn and evening and wide horizons on the upper snows are less beautiful; it means that their beauty has been reproduced too often to the best of men's ability, and that the readers of Alpine literature already carry in their minds pictures which show them how futile is the attempt to crush the infinite beauty of reality within the bounds of language.

There are two qualities in beauty more clearly revealed to me on high mountains than in any other place. One is harmony; the harmony of the infinitely small with the infinitely great, where perfection of beauty in detail is found at every stage of the building of the whole. The tiny six-pointed star that drifts down on to your coat has beauties that multiply with every increase in the power of the microscope. And yet these beauties are all eclipsed for our limited vision when we see them built up into the leaves and flowers of frost that grow under the winds of winter on the upper rocks of British hills, the consolation Nature awards to the smooth, hard slabs that can offer no lodging-places to the flowers of summer. Crevasses open to let us see translucent canopies, so delicate that a touch of the sun will shatter them, so beautful that we forgive the inconvenience they cause thereby to our material progress. Yet we almost forget they exist as we look at the glistening draperies that fall for thousands of feet over the form of a great peak like Monte Rosa or Siniolchum. In the light that beats upon you on a snow crest, out of the deep, palpitating blue of the dome of sky, and leaps up from the tiny facets of the ice-crystals around you, the countless waves of energy seem to be moving with one purpose, a purpose in which you must have your part.

The second quality is quiet strength. There is something in the serene loveliness of a scene in the High Alps more truly spiritual and undying than in the beauty of things whose life, like our own, may be measured in hours, in seasons, or in years. The following words of Théodore Camus may help to show you what I mean. Camus was one of the many young men of Lyons who have lost their hearts to the Alps by looking at their distant snows from the hills that rise above the Saône. Not long before his death, when he knew that the illness which had attacked him must be fatal, he was talking to his sister, a nun, of his increasing detachment from things that belonged to earth, and he added: 'There is just one thing to which I hold as close as ever, which for me shines with a wonderful brilliance that remains undimmed though it belongs to the things of earth; I mean the High Alps at heights of three or four thousand metres. This is the loveliest thing on earth, and how few there are who know it! When I die, it is to them that I shall send one of my last good-byes, and every day I thank God, not for having created them, but for having made me know them. It is as if, in doing that, He had allowed me to have a glimpse of the infinite, through a window open only to a few privileged beings, of that infinite which cannot be described, for all descriptions are so far below the truth.'

This is the beauty in mountaineering which, when we have made it ours, we can keep always with us.

There is also a beauty only seen in action, in the midst of vigorous play, when our heart is beating fast to supply our calls upon it, and our face is close up against the mountain's as we pause for breath. We struggle through the hours of a long day to make our will prevail and win the game, and all the time the mountain maintains its calm as though it knew it was its beauty that had conquered us. Nor can our idea of beauty be complete without the struggle. The Greeks are the people who have been most eager in the pursuit of beauty as an ideal, and it was in their games that it most often found expression. Nor is it only through the eye, but also through the sense of touch and other senses that beauty is gathered into our experience and helps to fashion our soul. It is no exaggeration of the fancy to claim that the climber knows the beauty of rock, its firmness, its variety of colour, form, and texture better than a mere walker. Many of the loveliest formations of ice and snow are only approachable by him, and only he knows the full fragrance of the cool air on the ridge that has cost him hours of toil on burning slopes to win.

And besides all the intimate charm that mountains reveal only to those who are not content to sit at their feet and watch, but are determined to win them, there is the beauty of artistry that is called into existence by all great sports. There is beauty in any action performed as perfectly as means permit—we may even concede that the action of a motor engine is in this sense beautiful at times. There was more than mere efficiency in the way Mallory or Franz Lochmatter would climb a slab, or in the action of a good step-cutter, where every blow is struck exactly in the right place and every ounce of effort tells in the result, while the poise of the body in the slippery steps responds to every movement of the swinging axe.

On high mountains there are never fifty thousand spectators as at a cup-tie or a test match, from whom the cry of: 'Beautiful! beautiful!' is drawn by a clever dribble or a glance to leg. There is only the breathless silence of two or three companions, strung out upon some narrow footholds, as they watch the series of well co-ordinated movements that carry a leader past a protruding boss. Nevertheless it is a spontaneous tribute to this beauty of action.

Guido Rey aptly compares the man who claims to know the charm of mountains without ever risking his life upon them to a man who would claim to be a navigator without ever having left the shore, or to have known what the love of a woman can be from having sung serenades beneath her window.

Only when men become as gods will they have full knowledge of the nature of beauty, and meanwhile they may follow all sorts of paths in their pursuit of it. It is the pleasantest of all life's quests, and the climber, as he pursues his pilgrimage, is reminded at every stage of it that he is in the right way. From start to finish he has the pageant of the sky enacted daily and nightly, and he is in the best place of all to see. He knows the clouds from within and from above as well as from beneath; he can watch the magic of their birth upon the crest, and of their reabsorption into the invisible. He can feel beauty in the morning air and in the soft grass, as well as in the rocks and snow. The meadows are dressed for him with a profusion of colour that any gardener would envy, not only in the valley levels but where the mountain form beneath the dress sets off their beauty; and high among the rocks he will find a gentian or a tuft of *Eritrichium* that will seem beside the wealth of the meadows like the widow's mite after the offerings of the rich—more than them all.

As he rises, the dome of sky grows vaster, and the clouds and colours that come and go within it show variations that are never seen at levels where intensity of tone is lost in a softer air. No sky in any part of the world has the depth of blue that frames a foreground of snow upon a great peak. There are men who seem to think the Alps in sunshine are not beautiful because they are unpaintable; one might as well refuse to see beauty in a symphony of Beethoven because it cannot be played on one octave of the piano.

When the summit is reached, it may happen that the details of the view, beautiful as they are, are lost in the impression of some all-pervading quality in beauty, that remains recognizable wherever nature is unspoiled. I never really saw the beauty of our Hampshire country till years after I was grown up. It was just after I came back from the Alps. It was not, of course, the contrast, but the realization of this same essential quality; I had been studying a *magnum opus,* and I now saw the same workmanship in the quieter tones of a different subject on a smaller canvas.

And now, if I want to travel on a magic carpet to the summit of an Alpine peak, I go to a certain place, high upon the downs, when the north-west wind is blowing (I cannot think how Charles Kingsley can have preferred the colour-destroying north-east), and I look between two beech trunks that might be the framing of a deep-cut col, and across the shadows moving on the lower ground, to a great

AN APPROACH TO REALITY

range of distant peaks built up into the sky. They have not the calm fixity of mountains, but they give a sense of truer reality than any picture I could hang upon my walls. Mountains may help us to see beauty in a work of art; they insist upon our looking for the nature of beauty at its source.

There is another instinct which has led men to climb: the desire to know, to get nearer to the truth of things. Fully alive as Saussure was to the beauty of Mont Blanc, he would not have made its ascent but for his desire to know what it could tell him. Looking from the summit over the array of peaks and valleys at last spread open before him, he says: 'I realized their relations to each other, their connecting links and their structure, and one look removed doubts which years of work had not been able to clear up.'

The scientific value of climbing has diminished; we have other ways of measuring heights and of solving topographical problems; the desire to get nearer to truth is still a motive. It may be nothing but a wish to test our skill, by matching it against the resistance of the mountain or against the performances of others; it may be a wish to know whether the human body can do its work at twenty-eight thousand feet—this is one of the reasons given by promoters of the Everest expedition; it may prove to still greater satisfaction that muscular effort successfully directed to a good end is one of the great sources of contentment; it may be to get above an atmosphere of doubt as to the direction of life; and it may be nearly all these things at once.

And from the mountain we shall get nothing but the truth. It lays bare our weaknesses, while opening to us a source of strength. We learn from it the limit of our capabilities, and while it rewards us for success and for unsuccessful effort more truly than we know, we must never expect it to pass over a mistake. Deceits and subter-fuges and vanities, on which a man may raise himself higher than he deserves in civilized life, slip away from under him in the field of sport, and most completely of all upon a mountain. Even those arch-impostors of Tarascon, Tartarin and Bompard, are exposed to one another among the stern solitudes of Mont Blanc. It is pleasant to have such a perfect testimonial to the truth-compelling nature of our effort from a great novelist who was not a mountaineer. 'Ecoutez-moi, ami, d'abord, je n'ai jamais tué de lion.' That from Tartarin! And when Tartarin says after a temporary re-inflation of spirit: 'Du courage, Gonzague, du courage!' Bompard replies: 'C'est justement de ça que je manque'!

x

You may remember the cricketer among A. A. Milne's 'Rabbits' who maintained a certain reputation on an M.C.C. tie and a faculty for getting run out. In an Alpine hotel it is possible to find men whose club badges, and continued bad luck in the matter of weather, lead you to form an estimate of their value on a mountain which is a good deal higher than that of the guides or amateurs who climb with them. I am sure such cases are rare; the certainty that a climb will disclose a man's true value discourages pretence. And a climber who can be trusted to say when he feels the slightest doubt as to his safety is a far better companion on the rope than one who may be too proud to ask for help, too self-confident or too ignorant to see the need for special care.

A big climb is done under ideally loyal conditions, when each member of the party gives ungrudgingly of his best, and each shares almost equally in the success. It is one of the drawbacks of a great game like cricket, that the unlucky man who has made naught and missed a catch or two has a very different share in the victory from the man who has made a hundred or taken half the wickets. The weakest member of a climbing rope, unless he is a mere passenger, hoisted up a climb far beyond his powers, has made a big contribution to success.

It is only when a spirit of rivalry intrudes itself, when the tale of achievement is told, in fact when men get away from the influence of the mountain itself, that we find climbers claiming special credit for their own exploits and belittling those of others. Balmat and Paccard climb Mont Blanc with a single aim and in loyal co-operation. It is the jealousy of Bourrit, the personal ambition of Balmat, and the desire to adorn a tale on the part of Dumas, that obscure the truth for over a hundred years.

We see the bare rock of the character of those who share our fortunes on a mountain. That is why the friendships—even that word may fail to convey the closeness of the bond—made by climbing mountains are unlikely to be upset by misunderstandings. Those who climb and continue to climb mountains for the love of them acquire a kind of mountain view of life; though the path pursued in common may occasionally divide, yet, provided the goal is kept in sight, they are bound to draw nearer to each other again.

It is not only our friends whose true nature is revealed by mountains, it is the character of the mountains themselves. They are always correcting or adding to our knowledge of them, if we climb to learn, and not to excel or anticipate a rival. My own possibilities of doing the latter are gone, and any young man who reads this chapter may well think that it is the attempt of an old man to console himself with the philosophic view. Let me, therefore, quote from a paper that I read to the Alpine Club twenty-five years ago, in the early years of my climbing with Gibson and Mallory, Bullock and Tyndale, which called forth a protest signed by numerous distinguished climbers against the temerity of my proceedings.

Each season as it passes leaves us some fresh indications of how to make a wise selection from our many sources of delight. And I have settled to my own satisfaction that mere novelty possesses but faded charms in the Alps. I cannot deceive myself into thinking I am an explorer because I am the first to scale a few hundred feet of rock which have been known to climbers before I was born. . . . And so far is novelty from being necessary to me in my Swiss expeditions, that whenever I have been wise enough to make a second ascent of a peak, I have enjoyed it no less and sometimes more than the first, and likewise with a third and even a fourth. Nevertheless, until we have followed one fairly difficult route upon a mountain we do not properly know it. One aspect of them we may see when walking over their snowfields on a fine day, but before we have come to grips with them we are mere acquaintances. There is an overpowering sense of personality about a peak when we feel his broad snowy chest almost touching our own, when his great rocky shoulder rubs against ours, and our hands clutch at his hard rough skin to get a hold. Some sort of struggle is an excellent beginning to a lasting friendship.

We soon learn to value mountains by other standards than that of fighting power. And it often rests with us to decide whether they shall restore or exhaust our energies, whether they shall develop or test our powers of endurance, whether they shall deepen or disturb the current of our lives. Occasions constantly arise when we underestimate the difficulties, or the weather plays us false. And then we can enjoy what is better than any self-imposed struggle; for the satisfaction of accomplishing a climb of catalogued severity is nothing to the joy of fighting a way out of difficulties and dangers that come unforeseen. The heroes of mountaineering are not those who have fallen in an attempt on some almost inaccessible pinnacle, but those who perished like Carrel on the Grand Staircase.

I would not alter anything I wrote then in the full enjoyment of youth.

We all helped to keep a record of those early years, and the paper from which I have just quoted ends thus:

When I read through the simple story of our climbs—it has reached its fourth volume—there is nothing that gives me more satisfaction than to find that we can still appreciate as of old the simple snow climb. We do a few audacious things, we should not be young if we did not; but we have tried to live up to our belief that there is an influence more purifying than danger in the beauty of the snows; and that among the countless ridges and recesses of the Alps we shall find an outlet for the energies of youth without having constantly before our eyes the immediate prospect of dissolution.

During the war, in Flanders, Mallory wrote an account of the last big climb he did with me. I will quote a few words from it. It refers to the moments when the difficulties were over, and the excite-ment of the struggle ended in the certainty of success up the final easy ridge of Mont Blanc.

The end was too certain. He began to fear an anticlimax, a disappointment in things attained. Wasn't it like a slice of bread and jam, the last unjammed portion? Wasn't the adventure ended, and this merely a depressing fatigue? But in the mere act of firmly planting the feet he found an answer to that last doubt; at each step upward and steeper there throbbed a dim faith refuting the heresy. The spirit didn't come so far to slip all down to nothing, all parts of such experience were significant; the dream stretched to the very end.

And on the summit of Mont Blanc, reached not long before sunset:

Is this the summit, crowning the day? How cool and quiet! We're not exultant; but delighted, joyful; soberly astonished. Have we vanquished an enemy? None but ourselves. Have we gained success? That word means nothing here. To struggle and to understand—never this last without the other, and such is the law.

After his very first visit to the Alps this habit of searching after truth, this desire to assign to things their true values, became charac-teristic of Mallory. That visit, I am sure, gave to a mathematical scholar, regarded as below rather than above the average ability of the scholars of his years, a philosophic outlook which made him an untiring learner. There was a Mallory termed highbrow by his companions on Everest in 1922 and 1924, the man chaffed by Long-staff: 'Mallory, you know the one good thing the Bolsheviks have done in Russia? They've obliterated the intelligentsia.' But it was not a different Mallory from Mallory the mountaineer, it was an essential part of the latter. To see the correct value of a thing, especially of mountaineering itself, was a purpose in his life. I have never been so proud of having introduced Mallory to mountains as when I found him saying after the great climb in 1922 to twenty-seven thousand feet, when there was a question of a third attempt: 'Though I was prepared to take risks with my fingers, I was prepared to take none with my heart, even had General Bruce allowed me.' It showed that Mallory put a true value on mountaineering, far higher than that of any mere achievement, even the conquest of Everest.

The great *truth* that climbing teaches us is that the physical struggle and the contemplative aim are parts of one indivisible whole. Every effort of the muscles that lifts us a little higher is giving us an assurance, absorbed unconsciously into our being, that in the right use of matter to a spiritual end we can fulfil our destiny. And, what is best of all, the enjoyment we find in so doing convinces us that the purpose that controls our destiny is a generous purpose.

Mountains are most trustworthy reminders of it. They do more than sweep away those medieval and puritanical ideas about the opposition of body and spirit, which made us wonder as children why a kindly Creator had given us appetites for our destruction; they give us something more attractive and more comprehensible in their place. They show us that beauty, if we understand its nature, is no snare, and that the gratification of instinct is a road to happiness; that it is something essentially beautiful in their form and structure and purpose that draws even a small boy to climb mountains, and that in the movements that satisfy the climbing instinct we find a thrilling gratification of sense, and learn the generous purpose that has endowed us with that and other instincts. In the whole field of sport, I can think of nothing that combines so perfectly a personal satisfaction with that of work for others as the cutting of a staircase in steep ice at the finish of a long climb.

Moreover, the climber finds that instinct is hedged about with safeguards which gently force him towards the way of gratification most beneficial to himself and others. He soon learns that a very long day's climbing at high altitudes without previous training is as much a misuse of a good thing as eating huge meals without taking exercise; that beyond a certain point of fatigue, capacity for physical and aesthetic enjoyment ceases, and the whole object for which he is meant to climb is lost. Abuse of the instinct for purposes of self-gratification, as in the case of certain climbers of the present day of the sixth-grade type, quickly produces death or a destruction of the powers. The mountains are a sure guide to the beneficent purposes of instinct. Nowhere else is the appetite for food so obviously a blessing as at great heights, and nowhere is its gratification more beneficial, or the purpose for which food is taken so clearly shown.

The climber, in fact, learns, more easily than others, that the rule governing the gratification of any instinct is that it shall be both in his own interest and in that of others. Those who for the satisfaction of personal achievement take definitely dangerous routes upon a peak—and all climbers know the difference between what is difficult or arduous and what is dangerous—do so in nearly every case at the expense of others, just as a motorist does who ignores the red signal at a cross-roads on the chance that nothing may dash into him at that moment. We may, by a prodigal expenditure of nervous energy and a successful gamble with our lives, achieve an ascent which is worthy of record at the cost of tortures of apprehension to those who care for us. Or, on the other hand, we may come down from our peak, as Guido Rey describes it, 'happy to bring back to those we love the serenity we have won on the heights, and to see them smile approvingly upon us because they know the mountain gives them back a son, a brother, or a friend, stronger, healthier, and more loving.'

And again, in bidding us be generous, the mountain sets us an example. As we approach that symbol of ultimate reality, the crest of snow that rises to the highest point, what perfection of generosity we find! The flower in the meadows opens its lovely calyx and gives its honey to attract the fertilizing bee. There is an element of self-realization in the act, and there is a touch of sadness in decay when its aim has been accomplished. But in those exquisite flowers and patterns of the snow that adorn the graceful architecture of the crest, is there a trace of selfishness to be found? They are just pure gifts of beauty offered to us by the master workman who gets such wonderful co-operation out of sea, sun, air, and mountain. They are born from the touch of the wind upon the ridge, and they grow there for men to draw the nectar of their beauty, till at the bidding of the sun they quietly return into the air or to the sea to begin some other generous act. And in our gratitude to them we do not forget our own gift of appreciation. Up there, where it is good for us to be, could any one think that all that beauty and that generosity was the product of his own brain?

If there is none but a materialistic basis to mountaineering or to anything else, if the conquest of matter and the conversion of its use to material ends is the purpose of life, then my philosophy of mountaineering collapses, built though it be in part upon the rock. If you admit there is a spiritual basis to it, if there is reality in the generosity of purpose that draws us upwards to seek for truth by the gratification of our physical desires, then you will forgive me if I introduce a part of a man's being which now and then impels him to get in touch with ultimate things, the part we generally call his religion. In making this one serious attempt to justify a mountaineering faith I cannot leave out the thought that matters most of all.

If there is reality in the beauty of form, of colour, and of action that attracts us, in the truth which we climb to find and do slowly seem to find, and in the generosity which that dawning truth reveals, then we must be glad to find confirmation of our belief that mountains are indeed a true guide to these things.

One figure stands out far above all others in the understanding of these great realities, one who is acknowledged to be a supreme authority on spiritual values. I mean, of course, the man who saw the glory of beauty in the lilies of the field, who tells us that the whole object of His life was to bear witness to the truth, and who bore witness by going about doing good.

How did He endeavour to reach the one source of these realities? How did He refresh himself at that source? 'He went up into the mountain to pray.'

For men of our calibre, any form of activity which helps us to reach upwards to that source, even the mere action of climbing, may be regarded as a form of prayer. Does it diminish the pleasure or the value it has for you, so to regard it, just for a moment? 'He went up into the mountain to pray, and He continued all night in prayer.' Men have been led to follow His example, though it may be quite unconsciously. Follow Dr. Kugy to a bivouac in the Julian Alps, and fill in from your own experience the sketch he gives us. 'Once more the sinking shadows, the distant song of waters, and infinite silence about us. So the mountain night passes in the beauty of a dream. If you have thus dwelt in the secret heart of the mountains, beholding the full glory of their revelation, as they unfold their signs and wonders from the going down of the sun to its uprising, nothing can efface the memory of such nights.'

The monks and hermits went up into the mountain to seek salvation, and they made two fatal mistakes. They made moral perfection their aim, and they forgot that the physical side of life is the one that must carry men towards their spiritual goal. Sport, and the sporting side of mountaineering in particular, has come to show us how much of beauty is to be found in harmonious action, how much of loyalty and generosity in defeat or victory. A great deal of what remains of religion in England at the present day is contained in the ideal of sport. The contemplative view of life is put aside, partly because it is more difficult for the majority of men, partly because they know that a contemplation of the ultimate end of things as foretold by the scientists is a cold, wintry prospect that only throws them back upon the momentary brightness which mechanical triumphs can shed upon a narrowed sphere of existence.

The sportsmen may fail as badly as the monks. Just as the latter lost their spiritual realities by neglecting to use their physical powers in active pursuit of them in the world, so also the sportsmen, if the spiritual aim is forgotten, will find that sport will teach them less and less of true values. They will cease to look for beauty, and be content with efficiency in physical action, will pursue material results, with less and less observance of loyalty and honesty in method or of generosity to opponents. They will look more and more for quantitative results, such as the position in a championship, the beating of records, gate-money, and applause.

Let us hold fast to the spiritual appeal of high mountains while actively pursuing mountaineering as a sport. As Guido Rey has well said: 'Climbing mountains is not an end in itself, it is a means to an end.' If it is fair to apply the word 'utilitarian' to anything which gives direction and purpose to life, then mountaineering is utilitarian. There is no baseness in utility. The most selfless and heroic actions in the whole history of man were not performed without some purpose in view. We know, for we have so often learned it, that if we climb mountains because our bodies and our minds are drawn towards them for what they are and for what they call us to be, we shall receive from them our reward in a renewal of vitality and strength, a refreshment of our minds, and a recovery of our happiest vision of life, which will keep us as anxious to learn as a child, and will restore for us 'the rapture of the forward view.'

I admit that we acquire some distaste for the smooth, hard road of habit along which some of our friends bowl smoothly along. Hill-sides are never quite of the same nature, and are always presenting us with unexpected problems to be solved. Moreover, men who have indulged in solitary climbing, and have loved mountains from infancy, are inclined to undervalue technique, so that their own professional work may suffer from the lack of it. Each difficulty presents its special features, and they trust to instinct and general experience, whether it be of youth or mountains, to carry them over. Inevitably, too, a man with a mountain philosophy, especially if he has climbed much alone, will, at times, find his eyes dwelling on the ridge above, heedless of the clamorous fellow-workers with whom he is roped; letters accumulate unanswered, appointments, functions, messages, are all, at times, forgotten!

40. A MOMENT OF THE PAGEANT

Human nature being prone to longings, and thought being the most unruly of all our faculties, he will find his mind wandering more often than it should to that period of refreshment that lies ahead. He may even be accused of corrupting the youth. The place of a certain scholar of Winchester (now a senior member of its staff) in the examination at the end of his last school year was deplorably low, and not without reason he was accused in the last report sent to his mother of having wasted his time on reading and talking of the mountains, which owing to me had come suddenly to occupy a large portion of his mental horizon. 'Ropes, axes, mattresses!' The complaint had ample justification. Such, however, is the generosity inspired by long and intimate contact with these mountains that he has forgiven me; and even his mother has done so too. I may dare to ask him to read the proofs of this book.

Not that there is any lack of moral sternness in what mountains teach; they offer a wealth of good material to the puritan. It is the weakness of a man's nature, coupled with the ardour of his affection, that makes him steal an hour to read, or better still to dream, about their beauties and their goodness. For the man who knows them well, they draw into one harmonious purpose and so revitalize his health, his work, his play, his desires, his affections, and his religion. For him the mountain is a symbol, not only of the way that leads to a perception of true values; it is also a symbol of a unity of outlook to which all men, however great their divergence, must gradually draw together.

If there is indeed one great source of all reality, then all ways that lead thither must converge. That is why a mountain is such a satisfying guide; it supplies men with unity of purpose, and it demands the use of every part of their physical nature in its attainment. In the plain, or on the low hills that rise above it, there are church towers and steeples that point as unmistakably upwards in the same super-worldly direction as the mountain itself; yet men have been sorely distracted in deciding which of the appointed guides is the best to follow, so that many of them decide to remain strolling aimlessly about the plain. It is not easy when you are within the walls of one of these churches to see how your path, and that of a friend in a church some distance off, are going to come together. It becomes easy if you both follow the example of Him in whose honour both churches have been built, and 'go up into the mountain to pray.'

It sounds too easy; remember it is only the beginning of a solution of life's riddle. I wish our mountain philosophy had been written by a man like King Albert of Belgium; because, in these days of publicity, whatever is said by those whose names are widely known finds far more willing listeners, and because we know that this king was a great man who loved mountains as only a climber loves them.

It is my one regret for being just an ordinary man, that I bring so little credit to the mountains that have done so much for me. Only one man knows the creature I should have been without them; it is in gratitude for his escape from that existence that he has tried to add something to the knowledge and affection with which men may regard them.

NOTES ON ILLUSTRATIONS

1. ' *Clear of the Brooding Cloud*' (frontispiece).
Mont Blanc de Courmayeur, seen across the Val Veni.

2. *Mont Aiguille.*
(*a*) From the north. (*b*) The west face in April.

4. *Mont Blanc from the Air.*
Mont Blanc de Courmayeur is seen to the left of the highest point.

5. *Jungfrau from Obermönchjoch.*
The Jungfrau is in the centre; on its left the Rottalsattel; then
the rocky Rottalhorn. Left of this is the saddle described by
Meyer as the foot of the Jungfrau, and on the left of this saddle is
seen the descent mentioned by him and difficult to account for
by any other theory of the route followed than that given in the
text. Meyer must then have gone close to the rocks of the
Rottalhorn and across the top of the great spur which comes down
from the Rottalhorn into the Jungfraufirn in the foreground of the
photograph. The 1812 route, the usual route now followed, goes
up the snow to the right of this spur and across the *bergschrund*
straight up to the Rottalsattel.

6. *Maps of J. R. Meyer's Explorations.*
On both maps L is the Lötschenlücke, C is the point where
almost level snow is reached just east of the Lauitor Saddle; M
indicates the direction of the Märjelen See and Alp, a little below
the edge of the map.
   On Meyer's map the only portion of the tracks shown that concerns 1811 is that joining L to the junction called Vohrjähriges
Nachtlager (i.e. the position, vaguely indicated, of the two 1811
bivouacs), and the track going north from this junction to the
Jungfrau. The track from M to the junction (perhaps continuing
over 1811 ground to L) was probably made during a week's stay
at the Märjelen Alp at the end of August 1812, when the weather
did not permit any big ascent. The track from M to the Zweites
Nachtlager (the 1812 bivouac) and on to the Jungfrau is the 1812
route up that peak, which Meyer describes as being made 'from

the opposite side to that ascended in 1811.' The description is a natural one if we think of the Kranzberg, as Meyer would, as being a continuation of the southern ridge of the Jungfrau.

Note on Meyer's map the vague placing of the Ebnefluh, almost where the Gletscherhorn should be, the latter peak having been regarded at first as the Jungfrau. The topography of the part near the Grünhorn is even vaguer, this peak being marked as a southern spur of the Trugberg, which has no name in Meyer's map. There are many interesting variations which those who know the country may be interested to note.

On the reproduction of the Siegfried map, A is the probable site of the first bivouac in 1811, B the second bivouac, near the point 3622m. D is the saddle to which the descent was made to the foot of the Rottalhorn. E is the point where the spur descend-ing east from the Rottalhorn is crossed, close to the Rottalsattel just left of it.

7. *Weisshorn and Mischabelhörner.*

Taken from Castor. The Weisshorn is on the left, its right-hand skyline being the ridge climbed by Tyndall. The Dom is the highest point of the Mischabel on the right of the picture, the Täschhorn is slightly below it to the right; the face it shows is the scene of Geoffrey Young's adventure, referred to in the text.

8. *The Italian Side of the Matterhorn.*

Taken from the Col des Grandes Murailles. The snow ridge partly obscured by the small cloud in the right-hand bottom corner abuts against the knob called Tête du Lion. Almost on a level and about half an inch to the left of where this snow ridge meets the rock some bright spots of snow mark the Col du Lion. The Italian route made by Carrel with Gorret goes up the rocks and past the upper bright snow-patch, above which it joins the ridge on the left and follows it to the Pic Tyndall, the level shoulder on the right below the final crags. The gallery followed by Carrel passes across the black rocks of the topmost triangular north-west face; the small patch of snow visible about a third of an inch below the Italian (left-hand) summit is near it. The photograph shows something of the nature of the slopes of the Swiss side of the Col du Lion.

10. *A Himalayan Spire.*

A pinnacle on the spur between the Baltoro and Godwen-Austen glaciers.

11. *Nature's Last Stronghold.*

The upper part of the Mustagh Tower from east of the Baltoro Glacier; probably the most inaccessible of all great peaks, for its immense precipices show no weakness in its defences.

12. *In the Canadian Rockies.*

Moraine Lake.

13. *Mont Blanc from the Tour Noir.*

A tele-photograph.   The Brenva route lies on the ridge that runs up to the ice-cliffs, shown about an inch below and very slightly left of the highest snowy point.   You can see the famous narrow portion of the ridge crossed astride by Moore's party where it runs level, nearly an inch above the left-hand edge of the rock which throws a long shadow across the snow in the centre of the foreground.   In the upper part of the picture the Brouillard ridge is the left-hand skyline till it falls behind the Péteret ridge, which joins it at the top in the summit of Mont Blanc de Courmayeur. The great face below the latter is the scene of the long, difficult climbs made by Graham Brown and Smythe.   The two snowy humps on the skyline about two inches right of the highest point are the Bosses du Dromadaire.   The small rocky point just reaching the skyline of the left-hand *bosse* is the summit of Mont Maudit.   The summit of Mont Blanc du Tacul is hard to distinguish, a third of an inch below and slightly to the left.

14. *Defences of the Aiguille Verte.*

The north-east face of the Aiguille Verte.   The route referred to is up the couloir that slopes down from the summit to the right and is clearly overhung by ice-cliffs.

15. *Human Granite.*

The subject is Alexander Burgener.

16. *Aiguille du Plan.*

The photograph shows the Chamonix (north-west) face, the scene of the climb described on p. 208.   The reverse side, which was traversed by M. de Lépiney on his ascent of the Pte de Lépiney, described on pp. 112, 114, is a dry, bare precipice in fine summer weather.

20. *Škrlatica.*

The north-west face, which is the one referred to in the text.

22. *Aiguille des Charmoz—North Face.*

The attempt which so nearly ended in disaster, described in the text, was made on or close to the rocks directly below the summit on the right of the ice-slope; it ended in the narrow right-hand couloir in which the ice-slope ends, at the level of the top of the Aiguille de la République, the huge spike on the left of the picture.

23. *The Matterhorn—North and East Faces.*

A tele-photograph from the Alphubel. The true angle of the ridges is better seen than from a lower view-point.

26. *Kanchenjunga.*

The spur ascended by Bauer's party is well shown in almost its whole length, running up from the bottom of the picture towards the right.

28. *A Favourite Swiss Playground.*

Two of the central peaks of the Dents du Midi are shown close at hand; farther off in sunshine is the Dent de l'Est, its rocky skyline being the ridge mentioned in the text.

29. *Clogwyn dur Arddu.*

The view is taken from a point near the Clogwyn station on Snowdon. The west buttress is the farthest part of the dark cliffs, in the centre of the picture.

30. *Raised to the Alpine Peerage.*

The Petit Clocher de Planereuse. The ordinary ascent lies up a couloir behind the long left-hand buttress shown in sunlight from its base to the top of the peak. The right-hand ridge is that descended by the two de Lépineys.

32. *Snow Banners of the Sierra Nevada.*

The peak throwing a dark shadow on the left is Grey Peak, in the Merced Group.

34. *The Right Place.*

On the east face of the Douves Blanches.

35. *A Winter Transformation.*

On the Rigi, looking towards Pilatus.

39. *An Approach to Reality.*

A col near the Gross Spannort, in the early morning.

40. *A Moment of the Pageant.*

From the slopes of Nanga Parbat; the Hindu Kush are shown in the distance.

INDEX

References in italics indicate that the subject is illustrated with a photograph or diagram

MADE AT THE
TEMPLE PRESS
LETCHWORTH
GREAT BRITAIN